Maja and Reuben Fowkes are co-directors of the Postsocialist Art Centre (PACT) at University College London and founders of the Translocal Institute for Contemporary Art. Their publications include *Central and Eastern European Art Since 1950* (Thames & Hudson, 2020), the edited book *Ilona Németh: Eastern Sugar* (Sternberg Press, 2021) and Maja Fowkes's *The Green Bloc: Neo-avant-garde Art and Ecology under Socialism* (CEU Press, 2015). Their extensive work on issues of art and climate change includes curatorial projects such as the exhibition Potential Agrarianisms, the Anthropocene Reading Room and the Danube River School, as well as numerous book chapters, journal articles and catalogue texts on topics from digital ecology to the socialist Anthropocene.

World of Art

D1106093

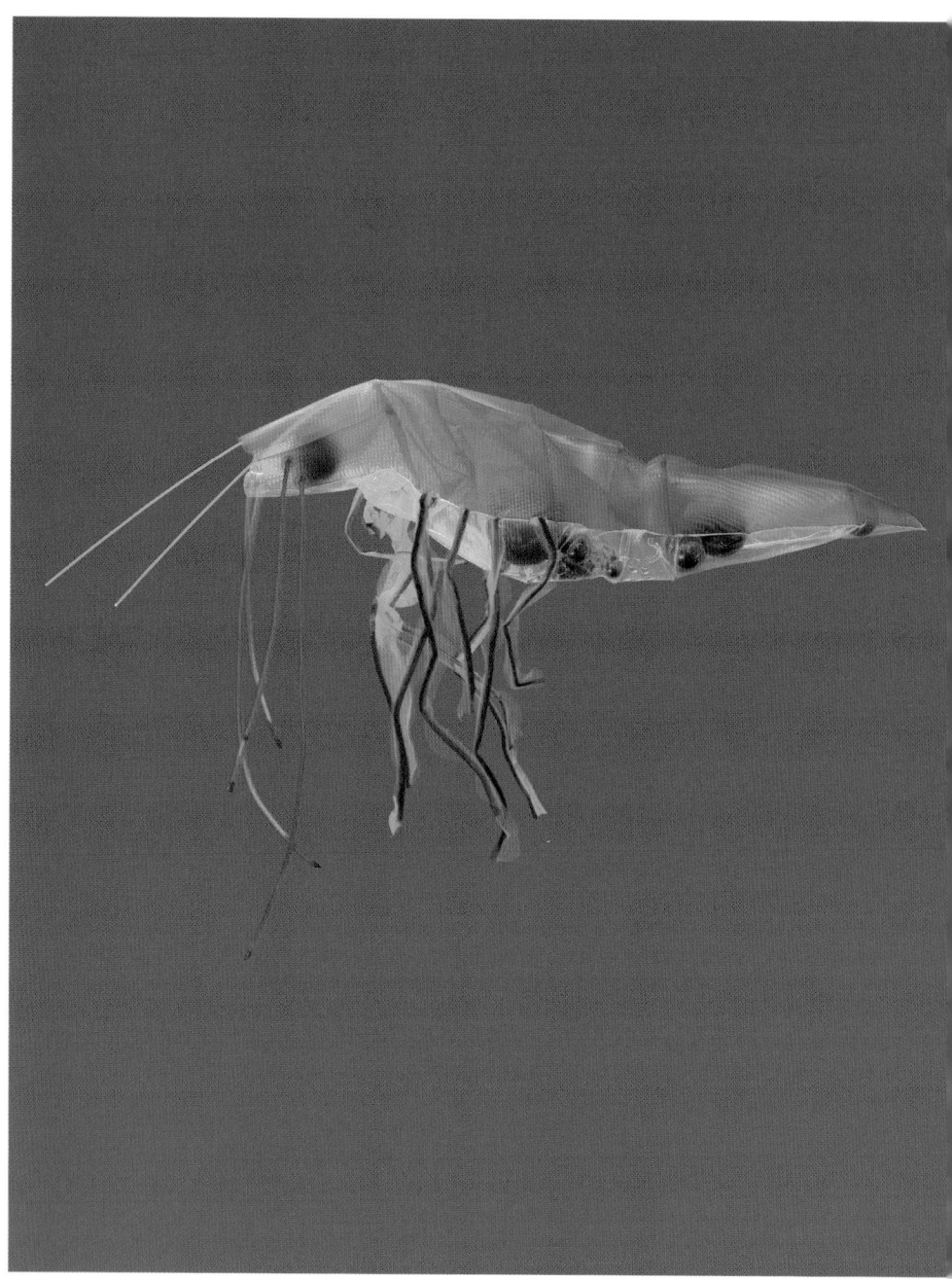

1 Anne Duk Hee Jordan, *Water Crab*, 2017–ongoing (detail)

World of Art

Art and Climate Change
Maja and Reuben Fowkes

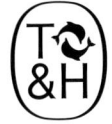

To Flora and Liam, whose youthful wisdom
never ceases to amaze and inspire

First published in 2022 in the United Kingdom
by Thames & Hudson Ltd, 181A High Holborn,
London WC1V 7QX

www.thamesandhudson.com

First published in 2022 in the United States
of America by Thames & Hudson Inc.,
500 Fifth Avenue, New York, New York 10110

www.thamesandhudsonusa.com

Art and Climate Change © 2022
Thames & Hudson Ltd, London

Text © 2022 Maja Fowkes and Reuben Fowkes

Art direction and series design by Kummer & Herrman
Layout by Adam Hay Studio

British Library Cataloguing-in-Publication Data
A catalogue record for this book is available from
the British Library

Library of Congress Control Number 2021943606

ISBN 978-0-500-20475-7

Printed and bound in China through Asia Pacific
Offset Ltd

Contents

Introduction

'Is my microphone really on? Did you hear me, because I'm beginning to wonder?' were the words teenage activist Greta Thunberg directed at global leaders in her plea to take seriously climate change and the interlinked emergencies of species extinction, soil erosion, deforestation, air pollution and ocean acidification, and to stop prioritizing economic growth over the future of Earth. Another of the principal voices cutting through the inertia and distractions to confront the enormity of climate disruption and its roots in the 'current global system based on the pursuit of financial gain' has been Pope Francis, who declared that 'we are not faced with two separate crises, but rather with one complex crisis that is both social and environmental'. Amazonian activist Alessandra Korap Munduruku has challenged the Western world to look beyond the climate symbolism of the forest in flames and realize that the 'Amazon burns with agribusiness, burns to make room for infrastructure projects', with the roots of global warming to be found in more than five centuries of colonial incursions into indigenous lands. These resounding voices articulate the magnitude of climate change, insist that it cannot be considered separately from the multiple signs of ecological breakdown and deepening social injustice, and underline the importance of understanding extractive capitalism and colonialism as its systemic origins.

Even the best-case scenario projected by climatologists, of keeping the global temperature rise within two degrees, will by the end of the century bring the chaos of ever more frequent extreme weather events, uncontrollable wildfires, desertification of land and coastal inundations as permafrost melts and sea levels climb. Correspondingly, climate change has transformed ecology from a single issue into an existential condition touching on and reassembling socio-political, economic and cultural life with implications for all fields of social activity. For theorist Bruno Latour, the 'climate question is not one aspect of politics among others, but that which defines the political order from beginning to end, forcing us all to redefine the older questions of social justice, as well as those of identity, subsistence and attachment to place'. The artistic practices discussed in this account are indicative of the ways in which issues around social justice, land rights, nutrition and wellbeing are today refracted and shaped by ecological concerns. The focus here is on research-based and situated artistic approaches that uncover particular socio-environmental matters in sites of crisis, yet engage in an international conversation that spans geographies and connects with planetary questions. Advocating and animating a new terrestrial politics, social art practices channel gestures of solidarity and care that encompass alternative community building and reach across societal and species divides to contest historical and present injustices. Confronting climate crisis therefore holds out the potential for turning from a perilous course towards ecological restoration, the reworlding of social relations and the resetting of terrestrial wellbeing.

The planetary scale of climate change and the unparalleled threat it poses to the continuity of biological life on Earth has called forth new critical tools and terminologies to comprehend the gravity of the moment. It was concern about rising levels of carbon dioxide in the atmosphere that first led scientists at the beginning of the millennium to propose renaming the current epoch as the Anthropocene in recognition of the unprecedented impact of humans on Earth systems. Ever since, the realization that human interference in natural processes has taken on geological proportions has captured the critical imagination and informed artistic thinking. Exposing the impact of extractivism, fossil fuels, monocultures, synthetics and nuclear power on Earth systems, artists partake in breaking the spell of the boundless promises of industrial modernity and technological progress to reveal their pernicious role in causing climate disruption. The insight that the roots of climate and ecological crisis lie in the mechanisms of capitalism, understood not just as a global economic system but a 'way of organising nature', has been defined by Jason W. Moore in terms of the Capitalocene. Further challenges to the West-centric assumption that responsibility for the planet-wide emergency is shared by a generalized Anthropos have emerged from black and indigenous perspectives. Philosopher Achille Mbembe has pointed out that in the wake of the dehumanizing histories of slavery and racism, black experience 'defeats the very notion of the human species', with the result that there is 'no longer a "human" who is not already enmeshed in the "non-human," the "more than human," the "beyond human," or the "otherwise-than-human"'. In emphasizing the notion of the colonial Anthropocene, theorist Macarena Gómez-Barris has foregrounded the underpinning logic of colonialism that 'continually wreaks havoc on localised social ecologies'. Artistic practices discussed in this book have uncovered the toxic dynamics between racial capitalism and climate change, exploring at the same time the coalescence of decolonial reparation and ecological restoration.

Emergent climate epistemologies that arise from critical reassessment of the atomized Western modernist mindset are articulated through art practices that form the building blocks of this account. Such artistic approaches draw equally on the insights of contemporary science and theory, as well as on traditional wisdoms and indigenous knowledges, to overcome the societal disconnect from nature. Among seminal eco-critical influences, theorist Donna Haraway has proposed the term Chthulucene to express the entangled coexistences of critters that 'writhe and luxuriate in manifold forms and manifold names in all the airs, waters, and places of earth'. Molecular biology has similarly revealed that organisms prosper not by competing for resources, but through biotic interdependencies and reciprocal relationships, pointing to what historian of science Isabelle Stengers has called the 'multiplicity of ways in which life forms compose the world together'. An interconnected understanding of the world that does not divide the human realm from the multitude of living beings and natural entities flows through many indigenous and traditional worldviews. As anthropologist Marisol de la Cadena has related, resistance to extractivism on indigenous lands is not just a matter of environmental conservation, but also a cosmopolitical struggle to recognize 'mountains as not only geology but also earth-beings'. In light of these insights, climate change is approached here as a planetary process that affects not only populations across the globe but also natural entities, interferes in vegetal worlds, conditions animal existences and demands a radical rethinking of the human in the terrestrial order.

The first part of the book, under the heading Many Anthropocenes, scrutinizes the growth mindset driving the operations of extractivism, militarism, petrocultures, synthetic environments and industrial agriculture as anthropogenic causes of climate change. Artistic practices discussed here expose the entwinement of colonial, military and mining complexes in extractivist machines that turn mineral-rich territories into sacrifice zones. They shed light on the operations of fossil fuel industries that infiltrate legal, political, cultural and environmental realms. Artists also investigate the proliferation of synthetic materials, with plastic waste reaching into the furthest polar regions, deepest rainforests and remotest maritime realms, and the effects of its decomposition in oceans and subsequent toxic dispersal in the biological systems of humans, animals and plants. At issue also is the biotechnological and energy-intensive model of industrial agriculture depleting the vitality of the soil, corroding rural communities, multiplying social injustices and diminishing the ecosystems on which planetary wellbeing depends. Artistic gestures of remediation examined here extend from disassociating sources of energy from their destructive uses to exploring the hybrid convergence of synthetics with the reparative potential of natural processes and carrying out performative acts of healing planetary wounds.

The second part, on Reconfiguring the Geosphere, discusses artistic investigations of how anthropogenic alterations to the biological, chemical and physical makeup of terrestrial matter are affecting natural entities such as soil, rivers, oceans, ice and air. Artworks analysed here address the devastation of the top layer of the lithosphere, contrasting the drone-eye view of territorial surveillance with muddy perspectives of entangled soil coexistences from within. Countering the control and domination of waterways characteristic of the industrial era, artists have uncovered hidden streams under city streets, seen rivers as protagonists of environmental insurgencies and advocated for their legal rights in line with non-Western worldviews that recognize rivers as spiritual beings. Drawing on research into marine ecosystems, these artists pose questions about the impact of tourism, overfishing, global shipping, pollution, deep-sea mining and surveillance on the furthest reaches of the ocean wilderness. The retreat of the permafrost as the most dramatic indicator of climate change is discussed through art practices that come to terms with the loss of ice, narrate fictional mythologies of polar landscapes and carry out empathic acts of care towards glacial entities. Directing our gaze through smog and light pollution up to the sky, this account also sheds light on the troubled connection between ethereal realms and terrestrial processes.

Artistic engagements with the vegetal world form the third part, entitled Floral Collectivism, which incorporates new scientific findings as well as traditional wisdom and plant knowledge, while also uncovering botany as a colonial enterprise and ideological playground. Through music, dance, rituals, performances and acts of tending, artists have turned to sensorial means to reach across the bio-epistemological divide and reveal the distinctive characteristics of vegetal life. Crossing into political territories, plants have become allies in liberation struggles, but have also been subject to instrumentalizing attitudes and practices from nationalist appropriation to propaganda gardening. Artists in this section pay particular attention to the agency of self-organizing weeds and societal attitudes to ruderal vegetation, rekindling appreciation of neglected botanical species and reawakening non-coercive relations to plants. Also discussed are artworks that disclose the hostile implications of the vilification of invasive species, siding with resettled and migrating plants to illuminate the role of the new wild in resuscitating degraded landscapes. Another question is what can be learned from the integral place of forests in indigenous cosmologies and ecosystems, the question of arboreal rights, the violence of deforestation and the conflicted role of forests and trees in mitigating climate change.

The fourth part of the book, on Animal Solidarities, considers the disturbed histories of animal and human relations through art practices that explore the ethico-legal and politico-cultural grounds for solidarity with non-human persons. In light of an unfolding extinction event of geological proportions, it asks how artists have engaged with campaigns for rewilding and de-extinction and approached the memorialization of lost species. Decoding the representational strategies of natural history museums to unveil the colonial origins of their collections, artists considered here propose strategies to decolonize museums and rethink natural histories from an animal perspective. Examining the ways technology has transformed attitudes to non-human persons, this account explores artistic approaches to restoring dignity to animals, the de-industrialization of factory farming and the revival of human–animal relations based on kinship and care. It directs the lens towards artistic engagement with a particular group in the animal kingdom, detailing the symbolic, political and ecological role of birds and exploring avian influence on the unfolding of historical events. A chapter on magnified natures examines artistic practices that focus on the vital contribution of microbes to the functioning of ecosystems, revealing symbiotic co-dependencies, but also the extent to which climate change is multiplying viral threats.

The final part of this account, on Pluriversal Ecologies, investigates the impacts of environmental crisis on humanity itself, from repairing troubled histories to envisioning potential futures and devising protocols for a just ecological transition.

The expansive and integrated understanding of climate crisis is directed towards rethinking the position of the human within the terrestrial order, also by probing the complexity of more-than-human entanglements in the technosphere. This part outlines the ways artists are actively reassembling the narratives of planetary histories and negotiating a plurality of critical standpoints, including the distinctive histories of socialist modernity, in order to confront and dismantle the infrastructures of colonialism and extractivism. It also explores artistic engagements with movements for land and indigenous rights in the global South and the precarity of disadvantaged communities in former colonial centres, expressing the commonality of the struggle for social and environmental justice. Focusing on the methodologies proposed by artists to bring about a radical ecological transformation, it investigates the reimagining of hybrid urban and rural spaces as sites for sustainable living and cooperative social organization in a post-carbon world. Devising radical protocols for climate survival, artists considered in the book are also anticipating a recentred Earth on which a plurality of possible worlds can coexist.

The destabilizing effects of climate change on all aspects of planetary life impel artists to go beyond illustrating or representing the crisis, to work through its cascading implications and uncover potential ways to instigate ecological change. At a time when the microphones of dissent are turned down by vested interests or tempered by the cautiousness of incrementalism, it is the collective voice of eco-conscious art practices emerging from indigenous communities, across the global South and in the progressive enclaves of the global North, that is amplifying the struggle for a just ecological transformation. What guides the artists gathered together here is an ardent concern for the living, breathing subject of the Earth and all fellow terrestrials caught up in this fast-moving climate drama, punctuated by the superlatives of the fiercest fires, thinnest icecaps, fastest extinctions and hottest temperatures since the end of the Ice Age.

Part I
Many Anthropocenes

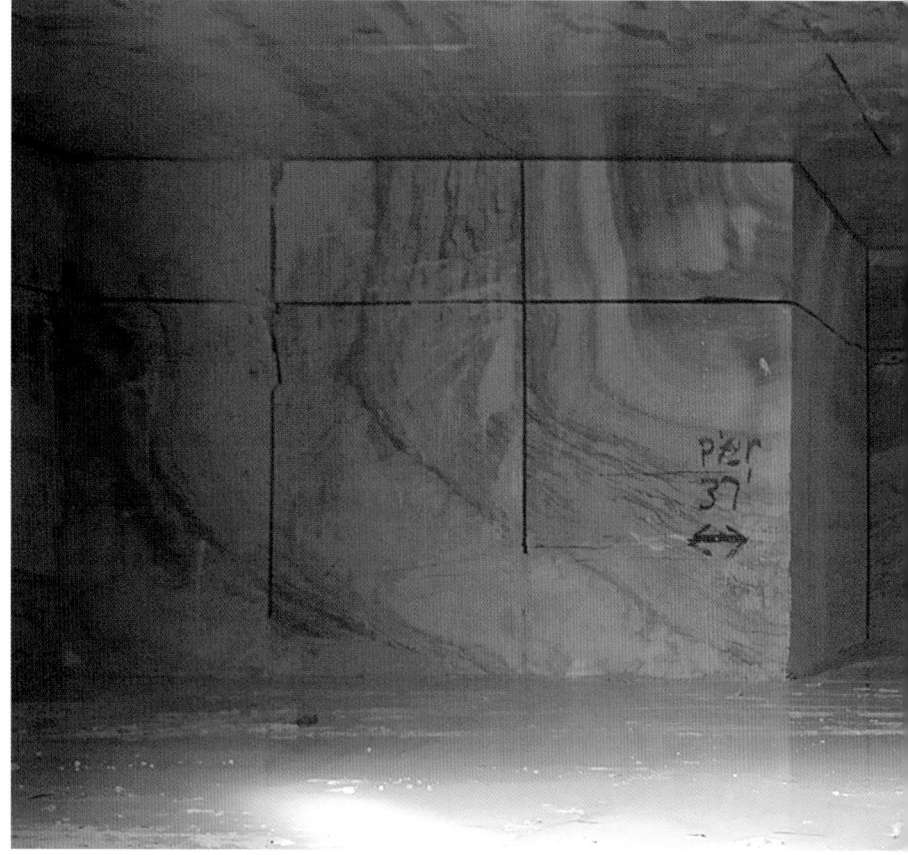

2 Amie Siegel, *Quarry*, 2015

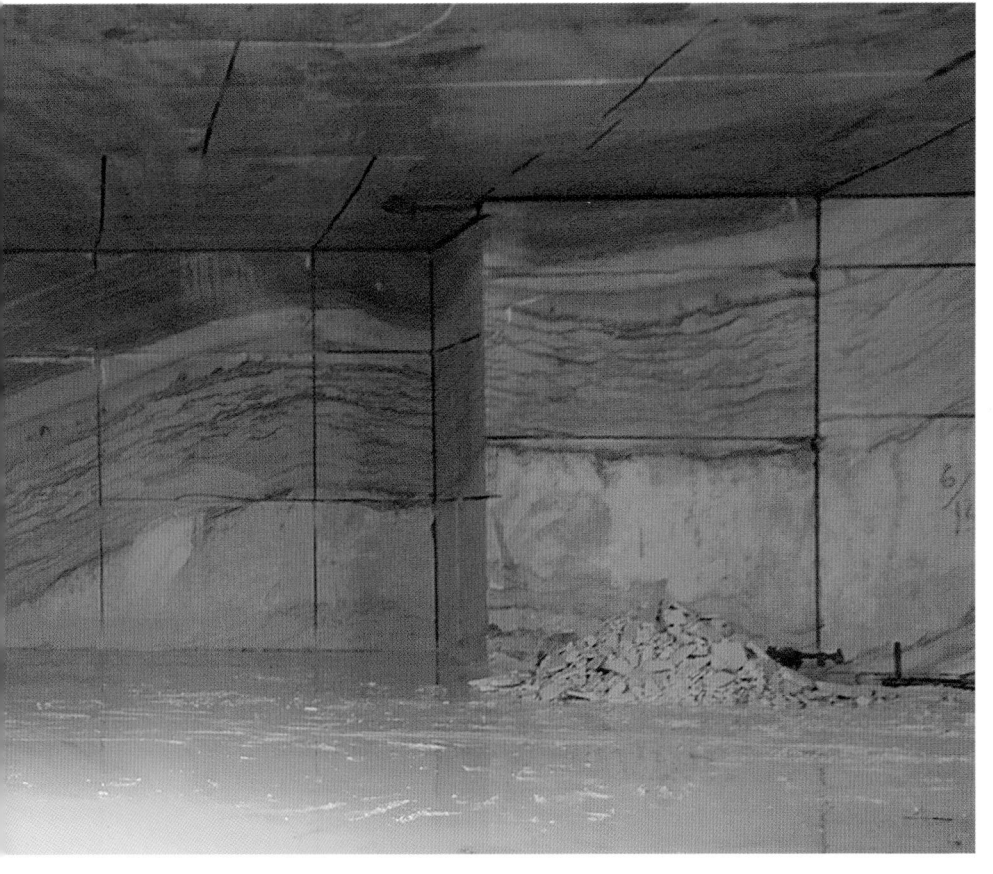

Chapter 1
Geological Records

'In order to have lived in a month where the world was not warming month-by-month, you need to have been born in 1985 or earlier', otherwise, as Nicholas Mirzoeff contended in *How to See the World*, 'you have never known what the pre-climate-changed world was like.' The bodily sensation of living in an anthropogenically transformed environment has conditioned the way we 'see the Anthropocene', with scientific investigation directed towards identifying potential turning points in planetary history when human activity first overwhelmed Earth processes. The megafauna extinctions caused by overhunting and the changing climate of the late Pleistocene are among the earliest signs of such 'golden spikes' in the geological record, while the upswing in atmospheric carbon dioxide levels etched in the permafrost by the Industrial Revolution is another contender for the start of the Anthropocene. The authors of *The Human Planet* pointed to an 'Orbis Spike' of reduced carbon dioxide levels due to the return of forests following the death of an estimated 50 million native Americans as marking 'the beginning of today's globally interconnected economy and ecology', drawing a connection between the crimes of colonialism and the onset of the Anthropocene. Indicators of intensifying disruption of the natural world have also been found in residues of plastic pollution, chemical fertilizers and skeletal remains of genetically modified chickens in the soil, while the first atomic test on 16 July 1945, which dispersed radioactive isotopes across the planet, is another stratigraphic marker. In that sense, over-exploitation, colonialism, industrial modernity, fossil fuel capitalism and the Cold War arms race are all implicated in the forceful reassembling of geological matter and contribute unequivocally to climate derangement.

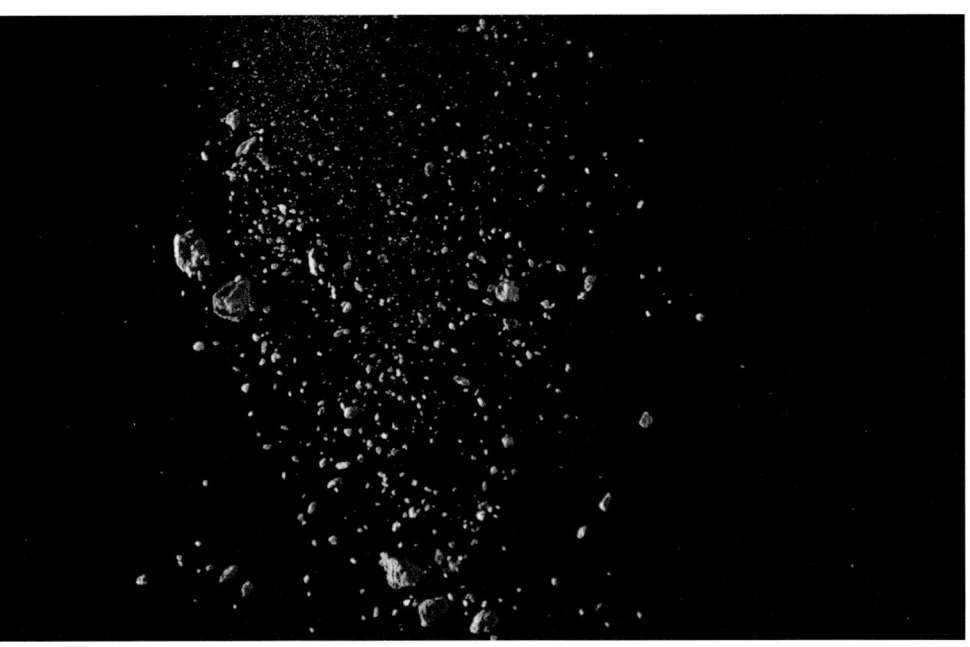

3 Nicholas Mangan, *A World Undone*, 2012

Nicholas Mangan's film *A World Undone* (2012) took as its subject zircon, the oldest mineral in the Earth's crust, which dates back 4.4 billion years to the long period of the planet's history before it became the stage for the emergence of biological life. Sourcing the aggregated red rock from the Jack Hills range in Western Australia where the most ancient fragments have been found, the artist reversed the geological process by crushing it back into particles. He then filmed their dispersal against a black background with a slow-motion camera. In the absence of a reference of scale and with the impression of gravity obscured through capturing the falling dust at 2,500 frames per second, the viewer could easily be inspecting microscopic substances in closeup or observing asteroids orbiting through cosmic domains. Metaphysical contemplation of the deep time of granular matter and the transience of human existence measured in the lifetime of the planet collide here with the brutal extractivism of open-cast mining of this ancient crystal in Mangan's native Australia. The geological understanding of 'earth as a set of stratified levels of being and time' is itself, as anthropologist Elizabeth A. Povinelli showed in her study *Geontologies: A Requiem to Late Liberalism*, closely entwined with the Anthropocene, since the history of science and the extractive mining of minerals developed in tandem at the onset of the new era.

The entanglement of ancient minerals in the economic and political microstructures of contemporary capitalism comes into focus in US artist Amie Siegel's film *Quarry* (2015), which took as its starting point the residential architecture of Manhattan luxury apartments. The work traced the journey of the polished slabs of marble used for worktops, floors and bathrooms in high-end penthouses back to the underground chambers deep beneath Vermont's Dorset Mountain, from where the white metamorphic rock was cut. The artist revealed the connection between the brutal process of extraction and the shiny showrooms that entice prospective clients by relying on the associations of marble with exclusivity and opulence in the speculative real estate economy. In a related work, *Dynasty* (2017), Siegel presented a fragment of pink marble from the lobby of the Trump Tower in New York, which she purchased online in the aftermath of the 2016 US presidential election. By exposing the links between political and economic forces and the extraction of geological matter, the artist challenged the blind spots of a narrow understanding of the Anthropocene that does not differentiate between branches of humanity or particular social groups in attributing responsibility for human impacts on Earth.

Prefiguration of the concept of the Anthropocene could be found in the work of early twentieth-century Soviet scientist Vladimir Vernadsky, who developed the notion of the Noösphere, or envelope of thought, to account for the magnitude of technological, scientific and military interventions in the biogeochemical processes of the Earth. Romanian artists Anca Benera and Arnold Estefan proposed the related term 'debrisphere' to denote alterations to the surface of the lithosphere as a result of the destructive power of the military–industrial complex of the modern era. Scale models and botanical drawings in their installation *Debrisphere: Landscape as an Extension of the Military Imagination* (2017) drew attention to the effects of war on specific environments, from the hilly mounds of rubble that reshaped the topography of post-war Berlin to the flattening of bombsites to create made-ground in London's East End. Another model dealt with the transformation of the British colonial territory of Diego Garcia, the largest island of the Chagos Archipelago in the Indian Ocean, into a US military base, at the cost of the eviction of its inhabitants and destruction of a finely balanced marine ecosystem. The persistence of the military–colonial mindset was exemplified by the British decision, following the legal

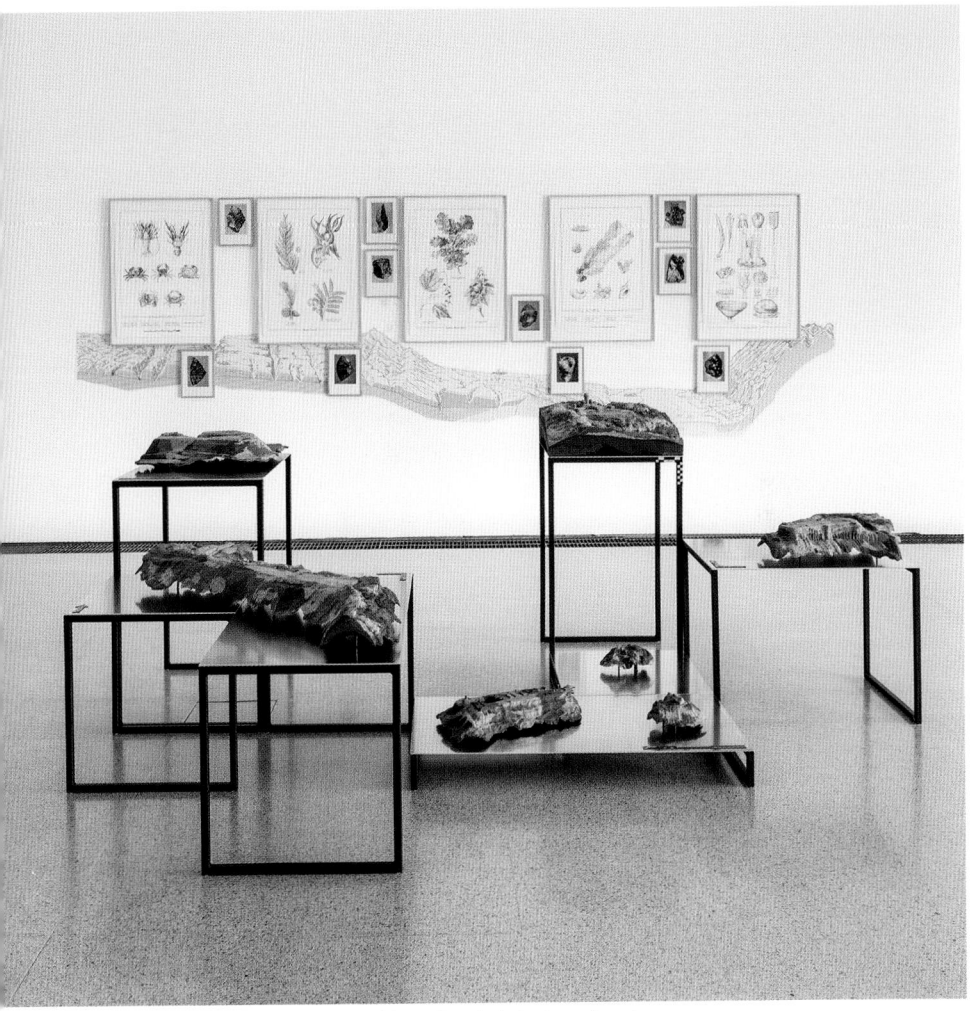

4 Anca Benera and Arnold Estefan, *Debrisphere: Landscape as an Extension of the Military Imagination*, 2017

recognition in 2008 of the islanders' rights to their ancestral home, to declare the Chagos Archipelago a protected marine biosphere in order to block their return.

London-based artists and filmmakers Sasha Litvintseva and Daniel Mann's film *Salarium* (2017) explored the geological phenomenon of sinkholes, which since the 1980s have frequently appeared around the shores of the Dead Sea in Israel and Palestine. As a result of hydro-engineering projects on the River Jordan and the extraction of minerals in mines to its

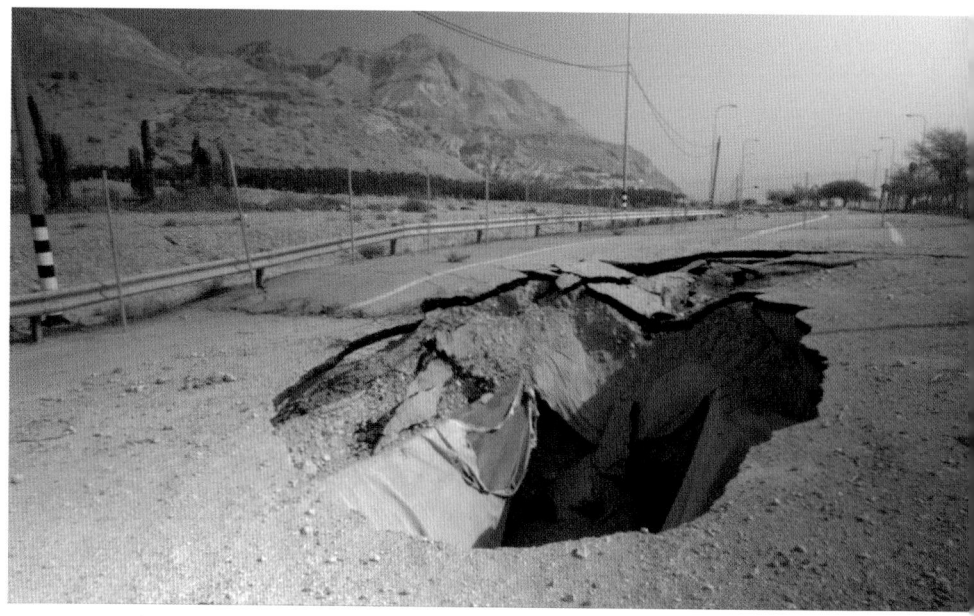

5 Sasha Litvintseva and Daniel Mann, *Salarium*, 2017

south, thousands of sinkholes have collapsed patches of the
land that stretches between the salty lake and the Judean Desert,
sucking in parts of the beach, water park and settlements. The
title refers to the common etymological roots of the words for
'salary', 'soldier' and 'salt', which are all at play in this work
that demonstrates the entwinement of economic, military and
geological elements. For the artists, the sinkholes represent on the
one hand 'the geological scale of gradual mineral sedimentation
and erosion', and on the other 'the human historical scale of
settler colonialism and resource extraction'. What is more, since
the sinkhole 'makes the invisible visible' and is therefore 'imbued
with political agency', the work vividly illustrated how schemes of
social engineering and environmental control come up against
implacable natural forces.

The contested history of nuclearization was the site of
intervention for Belgian artist Maarten Vanden Eynde, who
in his *Manhattan Project* (2017) attempted to recreate the
perfect dome that occurs 0.025 seconds after detonating an
atomic bomb. The artist used green antique uranium glass for
miniature explosions to create bubbles on a bed of sand that
came from White Sands Missile Range, where the first atomic
tests were conducted. Adding UV lights to this scaled-down
model, which turned the display fluorescent green and purple,

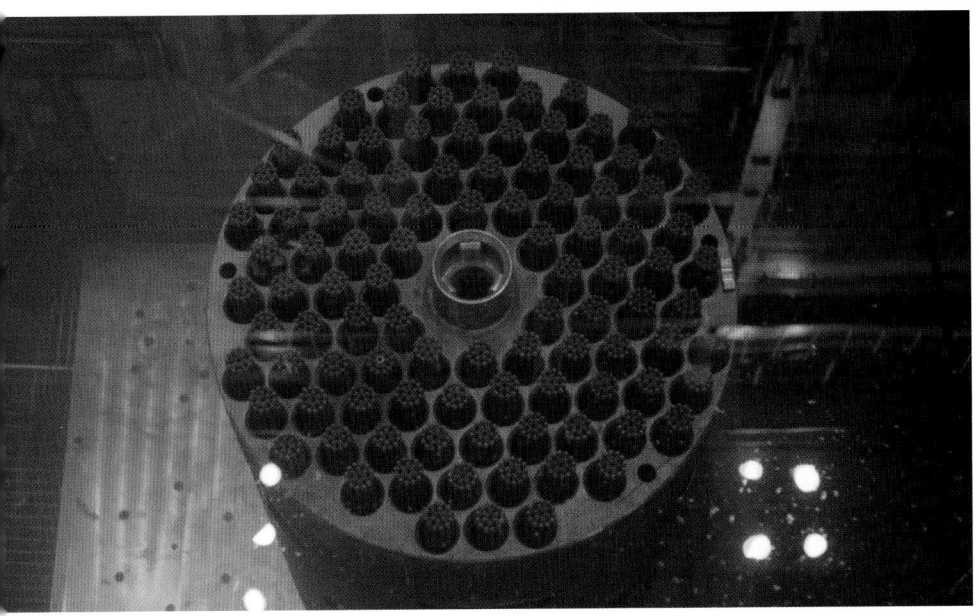

6 Emilija Škarnulytė, *T1/2*, 2019

had the effect of amplifying the menacing environment. Unravelling the entangled histories of cotton and uranium, his related installation made with traditional Belgian bobbin lace, *The Gadget 3D* (2017), referred in its title to the nickname given to the first atomic bomb that was detonated in the Manhattan Project. The work drew attention to the parallels between the colonial trajectory of the uranium mined for the first atomic bombs in the Katanga province of what was until 1960 a Belgian colony but is now the Democratic Republic of Congo, and that of the slave labourers, many of whom came from the Congo, destined for cotton plantations in the southern United States. These in turn provided the raw materials for the bobbin lace industry of Belgium, completing the circle of colonial domination, extraction and exploitation.

The ruins of Cold War nuclear culture and its unforeseeable impacts on the health of the planet were the focus of Lithuanian artist Emilija Škarnulytė's futuristic archaeological exploration *T1/2* (2019), which in its title referred to the abbreviation for half-life that in nuclear physics is a measure of the rate of radioactive decay. Slowly panning shots of a hi-tech fusion of speculative and historic atomic architectures equipped with fuel rods and cooling pools are devoid of human presence, pointing to the geological timescale of nuclear waste with

6

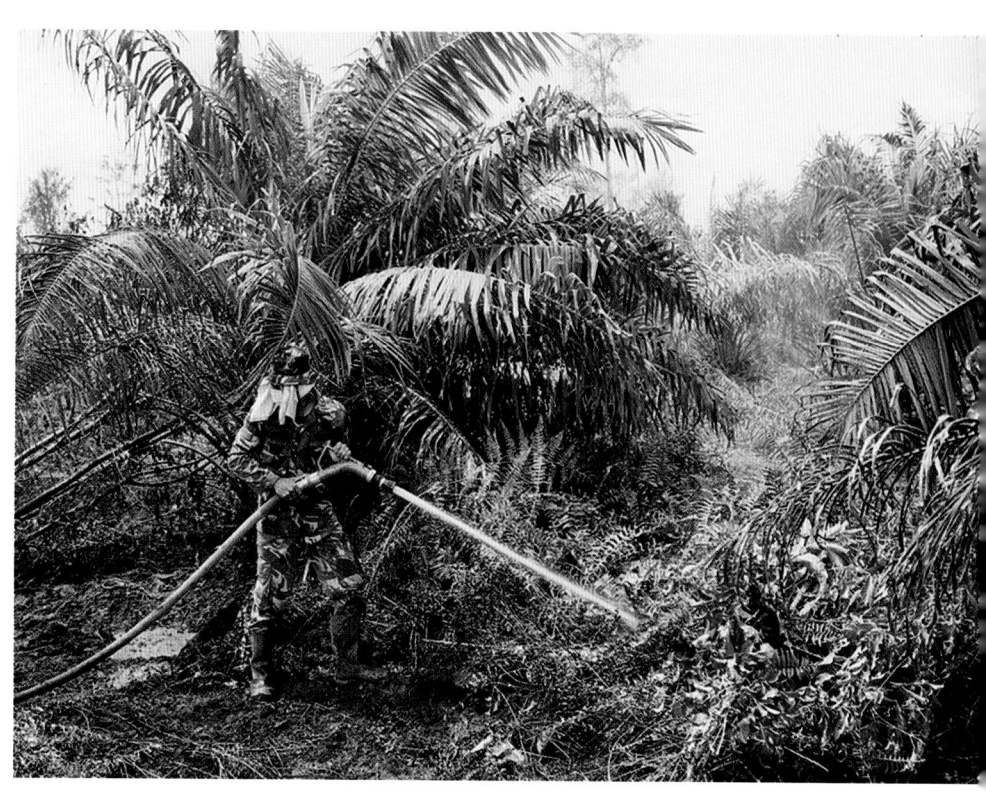

7 Armin Linke, *Blind Sensorium: Il Paradosso dell' Antropocene*, 2019

a half-life of hundreds of thousands of years. A mythological siren swims past submerged archaeological ruins and along the waterways of deserted atomic facilities, including the twin of the Chernobyl power plant still operating in present-day Lithuania, the Large Hadron Collider at CERN near Geneva and a nuclear submarine base within the Arctic Circle. Illuminating the relics of East–West nuclear competition, the work points to the indelible scars left by military and civil atomic infrastructures and the radioactive waste they generate on the natural environment and wellbeing of future generations. Seeking to explain the willingness of those in power on both sides of the Iron Curtain to create radioactive 'sacrifice zones', environmental historians John McNeill and Peter Engelke have pointed in *The Great Acceleration* to the use of 'the security demands of the moment' to justify 'lethally contaminating chosen sites for millennia into the future'.

The Cold War rivalry between opposing economic and political models, which were also competitively exported to the countries of the global South, took place against the backdrop of a surge of economic and social activity since the mid-twentieth century. The rapid growth measured in the indicators for urbanization, transport and communications was mirrored in the scaling up of human interventions in Earth systems, such as water use and soil degradation. In his collaborative work *Blind Sensorium: Il Paradosso dell' Antropocene* (2019), Berlin-based artist Armin Linke devised an archive to register the impact of anthropogenic changes on the planet, depositing footage from laboratories, data centres and conference settings, as well as photographs of sites of resource extraction, from a Chilean copper mine to abandoned oil platforms in the Caspian Sea. The work disclosed the central 'paradox' of the Anthropocene, namely that despite the oversaturation of images in the contemporary interconnected world and the employment of various sensory mechanisms, from satellites to sonars, to observe and collect data about the Earth, the majority are still blind to the effects of climate change. For Linke, this reflects the fact that knowledge generated by the 'technological sensorium' is deeply implicated in the accelerated exploitation of nature, while such images fail to narrate the complexity of the present moment on Earth in which technology, finance, politics and culture are interlocked in a self-reinforcing cycle of unsustainable growth.

Challenging the supposed neutrality of new technology, French Guianese artist Tabita Rezaire drew attention in her film *Deep Down Tidal* (2017) to how it functions as a tool to maintain and reinforce global structures of colonial power.

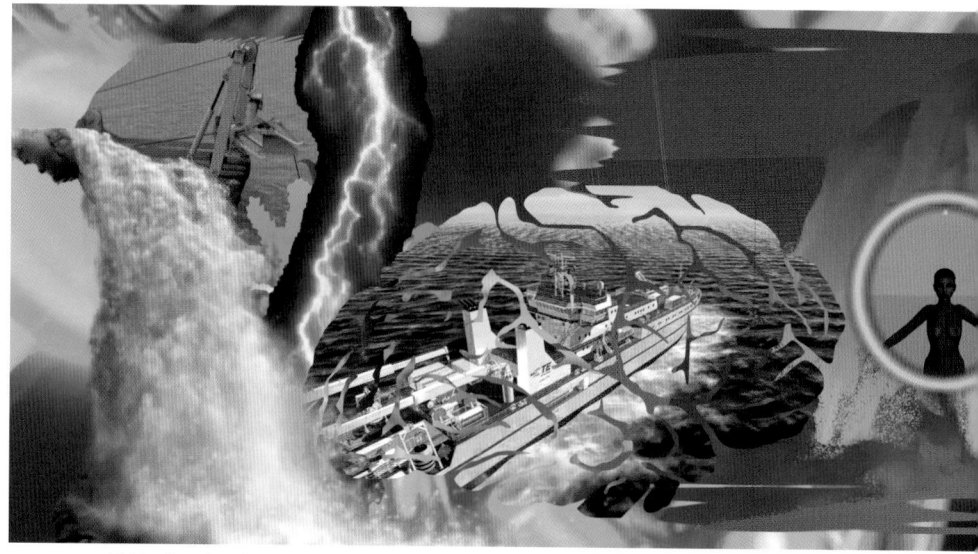

8 Tabita Rezaire, *Deep Down Tidal*, 2017

Exposing the prejudices and inequalities that thrive on social media and bolster Western domination of cyberspace, her work is a vibrant call to confront structural racism and decolonize the internet. The optic cables on the seafloor appear not just as infrastructure for the data transfers on which the globalized world depends, but also as a conduit for the transmission of 'exploitation, exclusion and eco-system disruptions'. What is more, due to the fact that these cables mostly follow the submarine paths of nineteenth-century copper telegraph lines laid along colonial shipping routes established in the slave trade era, they can also be considered as the hardware of a new 'electronic colonialism'. For the artist, the process of cleansing and healing in the face of the destructiveness of the Anthropocene is to be achieved by reviving the methods of 'ancient African spirituality' to reconnect to ourselves, each other, the Earth and the universe.

   The artistic practices discussed here outline the ways in which anthropogenic interventions in the biogeochemical processes of the Earth system have left an indelible record in the geological materiality of the planet. These ruptures are detected in mineral deposits, the pulverizing of the lithosphere, the reconfiguration of topographies and the secretions of atomic radiation, as well as in the deep time components of new technologies. Manifestations of geological evidence are approached in these works through the lens of geopolitical

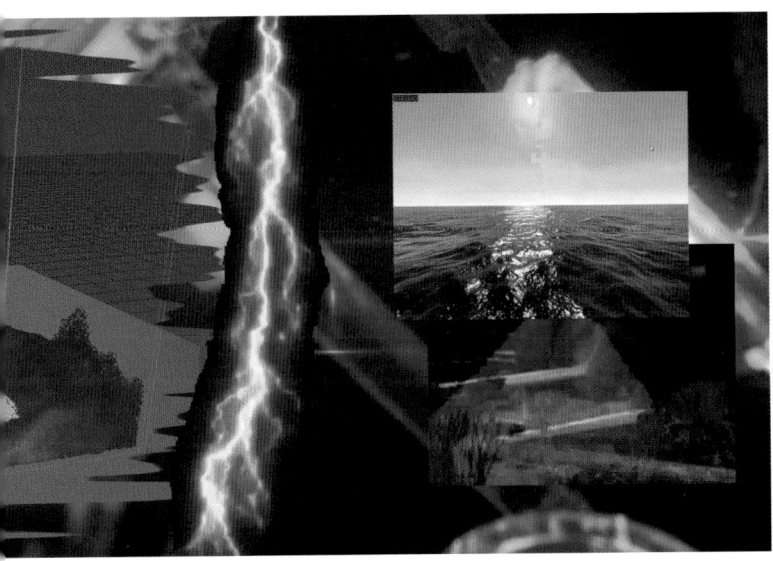

power relations, illustrating the entwinement of capitalist and political interests, the ongoing encroachments of the military–colonial complex and the extractivist agenda of cybertechnology. The exposure of toxic geologies and their climate-altering impacts goes hand in hand with tentative gestures to remythologize, re-enchant and spiritually cleanse contaminated grounds.

Chapter 2
Scars of Extraction

At its most tangible, extraction entails the removal of mineral matter from the Earth's crust by drilling, pumping, quarrying and mining in order to render it as raw materials that can be traded as commodities and processed in industrial operations. Extractivism can also be understood more broadly as a mindset that has infiltrated economic and social relations, succinctly defined by Naomi Klein in *This Changes Everything* as a 'non-reciprocal, dominance-based relationship with the earth, one purely of taking'. Historically the impact of extractive capitalism has been most intensively felt in colonized territories where, as theorist Macarena Gómez-Barris has described in *The Extractive Zone*, it seeks out areas of high biodiversity, systematically engaging in 'thefts, borrowings and forced removals' in order to 'reduce, constrain and convert life into commodities'. Today, as the finite reserves of what environmental historian Jason W. Moore has called 'cheap nature' are depleted, the competition between global corporations for the Earth's dwindling supplies of precious metals, copper, uranium, tungsten, cobalt and the rare earth minerals used in miniaturized electronic devices is accelerating. The practices discussed here examine how the extractivist machine turns mineral-rich territories into toxic sacrifice zones, with devastating impacts on local communities, expose entwined colonial, military and mining complexes, and problematize the ever more intrusive technologies and methods deployed to make natural wealth available for exploitation.

Lise Autogena and Joshua Portway's film *Kuannersuit; Kvanefjeld* (2016) is a collective portrait of the mostly indigenous community of Narsaq in southern Greenland as it faces the prospect of the opening of a large-scale pit mine that would change the city and its surroundings forever. Perched in the

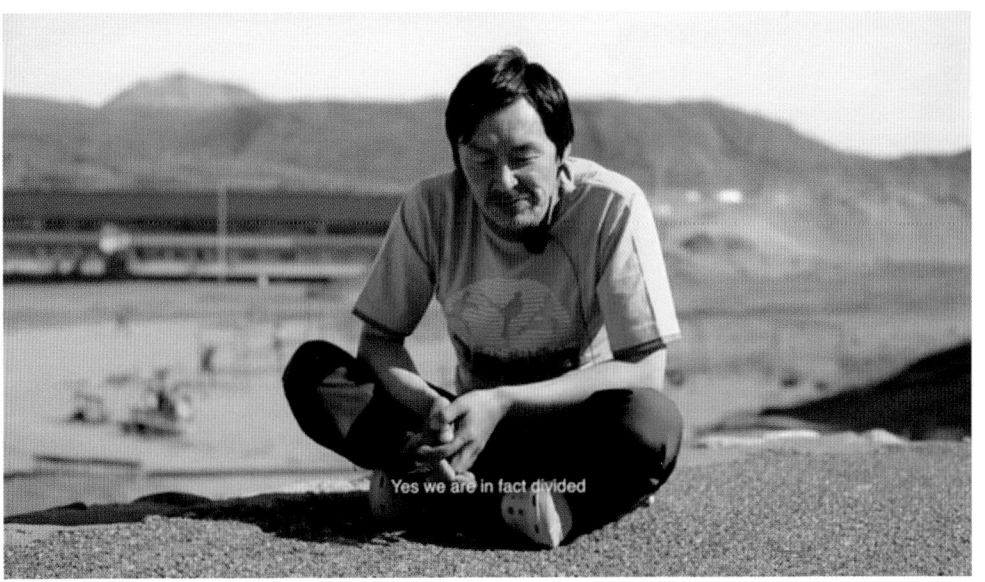

9 Lise Autogena and Joshua Portway, *Kuannersuit; Kvanefjeld*, 2016

foothills of the Kvanefjeld volcanic mountain, which holds
one of the richest rare earth mineral and uranium deposits in
the world, the city is divided over its future, due to the mining
industry's keenness to exploit the opportunities arising from
the melting of Greenland's inland ice. Some see it as a way out
from the unemployment and impoverishment that was caused
by the demise of the fishing industry and as a move towards
economic independence from Denmark. Others question such
self-sufficiency in which dependence on the former colonial
power would be substituted with that of the Australian–
Chinese multinational consortium that owns the mining rights.
They point to the pollution, toxicity and health hazards this
development would bring to the community and the natural
environment, as well as the unforeseeable consequences for
traditional sheep farming, ways of life and cultural integrity.
London-based artists Autogena and Portway lay bare the
complexity of the choices that the mining industry is imposing
on local communities caught between the desire for sovereignty
and the social and ecological trade-offs of extractive operations.
Their in-depth portrayal of this microsite on the edge of
the Arctic Circle vividly demonstrated how local politics,
financial speculation, cultural identities and natural entities
are inextricably entwined on the ever-expanding frontier of
extractive capitalism.

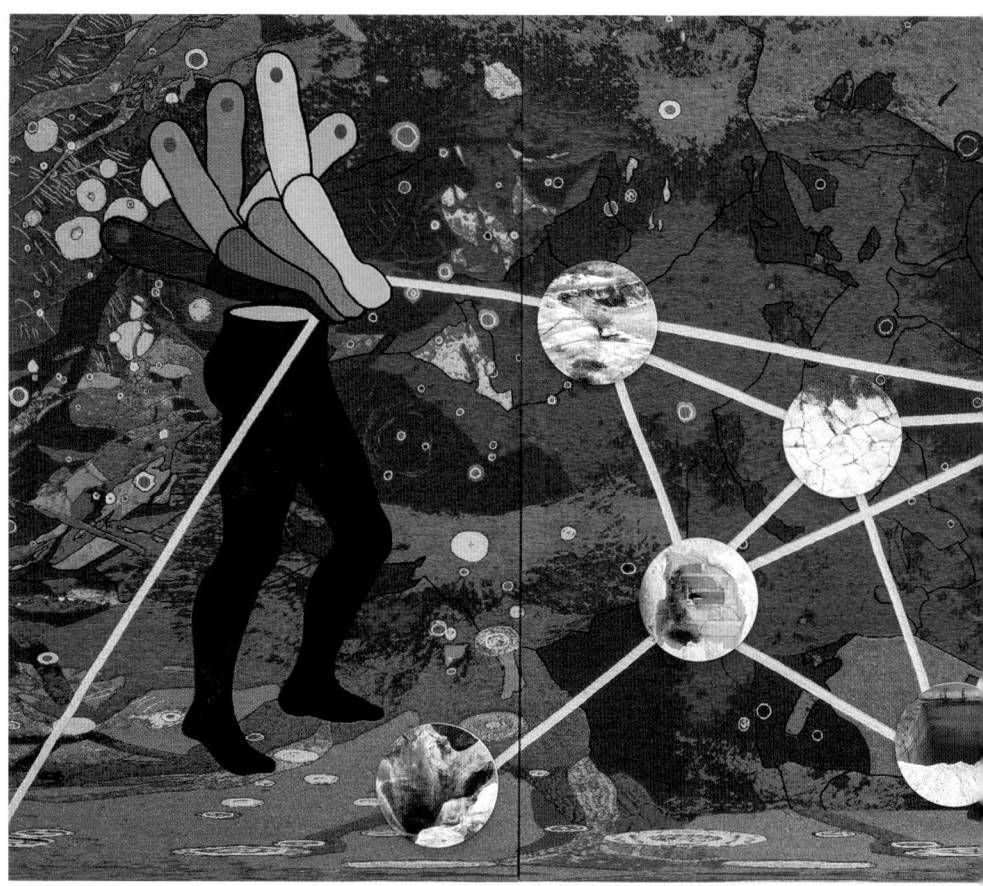

10 Otobong Nkanga, *The Weight of Scars*, 2015

The consequences of pursuing a path of extreme extractivism were laid bare in Nicholas Mangan's video essay *Nauru: Notes from a Cretaceous World* (2009–10). The film investigated the infamous history of phosphate mining on Nauru, the smallest island nation in the Pacific, which during the twentieth century was turned from an island oasis into a paradigmatic case of a sacrifice zone. The strip-mining of phosphate, the main component of agricultural fertilizer, accelerated after the island gained independence in 1968, making Nauru the second richest nation per capita on the planet, before the mineral deposits were completely depleted in the early 2000s. This left eighty percent of the island's land area barren as the topsoil was removed down to the coral backbone, while the population, now dependent on imported canned food and struggling with

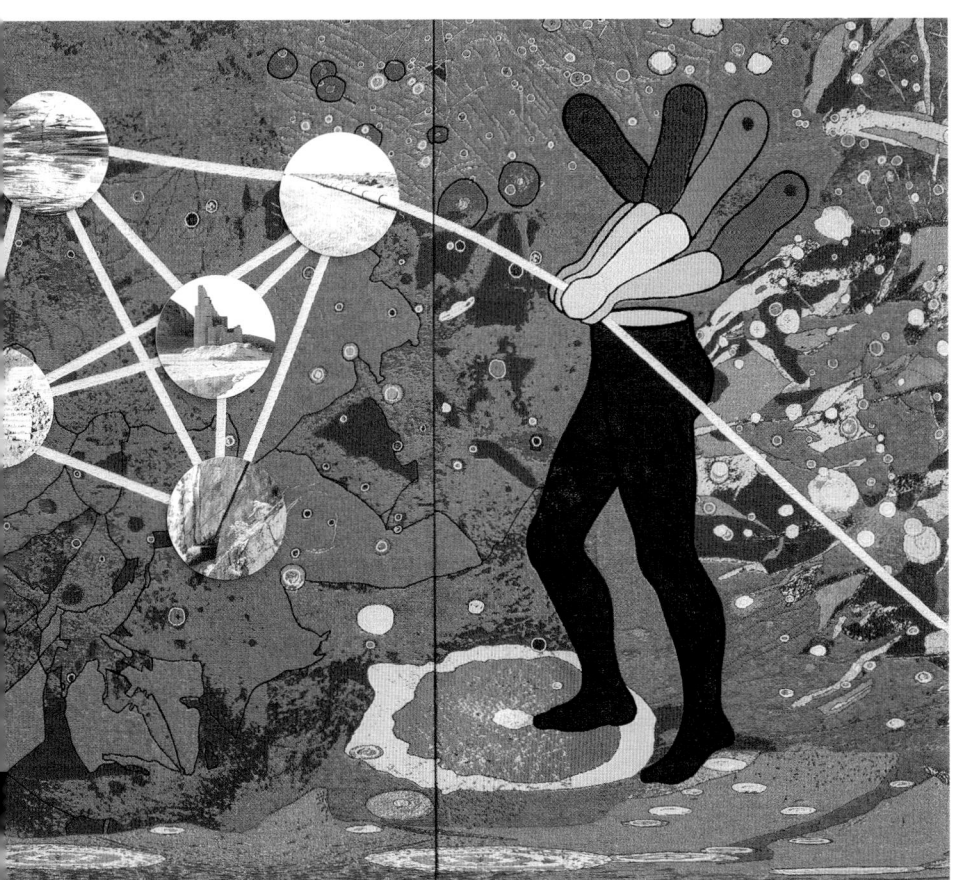

obesity, faces an even more uncertain future as rising sea levels threaten to turn them into climate refugees.

Erasing the heads of her figures to express the overload of information, too much for a mind to comprehend, Nigerian-born artist Otobong Nkanga equips them instead with multiple arms to emphasize gesture, action, work and connection to the land. This is visible in her work *The Weight of Scars* (2015), a set of four woven tapestries made in the aftermath of the artist's visit to the mines of Namibia. The work draws attention to the scars that such sites of extraction have left, equally on landscapes and on people's bodies, minds and emotions. Although the Namibians carved out minerals before the arrival of German colonizers, the scale and technology used in aggressive mining have made the damage a great deal more acute, especially around Tsumeb, one of the most diverse and richest crystal areas in the world. *Remains of the Green Hill* (2015) is a recording of the spontaneous performance by the artist upon seeing the site that used to radiate a bright green colour of oxidized copper, but is now a cavernous hole, instead of a hill. The voiceover from the interview with the last manager of the mine narrates the story of the development, yet Nkanga augments it with toxic remnants in the land and air of the mining district, considering the barren pits as social, political and emotional monuments to this destructive history.

The mineral-rich lands of the Congo River basin are another hotspot of extractivism, where copper, coltan, lithium, uranium, diamonds and sixty percent of global production of cobalt are ripped from the Earth through environmentally ruinous mining practices. Addressing the enduring impact of colonial domination on his country of birth, Sammy Baloji's installation *Untitled* (2016) consisted of soil-filled copper shell cartridges from which various plants grow. Such shell cases, widely used in both World Wars, were made with copper from the Belgian colonial territory of the Congo, and were later repurposed in peacetime as vases that were therapeutically decorated by shell-shocked soldiers. By planting them with species that are native to the mining areas of the Democratic Republic of Congo but are now used as ornamental plants in Europe, the artist drew attention to the erasure of the tragic history of the impact of the World Wars on Africa. The work also shed light on the unacknowledged presence of vegetation and natural materials extracted from Congo, including rubber for tyres, uranium for atomic bombs, copper for electrical wiring and rare earth minerals for mobile phones, in the globalized economies of the Western world. The related film *Tales of the Copper Crosses Garden: Episode I* (2017) incorporated footage of workers in a copper factory, the soundtrack of a hymn sung by the Copper Cross Singers choir and extracts from the work of Congolese philosopher Valentin-Yves Mudimbe challenging the Eurocentric myth of Africa as a *terra nullius* ready for conquest.

'We are all carrying a piece of Congo in our pockets, constantly connected to its conflicts,' observed Revital Cohen and Tuur van Balen, a London-based duo of Israeli and Belgian origin respectively, referring to coltan, a metallic ore used in electronic products including smartphones. Most of it comes from the artisanal mines of eastern Congo, a region caught in a spiral of violence over control of the extraction sites and trade routes. The duo's filmed performance *Trapped in the Dream of the Other* (2017) recorded the setting off of fireworks

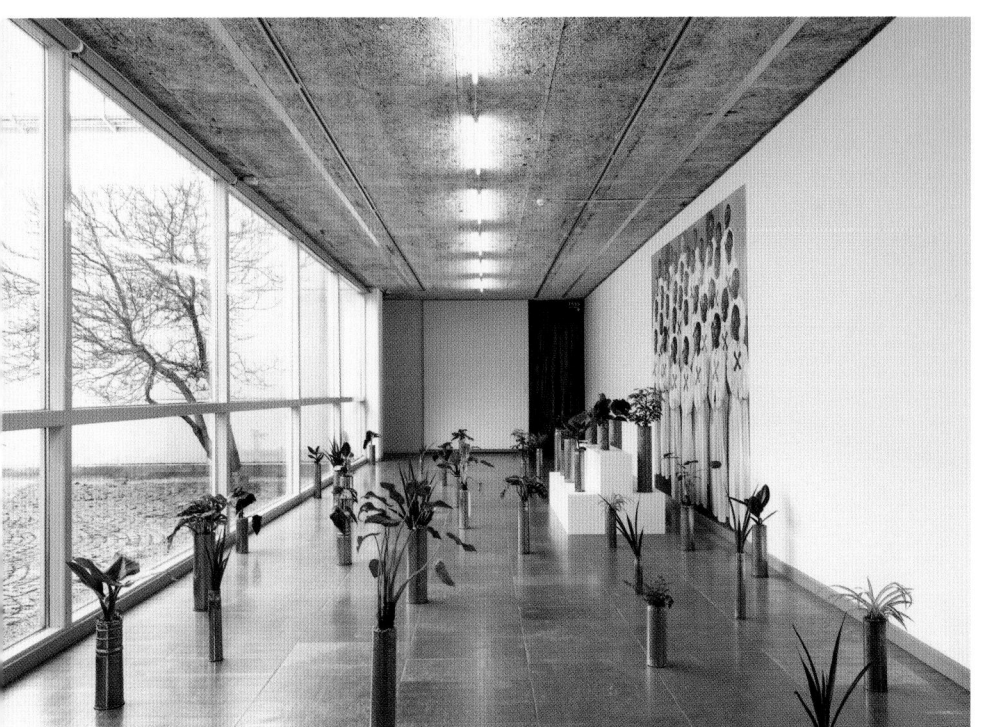

11 Sammy Baloji, *Petits Chanteurs à la Croix de Cuivre*, 2020, and *Untitled*, 2016

in one of DR Congo's coltan mines, for which 100 kilograms of pyrotechnics were procured in Hunan Province, the centre of the Chinese fireworks industry. The consignment only reached the site after overcoming various logistical obstacles, suggesting also a reversal of the journey of the region's minerals: namely, day labourers using basic tools dig coltan from the rubble of the ditches and carrying it in heavy sacks to sell to middlemen, who in turn take the load to cities, where the raw minerals are refined before being shipped to China to be processed in giant electronic factories. By setting off fireworks and creating a screen of smoke and sparkles, the artists alluded to the impossibility of getting to the core of the problem, since just as global efforts to compel tech companies to establish ethical conduct in their supply chains remain of limited success, everyone is interconnected and implicated in the extraction of 'conflict minerals' used in electronic products.

London-based Chilean artist Ignacio Acosta's extensive body of work *Copper Geographies* (2012–16) also dealt with the metal that plays 'a key role in worldwide information and

12

Scars of Extraction

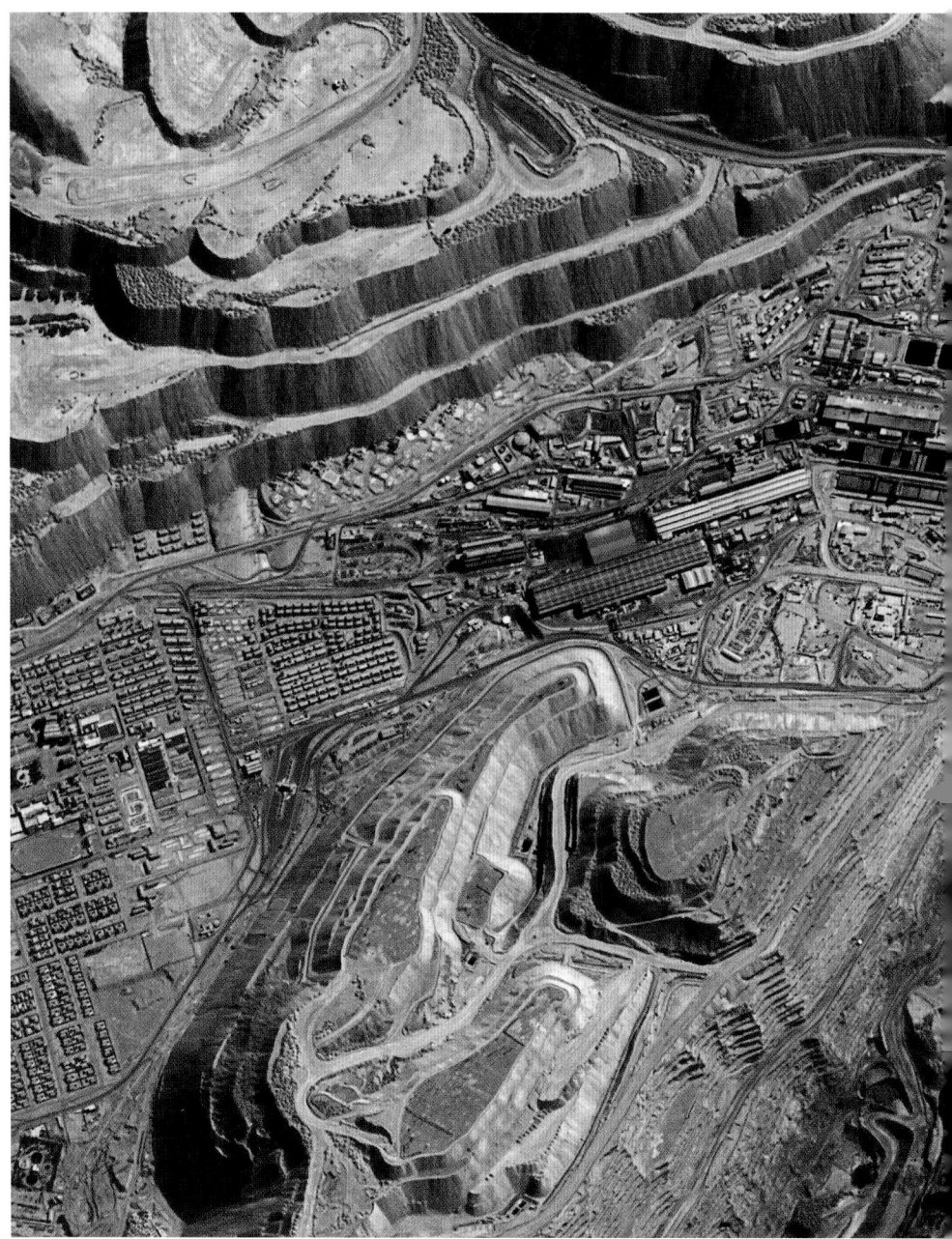

12　Ignacio Acosta, *Copper Geographies*, 2012–16

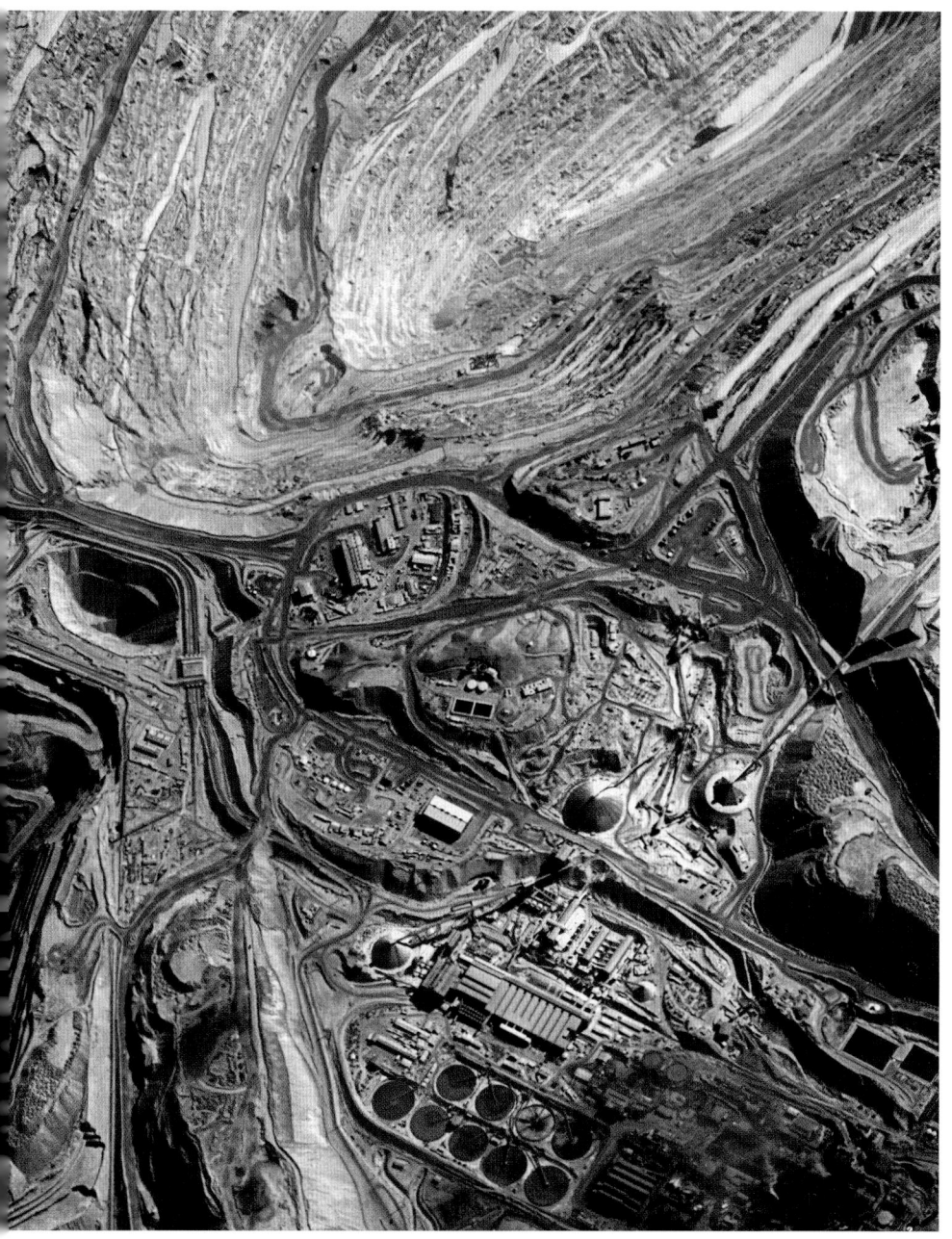

Scars of Extraction

communication technologies', as it is the core material for cables, tubes and wires used in infrastructure, transport and technology. However, in the artist's view, 'very little attention has been paid to how the industry impacts the ecologies in which it operates'. Through maps, photographs and texts, the work followed the copper on its journey from extraction through stock market speculation on metal exchanges to commodity trade, before ending up in recycling stations. Chile contains the world's largest deposit of copper ore, which is mainly located in the Atacama Desert, where Chuquicamata is now the world's biggest open-cast mine. Next to the mine is a model corporate town of the same name, which was designed in the offices of the Guggenheim brothers in the early twentieth century and inhabited until 2007, when due to high pollution levels its 25,000 workers were relocated to a nearby city, where social problems continue. As the artist reveals, throughout the decades of exploitation, the management of the mines has been in the hands of British, US and more recently multinational corporations, in cooperation with the state-owned mining company, while development is accompanied by legal battles and environmental disputes arising from the highly toxic and water-intensive process of extraction.

While the notion of the Capitalocene depends, as Raj Patel and Jason W. Moore have clarified, on understanding capitalism 'not just as an economic system but as a way of organising the relations between humans and the rest of nature', the issue of the specificity of attitudes and practices towards the natural world under socialism complicates this West-centric account. The socialist Anthropocene shared the modern industrial era's drive for economic growth, with terrestrial matter, vegetation and other species treated as an unlimited resource for building socialism, while at its height under Stalin, as Paul Johnson noted in *Environmental Histories of the Cold War*, nature was even regarded as a 'class enemy' that always threatened to evade Party control. The film *The Most Beautiful Catastrophe* (2018) by the Bratislava-based APART Collective opens with a matter-of-fact description of a socialist realist fresco from the early 1960s that includes three capitalists running away 'in their business suits', a worker with his 'chains broken', a metallurgist, a flag-waver and a woman with an open book who 'might be a person from the future recording the sacrifices of her socialist predecessors'. As disclosed in the film, the extensive development of heavy industry and mining during the socialist period has unexpectedly resulted in the appearance of new wetlands and marshes in the upper Nitra region as a side-effect of underground coal extraction.

13

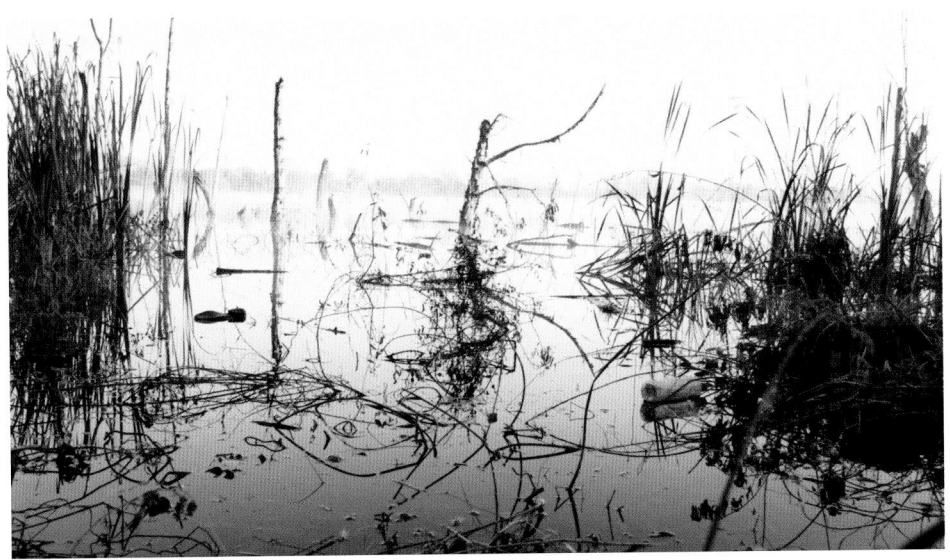

13 APART Collective, *The Most Beautiful Catastrophe*, 2018

These have become hotspots for the return of biodiversity to landscapes ruined by the socialist Anthropocene and its master narrative, summarized in the film through the motto 'We will dictate the wind, the rain, and nature WILL OBEY US!' However, the precariousness of all wilderness revivals on the margins of sacrifice zones is suggested by the fact that a recent mine accident resulted in the extinguishing of all insect life in the marsh, as toxic chemicals were released into the wetlands.

While the rise of a global capitalist system based on extractivism was inseparable from the colonial expansion of European powers, today its social and environmental effects no longer follow the territorial divisions of geopolitical hegemony, with zones of exploitation and enclaves of resource extraction operating across the global North and South. Berlin-based artists Angela Melitopoulos and Angela Anderson's video installation *Unearthing Disaster I & II* (2013–15) documented Canadian mining company Eldorado's construction of an open-cast gold mine in a mountainous region of northeast Greece and the mobilization of activists in protest. In addition to examining the environmental damage and future risks, such as the depositing of mine tailings in wooded stream valleys sacrificed for the storage of the toxic by-products of the chemical purification of ore, the work drew attention to the psychological toll on local communities of witnessing the destruction of natural places to which they are emotionally

14

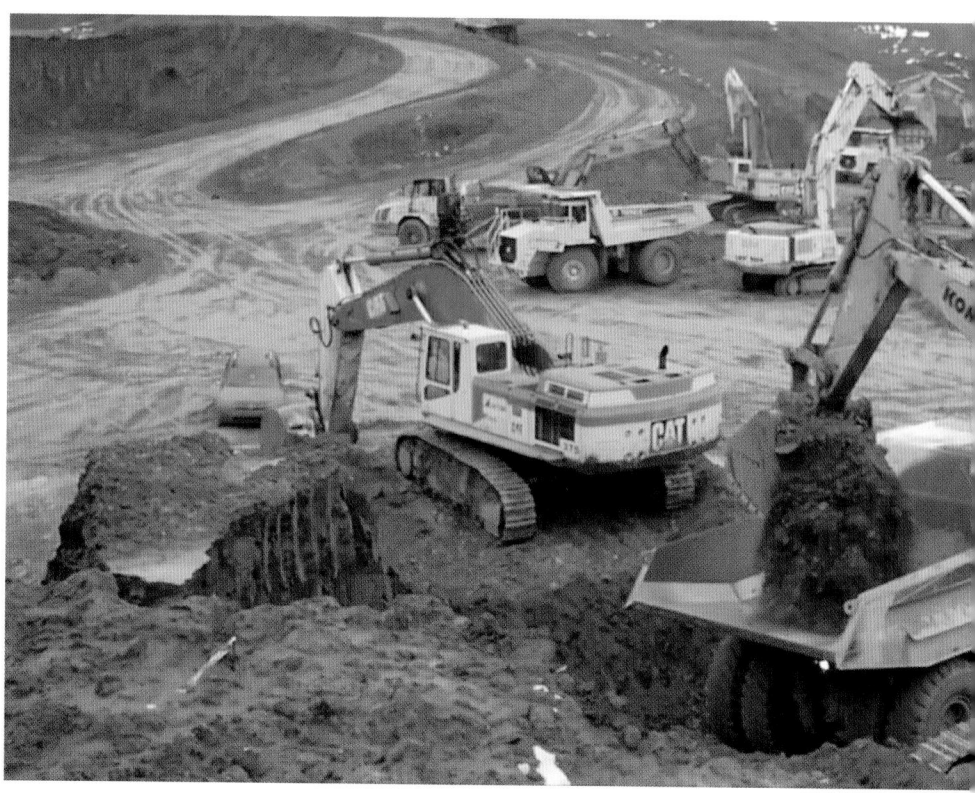

14 Angela Melitopoulos and Angela Anderson, *Unearthing Disaster II*, 2015

attached. It also makes clear that as global capitalism overrides local sensibilities to expand the extractive frontier, with traditional mining of veins of ore in underground tunnels giving way to vast mechanized open pits and intrusive technologies of high-pressure fracking, the stakes have never been higher in confronting an unsustainable economic system based on the domination and exploitation of the natural world.

With global warming making new regions at the polar extremes of the planet available for exploitation and mining, late liberal capitalism continues its menacing expansion. Meanwhile, soaring demand for fossil fuels and specific rare minerals as components for digital devices is driving a frenzied phase of extractive devastation across the world. Artistic projects discussed here investigated neo-colonialist exploitation in countries that remain deeply scarred by earlier waves of imperialist plunder of Earth's wealth, as well as the toxic legacy of the extractivist violence perpetrated by socialist

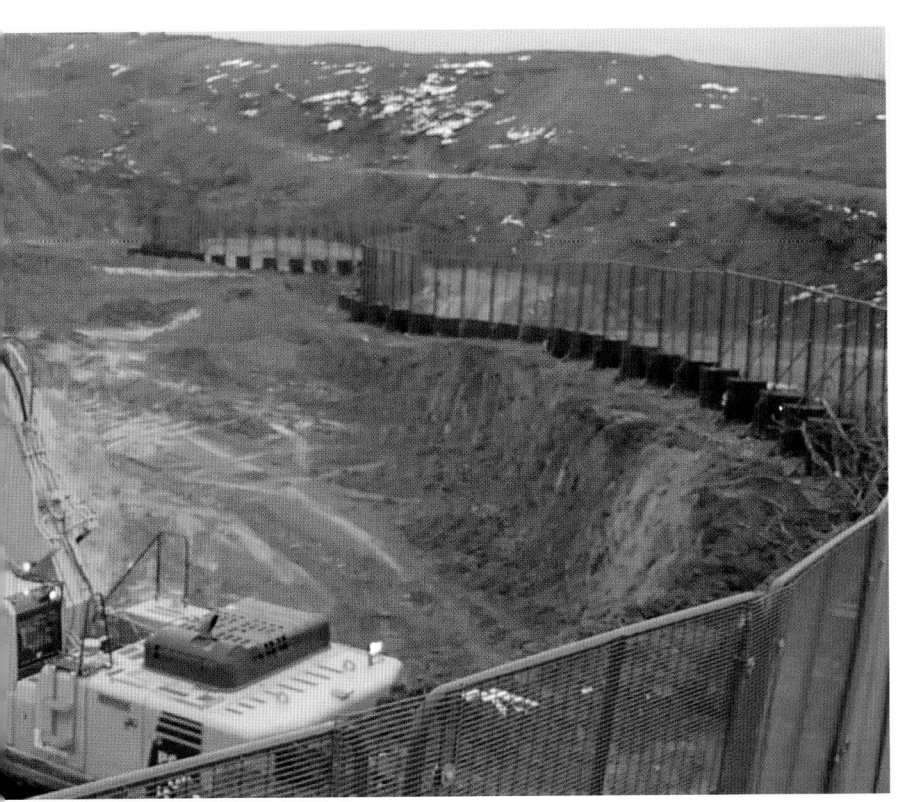

states, still visible in wounded post-industrial landscapes. They have also drawn attention to the opening up of new extractive frontiers in former colonial heartlands, while disclosing the deleterious effects of extractivism on mental and bodily wellbeing.

Chapter 3
Crude Oil

Since the first hard-rock drilling operation struck oil in Pennsylvania in 1859, the exploitation of petroleum has set in motion economic and infrastructural transformations that have defined the modern world. By tapping into reserves of ancient sunshine amassed over millions of years of photosynthesis and fixed in subterranean deposits of coal, oil and gas, industrialized societies have been able to take advantage of an unprecedented energy windfall. Oil reconfigured the geopolitical order, propelling the United States and Soviet Union to superpower status during the Cold War and generating conflict over the control of petroleum-rich regions, to the extent that, as Timothy Mitchell discussed in *Carbon Democracy*, wealth in natural resources became an 'oil curse' associated with oppressive and autocratic politics. Fossil fuel capitalism, and the swift economic growth it facilitated, made possible the rise of a global economic system in which petroleum-powered shipping, road and air transport accelerated international trade, while reinforcing structural inequalities and historical patterns of social exclusion. The correlation between economic globalization and global warming is underlined by David Wallace-Wells's observation in *The Uninhabitable Earth* in 2019 that 'more than half of the carbon exhaled into the atmosphere by the burning of fossil fuels has been emitted in just the last three decades'. Despite the fact that oil exploitation has left a trail of destruction in the natural environment through leaks, spills and fires, the petroleum industry has redoubled its efforts to obstruct the decarbonizing of economy, society and culture.

15   Conceiving their *Museum of Oil* (2016) as an institution in the making, London-based duo Territorial Agency (John Palmesino and Ann-Sofi Rönnskog) envisaged a climate scenario in

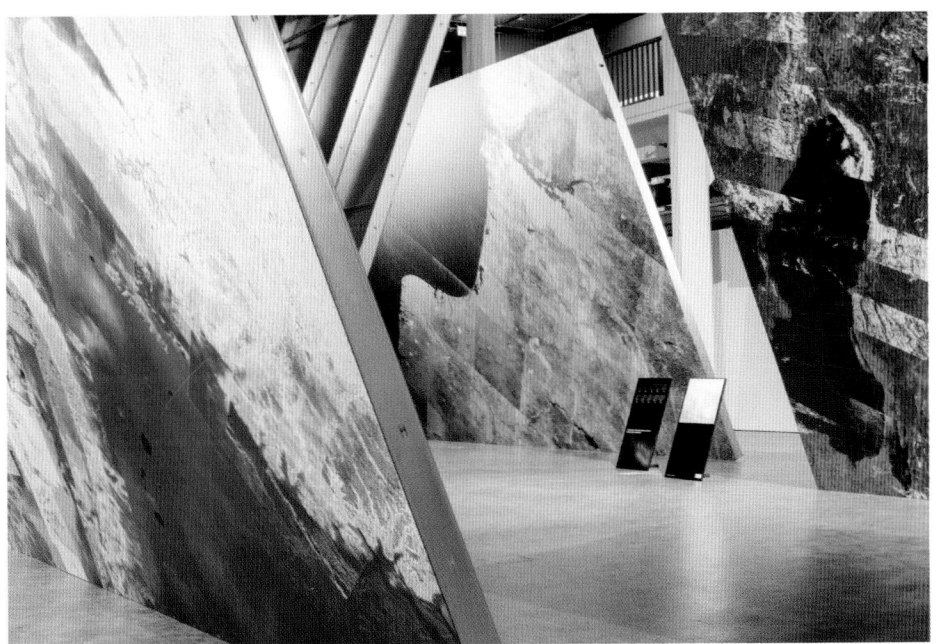

15 Territorial Agency (John Palmesino and Ann-Sofi Rönnskog), *Museum of Oil*, 2016

which petroleum stocks are left safely in the ground, while the destructive mechanisms of the oil industry are turned into historical artefacts. Consisting of large slanting panels, the museum display included satellite images, documentary footage and streams of data that disclosed the planetary imprint of oil drilling, pipelines and refineries, rendering tangible the sheer scale of such operations. This research detailed the damage inflicted by oil power on the natural world, from deforestation in Brazil and Peru to the regular oil leaks from rusting Soviet-era pipelines in Siberia and the upswing in fossil fuel prospecting in the Arctic as the ice melts. Equally, the artists drew attention to the destabilizing economic effects of oil investments, with companies driven to undertake ever more complicated and risky explorations by the constant need to secure new reserves as current fields are depleted. Oil power is revealed as operating behind the scenes, infiltrating legal, political, cultural and environmental realms, framing discussions of ecological disasters and intervening in climate policy agendas. The fact that the industry is never explicitly named in climate change agreements, which refer more neutrally to carbon emissions, was for Territorial Agency another reason to expose oil to public scrutiny in the museum.

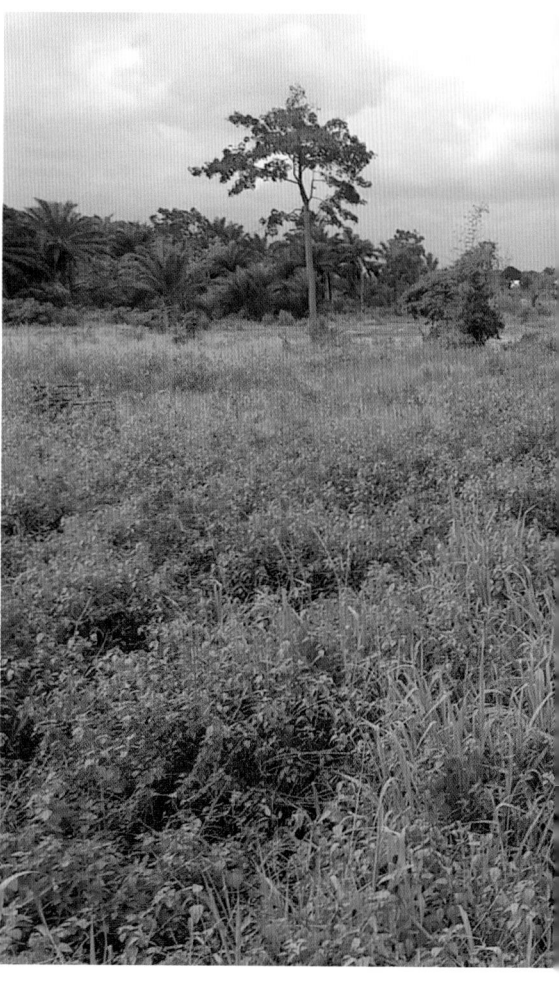

16   In the five-channel video installation *Karikpo Pipeline* (2015) by Nigerian-born artist Zina Saro-Wiwa, the camera glides through the low-lying expanses of the Niger Delta, showing palm trees and greenery occasionally intersected by corroded metal oil pipes or decommissioned flow stations. Every now and then ghostly apparitions of traditional Karikpo dancers wearing wooden antelope masks with horns emerge in the landscape. Their appearance and disappearance from view hint at what is hiding beneath the surface, namely the underground network of pipelines that have transformed the land and life of the inhabitants since oil was discovered there by Royal Dutch Shell in 1965. The harrowing environmental devastation of

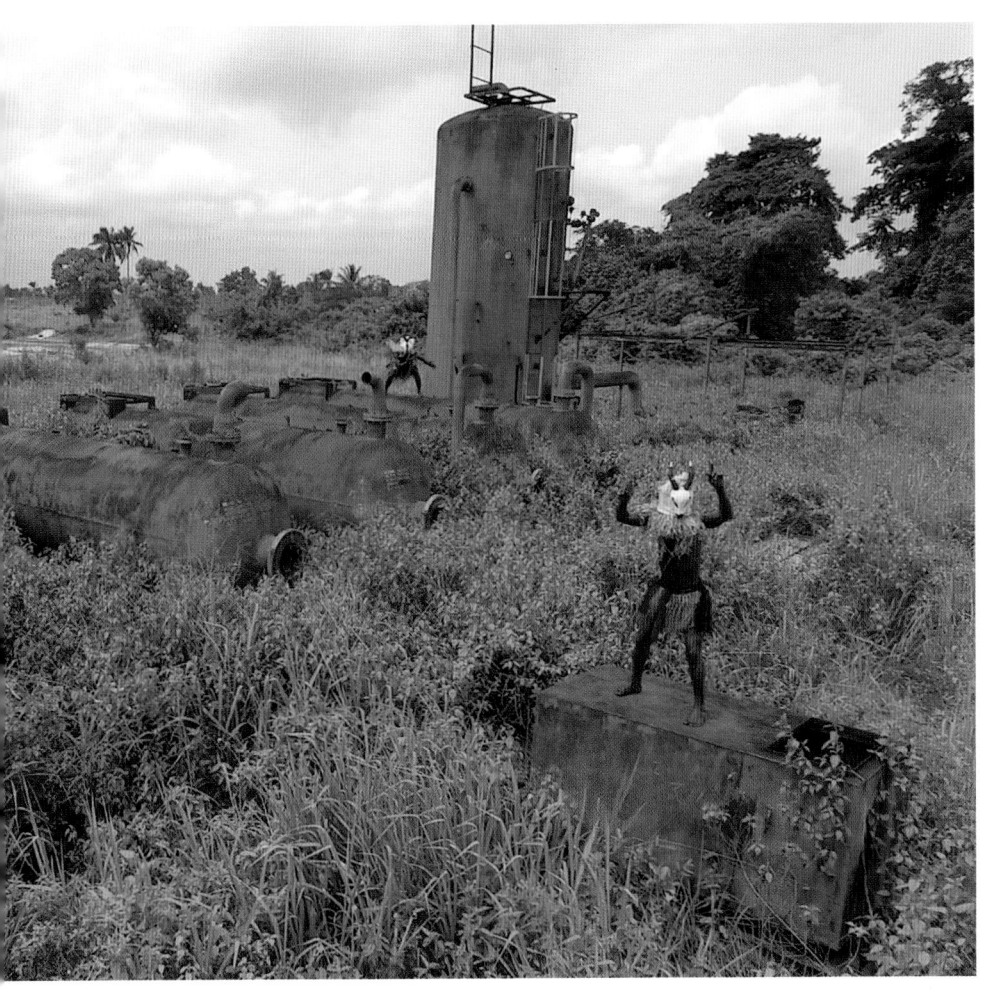

Ogoniland that followed is close to the artist's heart, since her father, activist Ken Saro-Wiwa, who established the Movement for Survival of Ogoni People to fight against the ecological destruction of the Niger Delta, was tragically executed by the military authorities in 1995. The use of drone footage in the film is suggestive of the surveillance techniques of the petroleum companies, but it also refers to the invisible spiritual forces that are believed to populate the scorched land of the Delta. In that sense, the work reaches beyond the violent, corrupting and toxic oil exploitation to uncover the hidden, rich culture of the Ogoni people and their unbreakable relationship with the land.

Crude Oil

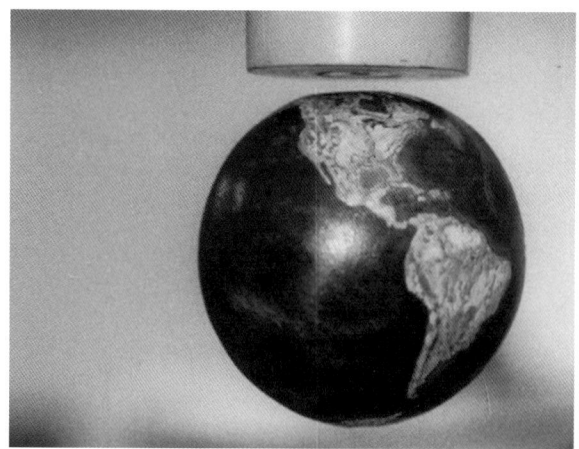

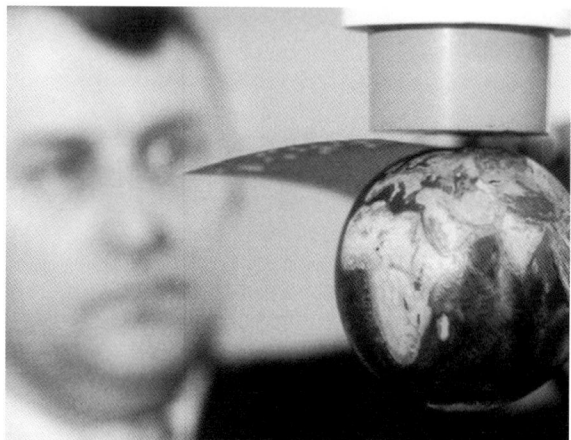

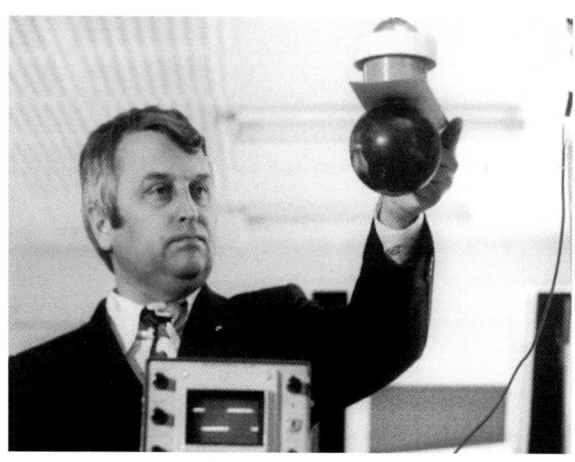

17 Kinotron Group, *Data Is the New Gas*, 2019

Taking the form of the research essay *Is Data the New Gas?* (2020), Ukrainian artist Oleksiy Radynski's inquiry into the structural interdependence of authoritarian politics and fossil fuel extraction investigated the controversy over the laying of the Nord Stream II (NSII) gas pipeline between Russia and Germany in the Baltic Sea. For Radynski, the biggest problem is not the fact that the undersea pipeline will deprive Ukraine of transit revenues and provide 'the Russian autocratic elite with another powerful tool to subvert European politics', but that the new infrastructure 'undermines the future of planet Earth by bringing the irreversibility of climate change one large step closer'. The artist traced the origins of German–Russian cooperation for the extraction of Siberian gas back to the signing in 1970 of the 'gas for pipes' deal, which enabled the building of the *Bratstvo* or Brotherhood pipeline to connect the largest gas reserves on the planet to the European energy market. While supplying hard currency to prop up the Soviet regime, this Faustian bargain laid the ground for the emergence in Russia in the post-communist period of an 'autocratic system based on a ruthless extractivist attitude to the Earth's resources'. Working also as a member of the Kinotron film collective, Radynski has investigated the role played by visionary cybernetician and inventor of the Soviet internet Viktor Glushkov in computerizing the world's longest network of pipelines. While publicly proclaiming the ability of computers to balance economic needs and environmental preservation, Glushkov warned in closed meetings of the future exhaustion of fossil fuel reserves.

Faced with the depletion of easily accessible oil reserves, the industry has resorted to unconventional methods such as pumping toxic chemicals into the lithosphere and using vast quantities of water to force the Earth to release hydrocarbons from shale rock. The technology of fracking is described by environmental theorists Sandro Mezzadra and Brett Neilson, authors of *The Politics of Operations: Excavating Contemporary Capitalism*, as the 'cutting edge of extraction' in that it allows it to 'continue beyond the point at which the gases it seeks to remove from the Earth have been otherwise depleted'. In *The Gas Imaginary* (since 2013), settler Australian artist Rachel O'Reilly investigated the profound social and environmental ramifications of the rapid expansion of new forms of fossil fuel extraction from the port of her hometown of Gladstone in the unceded territory of the Gooreng Gooreng people into new frontier spaces across the country. Through poetry, collaborative drawing, animation and performative lectures, as well as the feature-length documentary film

Infractions (2019), she traced the environmental devastation caused by unconventional gas fracking, vividly illustrated by the proliferation of shimmering ponds of toxic wastewater across the landscape of western Queensland. While *Infractions* platformed the current struggles of First Nations artists and theorists to protect water, earlier works addressed the continuation of colonial power brought about by unconventional mining, which is extending the ongoing indigenous experience of the environmental devastation of homelands and the technocratic usurpation of basic rights by the historically privileged settler population. Australia's climate-shaming status as the world's largest exporter of fossil gas has come at the risk of poisoning and depleting the underground aquifer systems of a country already facing extreme water shortages as a result of intensive agriculture and global warming.

Two distant geographies, the boreal forest in northern Canada and the coastal floodplains of Bangladesh, were set in dynamic correlation in Swiss artist Ursula Biemann's *Deep Weather* (2013) to underscore the profound changes in planetary ecology brought about by anthropogenic climate disruption. Aerial footage of the devastation caused by the open-cast mining and steam processing of the Alberta tar sands, turning the forest ecosystem and territory of First Nation peoples into a petro-capitalist sacrifice zone, is paired with scenes of the community effort to build protective mud embankments to hold back the flood waters of the Bangladesh Delta, swelled by melting Himalayan permafrost, rising sea levels and extreme weather. Biemann contrasted the hi-tech apparel of the Canadian miners tapping unconventional oil for delivery around the world, including to refineries on the US Gulf Coast through the disputed Keystone XL pipeline project, with the bare hands with which precarious communities in the global South desperately try to hold back the catastrophic local impacts of climate change. This work demonstrated the extent to which, in the interconnected Earth system, environmental devastation experienced in particular localities is inseparable from extractivist excesses taking place on the other side of the world.

With the warmest years on record, an unprecedented rate of melting ice and wildfires raging even in the Arctic Circle, the reality of climate disruption is becoming increasingly apparent, despite the efforts of a well-funded science of climate change denial to relativize the evidence. This was the starting point for Austrian artist Oliver Ressler's project *Carbon and Captivity* (2020), which set out to investigate how oil corporations are forging alliances in their efforts to develop sustainable technological solutions for continuing oil extraction. One

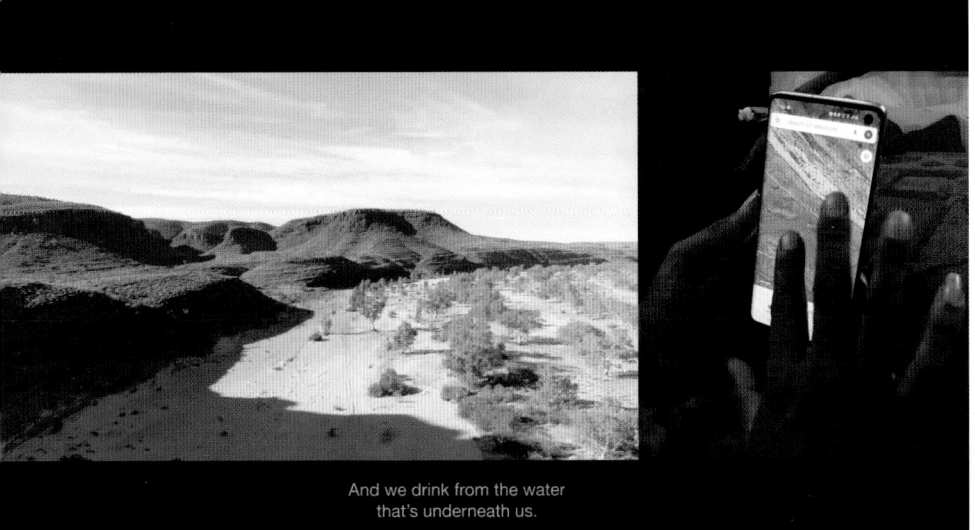

And we drink from the water
that's underneath us.

18 Rachel O'Reilly, *Infractions*, 2019

chapter of the film follows a guided tour of the world's largest facility for testing carbon capture technologies on an industrial scale at the Technology Centre Mongstad in Norway, with an industry representative laying out the prospects of carbon sequestration and storage on the seafloor. Such an approach mirrors the advocacy of technological solutions by signatories to the Ecomodernist Manifesto, who saw an opportunity for a 'good Anthropocene' to emerge in which geoengineering could be used to stabilize the climate. However, Clive Hamilton in his *Earthmasters: The Dawn of Climate Engineering* warns that we should be wary of 'any technology that claims to have found a way to immobilise for centuries huge quantities of carbon somewhere in the Earth system where it does not belong'. Also drawing attention to the unreliable premises of the technofix, Ressler insists on the environmental hazards posed by risky procedures to sink carbon into the Earth, the lure of subsidies for industry and the continuing global dependence on fossil fuel energy. 'Captivity' in his title stands not only for the technological system of carbon capture, but also for the state of humanity, kept in imprisonment by an oil industry determined to indefinitely postpone the post-fossil future.

Questioning its centrality as the fossil fuel of modern times, Kuwaiti artist Monira Al Qadiri pointed to the alternative histories of oil usage in her sculpture *Deep Float* (2017). Consisting of a free-standing bathtub filled to the brim with velvety black

20

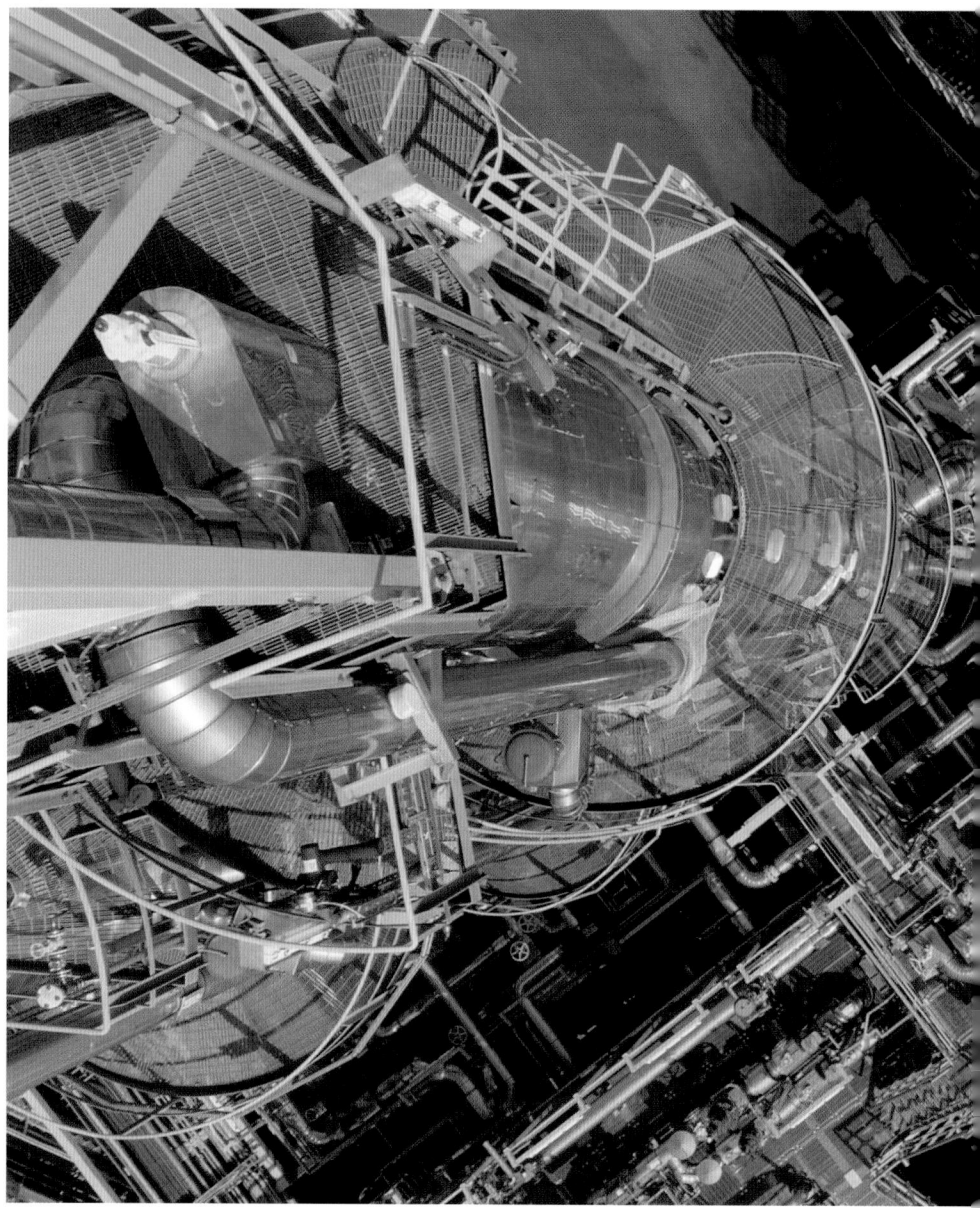

19 Oliver Ressler, *Carbon and Captivity*, 2020

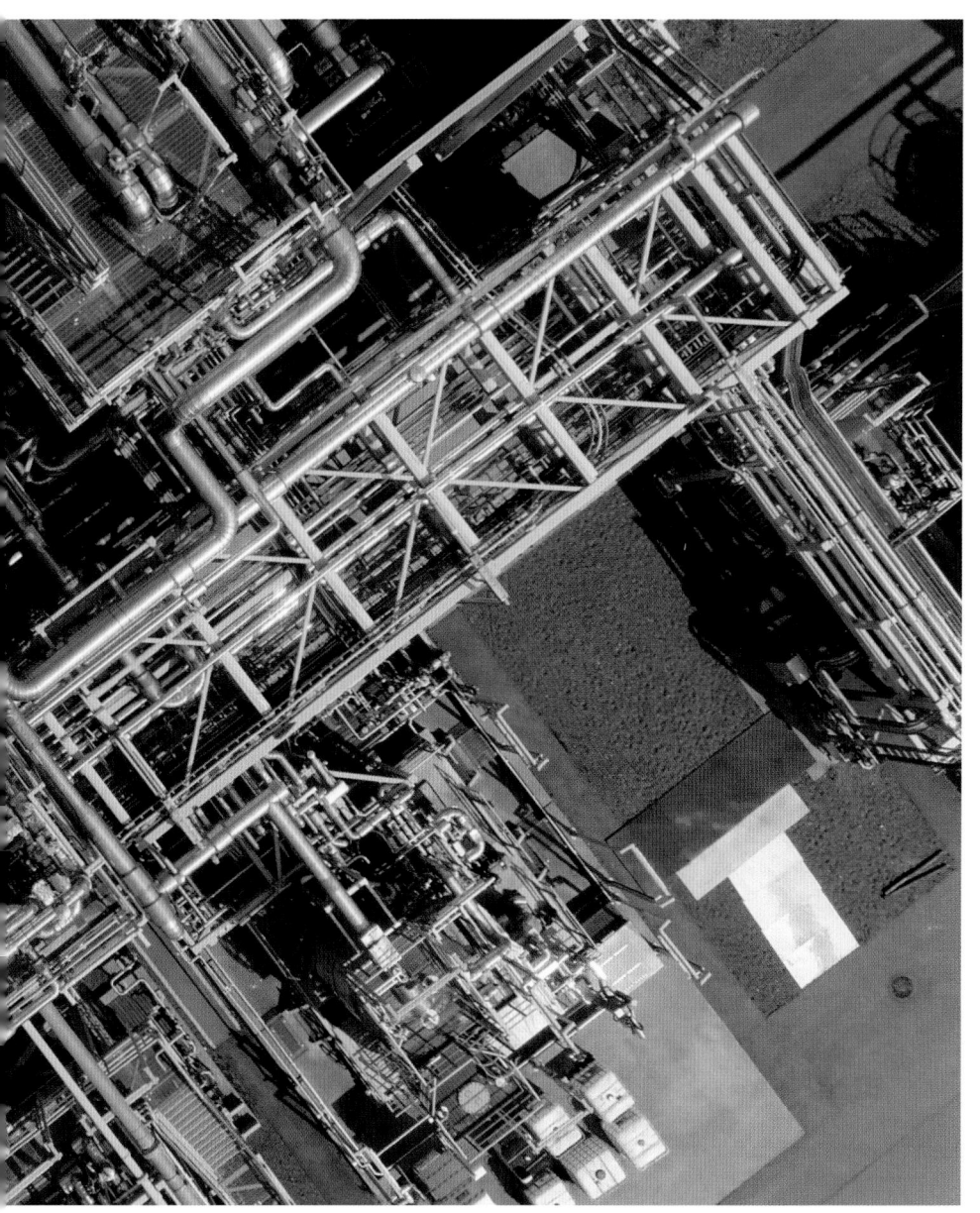

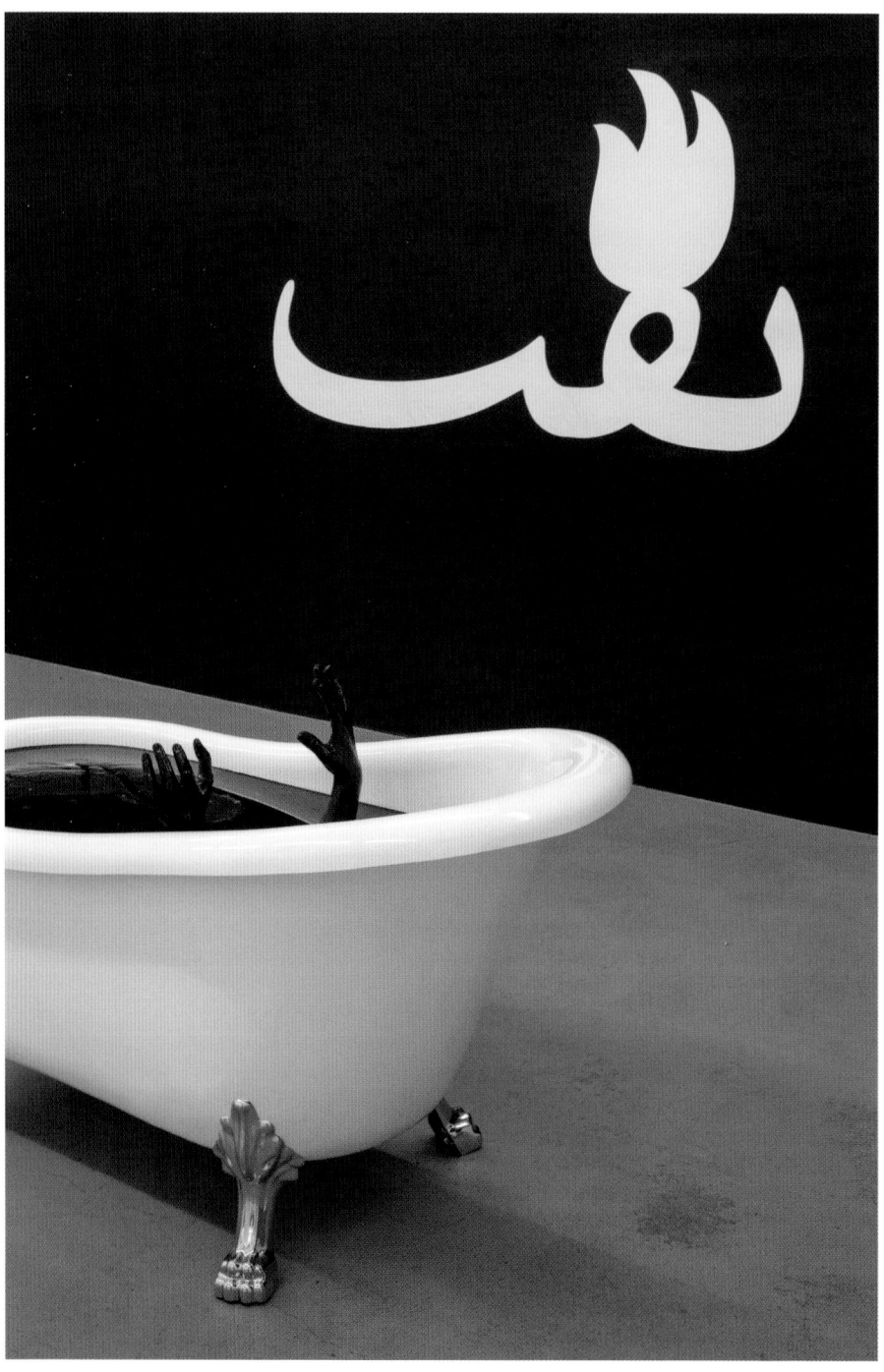

crude oil from which only a pair of outstretched hands emerge, the work is positioned in front of a black wall with a white calligraphic sign. In a reference to the Gulf States' economic dependence on oil, she appropriated the old Persian word *nft* – meaning oil – by adding flames to the cursive script. More specifically, the artist alluded to the city of Naftalan in Azerbaijan, where a centuries-old medicinal treatment involves bathing in a petroleum spa, a therapy that medieval traveller Marco Polo described as a 'magical solution to treat skin diseases'. This cure reached the height of its popularity during Soviet times when tens of thousands immersed themselves in the miraculous liquid that distilled the energy of ancient sunlight. *Deep Float* not only refers to the pre-history of the ruthless exploitation of petroleum, but also holds out the prospect of a post-carbon future in which oil's curative qualities eclipse its energetic power. One is left wondering whether the submerged figure is drowning or resurfacing, expressing the unease of a time in the planet's history when everything is at stake.

The environmental impact of oil drilling on natural environments and its contribution to carbon emissions have been addressed by artists in this chapter, who also expose the industry's attempts to evade scrutiny and the corrupting role of oil wealth in destabilizing democracies and propping up autocracies. As climate change and new technologies make ever more remote areas of land and sea accessible to exploitation, the threat posed by unconventional methods of oil and gas extraction, and the inevitable spills and accidents that accompany them, has only increased, while the industry promotes the pipedream of carbon capture to perpetuate fossil fuel dependency. By suggesting alternative ways to see, feel and understand the materiality of oil and its entwined geological and social histories, artists have also sketched the hazy outlines of a post-petroleum world.

20 OPPOSITE Monira Al Qadiri, *Deep Float*, 2017

Chapter 4
Synthetic Environments

In the era of advanced economic globalization, the increased use of material resources and reliance on synthetic materials generated a culture of disposability that spread across the world, 'eclipsing the practices of recycling' that, as Christophe Bonneuil and Jean-Baptiste Fressoz pointed out in *The Shock of the Anthropocene*, were fundamental to pre-consumerist economies of reuse. Synthesized from petroleum and designed to provide a cheaper alternative to natural materials for the mass production of goods, plastic exemplifies the consumerist boom of global trade that thrives on the circulation of shrink-wrapped necessities and packaged desirables. The colonial plunder of wild species and natural wealth, as well as growing resistance to imperial domination, were also factors in the development of plastic, with the first synthetic polymer, Bakelite, invented in 1907 at a time when the supply of ivory and silk was failing to keep up with demand. Paradoxically, the frequently short commercial lifespan of plastic is inversely proportionate to its lasting presence in the natural environment due to the resistance of synthetic materials to biodegradation. Equally, the 'planned obsolescence' of electronic machines that compels users to regularly update their technological devices, a marketing phenomenon described as early as 1960 by Vance Packard in *The Waste Makers*, has swelled the stockpile of e-waste. The worldwide proliferation of synthetic waste in terrestrial, atmospheric, aquatic and marine environments through the dispersal of polycarbonates, mineraloids, aluminium, concrete and tarmac calls for a further terminological refinement of the Anthropocene, with the notion of the Plasticene identifying another detectable layer of anthropogenic changes to the Earth's strata.

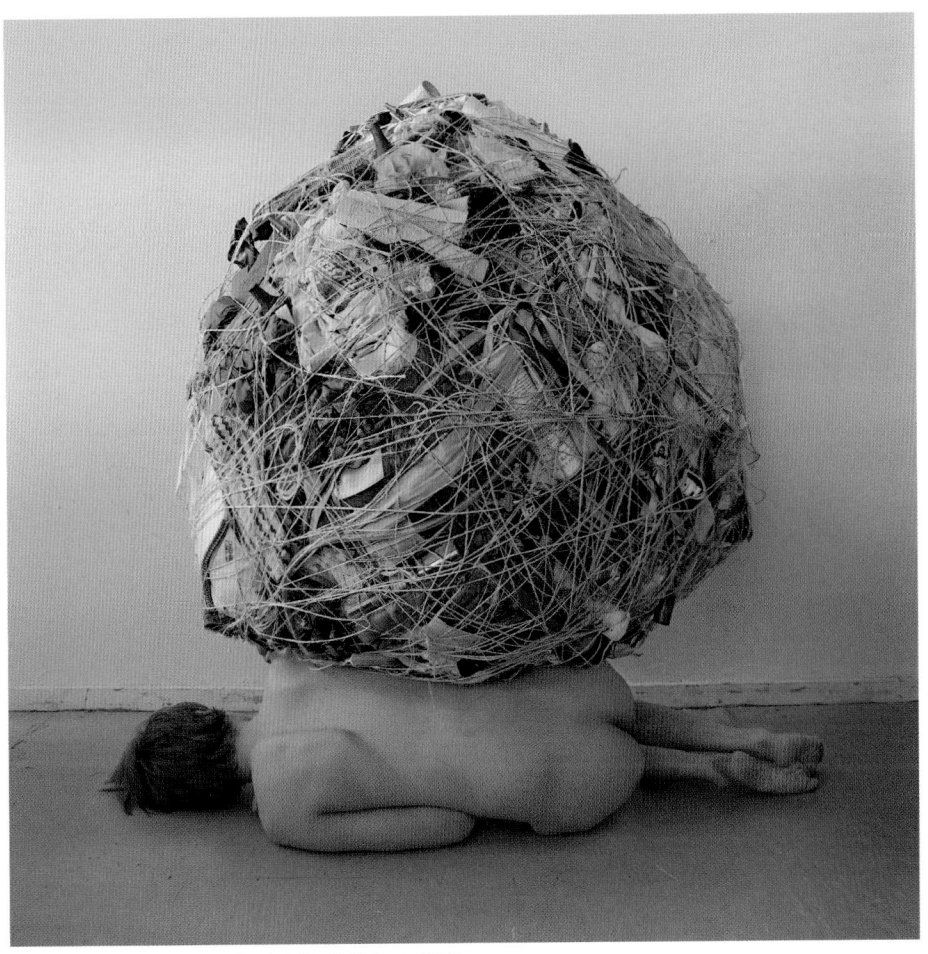

21 Mary Mattingly, *Life of Objects*, 2013

The ecological impact of an economic system based on the accumulation of objects, as well as the psychological burden on individuals of feeling trapped within a cycle of desiring, owning and discarding consumer goods, was investigated by New York-based artist Mary Mattingly in her sculptural series *House and Universe* (2013). Bundles of mass-produced objects the artist had amassed over the years were bound up with string into unmanageably large balls and then photographed in various settings. In one she is pictured engaged in the Sisyphean task of dragging her ball of possessions along a city street, another scenario has the bundle suspended pendulously from a hoist, while a third, entitled *Life of Objects*, depicts a hunched up

21

naked body crushed by the weight of the ball of superfluous objects. She also pulled her boulder across a bridge of strategic importance to the New York shipping industry, in order to draw attention to the journey made by the raw materials found in her personal possessions along global supply chains from zones of extraction, exploitation and toxicity. As Jennifer Gabrys et al. put it in *Accumulation: The Material Politics of Plastic*, things have become decidedly synthetic to the extent that 'plastic now appears as the archetypal material of invention, mass consumption and ecological contamination'.

The connection between consumption and contamination is also explored by Beirut- and Paris-based duo Joana Hadjithomas and Khalil Joreige in their series of three photographs *A State* (2019), which display the content of a drilling core sourced from an escalating rubbish dump in the Lebanese city of Tripoli. After accumulating waste for a period of twenty-five years, the open landfill, which is in close proximity to the sea, has reached a height of 45 metres. In fact, the country has made international headlines since 2015 when the failure of local waste management saw streets filled with rivers of rubbish, triggering a health crisis and rolling mass protests. The artists countered the sensationalism of media coverage to disclose how, as a result of political irresponsibility, urban waste is deposited in the Earth's strata. They pointed in particular to the toxic residues of plastic which, resisting biodegradation, pollute waterscapes and mingle with edible matter, before being ingested by animals and entering the food chain, turning us all indiscriminately into plastivores. Art theorist Heather Davis, in her study on plastics in the Anthropocene, has drawn attention to the 'porousness of our bodies and thoughts that leach into economics and materials, that transfer our wastes across the planet and into the deep future'. The accumulation of plastic waste as the end point for the discarded and obsolete outputs of techno-consumerist production chains is, in its subterranean layering, one of the most recognizable signs of the Anthropocene.

'Sometimes I imagine the world as a network of things moving from one place to another. Often their journey begins in China and ends at landfills in Africa. Europe is somewhere in between.' This is the rationale behind Polish artist Janek Simon's interest in an increasingly synthetic world, in which transcontinental synchronization is transforming cultural geographies governed by artificial intelligence and toxic post-

22 OPPOSITE Joana Hadjithomas and Khalil Joreige, *A State*, 2019

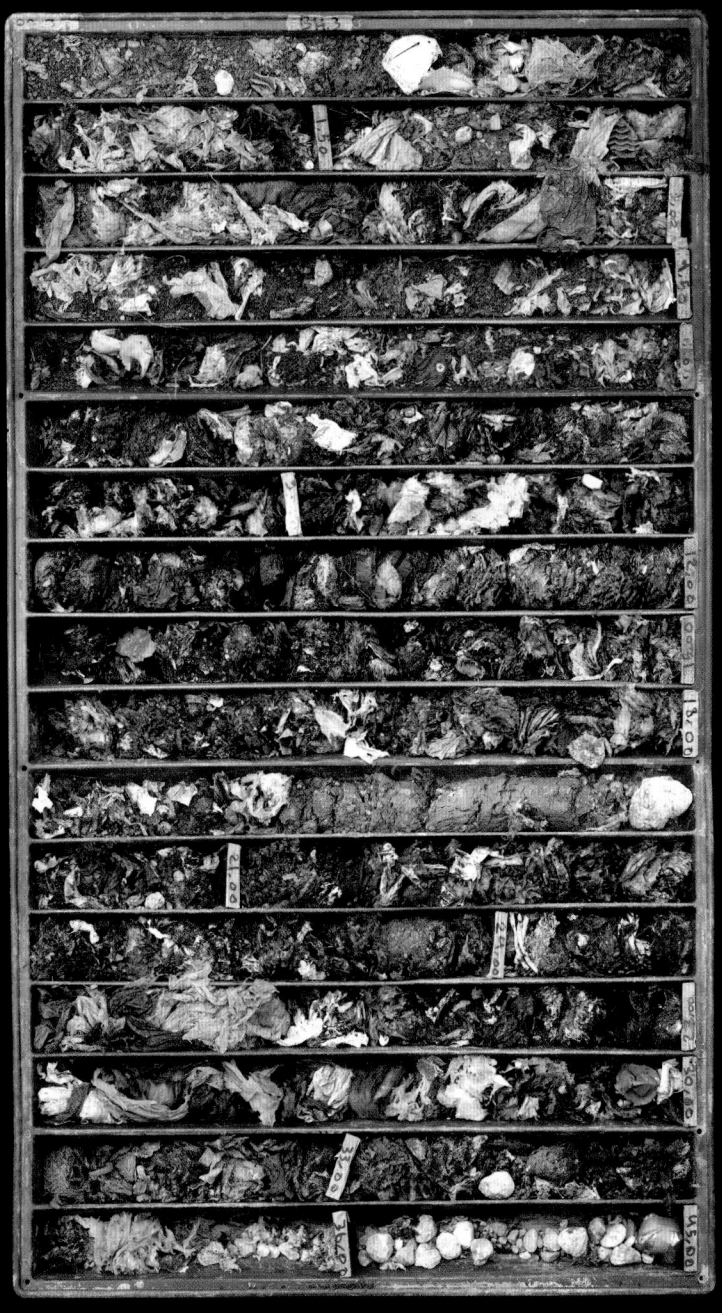

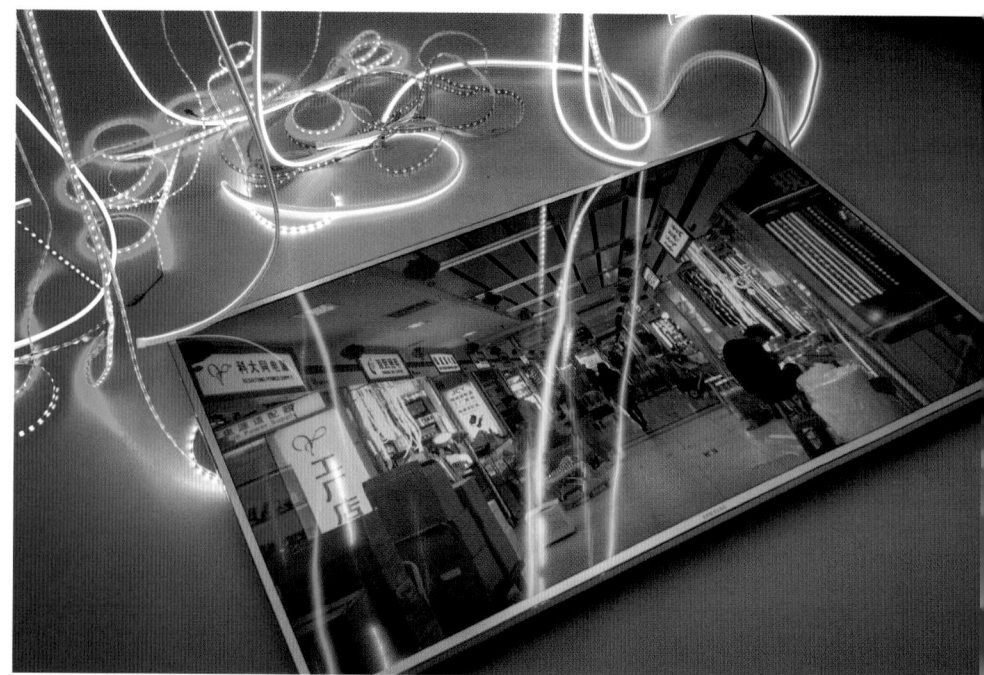

23 Janek Simon, *Huaqiangbei Commercial Street: A Selection of Objects from Shenzhen*, 2019

colonial economics. His sculptural piece *Alaba International: A Selection of Objects from Alaba, Nigeria* (2019) referred to Africa's largest open-air market in Lagos, where a sizable portion of the trade is devoted to *tokunbo*, second-hand electronics imported from Europe. The market also serves as a station for the disassembling of dysfunctional items into parts for recycling, to separate out gold and other precious metals for reuse, a form of hazardous urban mining. Such electronic waste is turning into technofossils, the geologically novel phenomenon of the material remains of the technosphere in the stratigraphy of the planet. Simon's related work, the installation *Huaqiangbei Commercial Street: A Selection of Objects from Shenzhen* (2019), dealt with the Pearl River Delta megalopolis, China's largest industrial hub and global electronics manufacturing centre, where the main factory of Foxconn, producer of electronic goods for companies such as Microsoft, Apple and Huawei, is also located. Through the investigation of these two conflicting trading sites, Simon delineated the unsustainable and unjust circulation of consumer products in the technosphere.

23

It is the scale of its production, with currently a billion tonnes made globally every three years, combined with the speed with which it has found its way through waste to the furthest reaches of the planet and its technofossil longevity that make plastic one of the most tangible markers of the Anthropocene. Conjuring its global spread, palaeontologist Jan Zalasiewicz has observed that 'if all the plastic made in the last few decades was clingfilm, there would be enough to put a layer around the whole Earth'. The intrusion of plastic into the makeup of the lithosphere is exemplified by plastiglomerate, a hybrid material composed of molten plastic debris and rock fragments. First observed in 2014 on a beach in Hawaii, this novel geological phenomenon was brought to critical light in an interdisciplinary paper co-authored by an oceanographer, a geologist and Canadian artist Kelly Jazvac, who also exhibited examples as readymade artworks. For the author of *Plastic Capitalism*, Amanda Boetzkes, plastiglomerate is a 'marker horizon' that stands as 'both a scientific measure of the Anthropocene and a cultural signifier of its impact'.

In his expansive sculpture *Plastic Reef* (2008–13), melted from plastic debris collected from five major gyres in the North and South Atlantic, the North and South Pacific and the Indian Ocean, Maarten Vanden Eynde pointed to the enormous accumulation of floating plastic waste collected

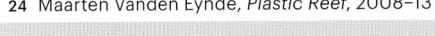

24

24 Maarten Vanden Eynde, *Plastic Reef*, 2008–13

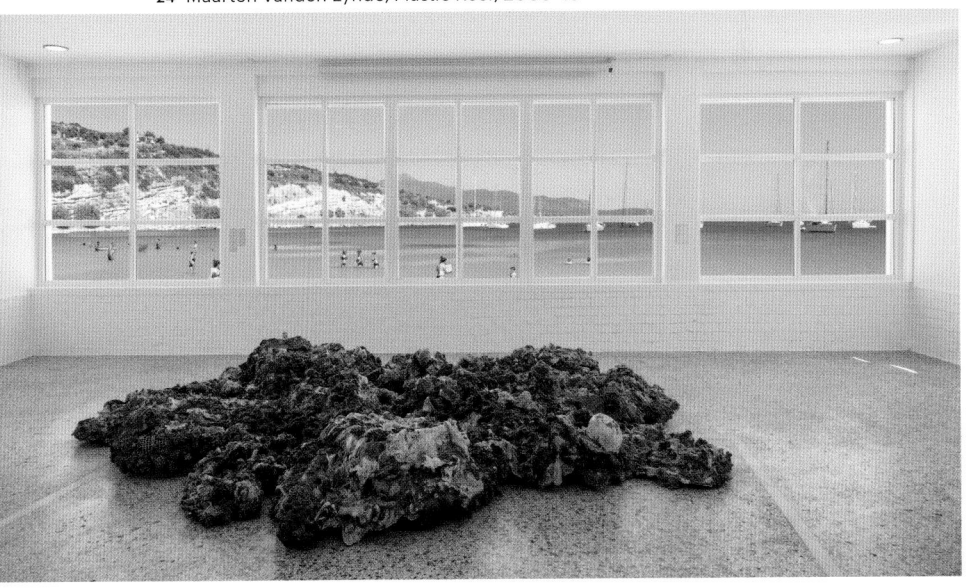

by the currents of the world's oceans. As an amalgam of discarded consumer products, the work could be considered a monument to capitalism as a system of waste, which has led to an estimated 250 pieces of debris in the ocean for every human in the world. What is more, by modelling the coral reef, the bleaching of which has become one of the starkest warnings of climate change, the artist drew attention to the fact that two thirds of the plastic debris that has entered the oceans through river deltas is not drifting on the surface, but actually dissolving into microplastics and sinking to the ocean floor. Floating plastic waste is not just a polluter of ocean life, but also a significant contributor to global warming, emitting greenhouse gases when exposed to sunlight and threatening plankton populations that play a vital role in absorbing carbon dioxide.

A critical aspect of the discussion of plastic and technological trash is its relation to colonialism, both in terms of a 'waste colonialism' that literally turns indigenous land into toxic sinks and of the wider issue of the intrusion of synthetics into the materiality of non-Western worlds. To assemble his *Herbarium of Artificial Plants* (since 2001), Colombian artist Alberto Baraya retraced the scientific expeditions of colonial botanists, borrowing their taxonomic procedures to classify exotic discoveries, but with the essential difference that he only collected plastic plants. The paper sheets of his herbarium contain artificial specimens, drawings and photographic documentation arranged on the page as a record of location and other data about the collected item. On the one hand, the work is an indictment of the role of botanical collections, and the rationally minded scientists who removed living plants from their native environment to study and categorize them, in establishing colonial domination and the knowledge conditions for the economic exploitation of conquered territories. At the same time, by collecting plastic plants from the most remote and biodiverse places on Earth, including the depths of the Amazon rainforest, Baraya drew attention to the global reach of the synthetic products of mass consumerism and the equally insidious infiltration of a throwaway culture in which artificial and natural worlds are interchangeable.

Post-styrofoam grounds, polymer habitats, post-electronic terrains and textile environments constitute the collection of the *Centre for Living Things* (since 2016), initiated by Polish artist Diana Lelonek to investigate the novel transformation of the biosphere into the plastisphere, the living micro- and macro-biotic communities that are now adapting to plastics. In her field research, the artist mapped and documented sites

25

26

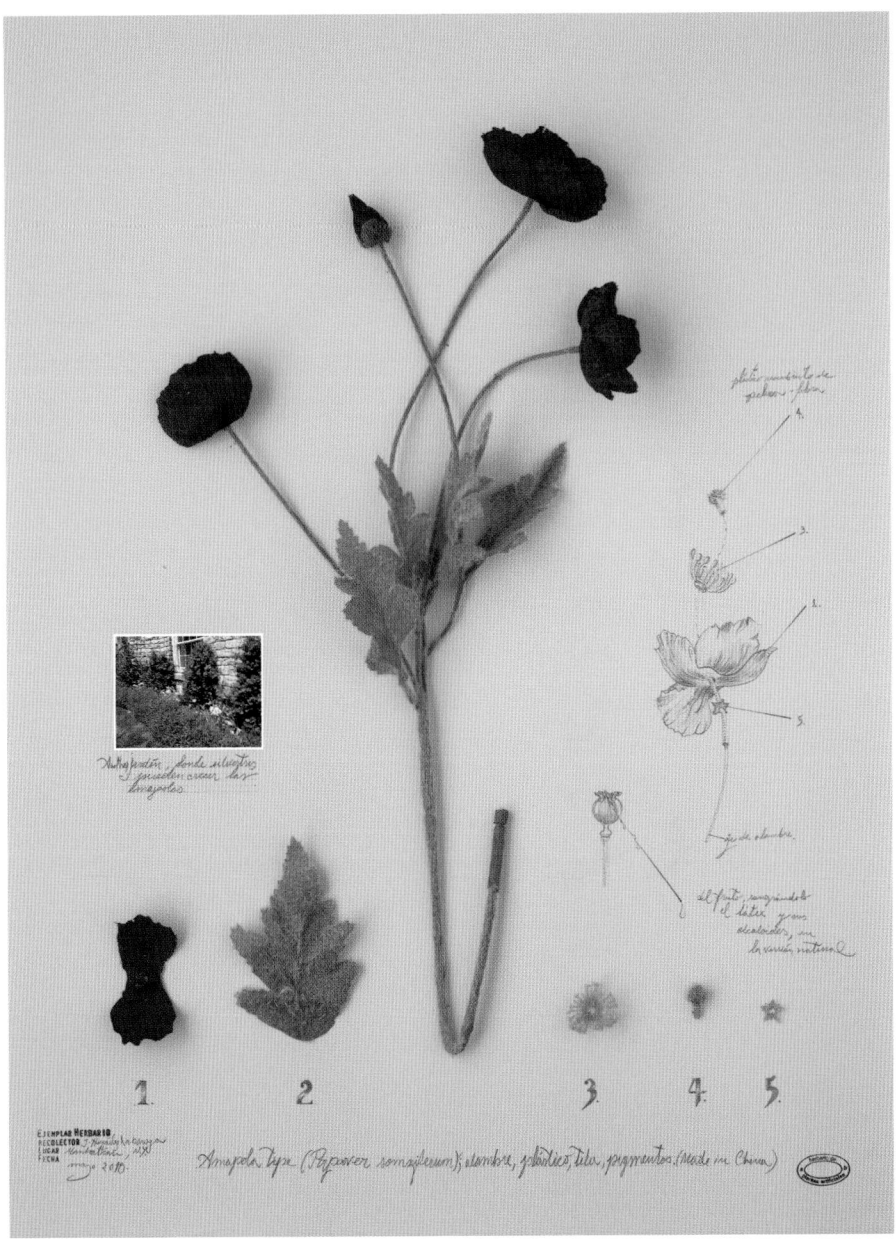

25 Alberto Baraya, *Another Amapola, NY*, 2018

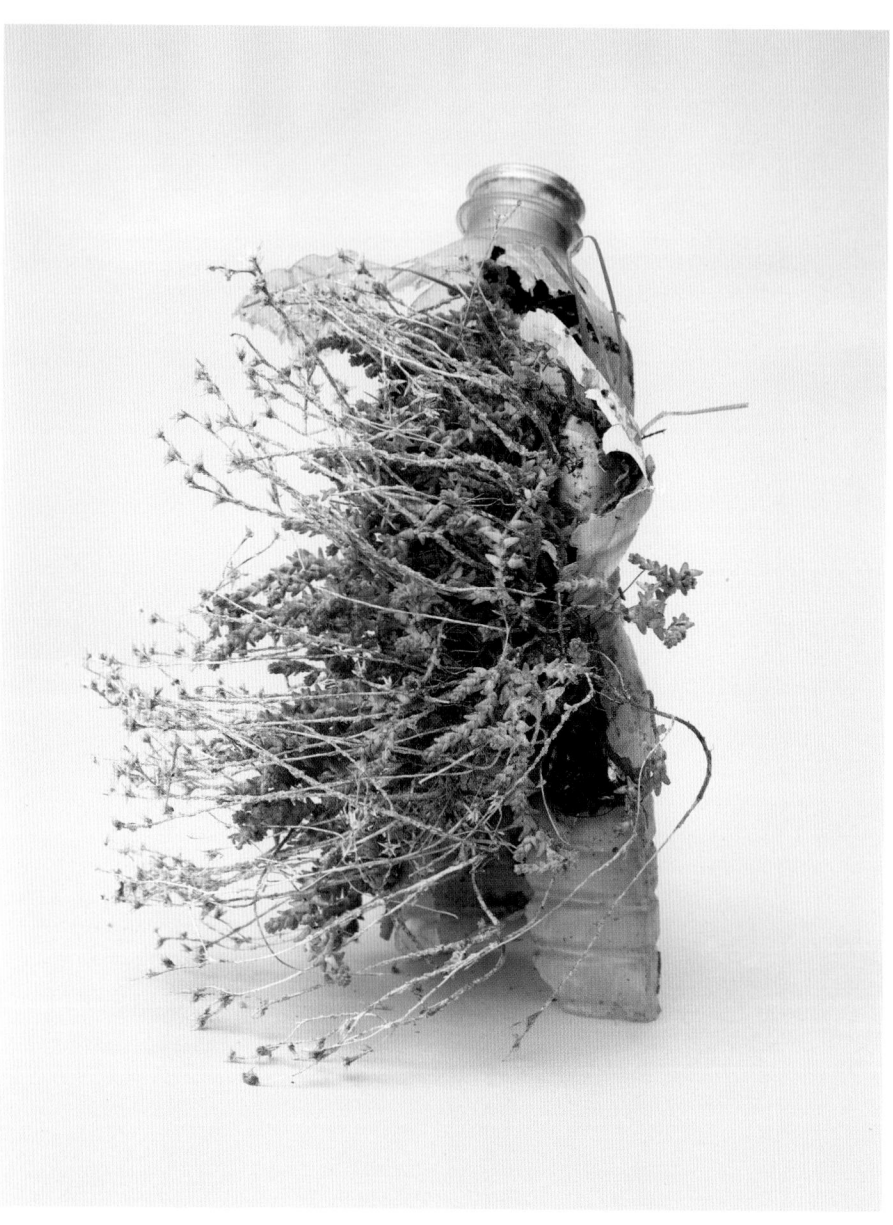

26 Diana Lelonek, *PET-environment*, 2017. Found object
from the collection *Centre for Living Things*, 2017

of urban and forest rubbish dumps, where illegal fly-tippers discard plastic, electro-waste and construction debris, observing that these environments have become hybrid habitats for local flora and fauna. She also selected some specimens of 'waste-plants' for resettlement in the Centre's premises in a disused greenhouse of the Botanical Gardens in Poznań. The created ecosystem of ruderal plants and synanthropes (species that adapt to artificial habitats), such as plants growing on discarded handbags, odd stilettos and worn-out mops, or moss covering styrofoam chunks and polyester carpets, is a testing ground for research into hybrid nature forms. By inserting them into the taxonomic regimes of highly managed botanical gardens, the artist destabilized the established classifications of scientific knowledge, pointing to the unsustainable division between natural and artificial categories in a world transformed by anthropogenic interventions.

The defining characteristic of the plasticene has turned out not to be the longevity of synthetic materials and their resistance to biodegradation, but rather that upon breaking down into microparticles they infiltrate into natural organisms and environments. The proliferation of plastic pollution is both extensive, reaching to the extremities of polar regions, rainforests and maritime realms, and intrusive, entering the corporal makeup of plants, animals and people. The artists also point to the personal and societal dimensions of petrochemical synthetics and their role in intricate global relations of capitalist production that depend on and deepen social inequalities.

Chapter 5
Expanses of Monoculture

On the wheels of petroleum-powered machinery the traditional, small-scale, biodiverse practices of farming based on crop rotation were transformed into a monocultural industrial agriculture reliant on chemical additives, pesticides and a narrow selection of seeds. The intensification of agriculture advanced at the onset of the Cold War, with the Soviet side introducing a model of cultivation based on the collectivization of smallholdings and the ploughing up of the Eurasian Steppes, while the United States exported the programme of the Green Revolution as an antidote to the spread of communism in the global South. Promising a new age of abundance, their patented recipe of cash-crop monoculture ended up dramatically impoverishing and polluting the soil and aquifers, which seed activist Vandana Shiva berated as 'a war against ecosystems' with agricultural chemicals becoming 'real arms of mass destruction today'. A new frontier was opened up by genetic modification, enabling the deployment of ever stronger pesticides, while terminator seeds made farmers inextricably dependent on agribusiness. The beginnings of the industrial system can be traced, as Jason W. Moore and Raj Patel have surmised, to the 'original factory' of the colonial sugarcane fields of the Caribbean, where relations between humans, plants and capital were violently transformed. Giving rise to another potent descriptor of the current geological epoch as the Plantationocene, intensive monocultural farming has depleted the natural vitality of the living soil, corroded rural communities, had a detrimental impact on biodiversity and made global food systems critically vulnerable to climate disruption.

Having grown up in a family of farmers, Italian artist Marzia Migliora engages with the issues arising from the intensification of agriculture through mechanization, dependence on chemical fertilizers and pesticides and the genetic modification of seeds,

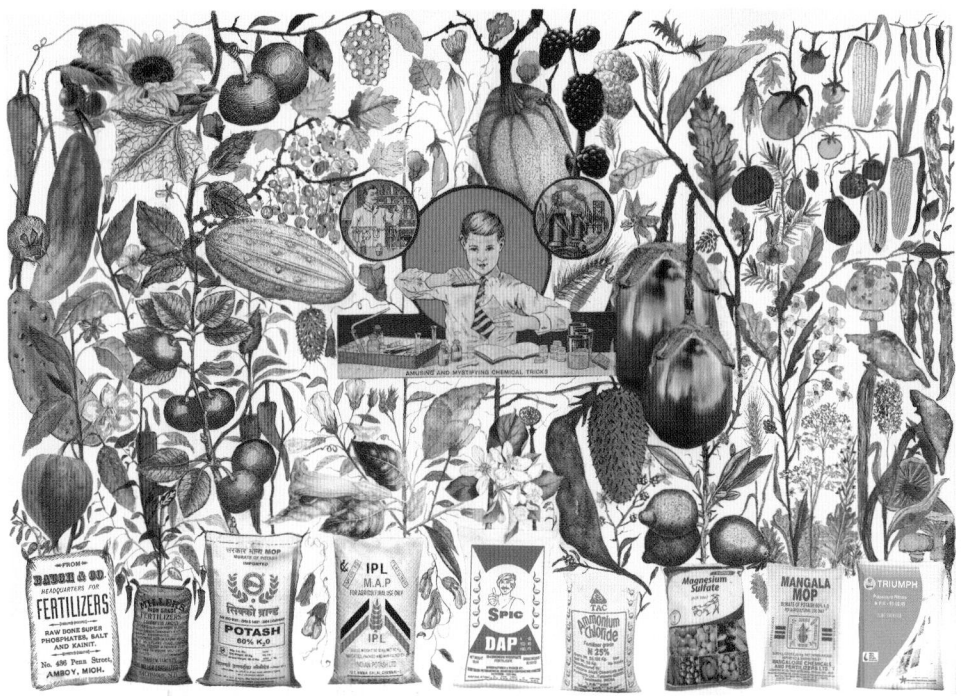

27 Marzia Migliora, *Paradoxes of Plenty*, 2020

which result in top-soil depletion, pollution and the 'complete transformation of products of the land we consume and the quality of life of those who cultivate that land, including my own family'. Her series of collages *Paradoxes of Plenty* (2017–20) investigated food production under global capitalism and its weighty footprint on people, animals and the planet. In outlining the costly path of development and its roots in the colonial past, Migliora also drew on her grandfather's collection of agricultural manuals, which bear the ideological imprint of twentieth-century agricultural history. The title of the work is a quotation from the book *An Edible History of Humanity* by Tom Standage, which situated modernity in relation to the ascendency of monocultures. The portrayal of agriculture that comes to the fore in these collages, which juxtapose the positions of farmers, their produce and global networks, speaks about the conflict between presumed progress and the actual expense of food industry extractivism, which is eating away the Earth, as if, in the artist's words, 'we were consuming our own body from within, in almost cannibalistic fashion'.

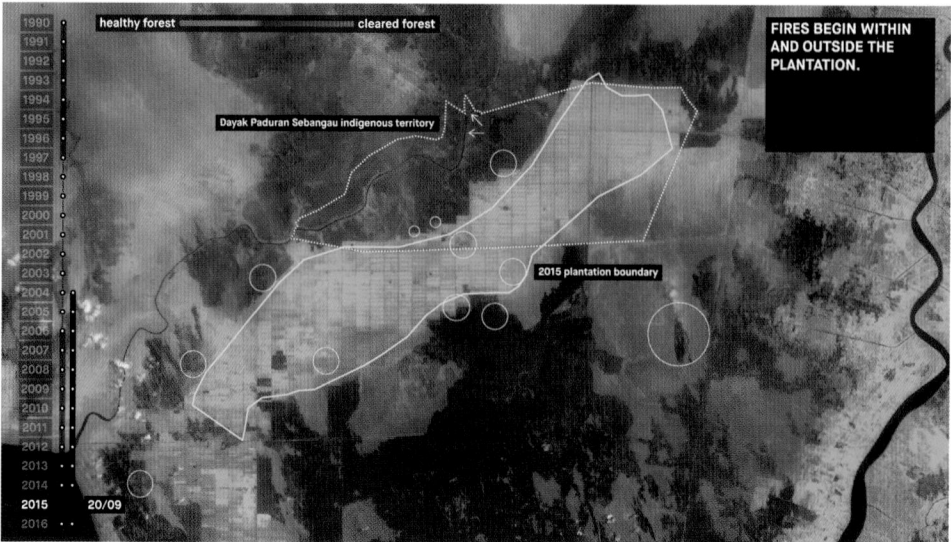

The following labels appear on the image:

1980–2016 (year scale)

healthy forest ▬▬▬ cleared forest

Dayak Paduran Sebangau indigenous territory

FIRES BEGIN WITHIN AND OUTSIDE THE PLANTATION.

2015 plantation boundary

2015 20/09

28 Forensic Architecture, *Ecocide in Indonesia*, 2017

In her work *Highway BR – 163 Cuiabá – Santarém* (2017–19), Berlin-based Brazilian artist Barbara Marcel shed light on the contested role of global agribusiness in altering the environmental and social fabric of the Amazon rainforest. The case in point was the American food corporation Cargill, whose maxim is 'committed to help the world thrive'. This privately owned company trades in grain, palm oil, cocoa, animal feed and other agricultural commodities and operates a soybean export terminal in Santarém, the city at the confluence of Tapajós and Amazon Rivers. Fuelled by the global meat industry, which uses soybean meal in animal feed, the expansion of soybean monocultural production in Brazil has come at the cost of deforestation, land grabbing, pollution and exploitation. For her work, Marcel collected bags used in the city's manioc market, which have been recycled by the local traders from industrial packaging. Some of these were plastic sacks that had previously contained chemicals for the processing of soybeans destined mostly for Chinese and European markets, while others had stored locally processed food made from Brazilian transgenic soy for internal consumption. By sewing the bags into a single fabric, the artist produced a tapestry of words and images that 'map the manufacturing cycle of the grain that most threatens the Brazilian Amazon Rainforest today'.

Evidence of the environmental destruction of ecosystems in the rainforests of the Indonesian territory of Central

Kalimantan was gathered in London-based research agency Forensic Architecture's investigation *Ecocide in Indonesia* (2017). The systematic clearing of forests and draining of peatlands for the large-scale cultivation of crops started with the soon-to-be-abandoned state Mega Rice Project in the 1990s and has intensified since palm oil plantations took over the agroindustry of the area. Today Indonesia is the leading producer of an ingredient that has a far greater yield at lower cost than other types of vegetable oil and is now found in more than half of all cosmetics and food products, with devastating environmental and health consequences. The research exposed the aggressive business practices of the palm oil industry, which exploits bureaucratic loopholes to avoid environmental impact assessments, invading indigenous territories and, in the wake of devastating wildfires in 2015, expanding into conservation zones. The resulting deaths of orangutans, whose name in the Malay language means 'people of the forest', is recorded as incontrovertible criminal evidence in the cartographic data. Tangentially, in his study *Palma Africana*, anthropologist Michael Taussig discusses monkeys 'kidding around' in trees at the edge of a palm oil plantation, throwing sticks at 'human marauders below', and uses this as a way to address the unspeakable trauma of such acts of ecocide.

In her video *Tropical Siesta* (2017), Ho Chi Minh City-based artist Thao Nguyên Phan addressed the agricultural history of rural Vietnam in the years after the Second World War, when the communist government put industrial agriculture at the centre of the nation's economy. Panoramas of rice paddies and the statement 'everyone is a farmer' feature in the opening scenes of the film, in which the main protagonists are school children wearing pioneer uniforms with red scarfs around their necks. The youngsters 'live in communes and work on self-sufficient farms' and choose their own curriculum, which happens to be the make-believe reading of the only book available, by seventeenth-century Jesuit missionary Alexandre de Rhodes from the era of French colonial rule. Their derelict primary school is however soon populated with painted animated figures of children sleeping and resting on desks and benches, whose dreams dispel the historical amnesia that has descended onto contemporary society. The work deals with the 'dark eras' of Vietnam's past, both colonial and more recent, when communist collectivist land reform entailed eradicating private ownership, and many citizens lost their livelihoods and some also their lives, a traumatic history that is not taught in today's schoolbooks.

The assemblage *Apotheosis of the Fertile Land* (2016) by Hungarian artist Tamás Kaszás was envisaged as a constructivist

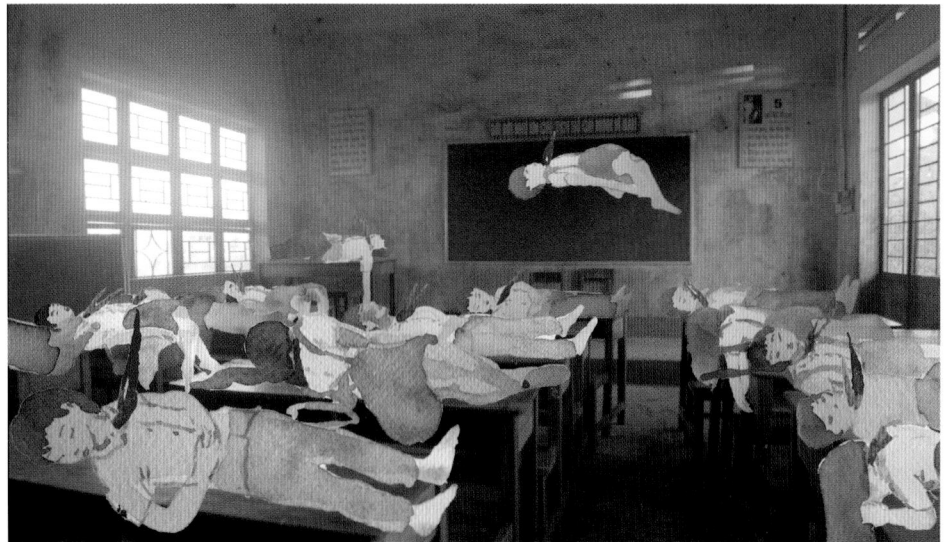

29 Thao Nguyên Phan, *Tropical Siesta*, 2017

relief consisting of a number of surfaces layered with
watercolours, photographs, prints and packaging materials
on the subject of agriculture. Visual references to peasant
uprisings are juxtaposed here with empty packets of industrial
cereal products and illustrations of agricultural machinery,
while the foreground is dominated by a wreath reminiscent
of the coats of arms of former Soviet states. Although cleaned
up from ideological insignia, with not a red star in sight,
the green wreath surrounded with depictions of various
types of grain still stands as a symbolic allusion to the
immense agricultural transformations brought by Stalinist
collectivization. Consequently, as recorded in *An Environmental
History of Russia*, the peasant became 'the rural proletarian'
who was 'working the fields that stretched to the horizon
with modern machines' in a system intended to increase
agricultural productivity, while at the same time centralize
control over rural populations and the natural world.
Reading between the lines of Kaszás's bright title reveals
how deeply engrained is the power and illusory optimism of
the Anthropocene doctrine of progress in its socialist and postsocialist forms.

The decline of the Slovak sugar industry in the post-communist
period could be taken as a test case of the impact of economic
globalization and its neo-colonial operations on local
agricultural practices. In her interdisciplinary project *Eastern*

30

Sugar (2017–20), Slovak artist Ilona Németh investigated the chain of events that led to the closure of the sugar refinery in her hometown of Dunajská Streda. She discovered that the pattern was repeated across Central Europe, shedding light on the social and environmental consequences of the demise of the industry. The artist traced the history of local sugar manufacturing from its inception in the nineteenth century, when sugar beet production allowed the Austro-Hungarian Empire to reduce its dependence on the mostly British-controlled trade in sugarcane from the Caribbean and India, to its privatization and acquisition by multinationals in the 1990s. Sugar beet was long valued by peasant farmers in Eastern Europe as a break crop in field rotations, which, in contrast to sugarcane monocultures, actually restores nutrients to the soil. The artist's research revealed that the socialist period of sugar beet production is remembered as an era of job and social security in which community life was enriched by its seasonal rhythms. In the years of transition to so-called free markets, the regional sugar industry struggled in the face of monopolistic machinations and the arbitrariness of the European Union subsidy system, which ended up compensating opportunistic owners to close and dismantle their factories.

30 Ilona Németh, *Eastern Sugar Archive*, 2017–20

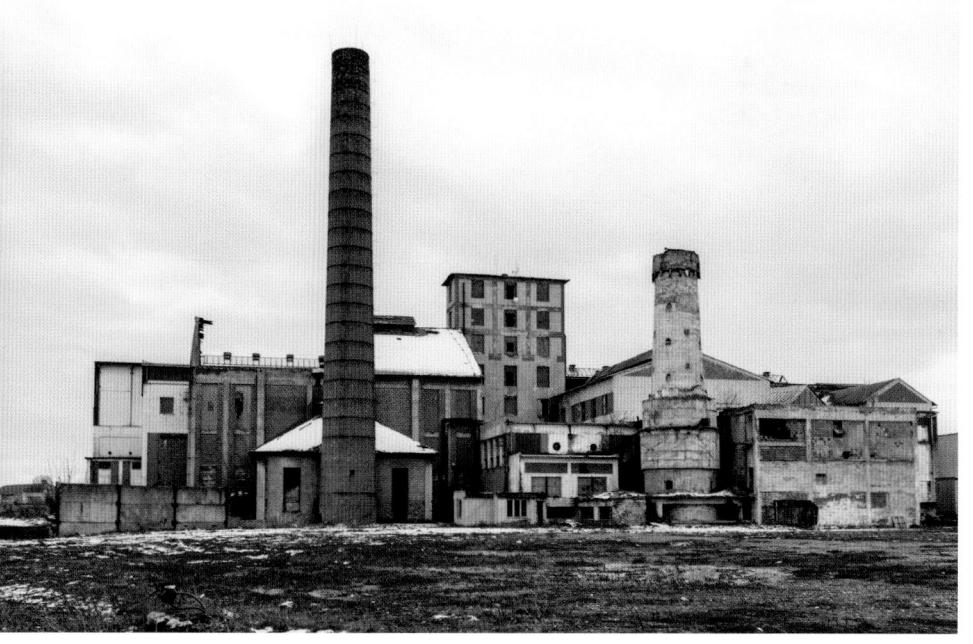

31

Carved from coloured candy, the crystalline sculptures displayed at the centre of Indonesian artist Elia Nurvista's installation *Sucker Zucker II* (2018) resemble giant cut diamonds, alluding to shared histories of slavery and exploitation in a world transformed by colonialism and capitalism. An accompanying mural visualizes key episodes in the development of the plantation economy by European colonizers and its spread to the subtropical territories of Africa, the Caribbean and Southeast Asia, emphasizing that the model of commodity production continues its domination up to the present day. The neo-colonial politics of food are a recurring question in Nurvista's artistic inquiries into the impact of global agribusiness on Indonesia, seen in the changes to farming methods and dietary habits brought about by technological innovations in rice production and in the rampant corruption, land grabbing and deforestation engendered by the palm oil industry. In the artist's words, the influx of global capital was 'stimulated by the spectacle of colonial fantasies of conquest and discovery, including risk,

31 Elia Nurvista, *Sucker Zucker II*, 2018

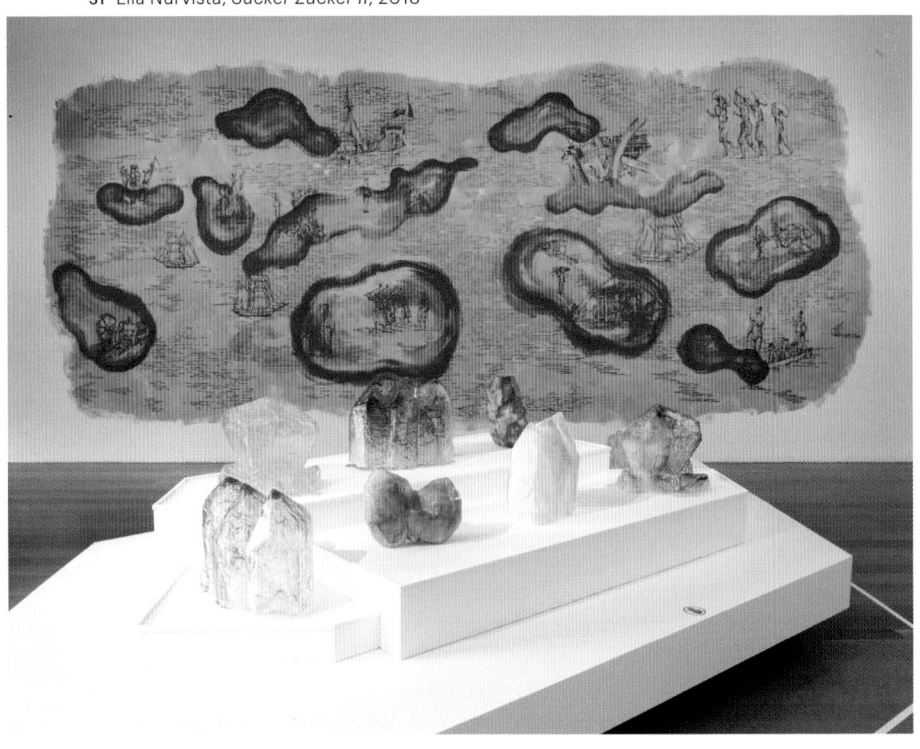

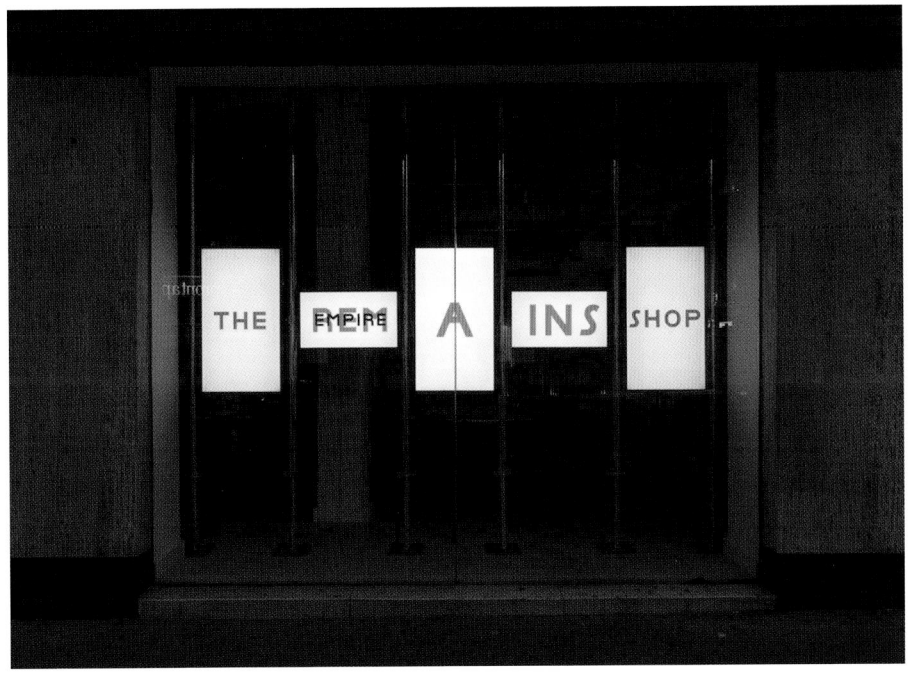

32 Cooking Sections, *The Empire Remains Shop*, 2016–ongoing

virility, and violence', while self-interested elites justified the destruction it wrought on the social and ecological balance of the country with the mantra of economic development.

Approaching food as a tool to question current forms of power exchange across the planet and revealing its histories as often 'deeply embedded in commodity racism', Cooking Sections opened their first *Empire Remains Shop* in London in 2016. As a point of departure for their public platform in the guise of a store, the duo Daniel Fernández Pascual and Alon Schwabe took the 'gastronomic paradox' of the recipe for Empire Christmas Pudding, which was written down in 1928 by the chef to King George V. The paradox lies in the fact that all of the seventeen ingredients used for the making of the 'most English of dishes' originate from faraway places, such as currants from Australia, raisins from South Africa, cinnamon from India, cloves from Zanzibar and apples from Canada. The artists approached the list of ingredients in the recipe as a map that traces developments in the postcolonial food market and explored the economic logic behind it. Their updated version of the recipe showed how the produce that used to be promoted by mentioning its place of origin now bears labels that conceal

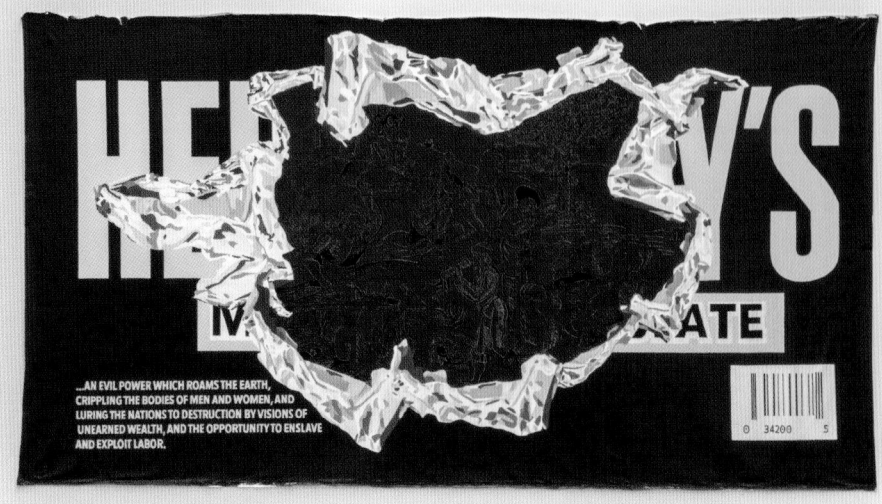

33 Minerva Cuevas, *Bitter Sweet – Hershey's*, 2015

such information with claims that it was 'packed in the UK' or 'produced in the EU'. Since the regulatory shift of the 1990s, the supermarkets control the sourcing, packaging and marketing of their groceries, and by capitalizing on consumers' trust in brands, they reduce transparency, also rendering opaque their ties to the mechanisms of global agrobusiness.

33

Minerva Cuevas's project *Feast and Famine* (2015), with the painting *Bitter Sweet – Hershey's* at its centre, problematized the cultivation of cacao crops in her native Mexico, an industry that also has a history stained by European colonialism and a present marred in conflicts and commercial interests. Consisting of prints made using cocoa powder, found objects and artefacts covered in chocolate, the project featured dozens of human ears cast in chocolate, referencing the pre-Hispanic practice of using the body as a unit of measurement, as well as the symbolism of the severed ear that recalls social repression and torture. For the casts, the artist used native cacao, Grano Real Xoconusco, grown in the state of Chiapas, but difficult to obtain in Mexico since most of it is exported to Belgium and Switzerland, while the domestic industry uses cheaper varieties imported from Africa. The installation also included a carefully calibrated machine that dripped chocolate into a pile on the floor at intervals of 3.6 seconds, replicating the rate at which someone in the world dies of starvation. While the export-oriented production dictated by the economics of globalized agriculture is disrupting local food supplies, communities in the region experience exploitative labour practices that are embedded in the legacies of colonial abuses, dispossession and the severing of ancestral and cultural ties. Nevertheless, one of the pieces is an appropriation of a Swiss chocolate brand, which instead of 'Toblerone' reads 'To Rebel', connoting the possibility of resistance.

Industrial agriculture is not living up to its promise to satisfy the nutritional needs of a growing global population, since any short-term gains were achieved at the cost of disrupting fragile soil relations. As the artists' works demonstrate, palm oil and soybean have followed in the path of monocultural sugarcane to a chemical, biotechnological and energy-intensive model of food production that multiplies social injustices while undermining the ecosystems on which planetary wellbeing depends. The entwined histories of capitalist and colonialist expansion in the global South, as well as parallel developments in socialist collectivization during the twentieth century, reveal the decisive role of the transformation of agriculture in the build-up to the climatic crises of the Anthropocene.

Part II
Reconfiguring the Geosphere

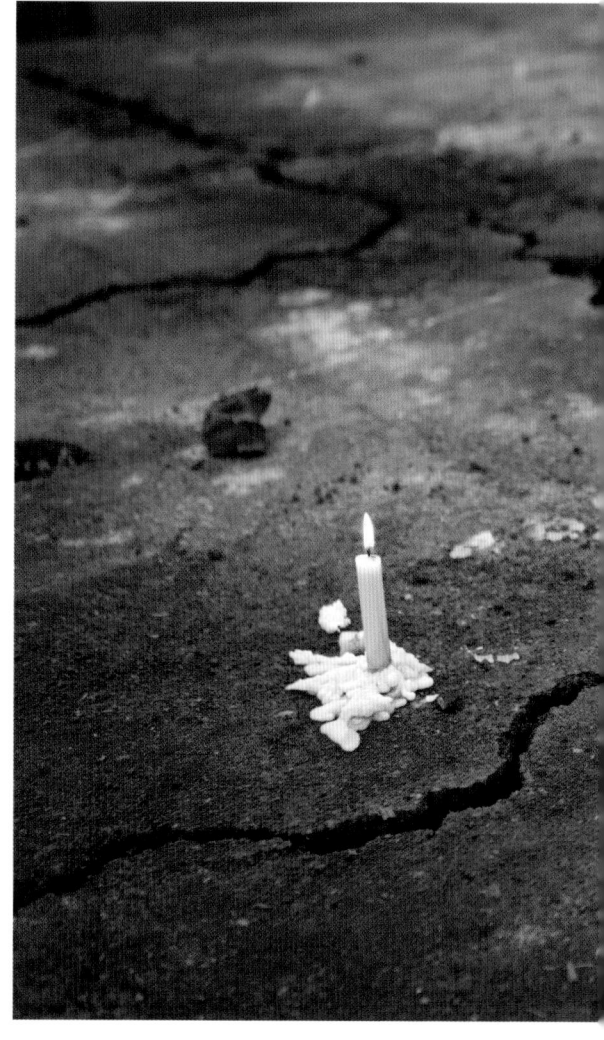

34 Dineo Seshee Bopape,
*Indeed it may very well be the
_____ itself*, 2016

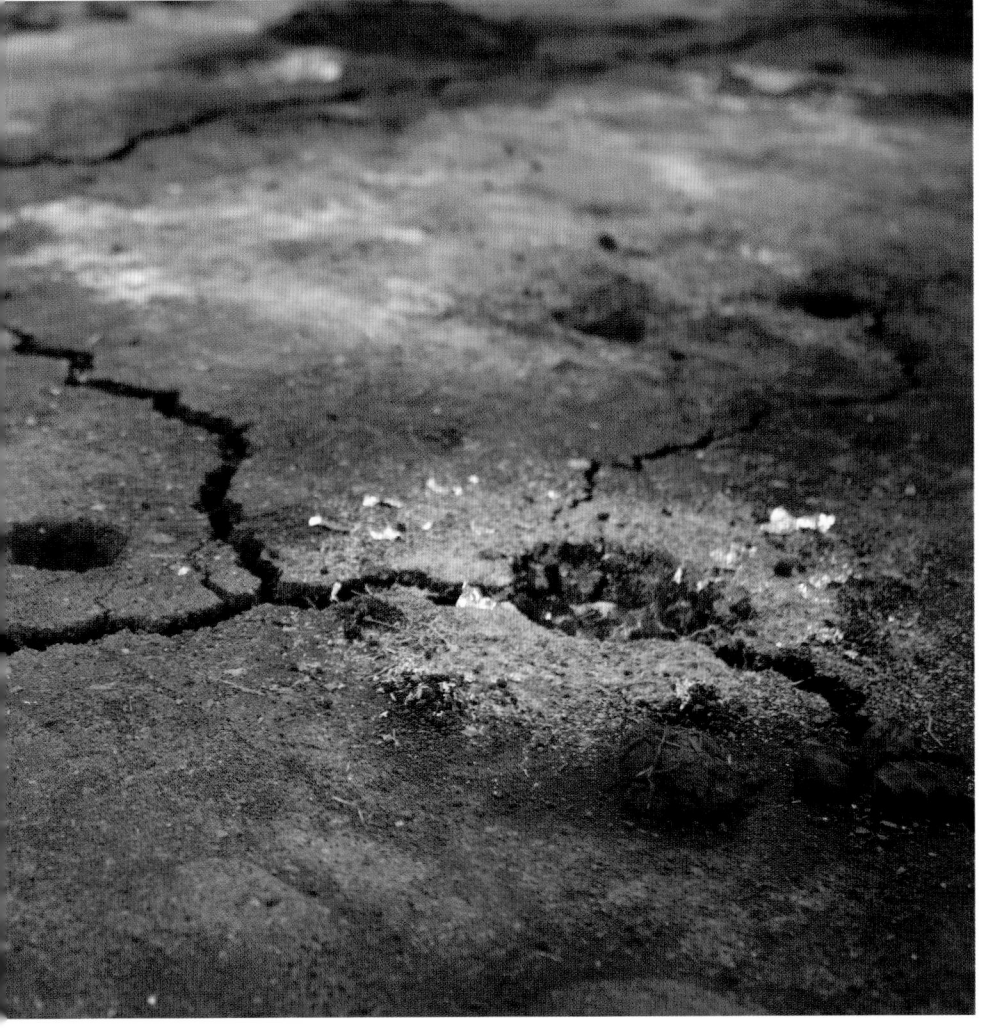

Chapter 1
Soil Reserves

Natural forces, such as volcanic eruptions, earthquakes and glaciers, 'have long sculpted the face of the Earth', but in the twentieth century, as environmental historian John McNeill observed in *Something New Under the Sun*, through brutal quarrying and accelerated erosion, 'humankind came to rival these forces'. The thin, life-giving membrane of soil, which can take millennia to form on the outer layer of the lithosphere, is the most vulnerable to processes of exhaustion, contamination and desertification. These have been accelerated by the expansion of crop and grazing land at the expense of forests and wild vegetation, while urban sprawl and concrete infrastructures steadily encroach upon fertile terrain, with the detritus of modern life adding another dose of toxicity. Annual soil loss, measured globally in tens of billions of tonnes, is compounded by the effects of climate change, with extreme heat and drought turning farmlands into desert within expanding tropical belts, while wildfires spread further, faster and more frequently. The realization that the world may be approaching the moment of 'peak soil', with by some counts barely sixty harvests left, is causing a reassessment of soil practices and attitudes. However, as anthropologist Kristina M. Lyons has pointed out in *Vital Decomposition*, one cannot talk about soil health without first inquiring into 'whose territories are being occupied; which enslaved and indentured bodies work now exhausted plantation fields; and which actors amassed tracts of land through violence and illegal contracts?'

Proposing the use of living soil as an alternative system of value to replace the petrodollar, Chicago-based artist Claire Pentecost sculpted units of the new currency from compost in the shape of gold ingots. Based on a financial abstraction, her *soil-erg* (2012) is impractical to circulate due

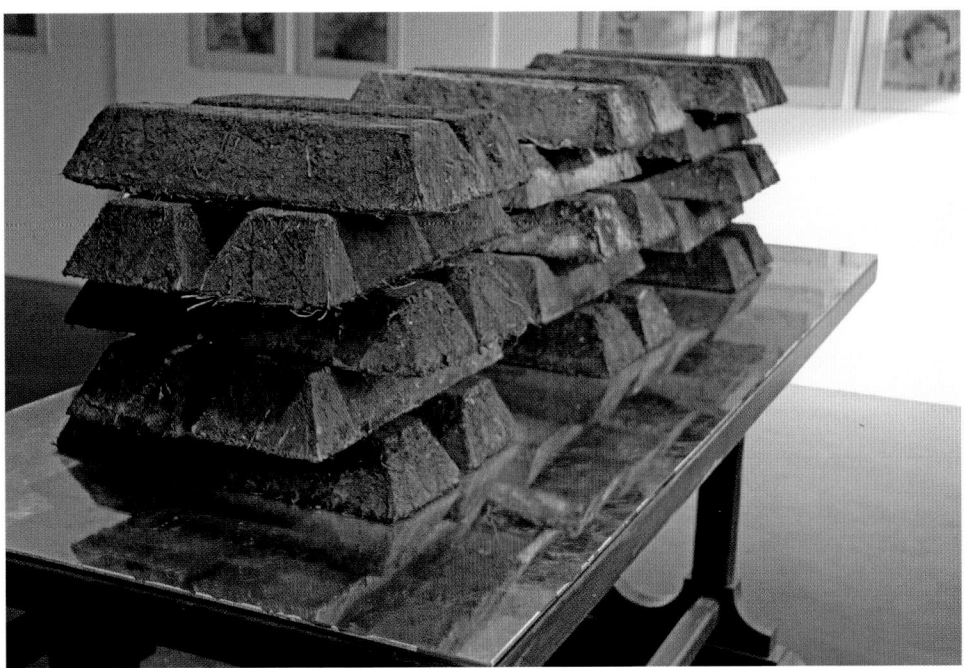

35 Claire Pentecost, *soil-erg*, 2012 (detail)

to its weight and crumbly structure, rendering it inherently territorial and intentionally place-bound. The sculptural installation is accompanied by a series of drawings depicting historical figures and theorists who contributed to an ecological understanding of agriculture, such as Indian theorist Vandana Shiva, marine biologist Rachel Carson and founder of the Kenyan Greenbelt Movement Wangari Maathai. Another element of the work was a wooden cabinet housing a composting bed with living worms who made soil for the duration of the exhibition, while inscriptions on its doors questioned the role of corporate capitalism in expropriating arable lands in the global South. Pentecost challenged here the economic foundations of the financial order symbolized by the gold standard, which was conventionally used to back currencies, instead pointing to the organic wealth of the soil as the ultimate reserve.

The damage caused by the actual financialization of earth came to the fore in Cooking Sections' project *For the Rights of the Soil not to be Exhausted* (2019), from their *Climavore* series, a body of work that poses the question: 'How do we eat as humans change climates?' The artists investigated the entangled histories and contemporary stakes in the exploitation of *chernozem* from the Ukrainian steppe, the uniquely fertile black soil that has made the country the 'universal breadbasket', but which is 'continuously stripped away and sold in international markets'. A display of propaganda photos and soil-related artefacts was exhibited in the cellar of the Bessarabka market in Kiev, which served as a mortuary during the Terror Famine of the 1930s that saw millions of Ukrainians perish as a result of Soviet grain requisitioning. Intending their project to engender conversations across political and environmental domains, the artists devised a programme of public discussions on issues such as soil reserves, biodiversity in the steppe and the adaptability of grain to the northward shift of climatic zones. They also initiated a collaboration with lawyers to draft a document to legally enshrine the defence of soil fertility against the extractivist strategies of predatory capital.

Technocratic interaction with the lithospheric mantle of the Earth is scrutinized by Los Angeles-based organization The Center for Land Use Interpretation (CLUI), with the aim to foster discussion of how land is 'apportioned, utilized and perceived'. Belonging to their *Landscans* series, the high-definition video
36   *Bingham Canyon Mine to Kennecott Smelter, Utah* (2018) surveyed from the air the second biggest open-pit copper mine in the

36 The Center for Land Use Interpretation (CLUI), *Bingham Canyon Mine to Kennecott Smelter, Utah*, 2018

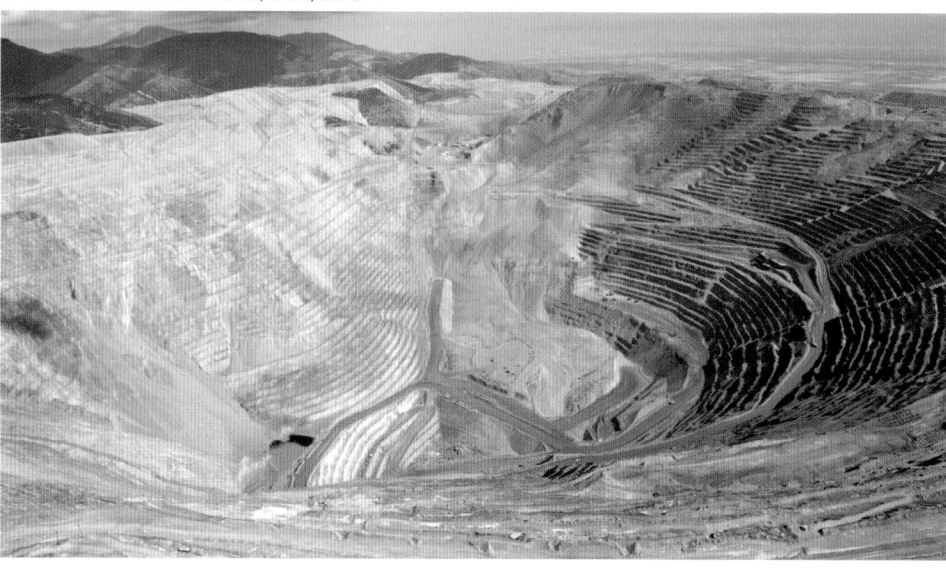

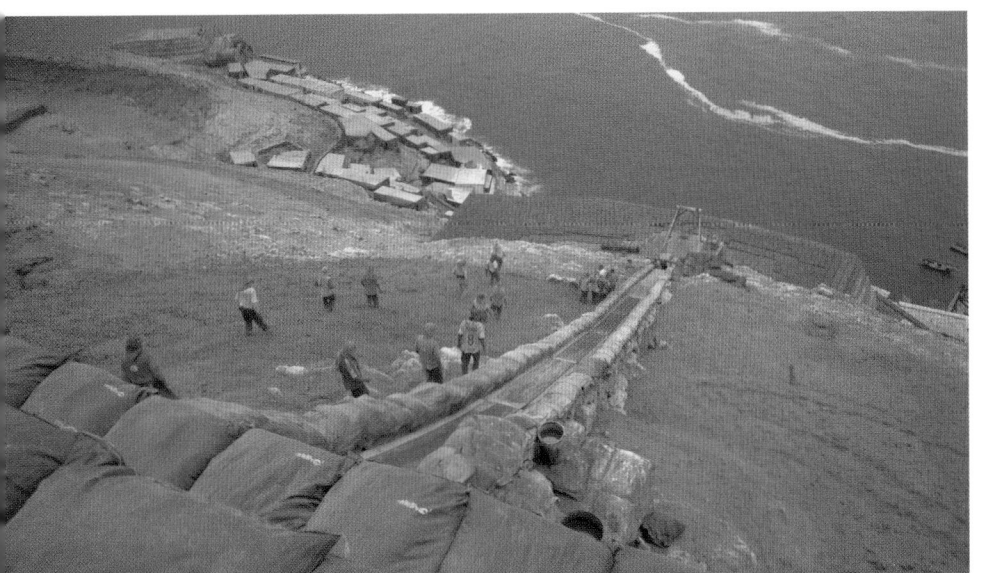

37 Dinh Q. Lê, *The Colony*, 2016

world, an active extraction site only slightly smaller than the
Chuquicamata pit in Chile. Overseen and operated by Kennecott
Copper Company, it was opened in 1904, and the crater – which
is still expanding – is now half a mile deep and more than two
miles wide. The slowly moving aerial footage shows the scale of
the excavation, the gaping hole of the pit, the network of roads
and the nearby smelter, while the approach to filmmaking
reflects the credo of the CLUI, based on maintaining the
appearance of administrative neutrality. Nevertheless, their
impartial documentation of a landscape scorched by the
systematic removal of the upper strata of the lithosphere calls
to mind the adverse environmental effects on natural habitats,
toxic encroachments on air and water, as well as the gratuitous
wastage of nourishing soil, reduced by the economic calculus
of the mining industry to worthless 'overburden'.

37   Vietnamese–American artist Dinh Q. Lê's film *The Colony*
(2016) examined the colonial history and present-day revival of
guano extraction on the Chincha Islands off the coast of Peru.
As a profitable alternative to crop rotation in restoring nutrients
to soils depleted by monocultural farming, guano from seabird
droppings was commonly spread on fields from the mid-
nineteenth century until the development of artificial fertilizers
in the early twentieth. During the 1860s, competition for control
of the lucrative soil supplement was the cause of a naval conflict

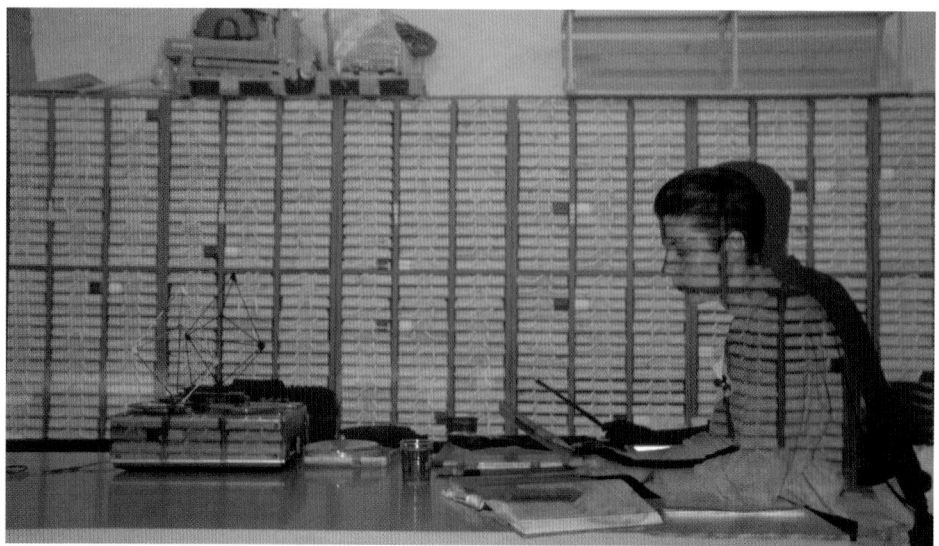

38 Filipa César, *Mined Soil*, 2013–14

between Spain and its former colonies of Peru, Chile, Ecuador and Bolivia, which ended in fiasco for the declining European power. Along with drone footage of the rocky shoreline covered with mounds of dried faeces and the abandoned dormitories of indentured Chinese labourers brought in by imperial forces to harvest the foul-smelling commodity, the film depicts pyramids of dark sacks awaiting loading to supply a new market of organic farmers, alluding to unsuspecting continuities in the methods and mentality of extractivism. At the same time, the overt and disconcerting presence of drones, reminiscent for the artist of the US Army helicopters that carried out murderous and ecocidal raids during the Vietnam War, draws attention to the technological weaponry with which rival powers now compete for control of resource-rich territories.

The troubled politics of soil becomes discernible when approached through the lens of 'colonial geology', which, according to Kathryn Yusoff in her *A Billion Black Anthropocenes or None*, 'generates a specifically racialised territorialisation of the earth'. In her film essay *Mined Soil* (2013–14), Portuguese artist Filipa César set out to explore the connections between the political trajectory of Amilcar Cabral as a revolutionary leader in the decolonial struggle of Guinea-Bissau and his research on soil and erosion. Assassinated in January 1973, months before the Portuguese colony declared independence, Cabral played a prominent role in African liberation

38

movements, but also worked as an agronomist in the colonial administration. César drew on digitalized footage from the militant cinema of Guinea-Bissau and a close reading of Cabral's published writings to suggest that he understood the soil not neutrally as 'an inert and static ground subjected to human agency', but as operating in dynamic relation to social structures and in response to the extractivist practices of colonialism. The domineering attitudes and practices towards the land that were challenged by Cabral in a colonial context have, as the film shows, resurfaced in contemporary Portugal following the opening up of the country to multinational mining corporations. In other words, under globalized conditions of resource depletion and climate disruption, the most extreme manifestations of extractivism are now indiscriminately spreading across colonial frontier lands and former imperial centres in Europe and North America.

Attention to earthy materiality and allusions to the imbrication of soil in colonial histories and African identities came together in Johannesburg-based artist Dineo Seshee Bopape's *Indeed it may very well be the_____ itself* (2016). Belonging to a series of related site-specific works, this installation made for the São Paulo Biennial consisted of circular and rectangular blocks of soil with dark mounds and cavities containing small quantities of symbolically or emotionally charged materials such as gold leaf, medicinal herbs, rose petals, gemstones and coal, as well as a cast of a uterus and handfuls of clay moulded by a clenched fist. Referencing in its layout the southern African strategy games of Morabaraba and Diketo, the work triggered a range of associations, from the erosion of memories of liberation struggles to issues of dispossession, landlessness and sovereignty. Surpassing anthropocentric social and political concerns, the artist also raised the geo-epistemological question of what bringing different soils together could mean 'for the materials themselves, for what they can experience of each other'.

Refusing the aerial perspective instrumentalized by colonial extractivism to delineate territorial boundaries, Taloi Havini's installation *Reclamation* (2019–20) privileged instead the earthbound epistemologies of the indigenous communities of the Autonomous Region of Bougainville. A layer of sandy ground provided an 'uninhabitable surface' for free-standing sculptures made from entwined cane by members of the artist's Hakö clan, one of the matrilineal peoples that have inhabited the Melanesian archipelago for tens of thousands of years. Using local materials and referencing the temporary

34

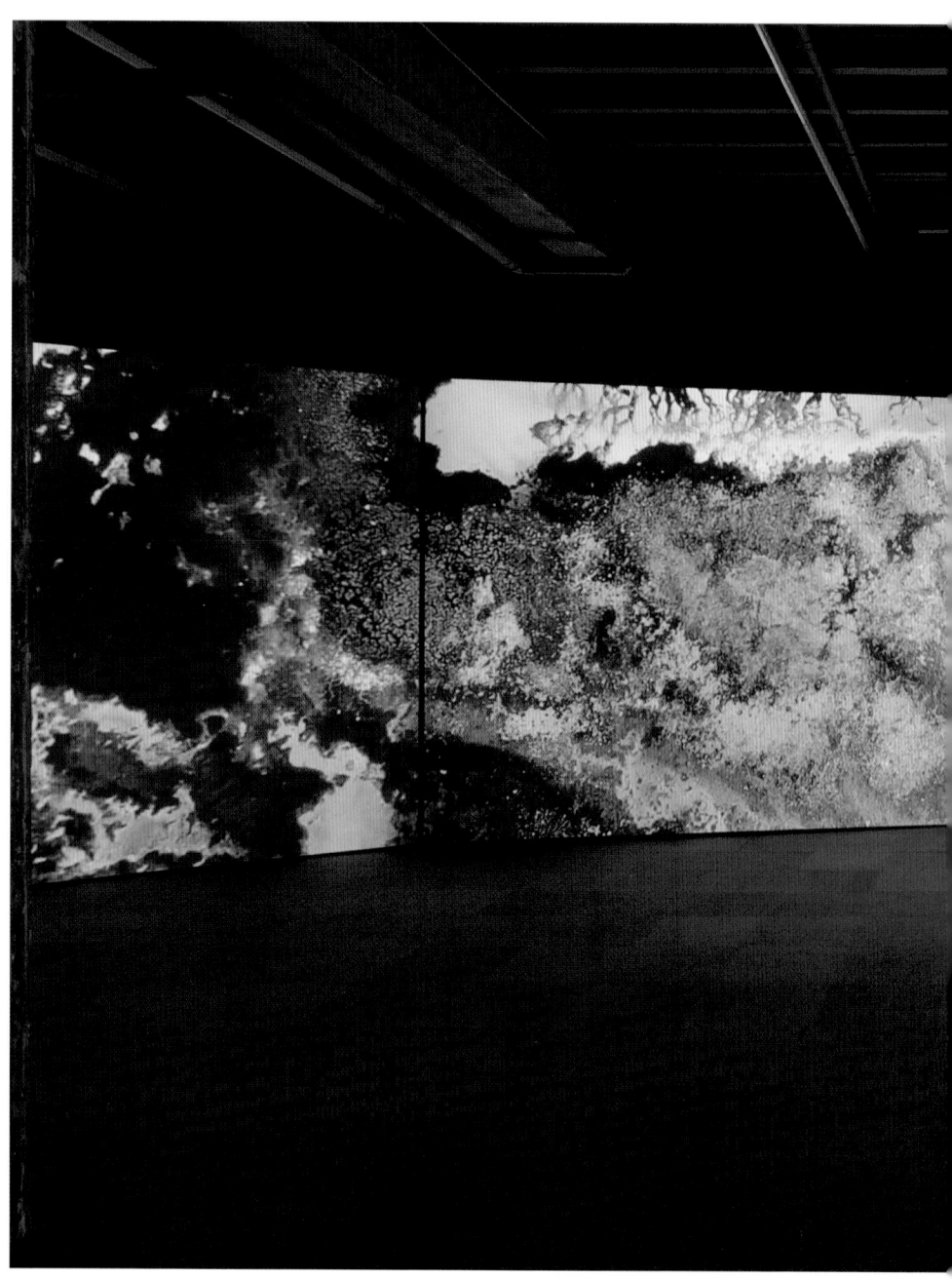

39 Taloi Havini, *Habitat*, 2018–19

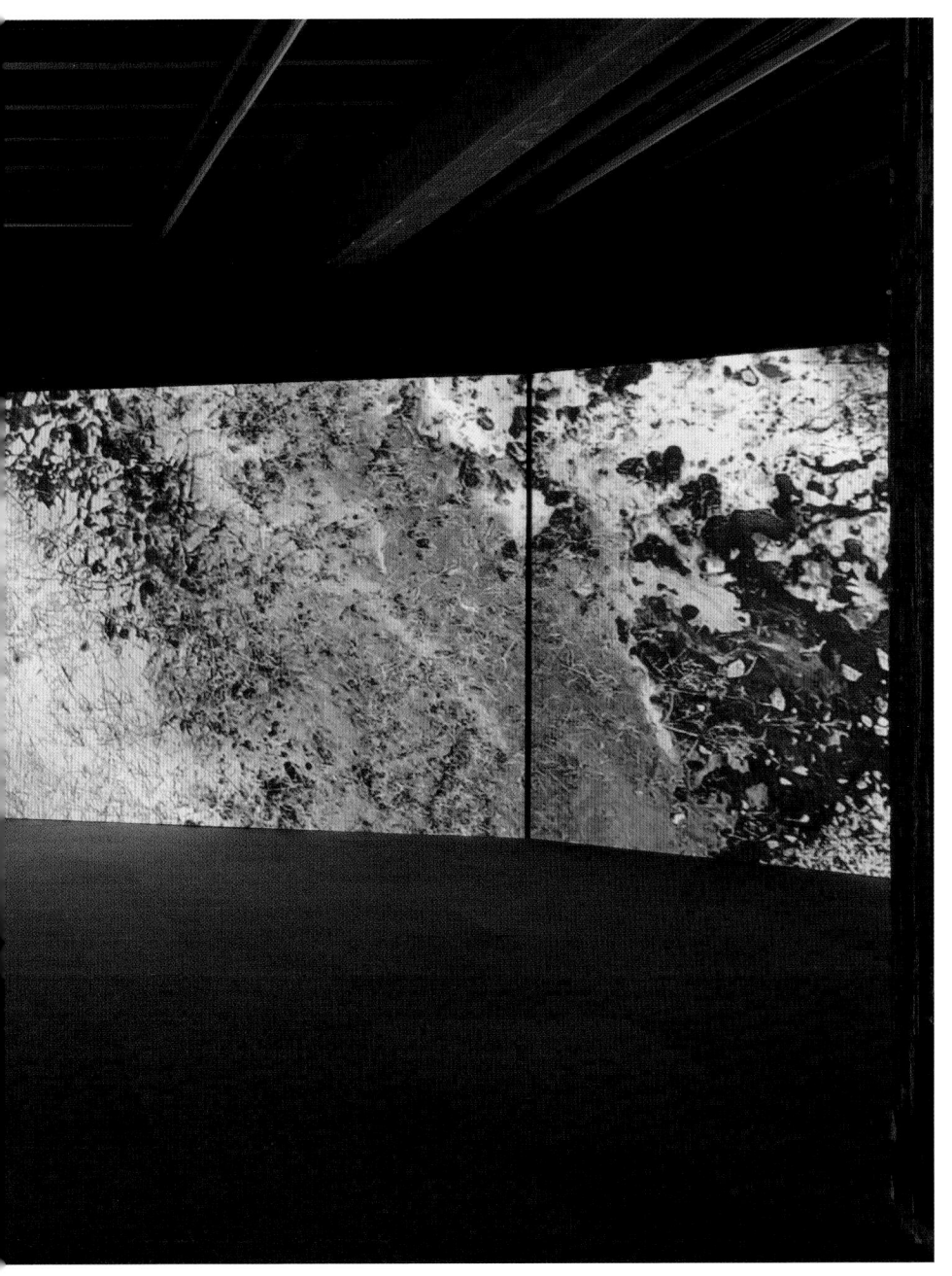

architectures of the region, the artist sees these structures as indicative of a non-Western 'form of navigation of space and knowledge' that, instead of looking down on the land, 'looks out and from within'. Havini's four-channel video installation *Habitat* (2018–19) focused on the origins of the uncertainty facing the local population and the reason why the reclamation of indigenous land rights is needed in the first place. Combining archival recordings of decolonial protests with family footage and newly shot film, the work dealt with the environmental damage caused by British–Australian mining giant Rio Tinto's massive Panguna copper mine, which for almost half a century contaminated agricultural land and waterways with poisonous tailings, leaving behind a barren terrain of waste rock. After a decade of military conflict in the 1990s, followed by a period of uneasy autonomy within Papua New Guinea, Bougainville is now on the brink of achieving independence, but as global demand for raw materials accelerates, indigenous communities face the prospect of renewed struggle around the precious minerals that lie beneath the land.

39

The toxic impact of the military–industrial complex on the lithosphere, which, as Bonneuil and Fressoz pointed out in *The Shock of the Anthropocene*, destroys 'even in peacetime', is most acutely felt in the training camps and firing ranges set up during the Cold War. In her black-and-white 16mm film *Black Beach/Horse/Camp/The Dead/Forces* (2016), San Juan-based artist Beatriz Santiago Muñoz delivered a silent meditation on the legacy for the Puerto Rican island of Vieques of six decades of contamination by the US Navy, which intensively used the Caribbean territory as a bombing range. The title reveals the film's montage structure of dream-like fragments, depicting at one point an energy healer handling magnetite stones washed by emulsified foam on an eroding beach and at another images of children playing in the waves, followed by shots of the rusting shell of a bombed-out ship. A further sequence shows a woman with cosmic markings on her forehead attempting to resuscitate a sacred ceiba tree poisoned by proximity to weapons testing, while wild foals lie vulnerably on the ground in forests still strewn with undetonated landmines. The human and non-human subjects in Muñoz's film channel the damage and distress etched in the lithosphere by the toxic histories of military occupation, while enacting gestures of spiritual and ecological recuperation.

The 'rush to grab land' has been given a new economic impetus as anxiety around imminent resource exhaustion intensifies, since, as Maria Puig de la Bellacasa has cautioned in *Matters of Care*, the less soil there is left, the 'more valuable an investment it becomes, and its intensified exploitation is further accelerated'. Aggressive interference into the biological, chemical and physical makeup of the soil that accompanied industrialization has left a lasting imprint in the terrestrial matter of the lithosphere, while climate change is further exacerbating land degradation. Artists are on the one hand providing a critical standpoint towards such harmful processes and on the other offering transformative perspectives from within to restore the vitality of the soil.

Chapter 2
Riverine Ecologies

The world's great rivers have found themselves at the mercy of the most forceful measures of technocratic control through damming and course straightening. Major waterways have been harnessed to provide energy and transport for industrial growth, while streams and brooks have been concreted over, drained and sluiced with toxic levels of pollution and waste. At the same time, the arteries of the hydrosphere have shown remarkable resilience, with biodiversity recovering when the chemical runoffs from fields and urban effluents are regulated and as the ecologically motivated removal of dams begins to outpace the construction of new barriers. Climate change is also testing the limits of the geoengineered domination of rivers, which enact their resurgent fluvial agency by bursting concrete fetters and reclaiming their floodplains. In place of the instrumentalizing attitudes towards waterways cultivated by rationalist modernity, river historian Peter Coates has advocated the 'view from under the bridge' that perceives 'change rather than destruction, and the production of new and different rivers rather than non-rivers, lost rivers, dead rivers or silenced rivers', which prevail in scholarly discussions. Abandoning the attitude of technocratic superiority and the logic of economic exploitability opens a channel to the cosmic rivers of folkloric and indigenous traditions, the geological rivers that charted fluvial corridors through primeval landscapes and the physical rivers that seamlessly collaborate in the hydrological cycle of the biosphere.

The connection between the suppression of waterways within the urban landscape and colonialist mapmaking were explored in Berlin-based Taiwanese artist Su Yu Hsin's film essay *water sleep II: Akaike river under Xizang Road* (2019). Sweeping over a map of the city of Taipei drawn from a bird's

40

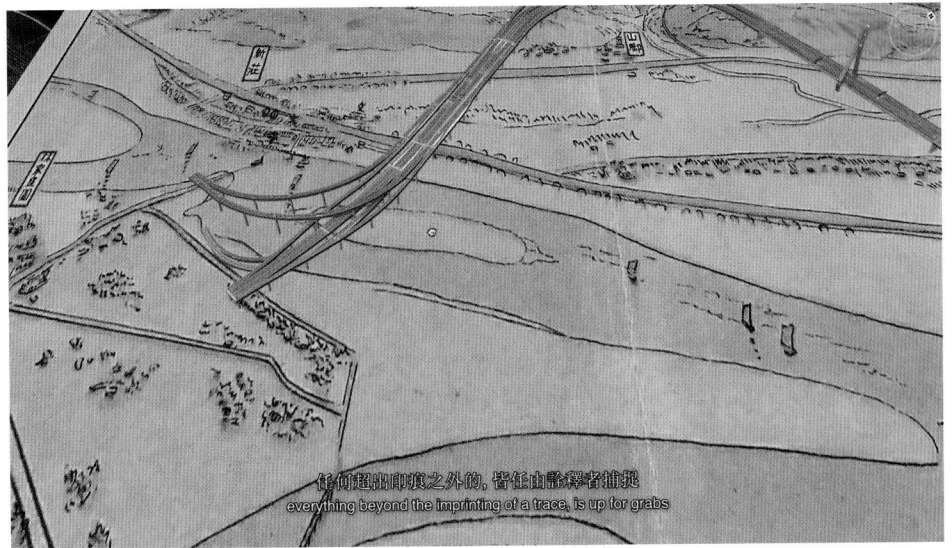

40 Su Yu Hsin, *water sleep II: Akaike river under Xizang Road*, 2019

eye view in 1935 during the period of Japanese rule, the camera exposes the distortions of colonial cartography that privileged Japanese settlements over Chinese villages and shrunk the distance between Taiwan and the faraway mountains of imperial Japan. A second map from 1944, made by the American military using aerial photography to identify bombing targets, further illustrated through its strategic choice of details the lack of neutrality in cartographic representations. What the colonial maps did reveal was the presence of the River Akaike, which was first demoted by the authorities from a named river to Drain No. 3 and then concreted over in the late 1970s to 'improve the cityscape and transportation', but is missing from today's digital visualizations of the city. The artist used this historical data to retrace its path on Google Earth, following its course along the Xizang Road and calling on viewers to imagine they are 'on a motorcycle riding above an invisible river under the asphalt'. In the finale of the film, emerging from a pumping station into the estuary, the river meets the horizon, asserting the continuity of its fluvial existence.

In her long-term project on the effects of hydroelectric dams on the natural and social environments of Latin America, Carolina Caycedo has emphasized that 'in indigenous cosmogonies of the Americas all bodies of waters are connected, and rivers are the veins of the planet'. *Be Dammed* began in 2012, when the Los Angeles-based artist read about the plans of a multinational

Riverine Ecologies

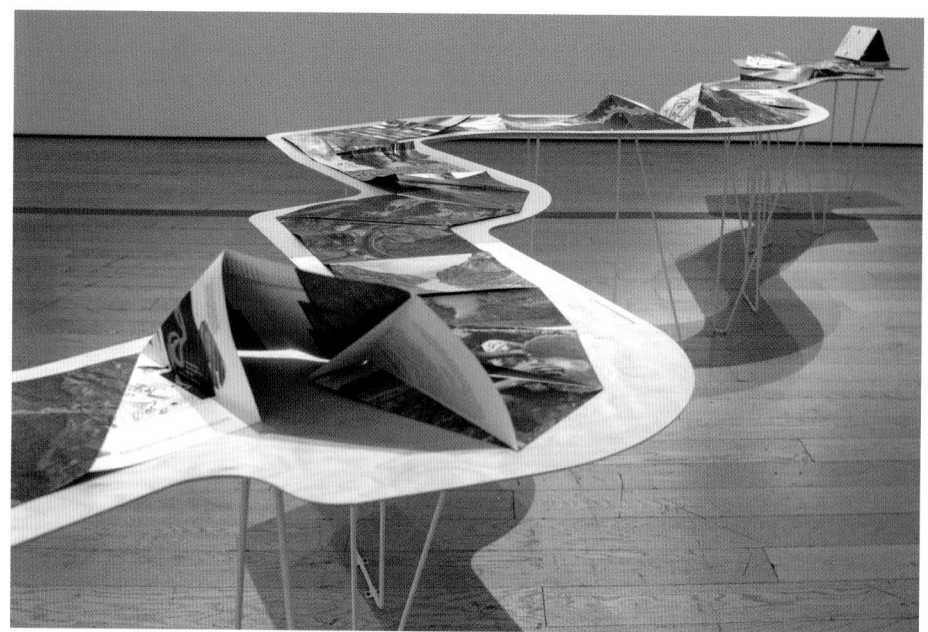

41 Carolina Caycedo, *Serpent River Book*, 2017

company to build a dam on her childhood Magdalena River, the longest in Colombia. On the day works were supposed to start, the river flooded, which in the local community was interpreted as the river protecting itself, while for Caycedo it indicated that the 'spirit of the river was a political agent in environmental conflicts'. Pointing to the fact that transnational corporations are involved in building or planning more than 250 dams across the continent, the artist raised questions about the transformation of water from a commons into a privatized resource, while observing that in the United States the trend has reversed, with the removal of dams creating conditions for the restoration of river ecologies. Comprised of videos, sculptures, geo-choreographies involving local communities, audio-visual essays and the experimental publication *Serpent River Book* (2017), the project furthered the understanding of rivers as part of complex ecologies shaped by more-than-human interrelations.

Canadian artist Genevieve Robertson's film *Still Running Water* (2017–19) followed the Columbia River over 2,000 kilometres from a spring close to the Kootenay Glacier in British Columbia to its estuary on the Pacific coast in Astoria, Oregon. Surfacing in a barren plateau of decapitated trees, the

41

42

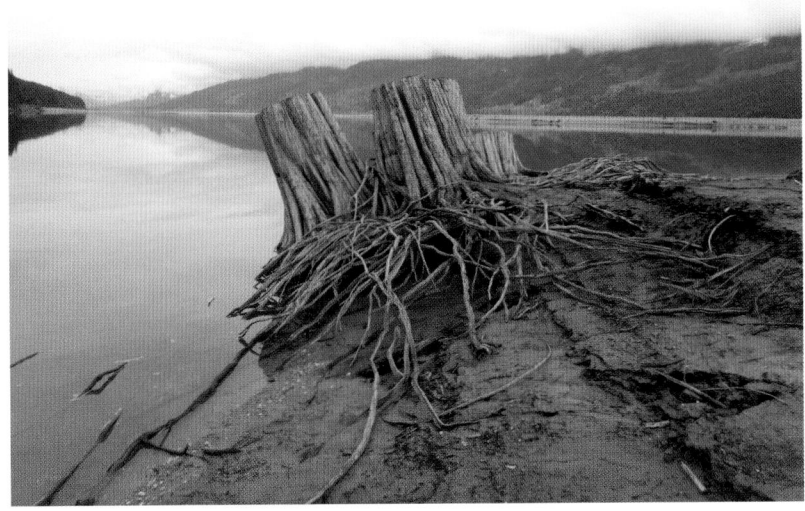

42 Genevieve Robertson, *Still Running Water*, 2017–19

river travels between gravelly banks; its waters appear lifeless and unenticing, flowing silently against a discordant electronic soundtrack. There is no trace here of the romantic tradition of wilderness landscape painting. Nor are we in the world of the modernist technological sublime, as the fourteen dams on the river's main course are viewed from a wary distance, deprived of associations with the mastery of nature and revealed as banal concrete edifices cutting across hilly terrain to disturb the river's flow. Instead the artist draws attention to the ecological and cultural costs of hydropower projects that have left the Columbia 'monitored and monetized down to the millilitre', blocking the upstream journey of Pacific salmon, degrading aquatic habitats and impacting the lives of indigenous nations whose ancestral territories and spiritual practices centre on the river. And yet at an elemental level the river still runs; by submerging us in its cold grey waters or closing in on cell-like bubbles, white foam and rippling textures, the camerawork insists on the liquid materiality of H_2O. Where the river meets the ocean, the sound of denatured industrial chords is replaced by the insistent crashing of waves, as the untrammelled power of the sea engulfs and absorbs even the powerful Columbia, erasing its ephemeral, human-tarred histories.

From its source in Tibet, the mighty Mekong River flows for 4,350 kilometres through China, Myanmar, Thailand, Laos and Cambodia to Vietnam, where it meets the sea, with its muddy waters bringing downstream an abundance of nutrient-rich sediments. However, over the last decades the building of hydroelectric dams upstream has significantly obstructed the distribution of lifegiving alluvial deposits to its delta. Thao Nguyên Phan's film *Becoming Alluvium* (2019) was conceived as a tribute to the 'beauty and suffering of the Mekong', whose currents bring cultural, religious and economic affluence to Southeast Asia, yet the 'human interventions to the river have been so violent that [it] is now forever transformed'. The single-channel video combined fairy tales from the countries the river passes through with materials from literary and historical archives to create a fictional narrative, switching between film footage and animated sequences made with watercolour drawings over illustrations by nineteenth-century French artist and Mekong explorer Louis Delaporte. Structured around three parts, or 'reincarnations', in a reference to the artist's Buddhist upbringing, the film portrays the industrial river with boats, interchanging scenes of family picnics and vistas of rubbish strewn along its shores and finally the story of a princess who asked for jewelry made from monsoon dew. With climate change affecting the water cycle, causing more extreme droughts and floods, Phan's identification with the Mekong's fertile alluvium and the environmental degradation it suffered is also directed towards shared uncertainty over the future.

43   In *Have You Seen the Flowers on the River?* (2007–10), Indian artist Ravi Agarwal investigated starkly contrasting attitudes and relations to the River Yamuna as it passes from a rural setting to enter the city of Delhi, where 'vegetables, flowers, water, sand and livelihoods give way to concrete, dirt, filth, criss-crossed roads and displaced, unconnected lives'. Based on anthropological interviews and a long-term engagement with upstream communities, the work included a video tracing the centuries-old traditional economy of marigold picking along its fertile banks, a sustainable form of family harvesting of flowers destined for the Fatehpuri Market in Old Delhi. The artist drew attention to the threat posed to these interconnected social and natural ecologies by the activities of real estate speculators and city modernizers, who after relocating the flower market to a landfill site on the outskirts of Delhi are now concreting over the flower-rich floodplains and displacing the disadvantaged communities who live along its banks. Going against the tide of urbanization, gentrification and engineering schemes to embank and canalize the river's flows, Agarwal made the

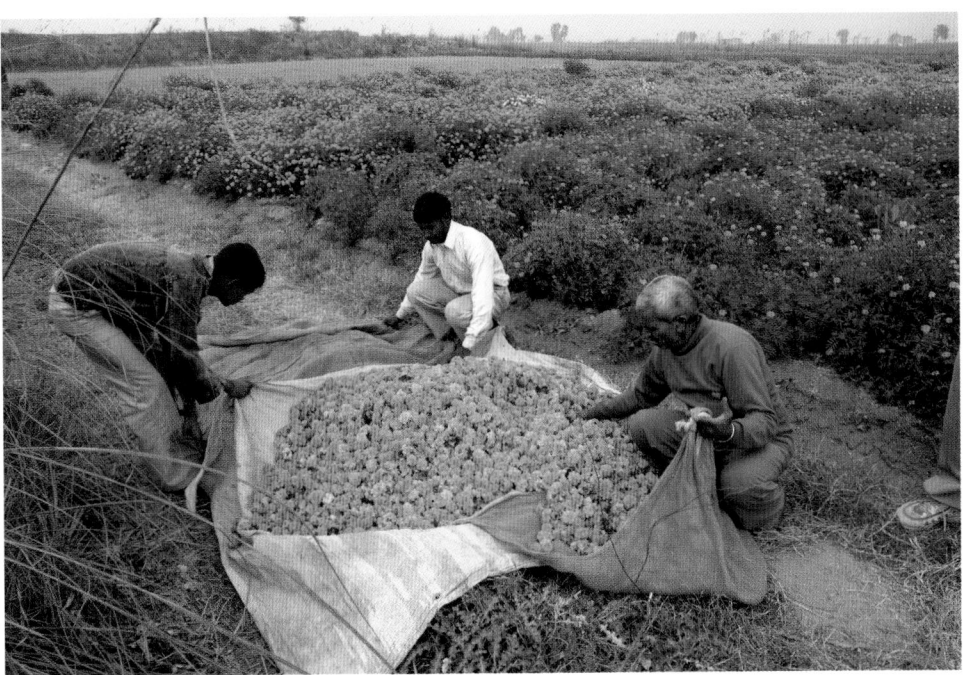

43　Rawi Argawal, *Flower Packing*, 2007

case for coexistence with the sacred Yamuna, based on the recognition that rivers are governed 'not only by the laws of hydraulics, but also those of biology, zoology, sociology, geography and politics'.

As of 2017, there is a precedent for bestowing rights historically reserved for humans in the Western legal tradition onto rivers, with the recognition by New Zealand of the legal personhood of the Whanganui River. Acknowledging the Maori belief that the river, together with all its physical and metaphysical elements, is an indivisible living whole, the government also apologized for the harm done to the sacred river, a litany including polluting it with urban effluent, damaging its bed by extracting gravel, diverting its waters to a hydroelectric plant and dynamiting its bends to ease tourist steamer access to the 'Rhine of New Zealand'. Artist Natalie Robertson's project *He wai mou! He wai mau!* (2017) addressed water as the sacral life-blood of Mother Earth, or Papatuanuku, and as an element of everyday existence. It included photographic works documenting the impact of deforestation at the mouth of the Waiapu River and the effects of increasing sediment deposits from anthropogenic erosion.

44

Riverine Ecologies

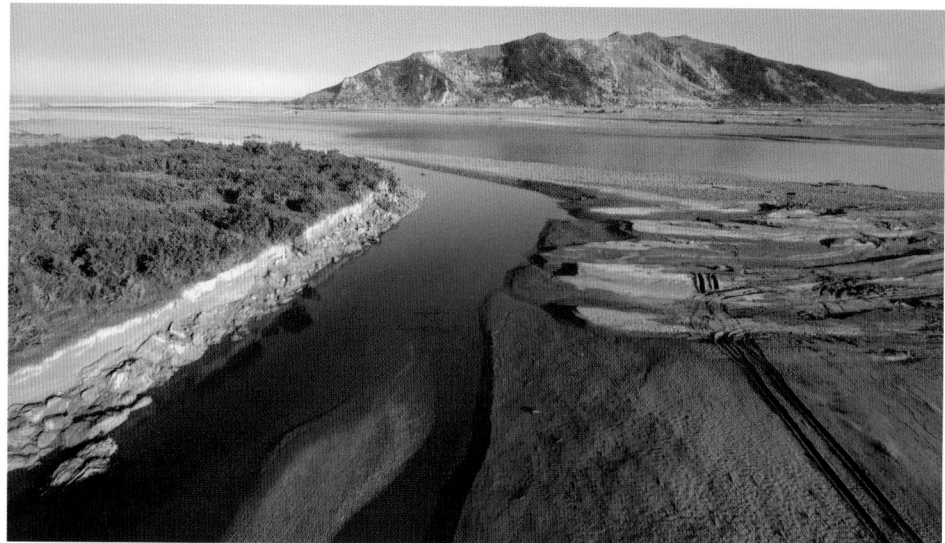

44 Natalie Robertson, *Waiapu River Confluence to Sea*, 2017

An accompanying video showed grey mullet swimming downstream to the ocean to spawn, capturing at water level and from drone footage the tell-tale signs of human interventions on the riverbanks. The mournful tones of an ancestral lament on the soundtrack express anxiety about the heightened threats to the wellbeing of the sacred and life-giving Waiapu River in an age of climate change, while advocating the Maori values of connectivity with nature, an ecological ethics of reciprocity and deep respect for the living world.

45   The River Kushuimi, as it is called by indigenous Shuars in the Ecuadorian Amazon, was the subject of *How Rivers Think* (2018) by Netherlands-based Ecuadorian artist Oscar Santillán. The work was composed of eighty customized slides that contained actual samples of water collected by the artist at regular intervals while canoeing down the river. The enlarged projections of the fragments of the rainforest, containing leaves, twigs, plants and sediments of the river, represent the intertwined elements of the complex ecosystem. Rather than depicting the river, through these liquid herbariums the artist let the river portray itself. This fluviocentric work was a tribute to Eduardo Kohn's ethnographic study of the region *How Forests Think: Toward an Anthropology beyond the Human*, in which the author also observed that humans are 'not the only ones who harness the unidirectionally nested river pattern',

since for instance fish distribute seeds along its course, intertwining floristic and riverine worlds.

The apparent disconnect of citizens of her native city of Kraków from the neglected rivers that flow mostly unnoticed through the urban conglomeration was the motivation for Cecylia Malik to embark on her *Six Rivers* (2011–12) journey. The artist set out to paddle down all six waterways within the city boundaries in a self-made boat assembled from found materials, overcoming on the way obstacles such as fences, concrete infrastructures and post-industrial ruins. Photo documentation and film footage of each river journey, ranging from rubbish-filled vistas of environmental degradation and urban sprawl encroaching on the fluvial course to hidden enclaves of flourishing biodiversity, were shared through social media feeds. Once completed, the work premiered in a public screening under a city bridge, bringing the artist's individual experience into the realm of the social in order to foster awareness of the coexistence of riverine environments in the urban tissue. It was soon followed by the grassroots initiative *Critical Water Mass* in which the public was invited to reclaim

45 Oscar Santillán, *How Rivers Think*, 2018

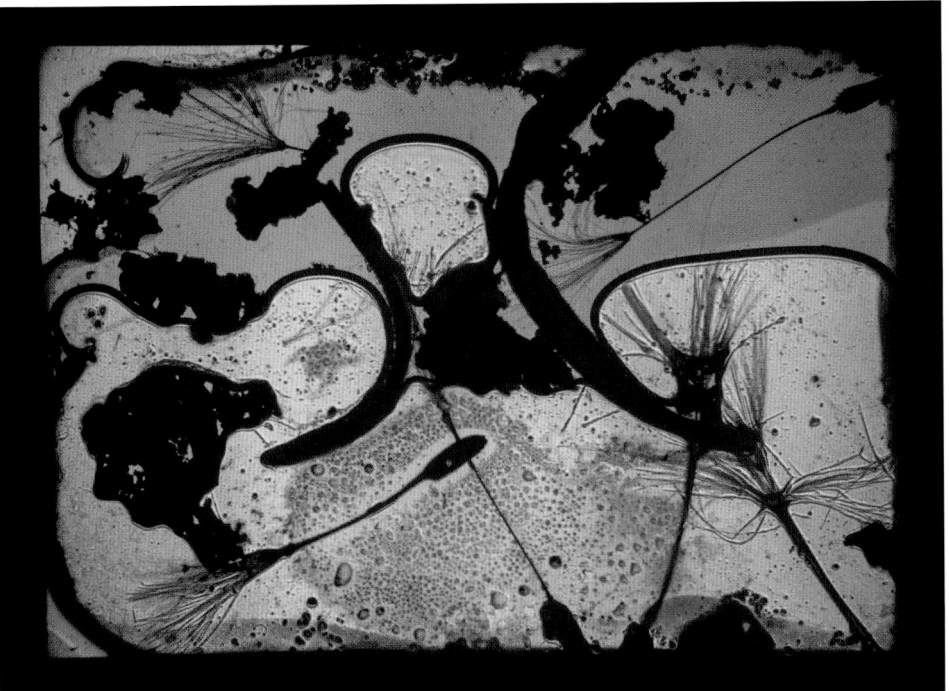

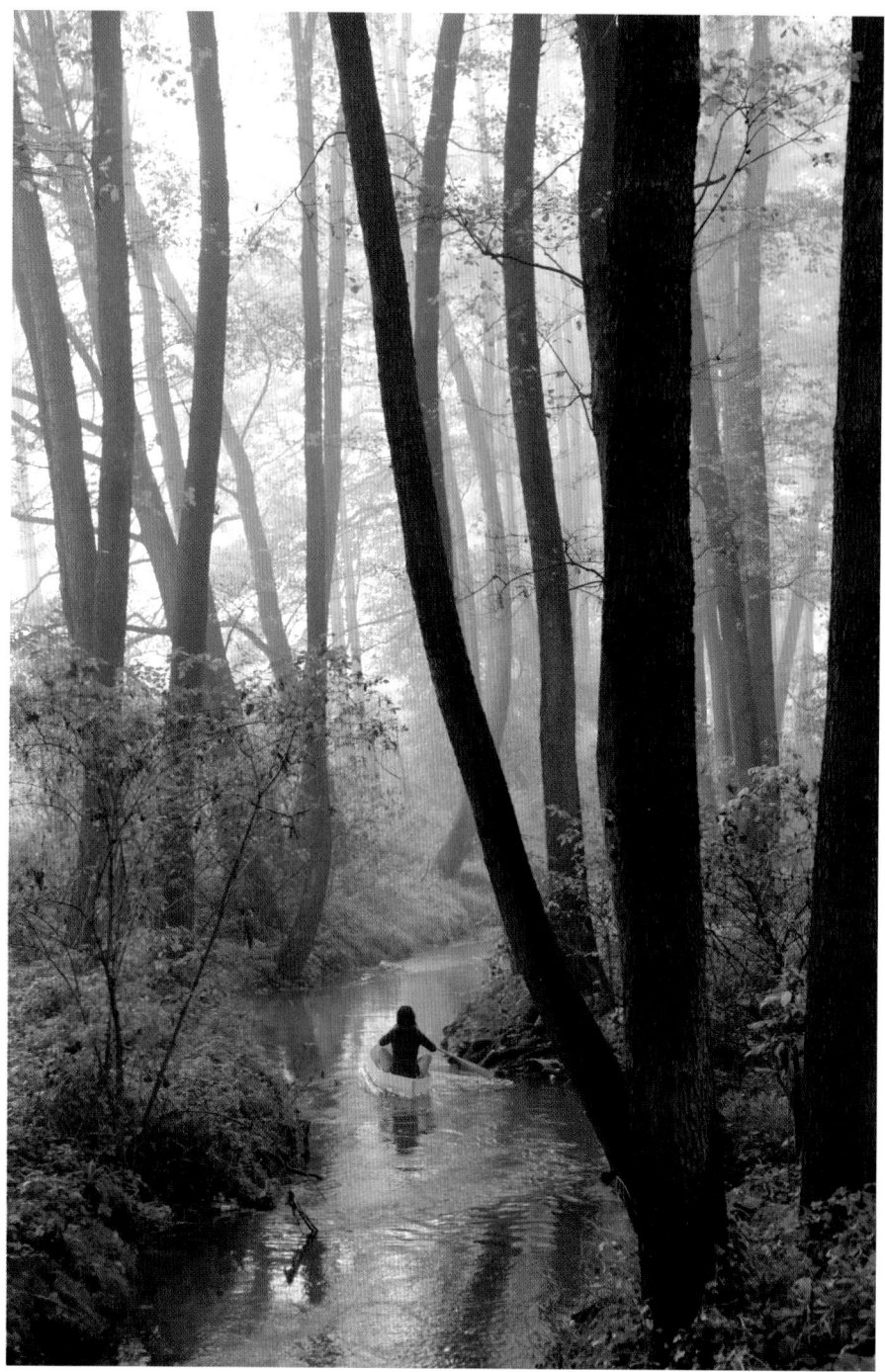

the Vistula, Poland's largest river, which flows through the centre of Kraków. The launching of festively adorned boats and homemade floating pontoons has since become an annual occasion for ecologically minded city dwellers to 'make friends with the river'.

In contrast to many large European rivers that flow westwards, the eastward course of the Danube passes through ten countries on its way from the Black Forest to the Black Sea. Many linguistic variations of its name preserve the proto-Indo-European root meaning of the primeval cosmic river, alluding to its millions of years of history before it became an Anthropocene river. A large-format billboard by Oliver Ressler depicted a panoramic view of the Danube with the baroque monastery of Melk perched familiarly above its bank in the distance, while in the foreground four large cargo vessels were criss-crossed in an apparent accident, with outbreaks of fire on deck and an oil spill in the river completely blocking the waterway. The artist addressed here the economic use of the river as a transportation channel, on which not only large tourist boats cruise, but also millions of tonnes of freight are shipped annually. Part of the photographic series *The economy is wounded – let it die!* (2016), the work referenced one of the slogans that emerged from the revolutionary upsurge of May 1968 in Paris, which for the artist not only anticipates the imminent catastrophe, but also contains the possibility of a 'deliberate act of sabotage', a river barricade as a site of mass protest interrupting the seamless flow of capitalism.

Rivers are revealed in these works as active protagonists that, despite being subjected to utilitarian and developmentalist agendas, continuously assert their fluvial agency. Uncovering the hidden waterways within the city, artists also exposed the correlation between the mistreatment of rivers and manifestations of social injustice along their banks. With their continuously renewing flows, rivers are a constant reminder of the limits of technocratic power. The demand to stop seeing rivers as part of the capitalist machine and to acknowledge their legal rights converges here with older traditions that recognize them as religious and spiritual beings within wider ecosystems.

46 OPPOSITE Cecylia Malik, *Six Rivers*, 2011–12

Chapter 3
Marine Permutations

The deep-seated sense of elemental connection with the sea derives from the shared oceanic origin of all terrestrials, whose corporeal makeup pulses with its salty flows. Even the 'protoplasm that streams within each cell of our bodies', as pioneering ecologist Rachel Carson observed in her 1951 book *The Sea Around Us*, bears the 'chemical structure impressed upon all living matter when the first simple creatures were brought forth in the ancient sea'. Today, the unfolding ecological crisis is impacting marine environments in manifold ways, including through overfishing, extinctions, the bleaching of coral reefs, acidification, plastic pollution and rising sea levels. At the same time, faced with the uncertainties of climate change, the oceanic imaginary is being reinvigorated through a radical questioning of societal, cultural and emotional relations to the sea. The blue humanities herald a shift from the imperialistic modern approach to the sea as a flattened blank canvas, or *aqua nullius*, for voyages of trade, discovery and maritime domination to the refiguring of the ocean, in the words of Elizabeth M. DeLoughrey in *Allegories of the Anthropocene*, as an 'agent, as embodied place, or as ontology itself'. The future of the oceans is torn between a renewed 'sea grab' for deep-sea mineral mining, accompanied by intensified exploitation of marine organisms, and oceanic stewardship that seeks a global return to an ethics of care and responsibility for the sea.

47   Set on a sandy beach, *Sun & Sea (Marina)* (2019) is an opera in seventeen voices, which through its enticing singing and easy-going scenes plays out the entwinement of leisure, consumerism, global travel and tourism with the climate crisis. Under the direction of Rugilė Barzdžiukaitė, with a libretto by Vaiva Grainytė and music by Lina Lapelytė, the work represented

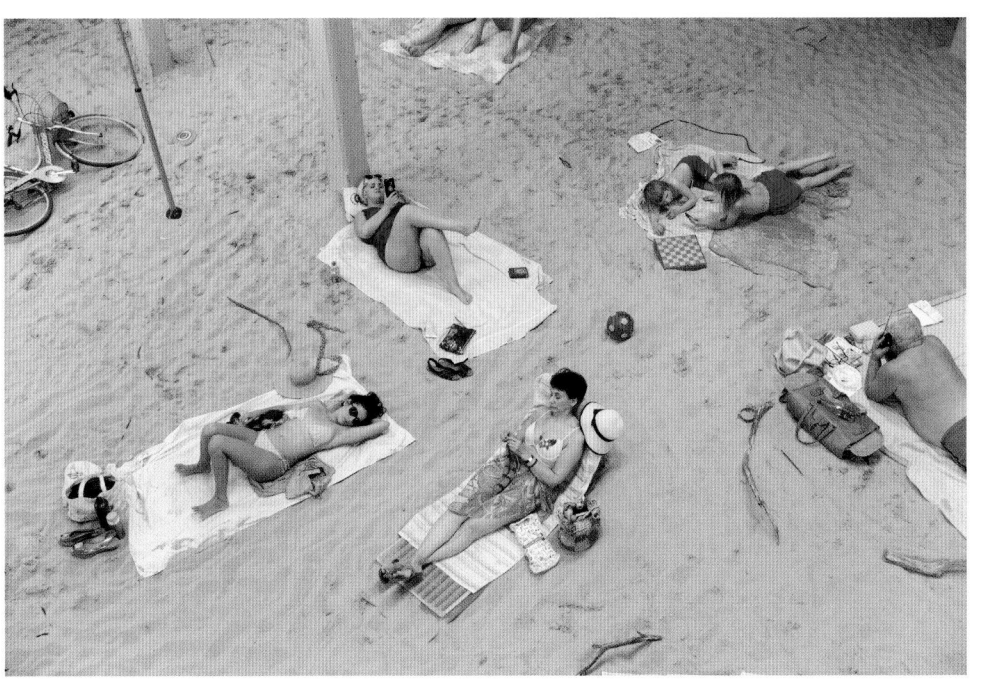

47 Rugilė Barzdžiukaitė, Vaiva Grainytė and Lina Lapelytė, *Sun & Sea (Marina)*, 2019

Lithuania at the 58th Venice Biennial. The performance was acted out on the ground floor of a warehouse and observed from a mezzanine, where viewers could watch protagonists sunbathing on their colourful towels, having picnics and playing with inflatable beach gear. A mother sang of her pride in her eight-and-a-half-year-old son, who had already swum in the 'Black, the Yellow, the White, the Red, the Mediterranean and the Aegean Seas... He has already visited two of the world's great oceans, and will visit the remaining ones this year.' A young man, who flew to Portugal for 'a short trip just for fun', chanted nonchalantly that 'not a single climatologist predicted a scenario like this'. The melodies, which interchanged between lively arias and dreamy lullabies, accentuated the air of obliviousness to a climate disaster that, despite the sun cream, turns sunworshippers' skin lobster red and leaves their bodies covered with a 'slippery green fleece' of proliferating algae. In that sense, as theorist Astrida Neimanis has noted in *Bodies of Water*, 'climate change, ocean acidification, aquifer depletion and toxic transits halfway round the world' are among the 'hard to fathom phenomena' that are giving rise to 'more-than-human scales of planetary distress'.

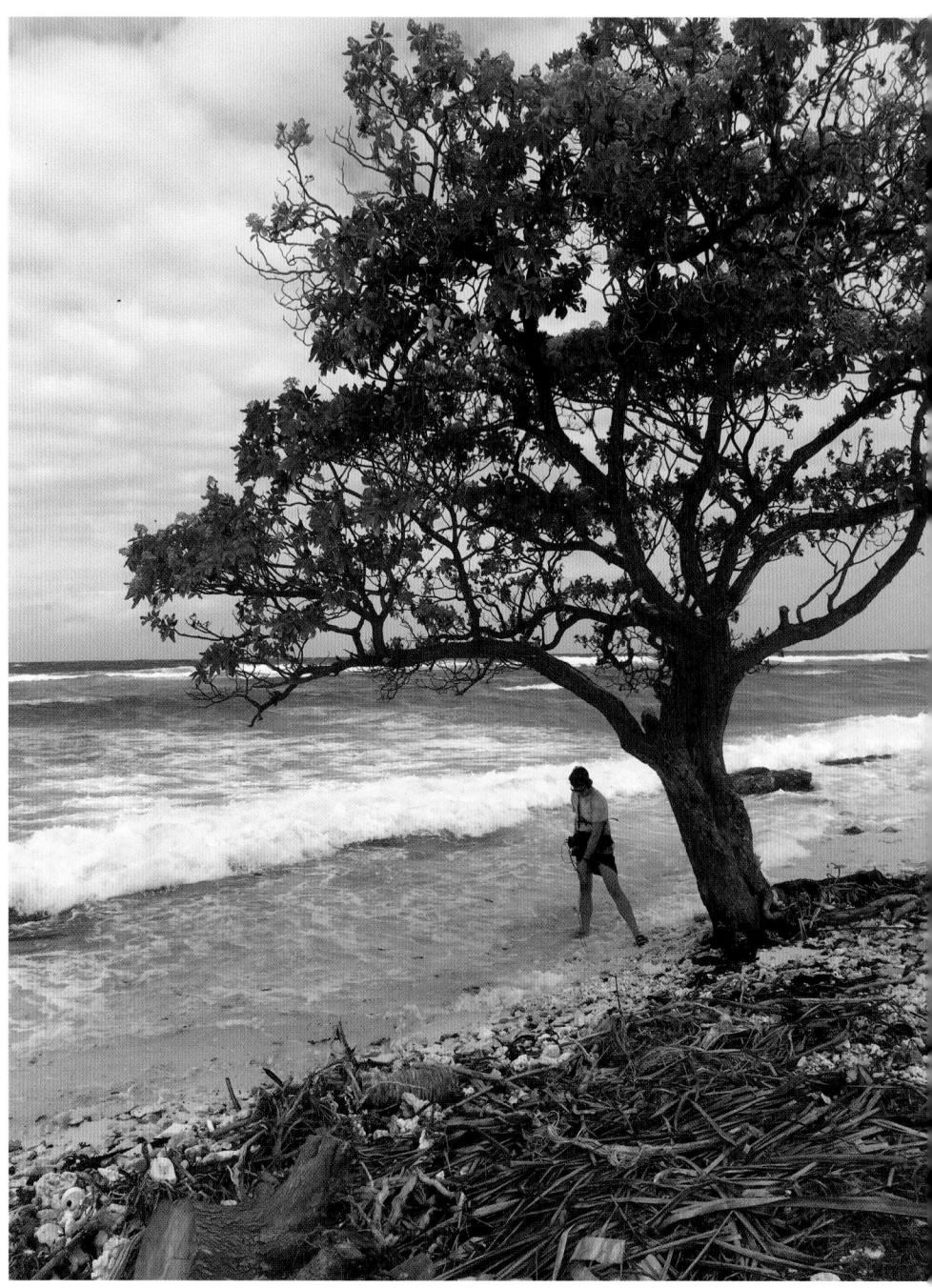

48 Anja Kanngieser, *Submersion*, 2019

Rising sea levels are one of the most visible manifestations of global warming, caused not only by the dramatic melting of glaciers, but also by thermal expansion as water molecules become agitated at higher temperatures. Gravitational effects and weather systems make some micro-geographies more immediately vulnerable than others, magnifying the uneven global distribution of the impacts of climate disruption. Born on a boat in the South Pacific to German parents and raised on a small island, artist and geographer Anja Kanngieser has engaged with the predicament of the region's remote coral atolls, whose communities find themselves on the frontline of the rising ocean. In her audio work *Submersion* (2019) she invited an audience in Melbourne to consider the connections between the long-term threat posed to the city's Southbank district by the River Yarra if sea levels rise by 3 metres and the imminent danger facing the island of Tarawa in Kiribati in the Central Pacific, which sits less than 3 metres above the ocean. In the first case, unceded land that was cared for by Aboriginal peoples for tens of thousands of years would be 'stolen twice', first by 'white men in ships seeking to extinguish everything that existed' and then by the sea, while in Tarawa, homes, wells and gardens are already being inundated by saltwater and the indigenous community faces the prospect of abandoning their ancestral lands. Her 'story about submersion' concludes with the warning that since the waters of Kiribati and the River Yarra are connected by the ocean, 'our futures are held together in common by this tidal force'.

48

Despite mounting evidence of the threat to marine ecologies posed by climate change and chemical pollution, mining corporations are gearing up to expand their operations in the submarine frontier lands of the high seas. The novel procedures of deep-sea mining were exposed in Armin Linke's installation *Prospecting Ocean* (2018), which juxtaposed footage of the deep ocean with shots of the machinery used to extract minerals and specimens. The inscrutable aesthetics of futuristic technology collide here with the casual brutality of the process of cutting and scraping the seabed, hydraulically sucking oceanic matter up to barges to be washed and separated, before discharging the slurry back into the ocean depths. Video of the meetings of the International Seabed Authority, responsible for drawing up a code for the commercial exploitation of the seafloor, are also included in the work, along with documentation of protests against underwater prospecting off the coast of Papua New Guinea. The work dramatized the clash between the legal-bureaucratic apparatuses of extractive capitalism and the ecological outlook of those seeking to protect the ocean from

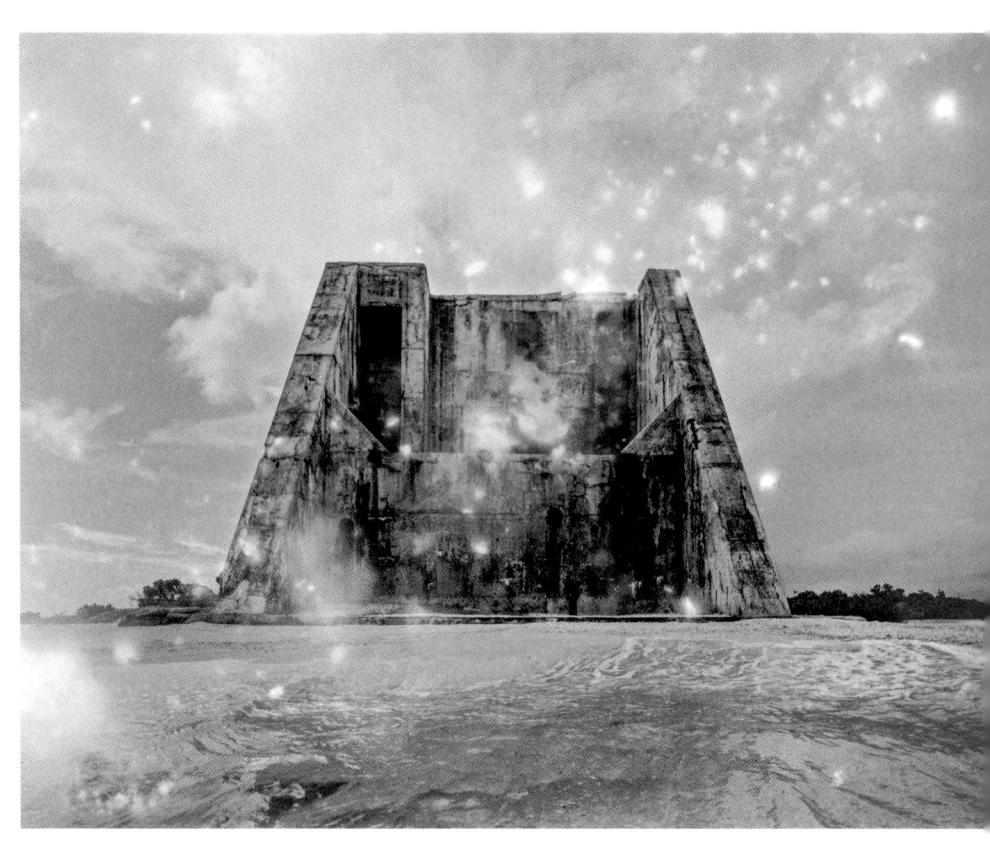

49 Julian Charrière, *Aomen I– Terminal Beach*, 2016

economic and political exploitation. The transformation of oceans into 'highly instrumented sensor spaces' has also been noted by theorist Jennifer Gabrys as exemplifying the hopes of marine science to deploy new technologies to steer 'Spaceship Earth through the gathering storms of planetary collapse'.

49   The atomic age of the oceans was explored by Julian Charrière in his project *Terminal Beach*, inspired by J. G. Ballard's collection of sci-fi stories. The artist set out on a field trip to the desolate Bikini Atoll in the Marshall Archipelago of Micronesia, approaching it as a site of speculative future archaeology. One of the outcomes of the journey to the coral reef, chosen by the United States as an ideal location for nuclear testing, was the film *Iroojrilik* (2016), in which the artist portrayed the verdant palm growths on the island, intersected by the remains of decaying bunkers and other military infrastructures, and dived into the ocean depths to reveal a seabed full of sunken ships. Famously lending its name to a style of swimsuits, Bikini Atoll was in 1954 the site of the powerful Bravo test, which resulted in an environmental catastrophe as radioactive fallout carried by strong winds blanketed nearby inhabited atolls of Remote Oceania. According to the authors of an *Environmental History of the Cold War*, the readiness of nuclear rivals to test weapons of such magnitude demonstrated both the intensity of the conflict and 'the superpowers' lack of environmental sensitivity'. By referencing Bikinian mythology in the title of the film, Charrière reflected on the primordial entanglement of the fish, coconuts and people of the archipelago, which through the project of nuclear colonialism have been expelled from paradise, with coconuts becoming radioactive mutant plants – the 'forbidden fruit' of the nuclear age.

50   Simryn Gill's photographic series *The Channel* (2014) takes as its subject the coastal town of Port Dickson in Malaysia, a colonial hub turned seaside resort marred by overdevelopment, pollution and its proximity to offshore oil refineries. Exploring the social and environmental effects of globalization on her hometown, the artist focused on its mangrove forest and in particular on the plastic and fabric remnants washed up by the sea that hang from low-lying branches. The colourful bags and strips of synthetic clothing adorning mangrove trees are reminders that plastic pollution is poisoning the sea and disrupting fragile beach ecosystems, while a solitary photo of a container ship passing through the Strait of Malacca points to the roots of the problem in the global capitalist system. As the only tree species that can survive in saltwater, protecting coastal populations from

tsunamis, providing through their underwater roots a nursery for juvenile fish and sequestering ten times as much carbon as inland trees, mangrove forests are key allies in the struggle against climate change. Reminiscent of Buddhist prayer flags, the synthetic rags blowing in the wind call attention to the endangerment of the mangroves and despoilation of the beach environment by the traces left in the ocean by wasteful global economies.

'International waters seem to be full of invisible walls,' observed Chilean artist Enrique Ramírez in relation to the obstacles he encountered from local maritime bureaucracy

50 Simryn Gill, *The Channel*, 2014

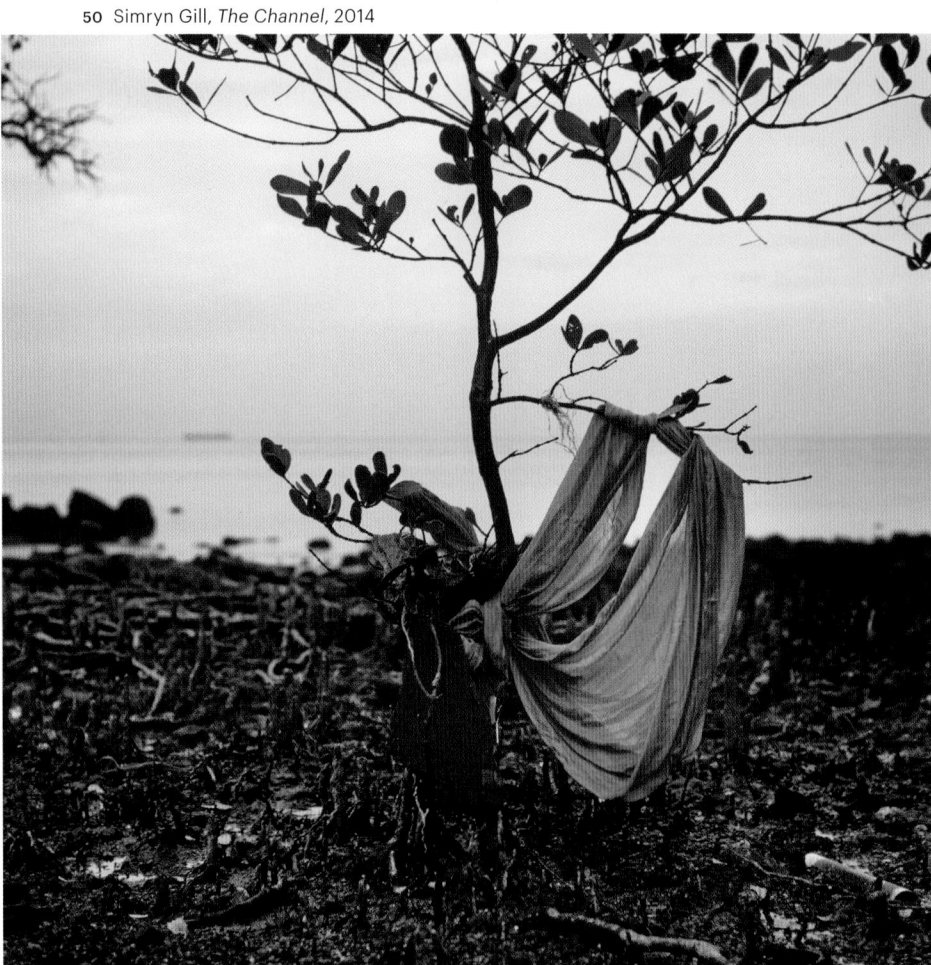

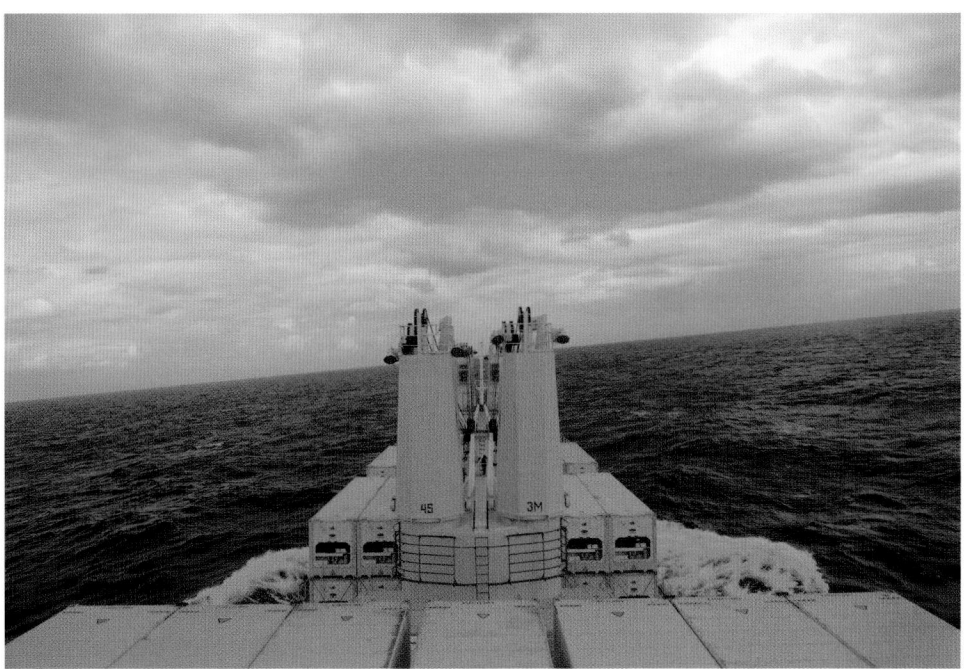

51　Enrique Ramírez, *Océan 33°02′47″S / 51°04′00″N*, 2013

in preparation for his voyage on board a cargo ship from
South America to Europe. After missing several ships, he
managed to set sail on the *Pacific Breeze*, a container ship
with a Ukrainian crew transporting fruit from Valparaiso to
Dunkirk. The result was *Océan 33°02′47″S / 51°04′00″N* (2013),
an uninterrupted sequence shot in real time over twenty-four
days that took the artist on a journey on the Pacific Ocean,
through the Panama Canal, into the Caribbean Sea and across
the Atlantic. Ramírez, born in Santiago during Pinochet's
dictatorship when many executed victims found their final
resting place in the sea, used the time on the boat to write
down his reflections on the political histories and personal
memories attached to the sea, the meaning of trade routes in
the age of globalization and the poetic challenge of transferring
the vastness of the ocean into visual form.

　　In her series of performative lectures *Black Atlantis* (2015–19),
London-based artist Ayesha Hameed reoriented oceanic
histories away from the master narrative of colonialist
expansion towards the experience of those who perished on
Atlantic slave crossings and those who continue to lose their
lives in desperate migration journeys. Among the episodes that

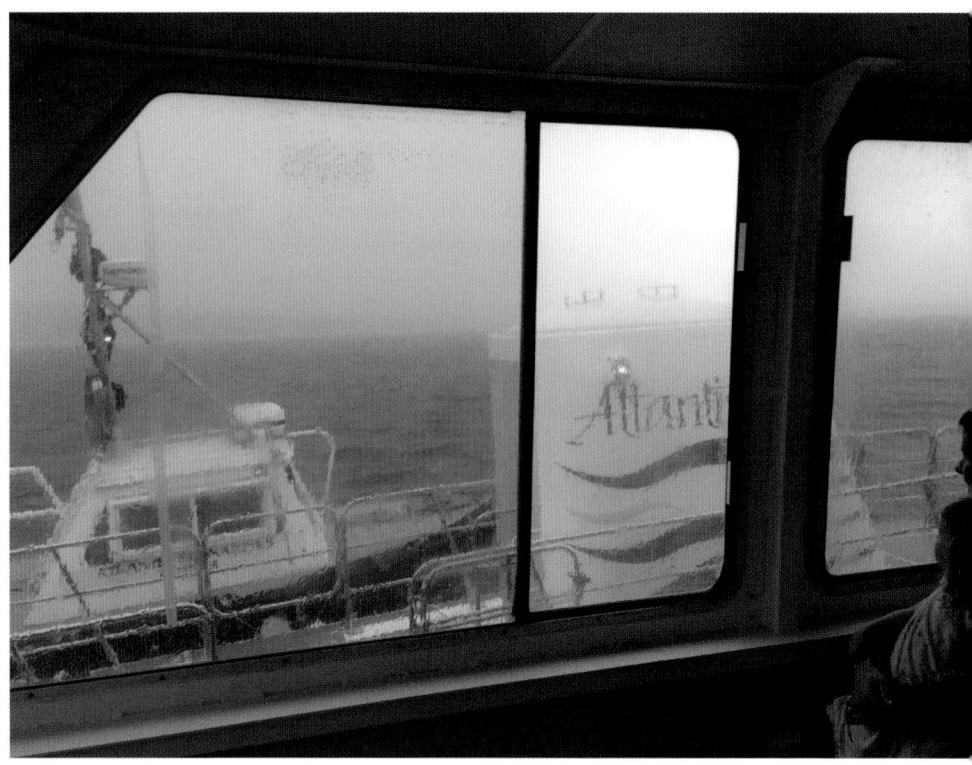

52 Ayesha Hameed, *Black Atlantis: The Plantationocene*, 2017

anchor her decolonial account of the sea is the story of
a small boat discovered off the coast of Barbados carrying the
desiccated bodies of eleven migrants, who were abandoned
by people smugglers en route to the Canary Islands having
left the Cape Verde Islands four months earlier. The artist
disclosed the connections between this contemporary tragedy
and the brutal history of slave transports that sailed the
same course on easterly trade winds, while drawing attention
to the mythological and geological process of petrification
that through the action of salt, sea and sun turns bodies
to stone. The speculative possibilities of alternative paths
through modernity are also visualized in the work through the
Afrofuturist scenario of a 'black Atlantis' inhabited by former
slaves who have adapted to underwater life.

The unravelling of the legacies of colonial domination
was also explored by Austrian–Australian artist Khadija von
53 Zinnenburg Carroll in *Te Moana* (2020), which addressed the
resurgence of indigenous sovereignties and ontologies and the

effects of ecological crisis on ocean species and island dwellers. For the Maori of the village of Muriwai in New Zealand, the rare event of the beaching of a female whale at the foot of a sacred mountain, or *maunga*, was cause for a funeral ceremony. While grateful that the whale chose not to die at sea but to come to their ancestral land, the community was also mindful that she died because of pollution, making her flesh too toxic to be eaten. As part of the ritual, cultural treasures or *taonga* were carved from her cured bones, while the softer cartilage was used to fertilize endangered kauri trees, enabling the whale to live on in healthy trees and carvings on the tribal meeting house. The work confronts the distinction between settler-colonial visions of ocean as alien space and what maritime geographer Katherine G. Sammler in her essay 'The Kauri and the Whale' has described as the Maori's 'genealogical relationship to the land, sea, and to nonhuman species'. Indeed, 50-metre kauri trees are seen as the father of the sperm whale, with shared traits of immense size, smooth exterior and the valuable oils contained in both bark and whale skin. As climate change threatens the existence of whales, the kauri and islanders, the work is a call to replace profit-oriented colonial worldviews with indigenous oceanic imaginaries of geo-hydro connectedness.

The commonality of the ocean as a shared and connecting element of planetary existence is weighed down by inequalities

53 Khadija von Zinnenburg Carroll, *Te Moana*, 2020

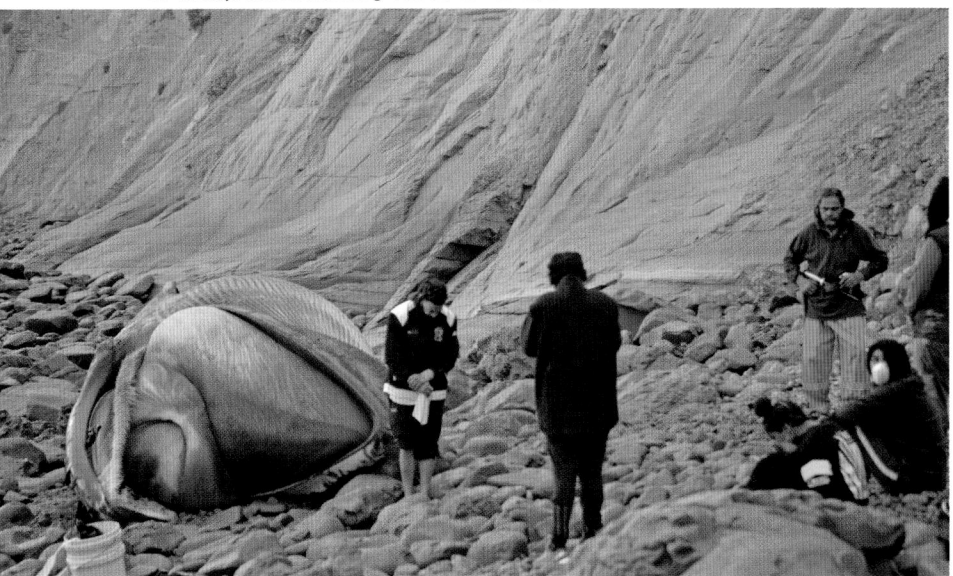

in maritime histories, with transported slaves and refugee castaways experiencing radically different seas from those sailed by Western explorers and traders. The boundlessness of the ocean in the colonialist mindset has been shrunk by the spread of consumerist flotsam and the infiltration of invisible particles into its remotest places, with the release of ballast waters further disrupting the fragile balance of marine ecosystems. As the art practices discussed here also investigate, Cold War militarism laid the foundations for today's all-encompassing technological surveillance of the sea, heralding a new era of underwater extractivism and enabling scientists to watch in real time the permutations caused by climate change registered in the vital signs of a rising and acidifying ocean.

Chapter 4
Post-Glacial Landscapes

Dramatic changes to the cryosphere, the cold zone of the planet where water is frozen into ice or snow, reflect the unprecedented rate of global warming, evident in the fact that to date nineteen of the hottest years ever registered have occurred in the new millennium. 'The distress signals from our overheated planet are all around us,' warned Dahr Jamail in *The End of Ice*, with glaciers 'vanishing before our eyes, having shrunk to the lowest levels ever recorded'. The melting of polar icecaps is destabilizing Earth systems by affecting weather patterns and raising sea levels, while at the same time contributing to climate change through the release of vast quantities of carbon originating in ancient vegetation trapped in thawing permafrost. This constitutes one of the unpredictable feedback loops that threaten to push the climate towards the tipping point faster than is anticipated in most climate change summit scenarios. In fact, as climatologist Peter Wadhams cautioned in his *Farewell to Ice*, the 'summer Arctic sea ice does not have long to live', and its demise will deprive the planet of protection from solar radiation and northern landmasses of cooling streams of ice-chilled air. The gathering speed of polar ice-sheet melt and the global retreat of permafrost are a unifying experience for the current generation on the planet, a predicament addressed by artists through works that internalize ice loss, consider glacial agency, recreate the mythology and memory of polar ice and take a stand for the rights of glaciers.

In 2015 Swedish artist Hanna Ljungh filmed a group of geologists taking annual measurements on the glacier of the south summit of the Kebnekaise mountain, the highest peak in Sweden. Entitled *I am mountain, to measure impermanence* (2016), the six-hour real-time footage of their scientific research

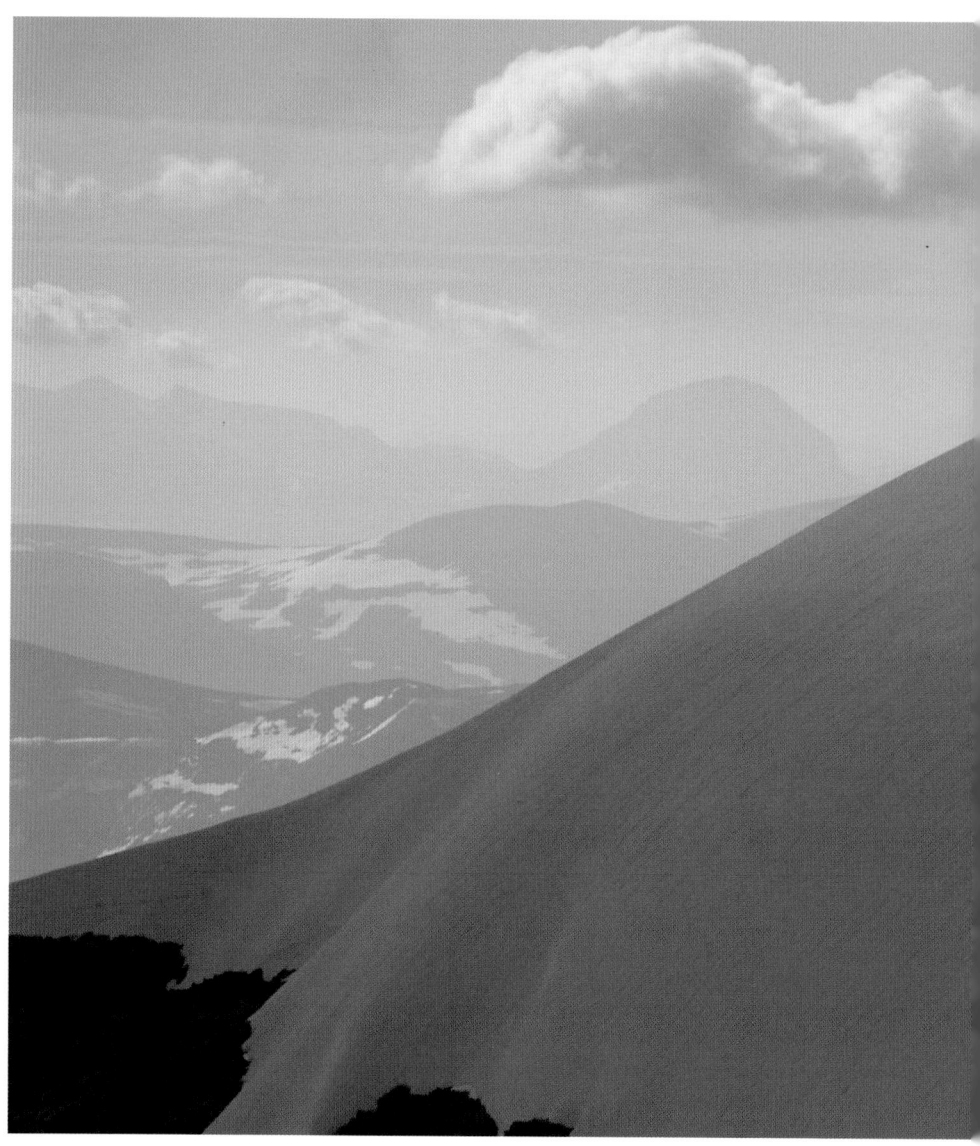

54 Hanna Ljungh, *I am mountain, to measure impermanence*, 2016

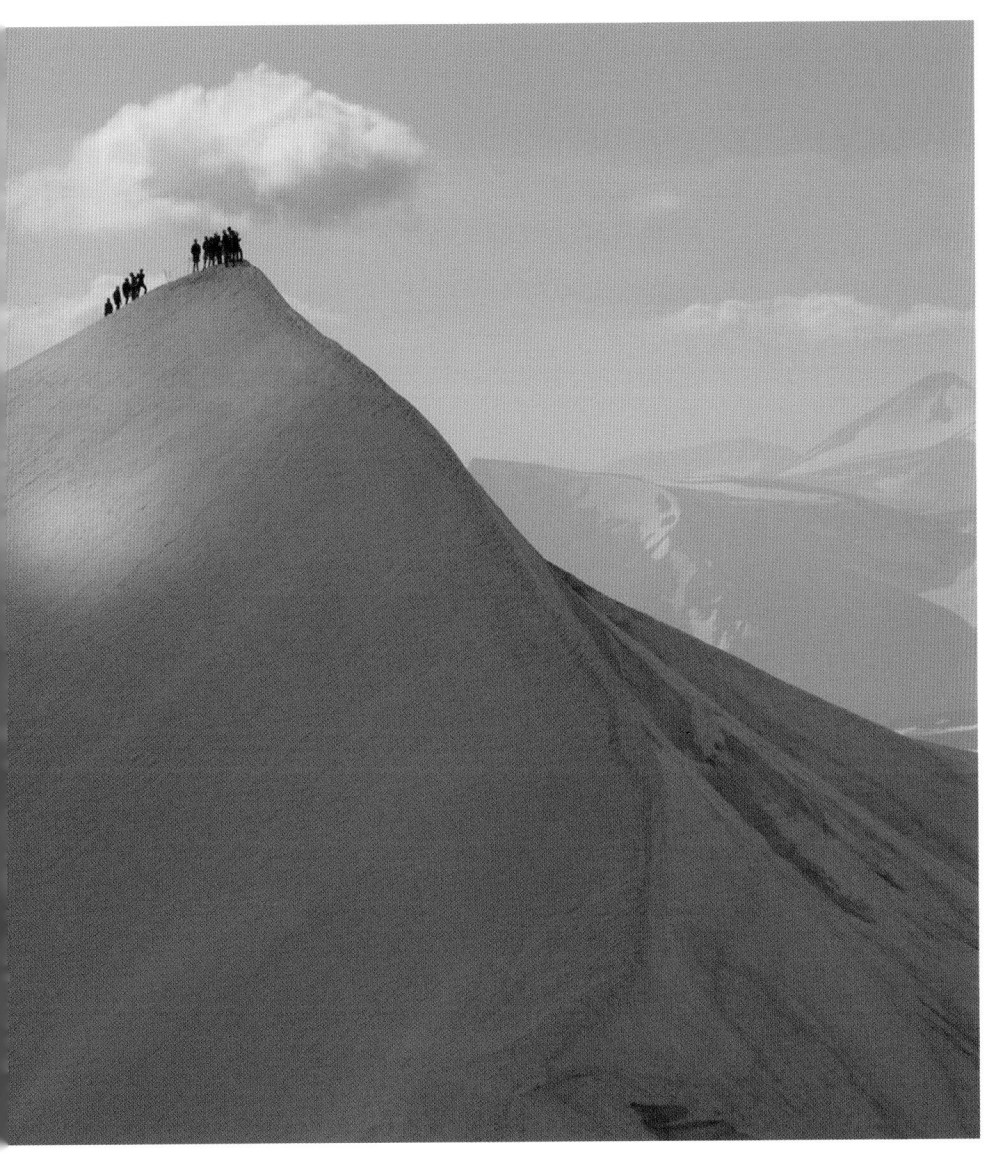

was recorded with a camera set on the rocky north summit, observing from a distance the small human figures on the ridge of the white mountainous landscape against ominous grey clouds. Measurements have been made at this location since 1902 and evidence was mounting that the glacier was shrinking, with the likelihood that the ice-free north summit at 2,096.8 metres would soon take over as the highest point in the country. In fact, the glacier shrank by 24 metres in twenty-five years and by September 2019 this scenario became a reality. The geological entities of the planet are tectonically active and Earth can be regarded as a 'highly dynamic system', 'its history not only unimaginably lengthy but also amazingly eventful', as Martin J. S. Rudwick observed in his book *Earth's Deep History*. However, the speed with which these changes are happening nowadays is the disturbing factor. In her practice Ljungh also reflected on the minerals and metals, such as iron and zinc, that are extracted from mountains and which are the same chemical elements that constitute building blocks of the human body. In that sense, as indicated by the title of the film, she personalized and internalized the geological changes to the mountain top, to which we are physically linked, but which is being transformed by anthropogenic climate change that brings about a planetary sense of impermanence.

In her project *On Glaciers and Avalanches* (2017–18), Argentinian artist Irene Kopelman explored the natural complexity and variability of the glacial environment of the Swiss Alps, turning to ephemeral pencil lines and fragmentary ceramic sculptures to express the fragility of the ice worlds she encountered on visits to the Aletsch, Gorner, Findel, Matterhorn and Rhône glaciers. Conversations with the geologists and biologists she trekked with are reflected in the precise attention the artist gave to the micro-environments of carbon-dioxide absorbing lichens or the evidentiary trail left by avalanches in the treeline. In series such as *Tree Lines Davos, Two Slopes from Below* (2014), the artistic process was conditioned by environmental factors such as visibility on the mountain and vicissitudes of the weather, which determined the length of each excursion and the subject of Kopelman's daily drawing, pointing to the potential of the glacier itself to shape artistic outcomes and impact scientific research.

The limitations of scientific rationality in fully apprehending natural phenomena that operate on more-than-human timescales and the potential of folklore and mysticism as alternative forms of knowledge are explored in Joan Jonas's performance lecture *Reanimation* (2010–13). This immersive work took as its starting point Icelandic writer Halldór Laxness's 1968 novel *Under the Glacier*. The US artist appropriated key passages in

55

56

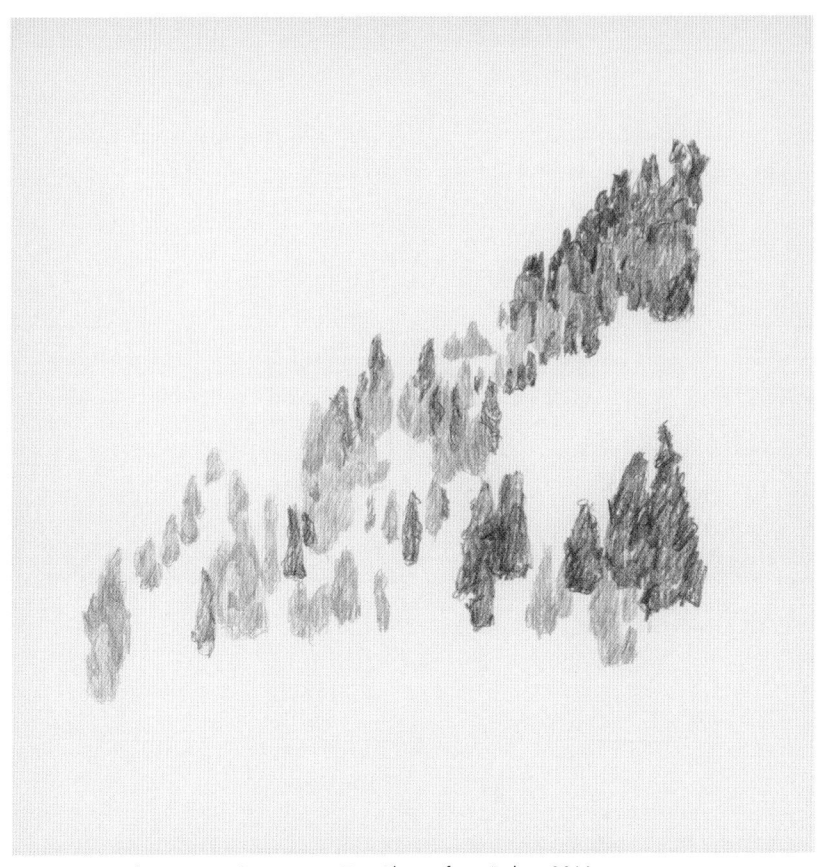

55 Irene Kopelman, *Tree Lines Davos, Two Slopes from Below,* 2014

her performance, including the line, 'If one looks at the glacier long enough, words cease to have any meaning on this earth.' Traversing the stage in a bird mask in front of a projection of a desolate post-glacial landscape and to a pulsating musical accompaniment, the artist carried out repetitive actions such as smearing ink onto paper with ice cubes or painting with tree branches. Amidst this discordant stream of indigenous, hi-tech and experimental methods of translating the incommensurability of the natural world into human terms, a map appears on screen illustrating the extent of glacial melt. While tapping into animist flows to reinvigorate societal relations to more-than-human realms, the work at the same time points to the existential threat posed by ecological crisis to the multiplicity and timelessness of nature.

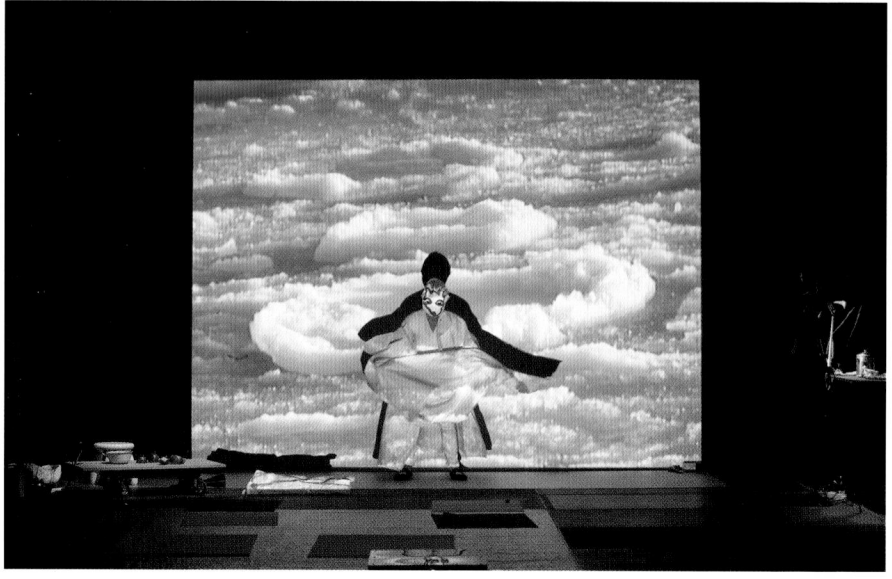

56 ABOVE Joan Jonas, *Reanimation*, 2012
57 OPPOSITE Ieva Epnere, *Four Edges of Pyramiden*, 2015

57

As four residents interviewed in Latvian artist Ieva Epnere's film *Four Edges of Pyramiden* (2015) explain, the allure of the former Soviet coal-mining town of Pyramiden on the Svalbard archipelago, deep inside the Arctic Circle, derives in part from its status as a frozen relic of the communist past. Nostalgia for a lost golden age is conjured by shots of the deserted pathways of a settlement that, before it was temporarily abandoned in the 1990s, was home to 1,000 people and equipped with a library, cultural centre, swimming pool, self-service restaurant, Lenin monument and other symbolic achievements of Soviet culture. Although mining coal beneath its frozen pyramid-shaped mountain was not economically viable, maintaining the enclave, which was established on the Norwegian island in the 1920s following the signing of an international treaty, enabled the communist regime to maintain its geopolitical influence over the Arctic region. Today, as temperatures on Svalbard rise twice as fast as the global average and its permafrost rapidly retreats, the tragic prospect of easy access to polar mineral wealth has made the revival of the Soviet ghost town a strategic interest of the Russian state. Yet as the film suggests, it is not the fading relics of Soviet power, but the disappearing entities of the natural world that make the inhabitants feel so privileged to live there. The hotel cook, for instance, whose family back in Ukraine cannot understand her attachment to this barren place, relates her experience of 'something vast, unfathomable and extremely beautiful' when she realized that 'the glacier has been there for a million years and I'm touching it with my hands!'

For the climate imaginary of the Anthropocene, glaciers signal extreme vulnerability to global warming, with the calving of ice sheets into Arctic seas heralding worldwide coastal inundations and the disappearance of seasonal melts from the Himalayas to the Andes threatening freshwater supplies as rivers run dry. In earlier times, especially during the Little Ice Age of the early nineteenth century, ice worlds figured as inhospitable, alien terrain and glaciers as sublime natural forces with the power to encroach on civilized realms. In the film *we are opposite like that* (2019), London- and Delhi-based artist Himali Singh Soin contrasted today's climate uncertainty of receding ice sheets with the opposite anxiety of the Victorians, namely that advancing ice would obliterate familiar landscapes. By annotating period drawings of frozen seas to reveal the 'illusion of ice as a looming, cosmic monster that sends shudders across the British Empire', the artist also suggested correspondences with the late-imperialist fear of losing political and cultural supremacy. Another recurring presence in the film is an otherworldly figure wrapped in silver foil, who emerges from a block of ice to narrate a story about her non-human origins in a fossilized past. The artist's

58

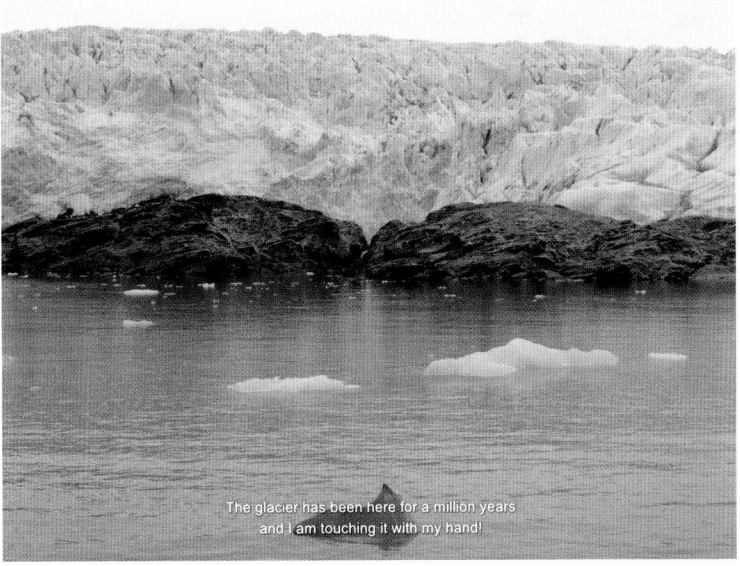

The glacier has been here for a million years and I am touching it with my hand!

quest to devise fictional mythologies for polar landscapes transformed by climate change draws attention to the potential erasure of memories of ice in a post-glacial future.

Registering the disruption of natural cycles and patterns in their daily lives, indigenous communities on the frontline of global warming are demanding the industrialized world take steps to restore the balance of the natural world, but are frequently also resigned to the inevitability of climate adaptation. Inuit artist collective Isuma's film *Qapirangajuq: Inuit Knowledge and Climate Change* (2010) gave voice to the experience of elders from across the Canadian Arctic Archipelago, who describe effects such as the disappearance of 'blue and solid' multiyear ice that 'behaves like living beings' and a reduction of directional 'tongue drifts' in the snow, as the wind blows now from the east, not the north. 'After the world tilted', as one hunter comments, the sun's rays hit more directly and the 'stars are no longer in the right position', while visual distortions brought on by more frequent mirages force fishermen to adapt traditional techniques and 'spear strangely', the Inuit term for which provides the title of the film.

After a visit to the Alps, Diana Lelonek produced a symphony on the theme of disappearing glaciers, in collaboration with

58 Himali Singh Soin, *we are opposite like that*, 2019

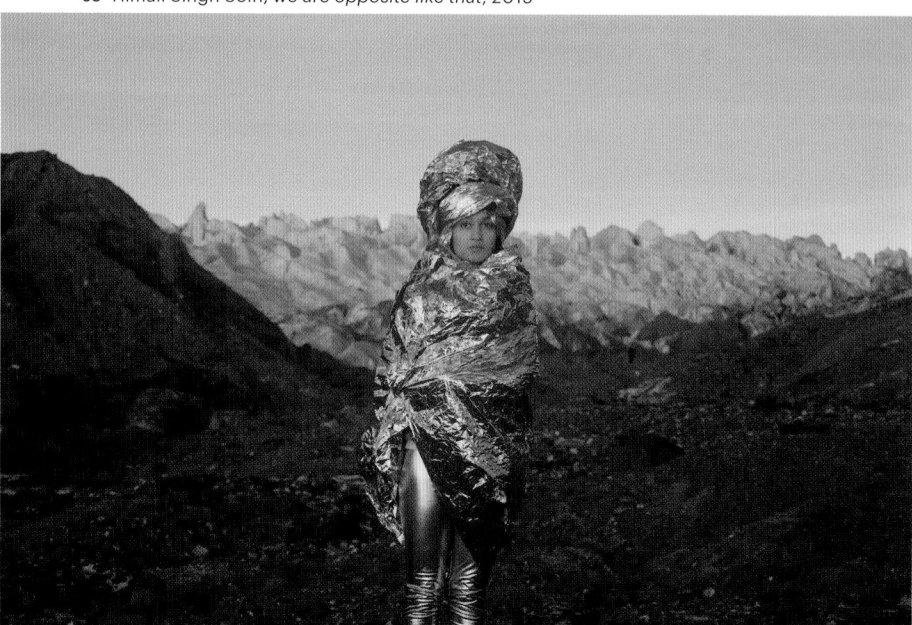

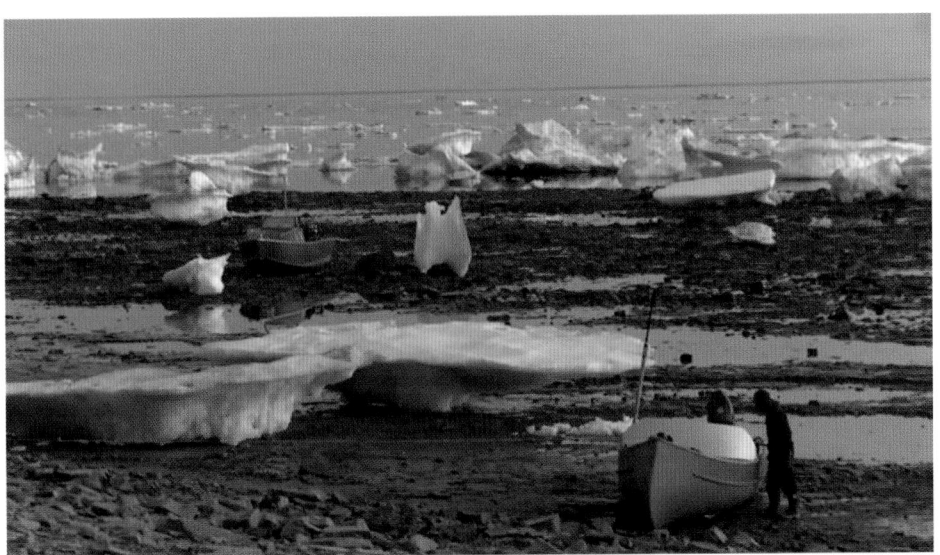

59 Isuma collective, *Qapirangajuq: Inuit Knowledge and Climate Change*, 2010

Swiss sound artist Denim Szram. Troubled by the unceasing sound of thawing ice, which she perceived as a 'slowly trickling catastrophe', Lelonek made in situ sound recordings, which were then converted into the disconcerting melody of this glacial song. One of the sites she travelled to was the Rhône Glacier, infamous for the fact that Swiss villagers whose livelihoods depend on tourists' visits have attempted to protect a historic ice grotto from the warming climate by covering it with white blankets every summer. This could be seen as a low-tech version of the 'good Anthropocene' approach to climate change, with proposals such as covering glaciers with artificial snow or using giant pumps to refreeze Arctic ice put forward by the advocates of geoengineering solutions to environmental crisis. However, the effort to protect the Rhône Glacier, with its weathered sheets broken by the wind, appears more like a Sisyphean act of labour in light of rapid ice retreat of more than 1,400 metres in the last 150 years. Instead of images, Lelonek's multi-channel sound installation *Melting Gallery* (2019) filled the exhibition space with the undulating yet persistent noise of ice loss and the realization that many of the planet's permafrost places have already passed the tipping point.

Rather than bringing the daunting music of melting ice to the exhibition audience, Slovak artist Oto Hudec decided to perform *Concert for Adishi Glacier* (2018) in the Caucasus Mountains. Playing one on one to the ice itself, in his recital

60

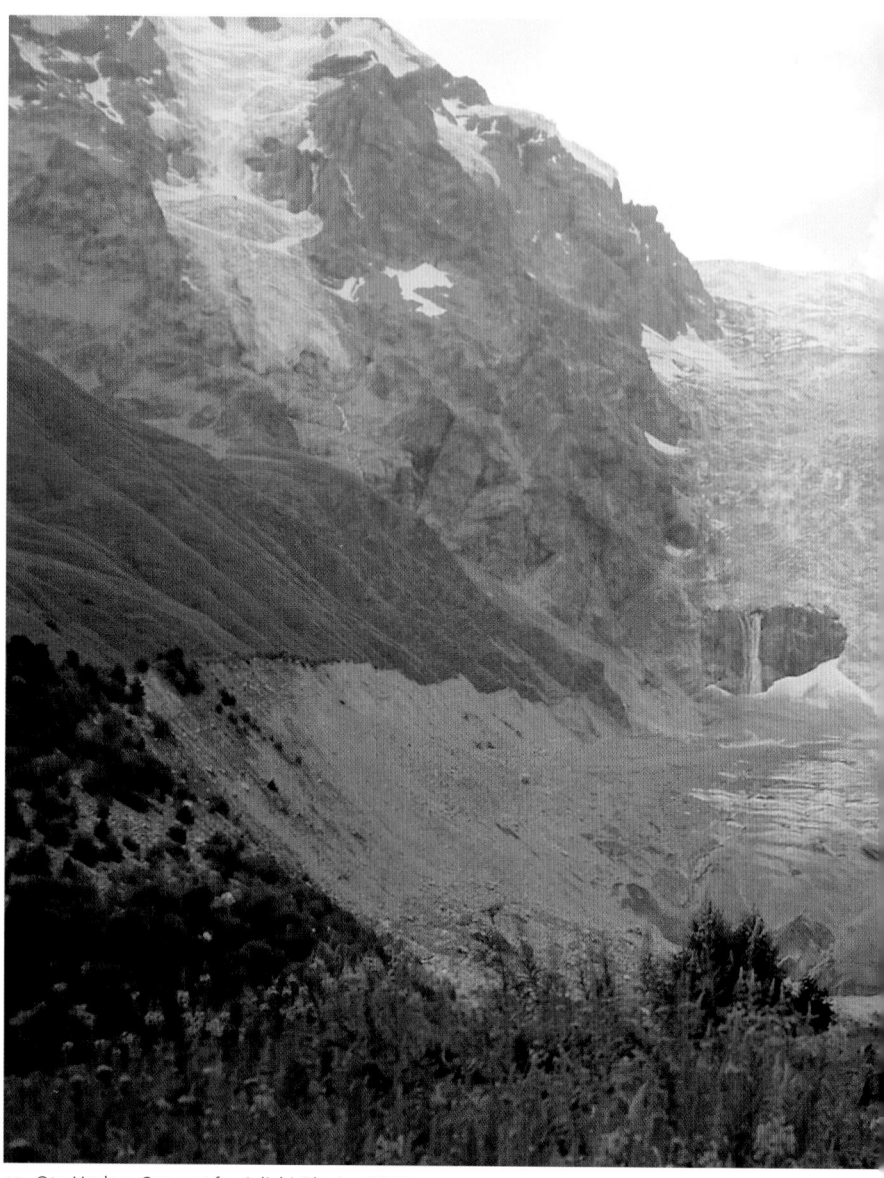

60 Oto Hudec, *Concert for Adishi Glacier,* 2018

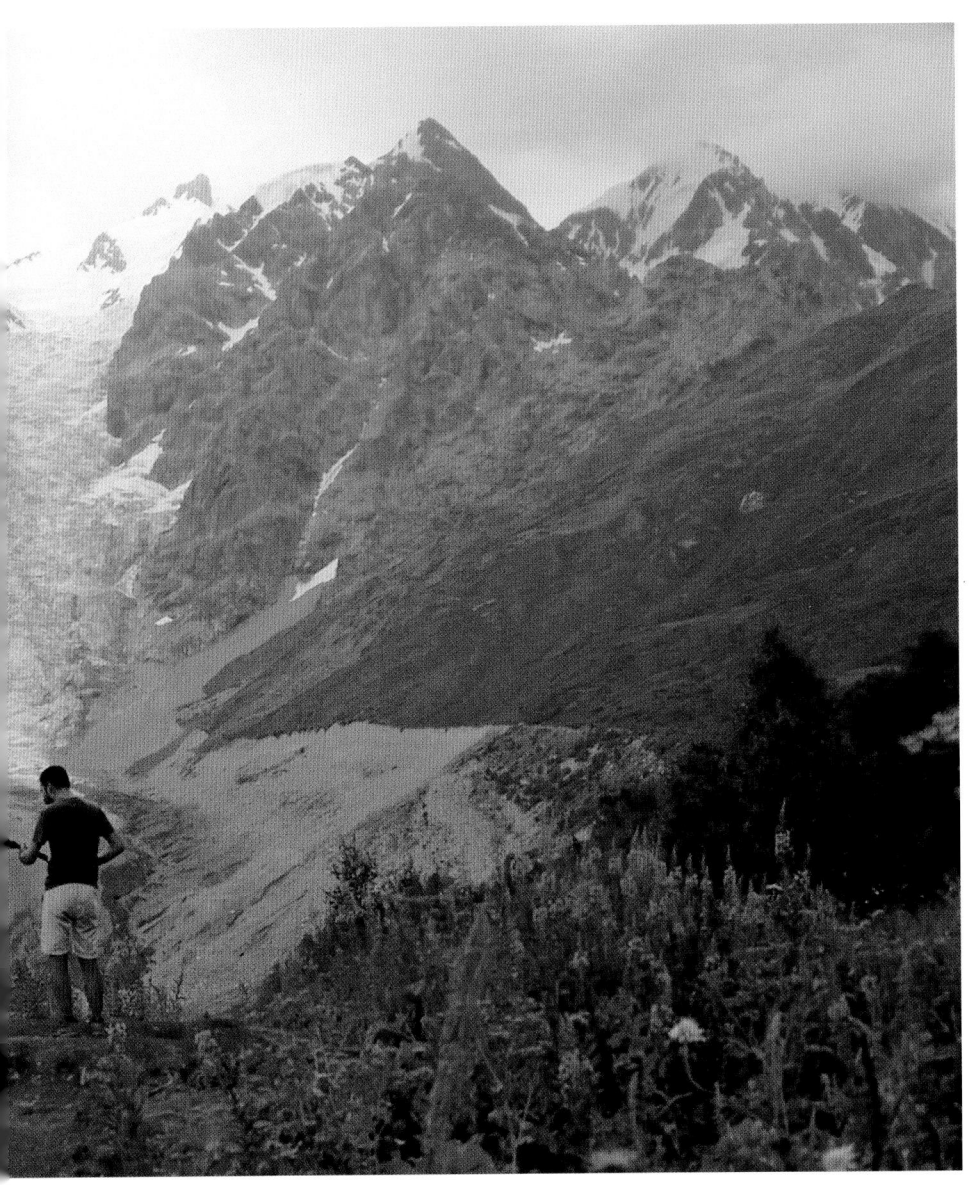

the intensifying sounds of the artist's guitar and mouth organ replicate the bewildering gush of meltwater. The film footage, shot from a discreet distance, does not intrude into the space between the Georgian glacier and the artist, whose back remains turned to the camera to preserve the intimacy of sonic exchange with the non-human entity towering above. Plants growing in the soil laid bare by the retreating ice indicate nature's resilience, yet also raise the question of whether the threat to biodiversity from climate change affects not only species but also natural entities. In that sense, Hudec's performance was an empathic gesture that recognizes the entangled fates of humans, animals, plants and other living organisms, as well as the physical forces and natural phenomena of the Earth. Care for glaciers is also manifest in a reassessment of anthropocentric constitutional concepts, such as through the extending of legal personhood to Patagonian glaciers in a pioneering act of environmental protection by the Argentinian Congress in 2010. The true political gravity of such legal gestures lies in the fact that in order to meaningfully protect the rights of vulnerable glaciers, a radical reconfiguration of the global economic and political order fuelling climate change is required.

Due to their role in the functioning of ecosystems and within world cultures, the frozen waterbodies of the cryosphere cannot be fully apprehended in narrowly scientific terms. The indigenous people of the formerly frozen north experience their melting most intensely as a dislocation of the cosmic order. At the same time, competitive extractive capitalism seeks short-term economic advantage in the melting of the polar ice caps, holding out the panacea of a geoengineering solution to glacial melt rather than dealing with its systemic causes. Performing empathic gestures of care towards these planetary entities, artists have investigated the dire prospect of a post-glacial world, in terms of its implications for rising sea levels, but also as the rapidly approaching collective trauma of a world without ice.

Chapter 5
Golden Age of the Sky

The sunlight breaking through saturated air was a compelling prism through which painters captured the nineteenth-century skyline. Climatologists examining Claude Monet's series of depictions of Charing Cross Bridge have established a correlation between the visibility of buildings in the paintings and the measurements of the London Fog Enquiry of 1901, enabling them to estimate the approximate concentration of pollutants in the atmosphere at the time. Several decades earlier, at the onset of industrialization, painter John Constable's curiosity for meteorological science was reflected in the large portion of his canvases devoted to the portrayal of clouds. His landscapes could be perceived as a record of 'the golden era of natural skies' when, according to meteorologist John Thornes, 'atmosphere was the last part of nature as yet uncontrollable and unspoilt by culture'. Today greenhouse gases from the burning of fossil fuels, sulphurous emissions from heavy industry and the lingering presence of radiocarbons from atomic explosions are all part of the gaseous materiality of the atmosphere, invisible yet toxic traces of the anthropogenic modification of air. In that sense, smoke, dust and other airborne particles released by human activity are, according to Mark Lynas, author of *The God Species*, equivalent in effect to a 'constant, medium-sized volcanic eruption, scattering sulphur and soot high into the upper atmosphere'.

The permutations of Croatian artist Dora Budor's site-specific exhibition at Kunsthalle Basel in 2019 were determined by external environmental factors, calling to mind the complexity theory of the 'butterfly effect'. First raised by a meteorologist in 1972 in relation to weather prediction, the question 'Does the flap of a butterfly's wings in Brazil set off a tornado in Texas?' eventually challenged the certainties of the Newtonian scientific

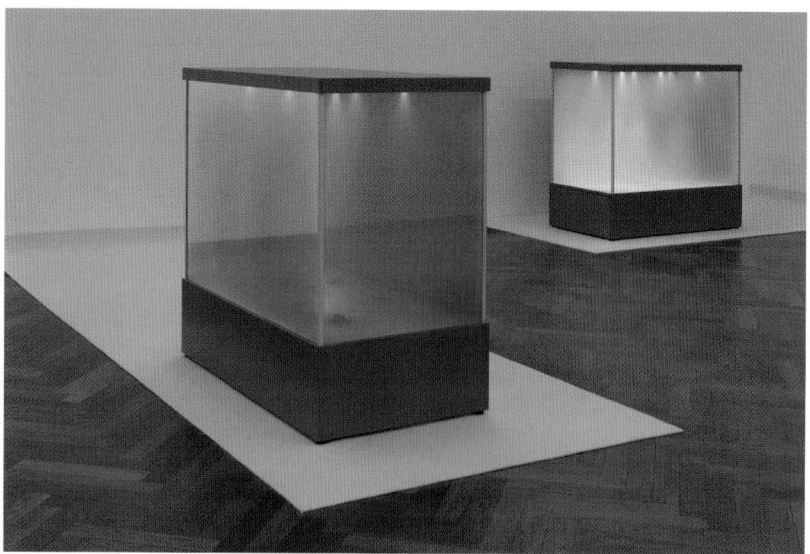

61 Dora Budor, *Origin II (Burning of the Houses)*, 2019, and *Origin III (Snow Storm)*, 2019

paradigm by highlighting the critical role of environmental variability. In Budor's installation, sound-sensitive devices placed in the building opposite – a concert hall in the midst of renovation – converted the clamour of construction drills, welding and hammering into electronic frequencies that modified the artworks in the gallery in unpredictable ways. For instance, sonic events on the building site triggered eruptions of pigment in a sculptural installation consisting of three glass chambers containing coloured dust. Entitled *Origins* (2019), each vitrine referred through colour to a particular landscape painting by J. M. W. Turner that captured atmospheric conditions at the dawn of the industrial era. The dynamic scenarios played out in the testing chambers of Budor's work demonstrated the complex interaction of natural phenomena, such as volcanic eruptions, with anthropogenic disruptions, including the dispersal of industrial particles, in the climatological feedback loops of the Anthropocene.

    In their search for the answer to the ostensibly straightforward question 'Where is the most blue sky on the planet?', Lise Autogena and Joshua Portway resorted to complex technological solutions. They devised a computer-generated installation, *Most Blue Skies* (2009), that measured the passage of light through the atmosphere and calculated the exact colour of the sky observable from numerous places on Earth, based on

61

meteorological information and data collected from several satellite monitoring systems. Notwithstanding their recourse to technological exactness and scientific objectivity, the artists also referred to the romantic connotations of blue sky, the relativity of the 'most blue' colour and its culture-specific relationship to the heavens, with climate disruption gathering like a dark cloud over the optimism emanating from the blue sky.

Certainly, the sky was not always blue. It became so as a consequence of the activity of photosynthetic cyanobacteria that produced oxygen as a side effect around 2.3 billion years ago. These bacteria turned Earth's atmosphere into an oxygen-rich one, which, as editor of *The Life of Air* Monika Bakke observed, 'gave the sky the blue colour it has today'. This transformation, also known as the Great Oxygenation Event, caused the mass extinction of life dwelling in a carbon-dioxide rich atmosphere and propelled forwards the formation of plant and animal organisms. The deep history of air is at the core of Australian artist Emily Parsons-Lord's research presented in the installation *Different Kinds of Air, a Plant's Diary* (2014), which attempted to recreate the gaseous composition, temperature, taste and smell of air as it changed over the course of geological history. For instance, air quality from 300–350 million years ago had oxygen levels that were nearly double what they are today, supporting the flourishing of megaflora and fauna. Over seven stages in the installation, the artist demonstrated how, in her own words, the 'history of the atmosphere on Earth is inexorably linked to the history of life'.

62 Emily Parsons-Lord, *Different Kinds of Air, a Plant's Diary*, 2014

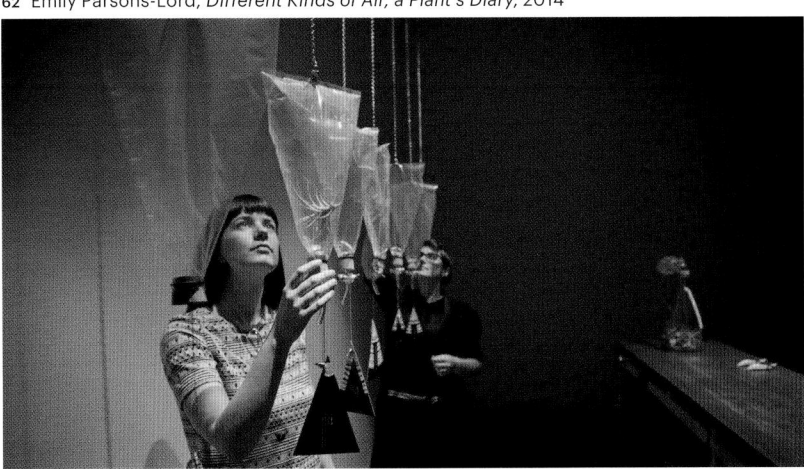

Artist Rohini Devasher's exploration of the sky dates back to her time at art school in New Delhi at the turn of the millennium, when she joined a group of amateur astronomers for regular 'star parties' on the roof of the Nehru Planetarium. Today, due to light and air pollution, the Indian capital's stargazers have to travel hundreds of miles to reach 'low threshold skies', leading the artist to speculate that entire generations 'born without stars' are being denied opportunities for celestial wonder. Collecting conversations with amateur astronomers in India and abroad, Devasher has investigated the transformative experience of gazing at the sky. In the sound piece *Shadow Walkers* (2010), she focused on the recollections of seven solar eclipse chasers. Lying on mats in an open space under the sky, the audience listened together to personal stories of a 'hair-raising experience' that 'occupies you entirely, consumes you' and which 'when it was over changed my life'. At issue here, and exceeding the confines of scientific understanding, were the sense of oneness with the cosmos and reciprocity between the vastness of space and intimacy of the self that arise in intense encounters with celestial phenomena. In other words, in conditions of atmospheric pollution, what sense of self can arise from gazing into smog?

Drawing on findings in the philosophy, politics, science and lived experience of air, Stockholm-based artist Hanna Husberg used her three-month residency in Beijing to conduct research into cultural and political aspects of urban air in the Chinese metropolis. The resulting audio-visual work *Often People Ask How Birds Are Affected by the Air* (2017) assembled interviews and dialogues with locals about the acute toxicity of the ground air in recent years. Respondents deliberated about the state's weather control measures attempting to ensure that no rain fell during the Olympic Games of 2008, when factories and traffic were also shut down for better visibility. Others wondered about the absence of once regular strong winds and how smog used to be a term related to English literature, before it became a permanent fixture of the local atmosphere. Husberg also pointed to linguistic adaptations to the new circumstances of hazardous air pollution, such as the changing meaning of *wumai*, which used to be a technical term for haze in optics, before it became a familiar meteorological condition. The artist showed how new technoscientific representations of air quality, notably phone apps giving daily updates of the PM 2.5 index measuring the level of 'fine particulate matter' or tiny toxic particles in the atmosphere, made people aware that what locals call 'white skies' is actually pollution'. Recent transformations in the air were envisioned through traditional aerial imaginaries as a disruption of the harmonious balance between *qi*, standing for energy

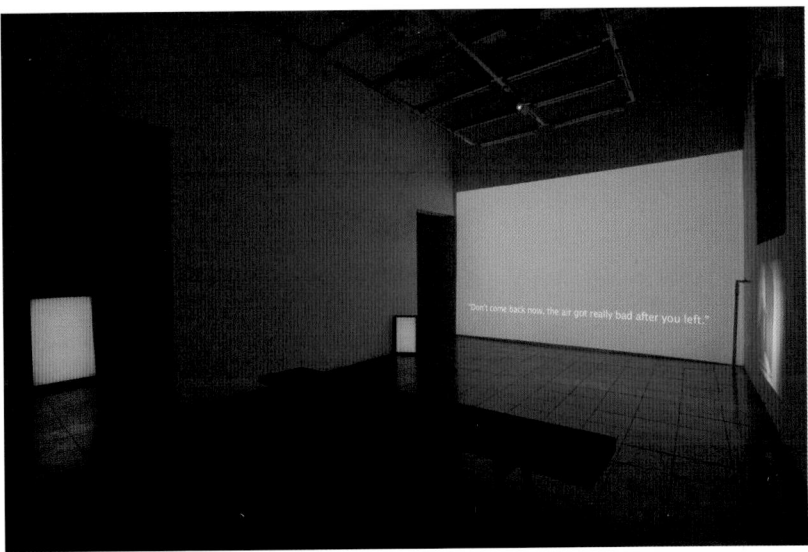

63 Hanna Husberg, *Often People Ask How Birds Are Affected by the Air*, 2017

or vital breath, and the dangerous wind, or *feng*, from which a 'hundred diseases' arise.

Taking as her starting point air pollution in her hometown of San Francisco, Amy Balkin conceived *Public Smog* (since 2004) as a clean air reserve made up of a lower park in the troposphere and an upper park in the stratosphere that fluctuates in size and location in response to changing political, legal and financial activities. The lower park addressed the noxious cocktail of airborne particles and invisible toxic gases hovering above the Earth's surface associated with coal burning, industrial processes and photochemical smog from vehicle emissions. The upper park was devoted to greenhouse gases, which have a vital function in sustaining life by trapping outgoing radiation, but which due to accelerating carbon emissions now endanger life on Earth by raising surface temperatures. The park was open to the public three times over the course of a decade through the purchase and retiring of offset credits in emissions trading markets, although the artist readily conceded that to 'buy back the sky on the open market' could only work if the entire supply of these virtual commodities could be acquired and removed from circulation. This ongoing project drew attention to the opacity of the emissions trading scheme, which, as Naomi Klein pointed out in *This Changes Everything*, by paying out 'real money based on projections of how much of an invisible substance is kept out of the air tends to be something of a scam magnet'. Repurposing

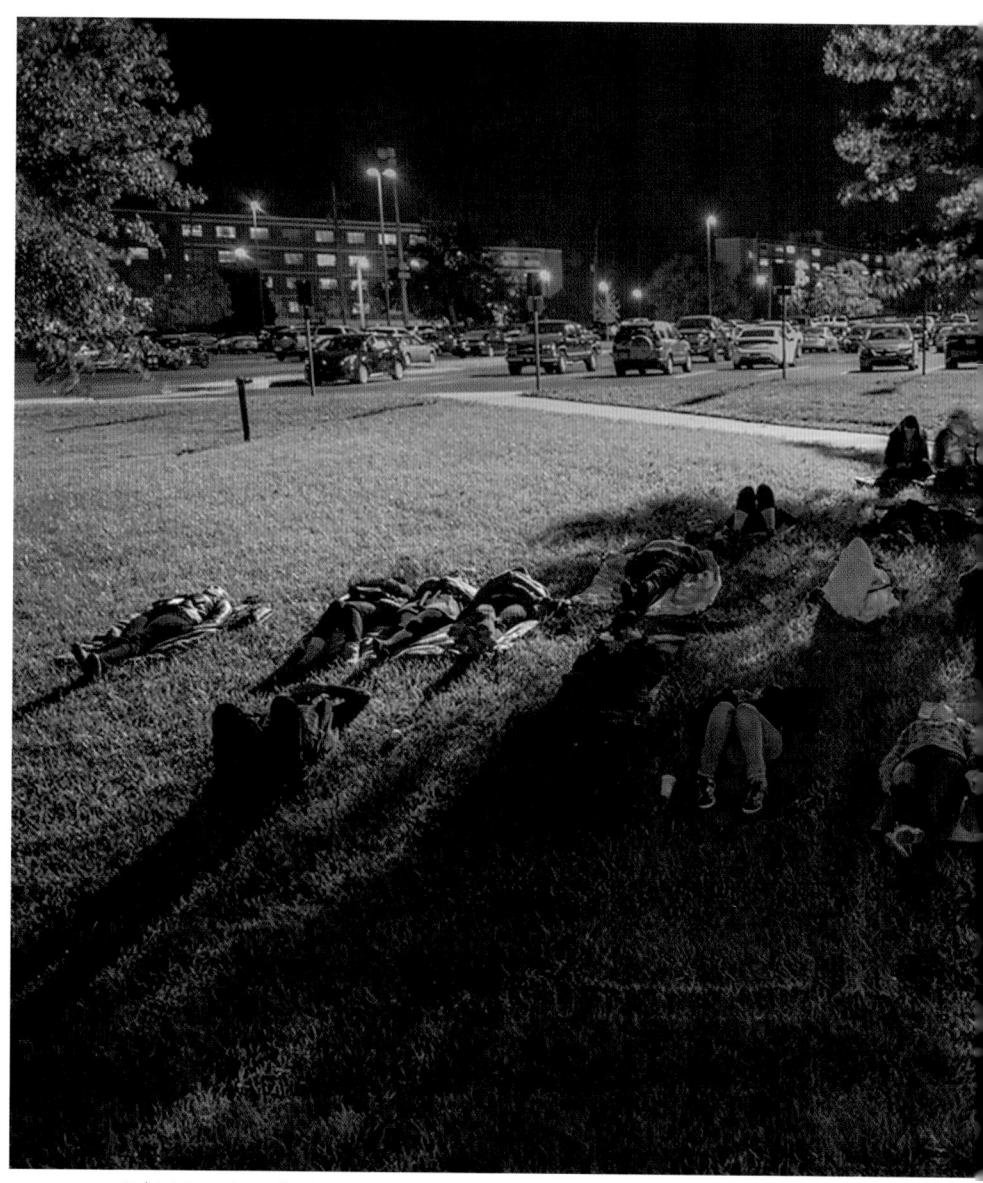

64 Rohini Devasher, *Shadow Walkers*, 2010

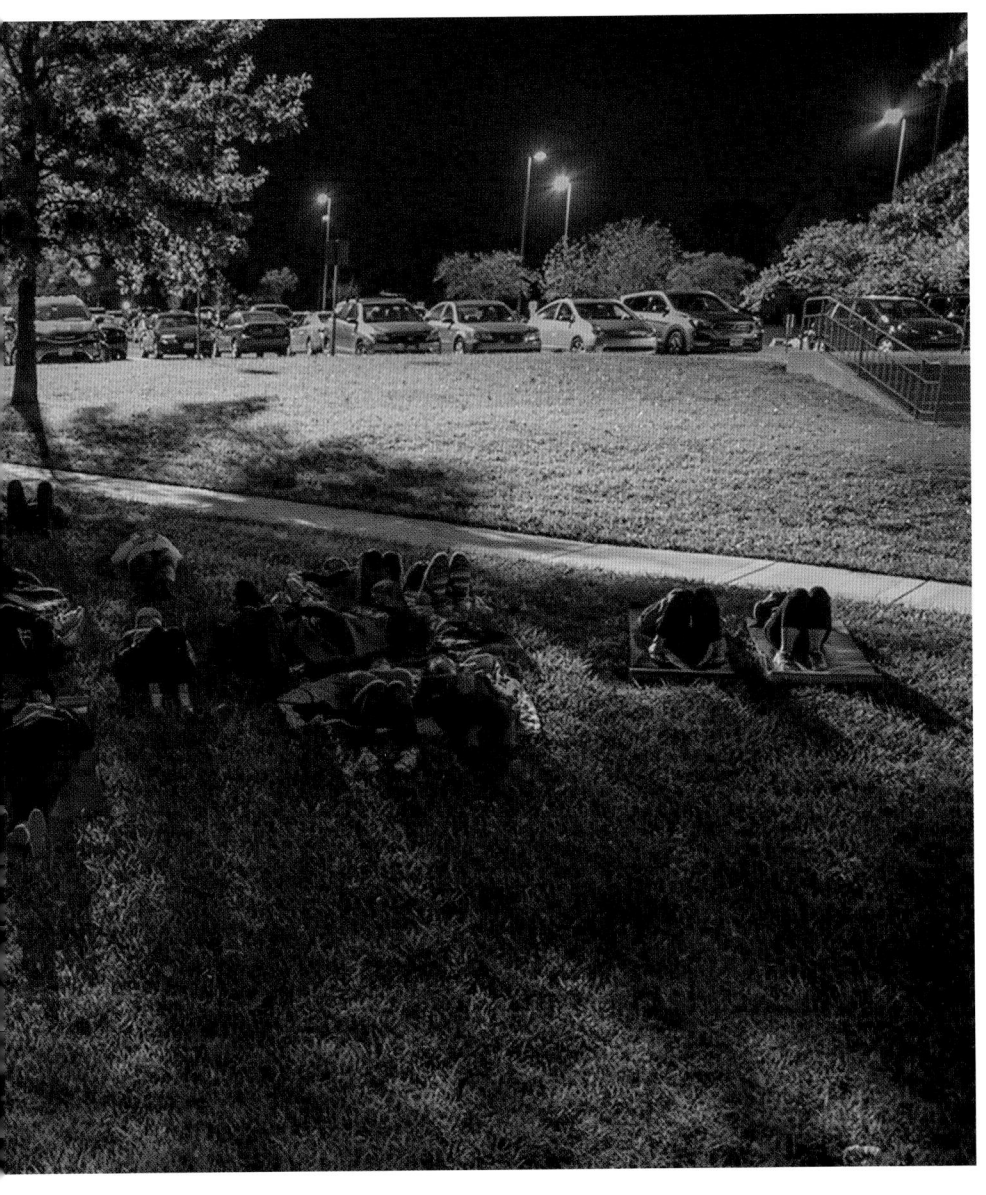

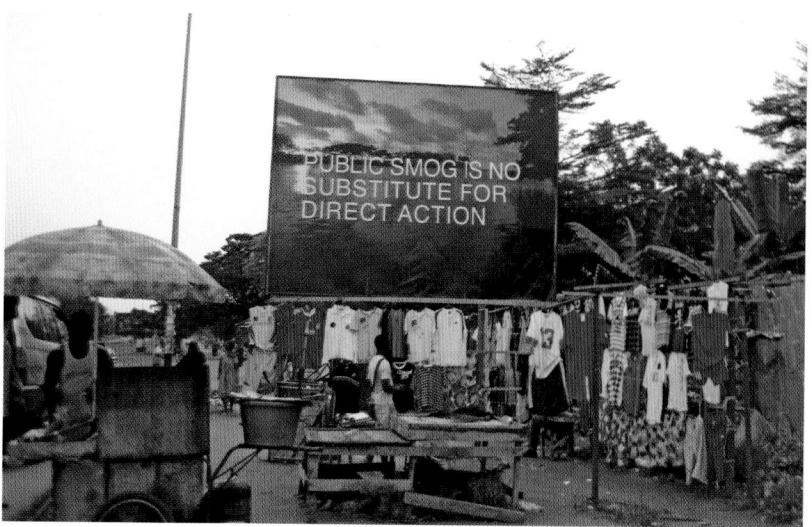

65 Amy Balkin, *PUBLIC SMOG IS NO SUBSTITUTE FOR DIRECT ACTION*, 2009

the dissembling rhetoric of the climate trade lobby, the artist's billboard *PUBLIC SMOG IS NO SUBSTITUTE FOR DIRECT ACTION* (2009) in the Cameroonian city of Douala explored the potential of opening a clean air park over Africa.

While transportation, industry, the energy sector and agriculture are commonly pinpointed as sources of carbon emissions, Barcelona-based artist Joana Moll directed attention to the emissions of atmospheric carbon dioxide from the internet, problematizing the hidden materiality of online transactions. Her work *CO2GLE* (2014) was a real-time, net-based installation that calculated the amount of CO_2 emitted each second from google.com, the most visited site on the internet. With the site receiving an approximate average of 47,000 requests every second, the artist estimated it produced 500 kilograms of CO_2 emissions per second. In other words, the physical properties of the internet do not only include infrastructures and the synthetic or rare earth components in electronic devices, but also extend to the transformation of the planet's air. Acknowledging that 'cloud computing is still rather dependent on non-renewable energy with heavy CO_2 emissions', media theorist Jussi Parikka in *A Geology of Media* also raised the question of the technological contamination of users' lungs that 'breathe the residue of metals and chemicals of digital culture'.

In contrast to the moon landing half a century ago, which was based on 'nationalist, colonial and patriarchal ambitions that have depleted the world', Tomás Saraceno's artistic experiment to realize the first fully solar-powered and untethered flight was achieved 'without lithium and batteries, without solar panels, without helium and hydrogen, without fossil fuels, only with the sun and the air we breathe'. The most ambitious of a series of investigations into the possibility of aerosolar flight and the wider utopian potentialities of living and moving in the air, *Aerocene Pacha* (2020) also articulated a critique of the polluting and exploitative technologies of extractive capitalism. Named after the Incan cosmovision of Pachamama and bearing the slogan 'water and life are worth more than lithium', the Argentinian artist's floating sculpture took its first flight above the Salinas Grandes, salt flats that are exposed to the environmental devastation of lithium mining, which for indigenous communities is also a sacrilegious act of violence against Mother Earth. Saraceno's vision of non-harmful and non-extractivist flight opened up the aerial imaginary to speculative immersions in the ephemeral materiality of the atmosphere.

67

Observation of atmospheric effects, by artists as well as scientists, at the dawn of industrialization and today, has revealed the interconnectedness of ethereal realms with terrestrial processes. Practices examined here destabilize assumptions about the constancy of air by investigating the deep history of Earth's transforming atmosphere, as well as considering the ways in which pollution is affecting the contemporary experience of the sky, giving rise to linguistic and cultural changes as urban dwellers adapt to airborne toxicity. Artists have also confronted the malleability of capitalism in rebranding itself as green and turning emissions trading into a source of opportunistic profiteering.

66 Joana Moll, *CO2GLE*, 2014

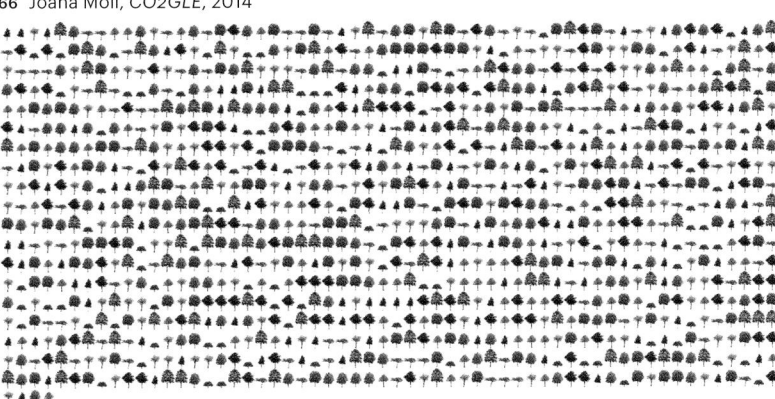

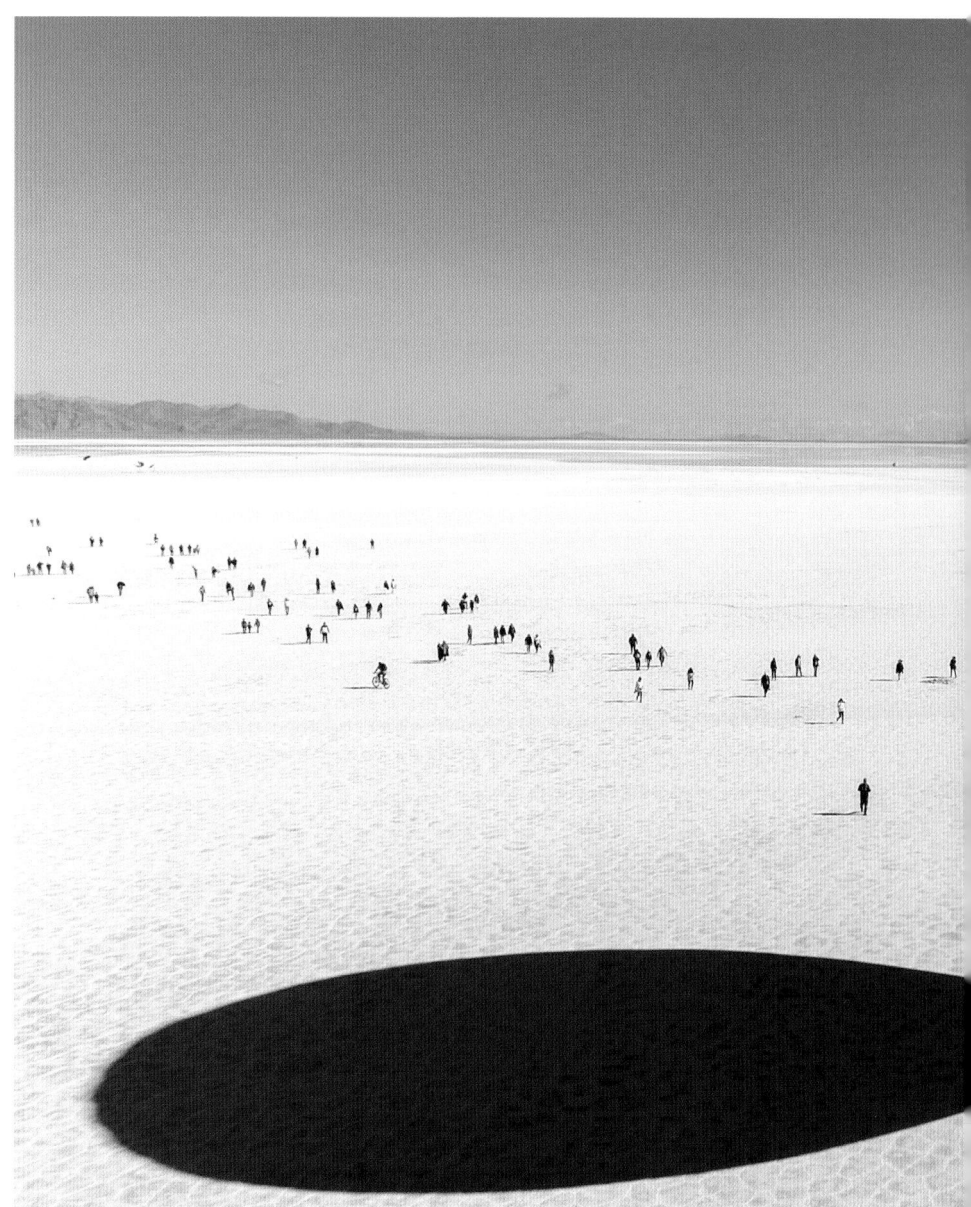

67 Tomás Saraceno, *Flight with Aerocene Pacha*, 2020

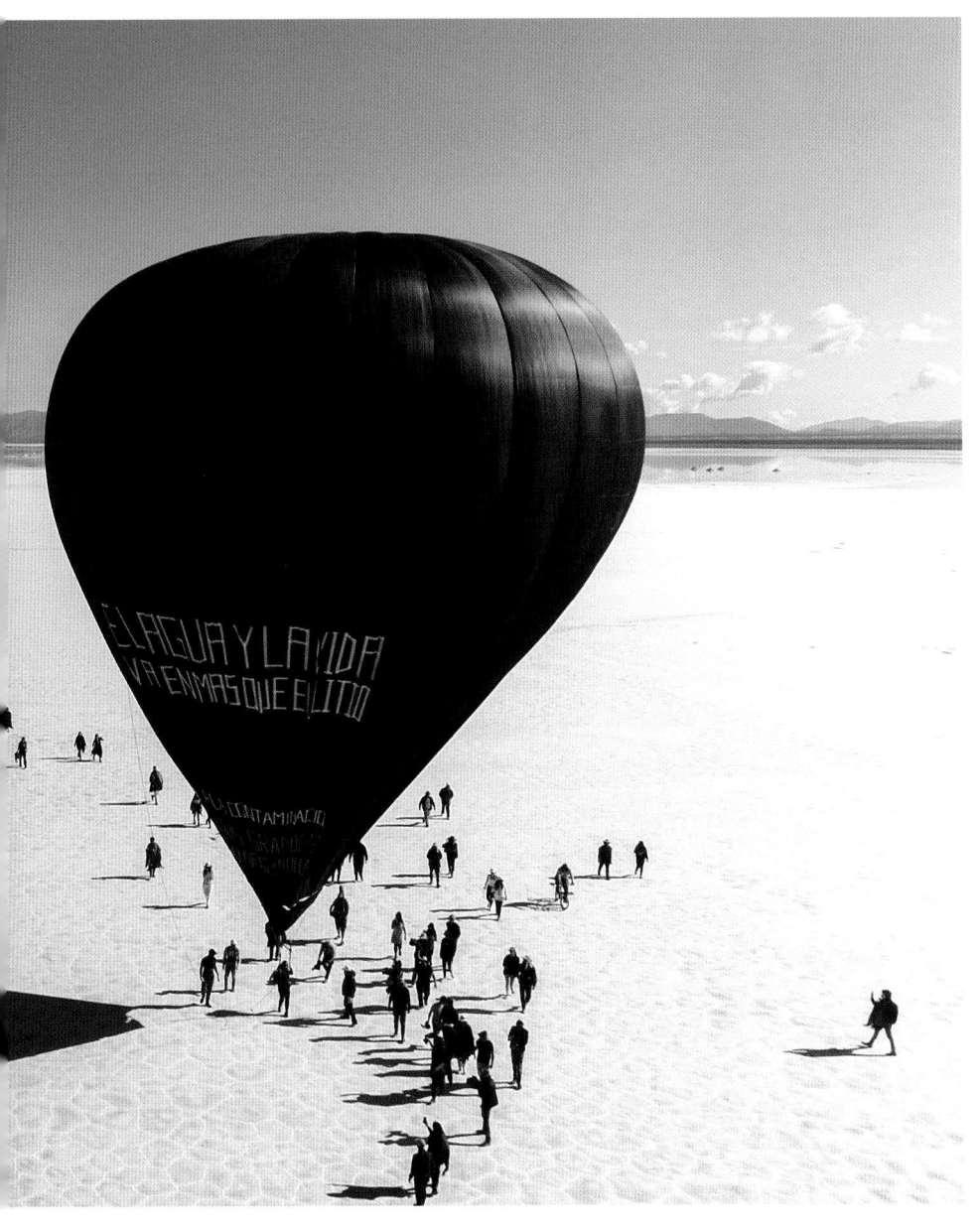

Part III
Floral Collectivism

68 Alexandra Pirici, *Describing in movement/Observing through embodiment,* 2020

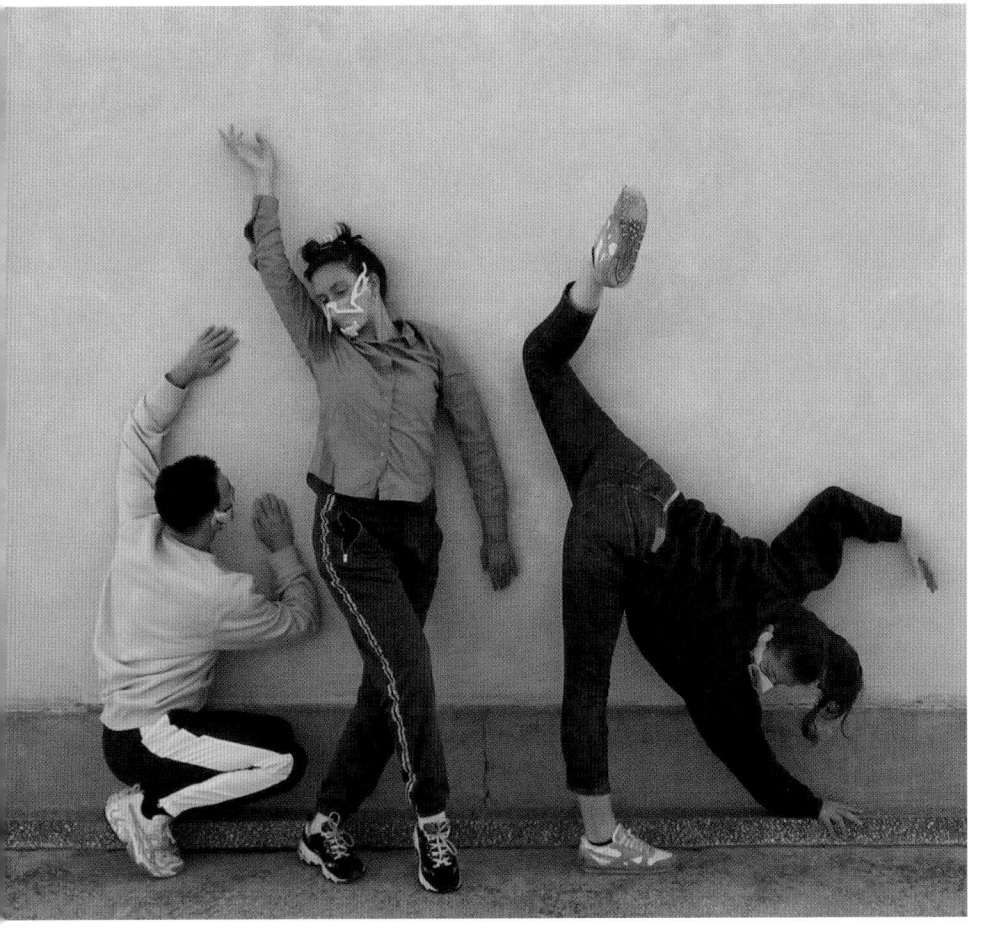

Chapter 1
Vegetal Agency

The threat to vegetal biodiversity posed by anthropogenic
changes to Earth systems is prompting a renewed alertness
towards beings that Western epistemology regularly dismissed
as unmoving, inactive, unthinking, unfeeling and inanimate.
It was on such grounds of treating plants as less developed
than their animal or human counterparts that, as Michael
Marder asserted in *Plant-thinking: A Philosophy of Vegetal Life*,
they became 'unconditionally available for unlimited use and
exploitation'. Opening up the modern discussion of vegetal
consciousness and plant agency, Austro–Hungarian botanist
Raoul Heinrich Francé observed in his 1905 study *Germs
of Mind in Plants* that 'the plant possesses everything that
distinguishes a living creature – movement, sensation, the most
violent reaction to abuse and most ardent gratitude for favours'.
Plants operate according to a specific set of principles based
on their modular and distributed strategy for interacting with
the world, which, as Stefano Mancuso noted in *Brilliant Green*,
enables them to 'breathe without lungs, nourish themselves
without a mouth or stomach, stand erect without a skeleton
and make decisions without a brain'. Plant neurobiologists
have explored the particular ways in which plants detect light
and dark, notice and react to touch, engage in sexual relations
and deploy chemicals and scents to warn each other of danger,
deter predators and attract pollinating insects. In contrast to
animals, plants acquire everything they need to live from the
earth, the air and the sun, moving to capture light and escape
danger and even migrating in response to climate change.
Vegetal agency is also demonstrated in their ability to start
symbiotic relationships with other organisms, such as bacteria,
fungi and insects, as well as humans, whose help they enlist in
getting transported across the world.

The disembodied rationale of modern science, which maintained 'mastery of intellect over body' through an insistence on '(masculine) objectivity' was at the core of the research project *Describing in movement/Observing through embodiment* (2020) by Romanian artist Alexandra Pirici. Challenging the traditional preference for the technique of drawing as a way of recording natural history, she proposed activating the entire body as a medium through which to perceive and learn about the world, devising a choreography for exploring the dynamics of plant life to expand the anthropocentric understanding of the notions of sociality, relationships and intelligence. A set of exercises dealt with vegetal phenomena such as crown shyness, when branches of different trees grow close to each other, negotiating space and access to light while avoiding direct contact. Another sequence was concerned with hanging or epiphytic plants, which, although they feed independently, need a support-body in order to grow, move and have access to light, seen in the wandering movement of the vine in relation to its assisting structure. Singling out dance as a means to reappropriate bodies that have been automated, alienated and enslaved by the capitalist system, feminist theorist Silvia Federici, in *Beyond the Periphery of the Skin*, has described it as 'a process by which we relate to the world, connect to other bodies, transform ourselves and the space around us'. In that sense, Pirici's choreographic exercises were also intended as a self-development tool for non-professional performers, a rehearsal for new forms of collaboration that hold out the potential to activate sensuous relationships in more-than-human worlds.

'The chemical language of plants is a complex form of communication, which our human senses are too dull to comprehend,' observed artist and composer Christine Ödlund in relation to her work on translating plant conversation into music. The score of her electro-acoustic piece *Stress Call of the Stinging Nettle* (2010) was based on scientific observation of the reaction of stinging nettles to being attacked by butterfly larvae, whose leaf-chewing results in the release of a chemical distress signal by the plant. Collaborating with ecological chemists at the Royal Institute of Technology in Stockholm, Ödlund developed a method of olfactory synaesthesia that entailed sniffing concentrated samples of the scented nettle signals and matching each with a colour and an acoustic effect. Compressing biochemical changes taking place on nettle leaves over a period of days into a musical composition lasting minutes, the artist set out to convey the extended timescale over which communication between plants takes

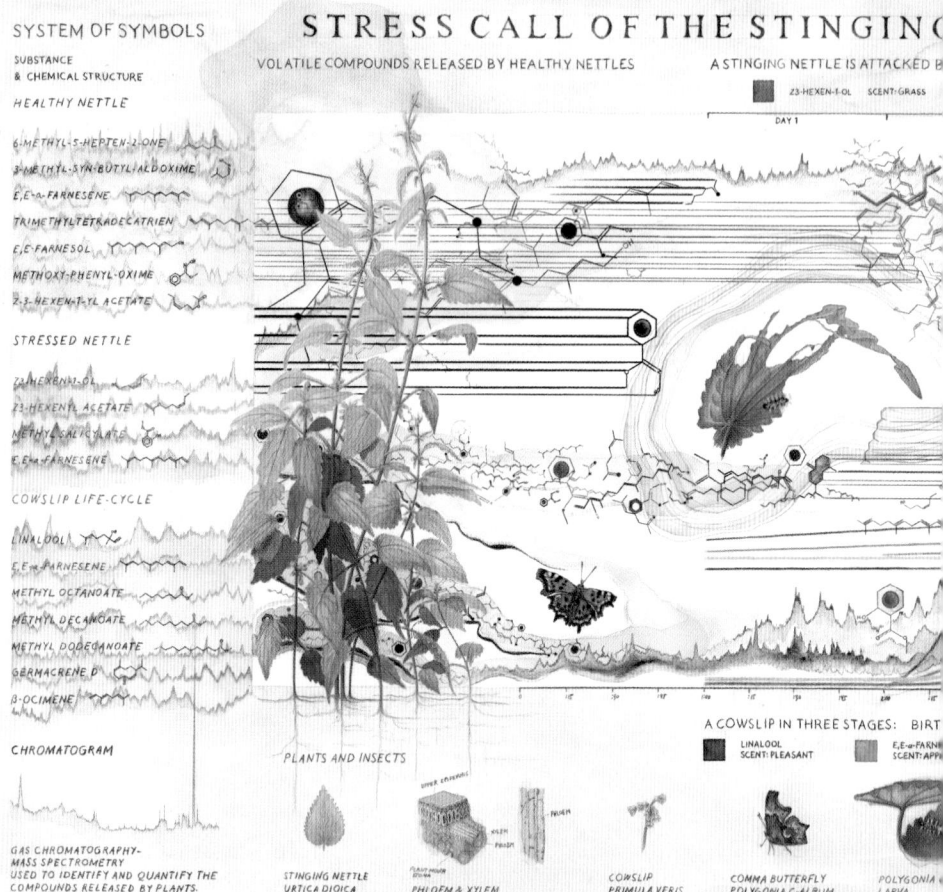

SYSTEM OF SYMBOLS

SUBSTANCE
& CHEMICAL STRUCTURE

HEALTHY NETTLE

STRESS CALL OF THE STINGIN(

VOLATILE COMPOUNDS RELEASED BY HEALTHY NETTLES

A STINGING NETTLE IS ATTACKED B

69 Christine Ödlund, *Stress Call of the Stinging Nettle*, 2010

place. Botanical illustrations on the score referenced further scientific evidence of plant intelligence, such as the reaction of neighbouring nettles, which in response to the chemical warning channel their energy into their roots until the danger of marauding caterpillars has passed.

Challenging heteronormative assumptions in plant science brings a new understanding of the multiplicity of vegetal life, or, as theorist Teresa Castro has put it, 'to queer botanics is to recognize plant nature is queer nature'. Such an expanded understanding of queerness was at stake in Chinese artist Zheng Bo's filmic exploration of sexual intimacy with plants *Pteridophilia* (2016), in which naked men interact with three

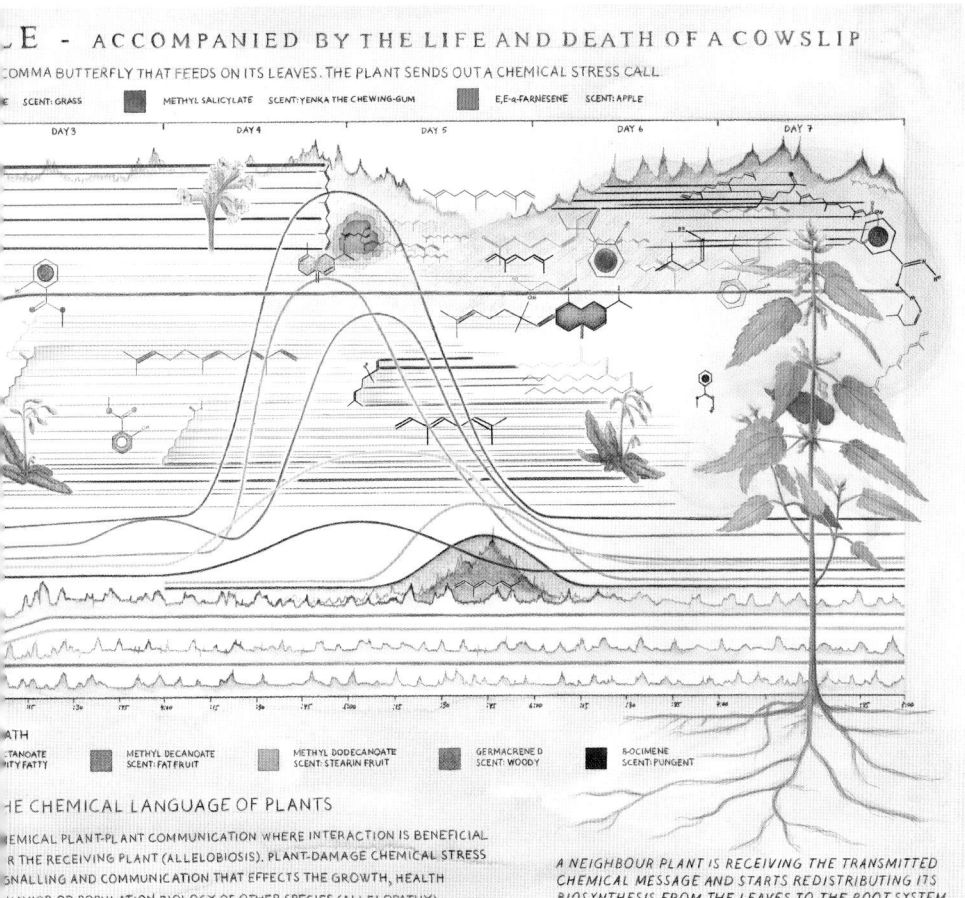

COMMA BUTTERFLY THAT FEEDS ON ITS LEAVES. THE PLANT SENDS OUT A CHEMICAL STRESS CALL.

E SCENT: GRASS METHYL SALICYLATE SCENT: YENKA THE CHEWING-GUM E,E-α-FARNESENE SCENT: APPLE

DAY 3 DAY 4 DAY 5 DAY 6 DAY 7

ATH
TANOATE METHYL DECANOATE METHYL DODECANOATE GERMACRENE D ß-OCIMENE
ITY FATTY SCENT: FAT FRUIT SCENT: STEARIN FRUIT SCENT: WOODY SCENT: PUNGENT

HE CHEMICAL LANGUAGE OF PLANTS

EMICAL PLANT-PLANT COMMUNICATION WHERE INTERACTION IS BENEFICIAL
R THE RECEIVING PLANT (ALLELOBIOSIS). PLANT-DAMAGE CHEMICAL STRESS
GNALLING AND COMMUNICATION THAT EFFECTS THE GROWTH, HEALTH
HAVIOR OR POPULATION BIOLOGY OF OTHER SPECIES (ALLELOPATHY).

A NEIGHBOUR PLANT IS RECEIVING THE TRANSMITTED CHEMICAL MESSAGE AND STARTS REDISTRIBUTING ITS BIOSYNTHESIS FROM THE LEAVES TO THE ROOT SYSTEM.

species of fern in a Taiwanese forest. Experimenting with love and desire between not just species but biological kingdoms made the artist aware of the queerness of the sexuality of ferns, which over generations alternate between producing sperm and eggs and just making spores, in other words between a 'binary' and a 'singular' sexuality. Motivating these transgressive entanglements between queer men and ferns was the artist's sense of the pressing need 'to develop truly intimate relations with other species', which alongside activism deepens the solidarities on which the survival of all depends.

70 In her film *Eyes of Plants* (2019), Chilean artist Patricia Domínguez considered the healing power of plants against

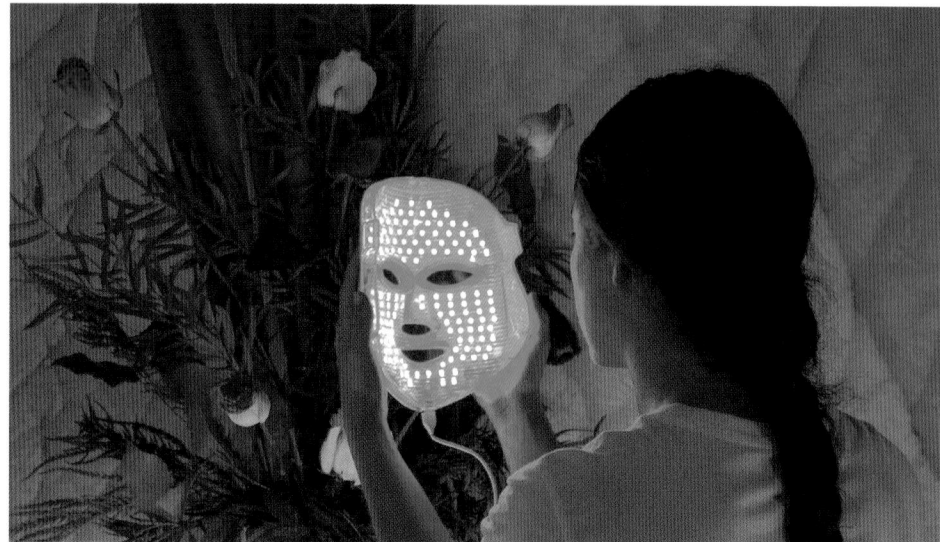

70 Patricia Domínguez, *Eyes of Plants*, 2019

the backdrop of a syncretic world in which indigenous lands
and beliefs collide with colonialism, extractivism and neoliberalism. The troubling cross-pollination of indigenous
cultures and colonial technologies is introduced in the film
through shots of a pre-Columbian crying vase and computer-
generated images of a bioprospecting drone, whose weeping
electronic eyeball echoes the tearful eyes painted on the
indigenous ceramic artefact. The artist's main focus was
on mestizo rituals involving roses, a species that arrived
from Europe with colonization but was absorbed by Central
and South American cultures, who recognized in the high
vibrations of the plant the energetic power to purify auras and
heal personal and collective traumas. Domínguez adapted
these traditional healing techniques to contemporary Chilean
bodies that in her words are 'subject to neoliberalism, tiredness
and cosmic debt'. Channelling the mixed ecological and
cultural heritage of her home country, Domínguez pointed to
the possibility of creating a globally understandable cosmology
based on the ethnobotanical knowledge of the curative
properties of plants.

Direct engagement with plants as a way to reconnect with
human–plant knowledges and re-establish relations that have
been lost through scientific handling and controls imposed
by agricultural corporations was the methodology employed
71   by Swedish artist Åsa Sonjasdotter in *The Order of Potatoes*.

Since 2010, her long-term project has entailed collaborative cultivation of potatoes in a self-organized and publicly accessible garden in Berlin in order to explore entangled natural and social histories of plant cultivation. In contrast to industrial breeding where 'human eugenics were deployed by representatives from the new, scientific field of plant breeding', pre-capitalist ways of growing plants were based, as the artist's research has shown, on 'skills developed through interspecies collaboration' in which 'plants and humans are both actors in the process of cultivation'. The work also incorporated the histories of potatoes, which until the 1600s were bound to the high altitudes of the Andes in South America, where thousands of wild and farmed varieties flourished before the colonial trade expediated their migration to other parts of the world. Responding to the risk that many varieties could become extinct as a result of bureaucratic regulations and the monocultural mentality of the food industry, Sonjasdotter set out to re-establish nurturing relations that take the 'potato perspective' into account.

Among the most distinctive properties of plants is their ability to produce an extraordinary variety of pigment molecules, which they deploy to attract the attention of animals that pollinate

71   Åsa Sonjasdotter, *The Order of Potatoes*, 2010

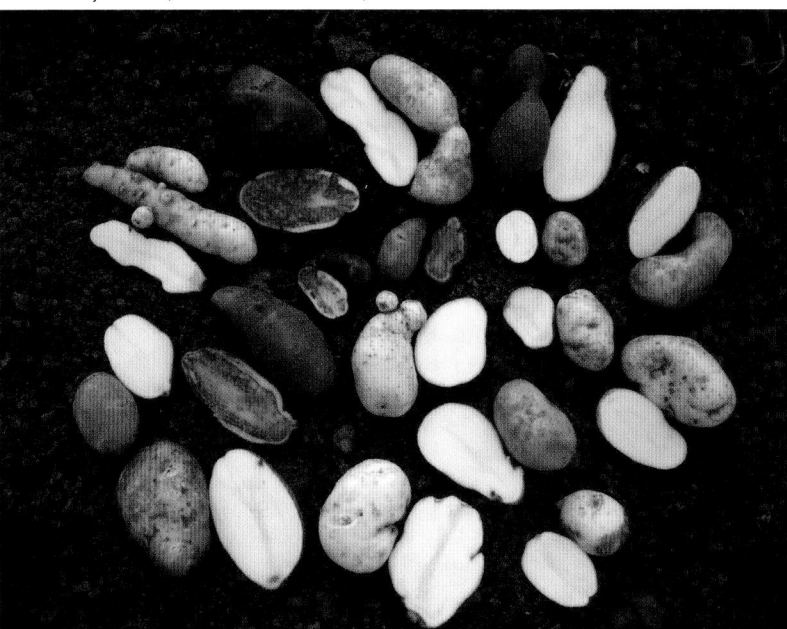

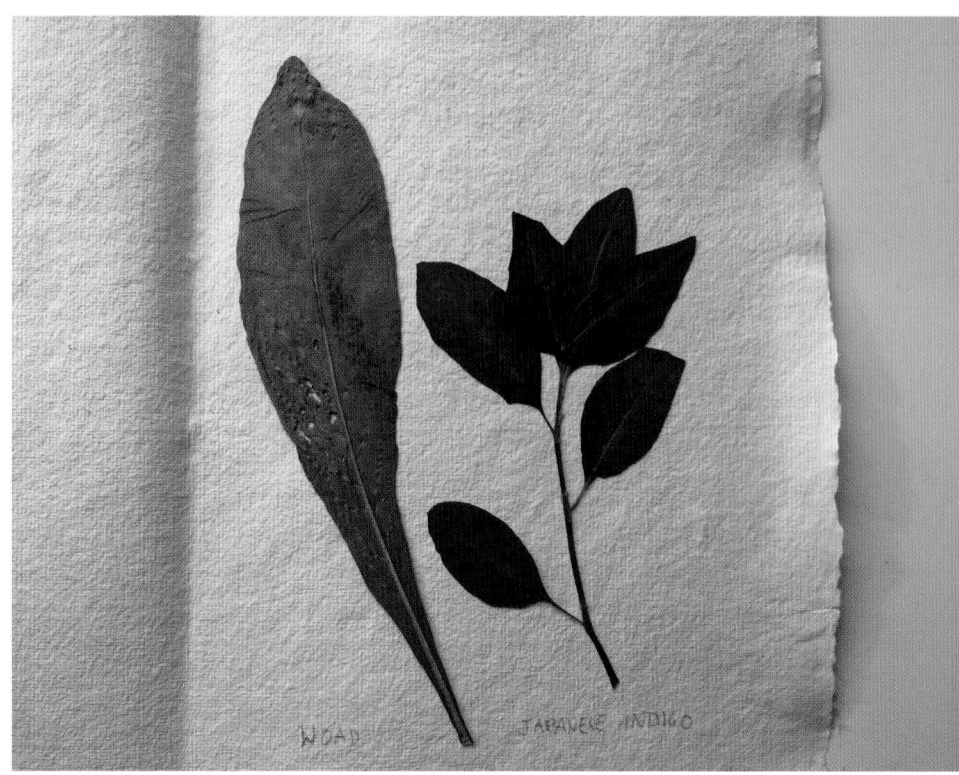

72 Woad and Japanese indigo, indigo-bearing plants best suited to a European climate, grown by Sigrid Holmwood, 2020

flowers and disperse seeds. By producing natural pigments, plants also made artists reliant on them for the colours on their canvases, giving rise to a particular form of cultural dependence on vegetal life. British–Swedish artist Sigrid Holmwood's project *Cultivating Colour* (since 2013) involved planting a pigment garden in the mountains of Sierra María-Los Vélez in Spain, making pigment as a public performance and researching the social history of plants. Referencing theorist Boaventura de Sousa Santos's call in *Epistemologies of the South* for 'ecologies of knowledge' as opposed to epistemological hierarchies, Holmwood interrogated the trajectory of Western modernity and art history through the figures of European peasants and pre-Columbian indigenous peoples. For instance, she wondered how the history of European painting would look if artists had had access to Mayan Blue, a pigment lost for five centuries either through the unintentional cultural ignorance of the colonizers or as a result of deliberate concealment by the Mesoamericans, until it was recreated using traditional procedures in the 1990s. The main European source of blue was woad (*Isatis tinctoria*), a plant also taken to 'New Spain' to grow on the plantations and which the artist used to recreate the Mayan Blue as 'a decolonial gesture' that acknowledges the hybridity of the post-colonial condition.

The history of vegetation on the Earth is much longer than that of humans, with plant historians estimating that it was the appearance of chlorophyll organisms 3.5 billion years ago that turned the planet green. In their work *Proxy Climates* (2019), Anca Benera and Arnold Estefan addressed the deep history of plants, examining the role of fossil pollen found in ocean sediments or sedimentary rocks in piecing together the puzzle of geological time. Due to their particularly resistant constitution, pollen grains and spores, as the authors of *Paleobotany: The Biology and Evolution of Fossil Plants* explain, 'have been extensively used as index fossils in biostratigraphy and in the correlation of rock units', as well as providing the proxy data for the reconstruction of past climates. Benera and Estefan's installation, made up of pollen grains, resin and desert sand in the shape of cylinders, referenced the sampling tubes from exploratory drilling for mineral extraction. However, instead of fossilized residues, the artists collected pollen from various desertification areas, such as Dăbuleni in Romania, 'where there is still some vegetation left, albeit not for long', pointing to the dire effects of climate change on the conditions for plant life in the geological present.

The art practices discussed in this chapter contest the deeply embedded misconceptions around plants in Western culture, epitomized by the use of 'vegetative state' to describe a condition of being incommunicative and insensitive to one's environment. Through music, dance, rituals, performance and acts of tending, artists have turned to sensorial means to reach across the bio-epistemological divide and draw attention to the distinctive characteristics of plants. As science converges with ancient wisdoms and indigenous knowledges of vegetal life, spurred on by the urgencies of climate change, vital awareness is emerging of our elemental dependence on plants for nourishment, oxygenating the air, energy and most medicines, as well as of their resilient agential power.

Chapter 2
Botanical Politics

The modern history of plant science has been strongly marked by political and economic interests, ever since botany was mobilized in the quest for 'green gold' during the long eighteenth century. As Londa Schiebinger wrote in *Plants and Empire*, botany 'worked hand in hand with European colonial expansion' to the extent that even the father of botanical taxonomy, Swedish naturalist Carl Linnaeus, 'taught that the purpose of natural history was to render service to the state'. Encouraged by imperial powers to unlock the botanical secrets of indigenous knowledge and capitalize on their medicinal and agricultural potential, botanists of the New World were also active in transplanting species across the globe. During the twentieth century, vegetal realms were drawn into the political arena in new ways. Under Soviet socialism, the Great Stalin Plan for the Transformation of Nature of 1948 gave state biologist Trofim Lysenko free rein to experiment with ideologically tinged theories such as 'floral collectivism', which saw trees planted in comradely clusters to protect against weeds and other class enemies. More recently, with the rise of neo-liberal global capitalism, pharmaceutical corporations have opened new frontiers for botanical extractivism, based on isolating and patenting compounds derived from traditional medicinal plants at the expense of the impoverishment of local communities and ecological disruption. Engraved in the political imaginary through floral inscriptions on national insignia, plants have also been utilized in state ceremonies and diplomatic protocols.

Exploring the correlation between plants and ideology, Zheng Bo's *Socialism Good* (2016) was a floral recreation in Chinese characters of the Communist Party slogan in the title, as a site-specific installation for the former CASS Sculpture Foundation in southern England. Flowers had previously been arranged to

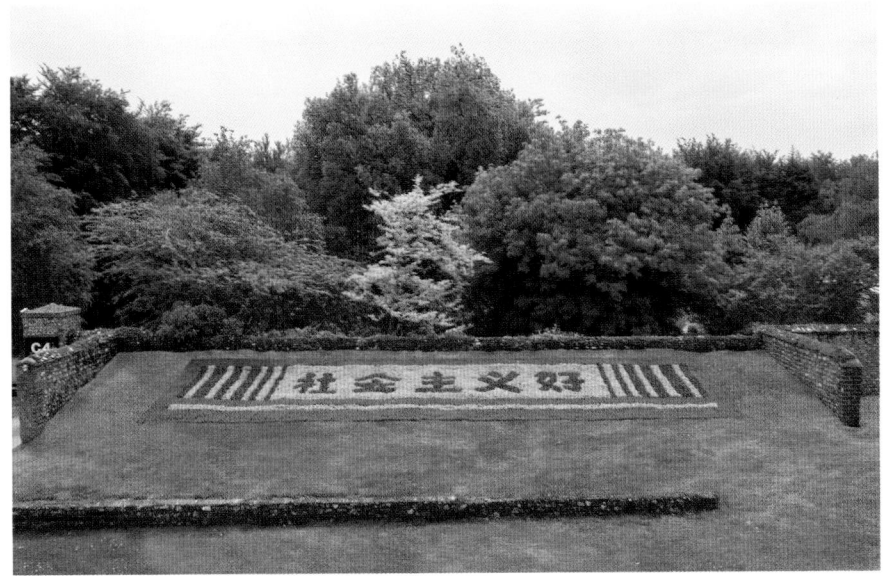

73 Zheng Bo in collaboration with plants, *Socialism Good*, 2016

deliver this propaganda message during the national celebrations of 1991 in Tiananmen Square, notably also the site of the brutal repression of student-led democracy protests two years earlier. Along with issues around the instrumentalization of plants to propagate ideological slogans and suppress freedom of speech, the work made reference to official Communist Party attitudes to the natural world, which since the 1950s had been guided by Mao Tse Tung's dictums 'man must conquer nature' and 'make the high mountain bow its head; make the river yield the way'. As Judith Shapiro put it in *Mao's War Against Nature*, 'the conquest of nature and prosperity of humankind were believed to be at hand through the miracle of socialism'. By deploying the floral slogan in the wake of the domestic turmoil of 1989 and the near global collapse of the communist system, the Party sought to enlist vegetal beings to reassert the correct Chinese path to socialism. While in the original scenario the propaganda plants were kept in line within a tightly controlled horticultural setting, in the artist's version the flower beds were left unattended and weeds were allowed to grow between the Chinese characters, raising the prospect of ruderal resistance.

Trees that have been adopted as national symbols by neighbouring countries with long-standing border disputes featured in Indian artist Reena Kallat's series *Siamese Trees* (2018–19), in which electricity cables were intricately braided

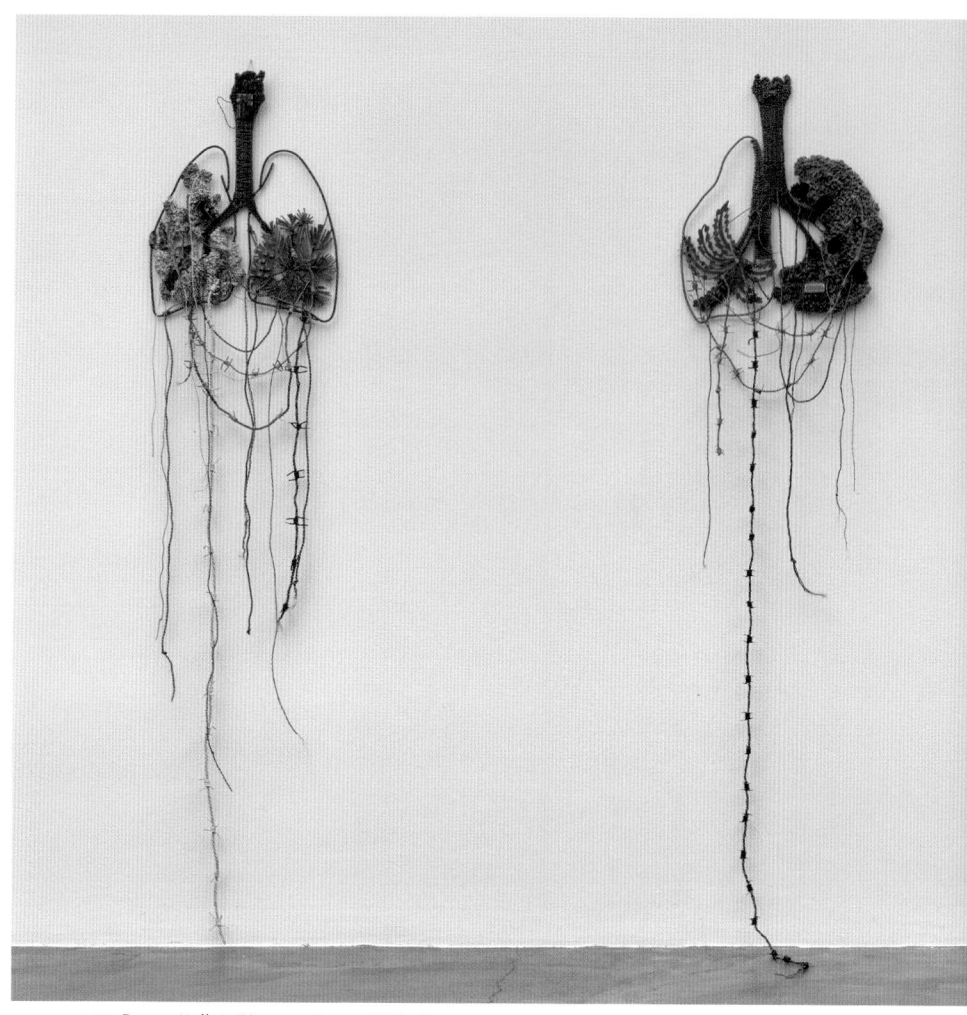

74 Reena Kallat, *Siamese Trees*, 2018–19

together to form two inverted and conjoined trees in the shape of human lungs. She fused ratchaphruek from Thailand with Cambodia's palm to form Ratch-yra palm, Mexican cypress with US oak to form Cy-Oak, mango from Bangladesh with Indian banyan to create Man-yan, and North Korea's pine with South Korea's hibiscus to form Pine-iscus. The chosen sculptural material carries associations of cables as conduits for energy and information, but when woven into draping barbed wire coils is also symbolic of the obstacles to the free flow of people and ideas across borders. By superimposing geopolitical conflicts onto

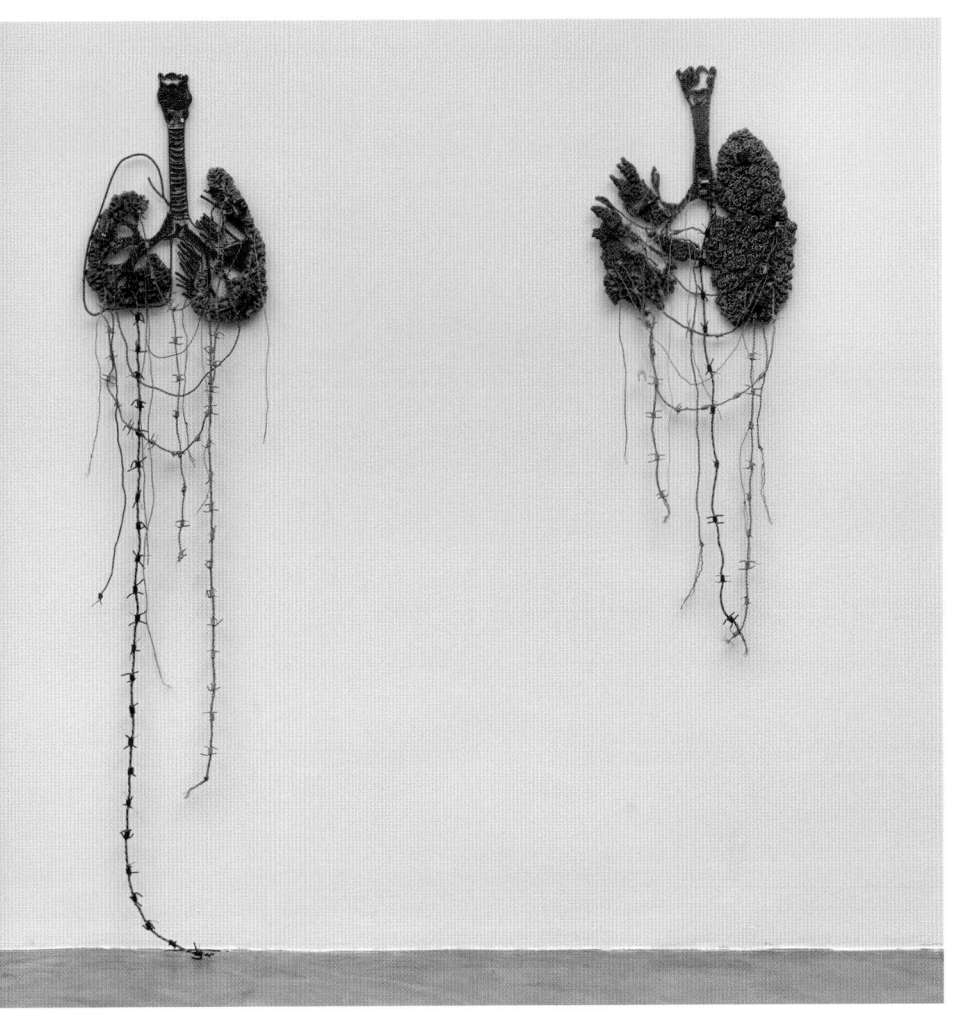

botanical realms, yet through her intervention demonstrating the integrated ecology of natural habitats, the artist considered these conjoined forms as 'an allusion to nature's defiance of artificially imposed, man-made divisions on the ground, a poetic provocation from the past or a proposition for an imagined future where indeed they may reunite'. Just as trees in ecosystems communicate through underground root and fungal networks and oxygenate air through their crowns, the interconnected arboreal bodies in this work reach across national, cultural and political boundaries and point to vital interdependencies.

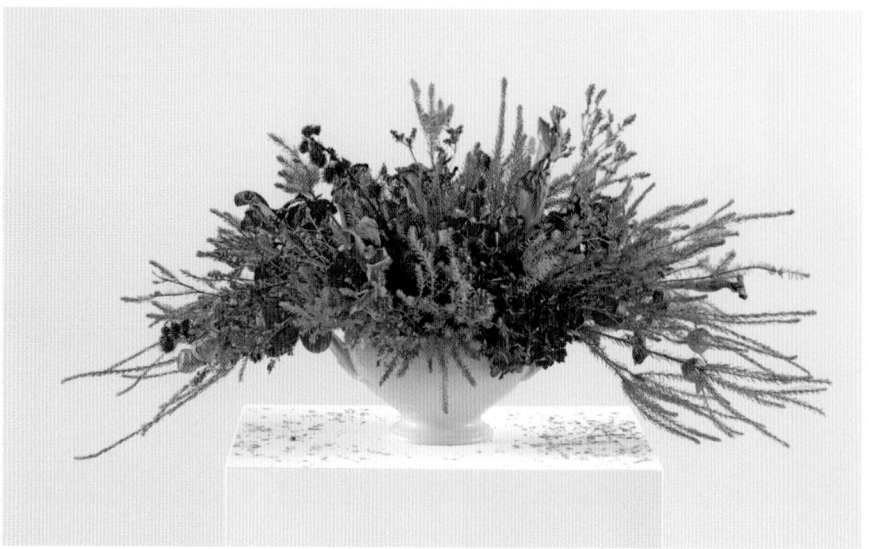

75 Kapwani Kiwanga, *Flowers for Africa: Cameroon*, 2020

Researching archival imagery of the transition of African nations from colonial rule, Paris-based Franco–Canadian artist Kapwani Kiwanga has uncovered the role of plants in various independence ceremonies. Her ongoing project *Flowers for Africa* started in 2013 during an art residency in Dakar, when she recreated floral arrangements corresponding to specific moments in Senegal's path to independence. Subsequently she developed a protocol to remake floral displays corresponding to the decolonial transitions of Rwanda, South Africa, Nigeria, Ivory Coast and eventually all fifty-four countries on the African continent. Drawing on archival photographs, Kiwanga worked with florists to reconstruct the elaborate bouquets, or in some cases simple boutonnières, with the fresh flowers and foliage then left to wilt and dry over the course of the exhibition. The deteriorating floral displays mirrored the creeping amnesia about colonial history and the waning of the optimism of the post-colonial era since, as the artist put it, 'just as the enthusiasm present during the period of independence has faded, pan-African dreams have been eclipsed by the everyday difficulties of the average African citizen'. Disclosing the botanical codes of floral diplomacy, the work showed how plants have been harnessed in the political symbolism of nation-building.

The supportive role of plants in the anti-Apartheid struggle in South Africa was unearthed by Swiss artist Uriel Orlow in his installation *Grey, Green, Gold* (2015–18), which dealt with the vegetable garden established by Nelson Mandela and other political prisoners incarcerated on Robben Island during the 1970s. Green stands here for the tiny patch of land in the grey prison yard cultivated by the ANC activists as an act of subversion against the racist regime, while gold is the colour of the strelitzia, a rare variety of a flower native to South Africa, popularly known as 'Mandela's gold' after he became president. *The Squirrel's Revenge* (2015–16), a photograph of the plant caged in chicken wire to protect it from marauding squirrels that were introduced into the country under British rule, alluded to the collision of botany and politics in colonial histories and decolonial struggles. Also belonging to Orlow's *Theatrum Botanicum* (2015–18), a body of work that examined the conflict between colonial botany and indigenous vegetal knowledge, was the experimental documentary *Imbizo Ka Mafavuke* (2017). Set in a nature reserve on the outskirts of Johannesburg, the film saw healers, activists, lawyers and the ghosts of colonial explorers, botanists and judges convene to revisit the 1940 court case against indigenous herbalist Mafavuke Ngcobo. The statement by a plant healer that 'plants and knowledge are not for us to sell' exposed the epistemological divide between the attempts of pharmaceutical corporations to use bioprospecting and genetic patenting to commercialize the biological resources of South Africa and the non-proprietary attitudes of local communities.

Medicinal plants used as abortifacients in the Caribbean during the era of colonial slavery were sites of contestation over

76 Uriel Orlow, *The Squirrel's Revenge*, 2015–16

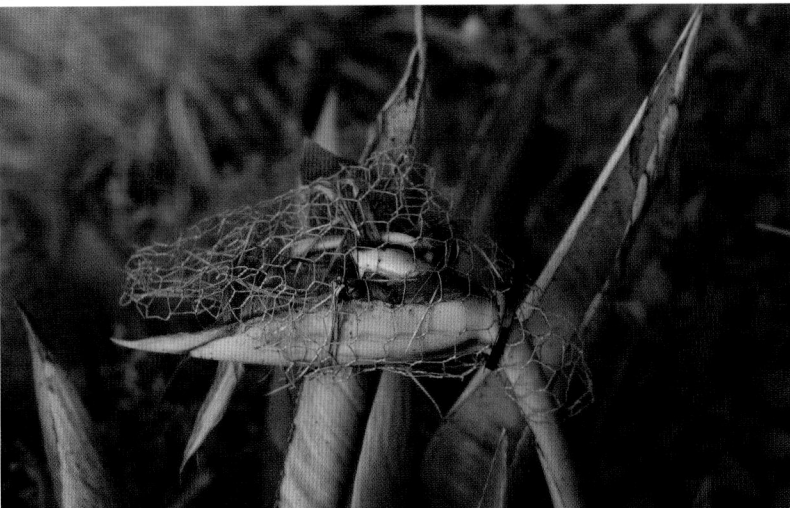

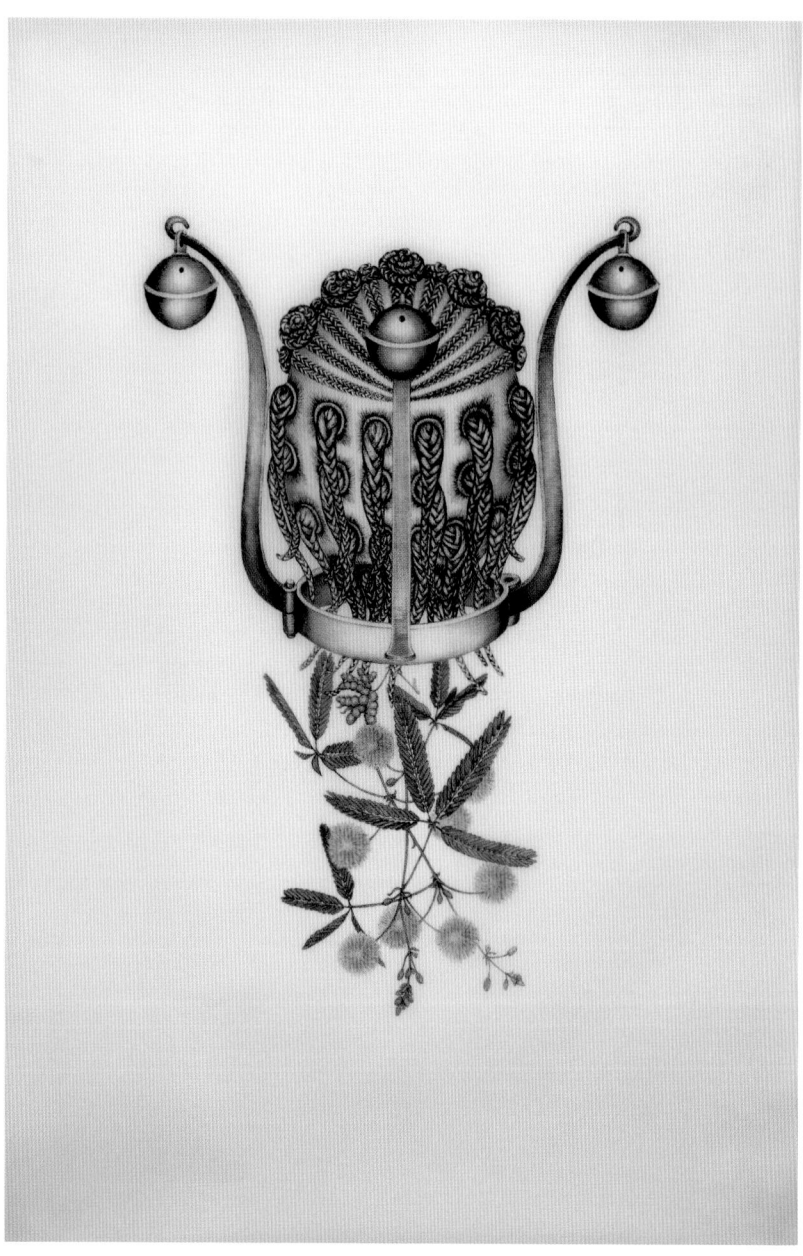

77 ABOVE Joscelyn Gardner, *Mimosa pudica (Yabba)*, 2009
78 OPPOSITE Beatriz Santiago Muñoz, *Farmacopea*, 2013

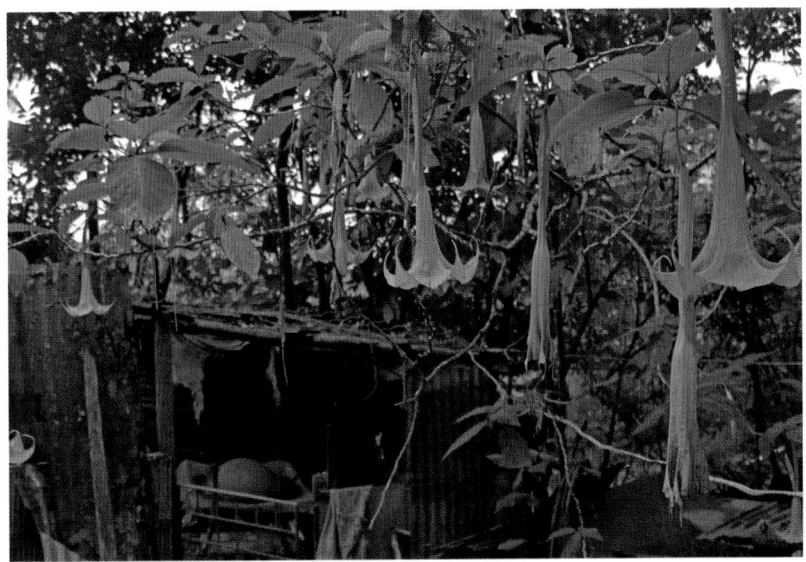

the ownership of women's bodies and access to indigenous
knowledge of plant-based techniques of reproductive control.
77 The series of watercolours *Creole Portraits III* (2009–11) by
Barbadian artist Joscelyn Gardner depict the backs of women's
heads with braided Afro hairstyles, from the base of which grows
a species of abortifacient plant. The iron torture collars around
their necks recall the punishment of women for their acts of
reproductive resistance in refusing to provide a new generation
of slaves. The artist also parodied colonial botany's categorization
of these exotic species by using the Linnaean taxonomic system,
along with the name assigned to each slave on the plantation,
in the portrait titles. As Schiebinger pointed out in *Plants and
Empire*, European botanists selectively chose not to collect
information about this aspect of Caribbean medical practices,
as it did not correspond to their political, economic, disciplinary
or personal interests. In that way, by suppressing knowledge of
such plant-based methods, Western science fostered 'bodies of
ignorance' that came to 'mould the lived experience of European
women' by restricting reproductive freedoms.
78   In her film *Farmacopea* (2013), Beatriz Santiago Muñoz
problematized the transformation of the Puerto Rican landscape
as a consequence of the government's agenda to turn the country
into a desirable travel destination. The title of the work referred to
the catalogue of plants used by indigenous people for medicinal,
hallucinatory or other purposes, with the artist paying special

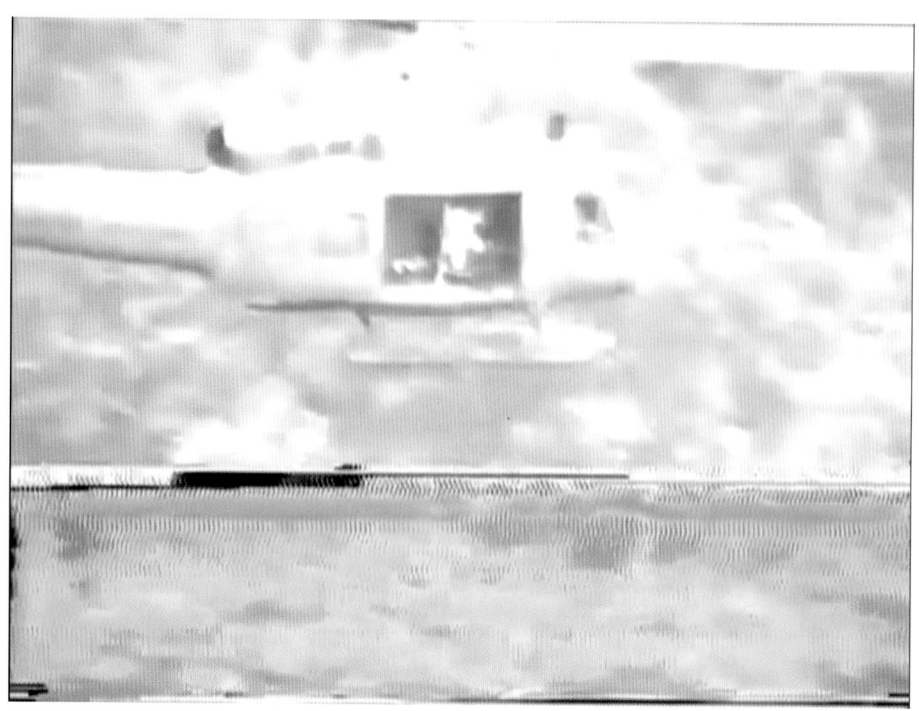

79 Hannah Meszaros Martin, *Falta de Luz*, 2020

attention to the disappearance of *Hippomane mancinella* or the manchineel tree. Locally known as 'the little apple of death', it is considered one of the most toxic trees in the world, since just sitting beneath it can cause sickness for days. While in the past the tree was responsible for many losses of life, nowadays it is incredibly rare, following the efforts of the Puerto Rican government to eradicate it and render the landscape harmless. As a result, the Caribbean island has, in the artist's words, been transformed into an 'undifferentiated tropical place for tourism, service and folklore', at the expense of biodiversity and native knowledges of local botanical uses. Endangering the richness of indigenous plant cultures, the loss of vegetal species is driven not only by climate change and agricultural encroachments, but also by the commercial and political project of sanitizing the forest to make it amenable for the travel industry.

Relying on the forensic methodology of collecting evidence from fieldwork, photography, films, remote sensing and ethnology, Hannah Meszaros Martin has investigated the eradication of the coca plant via aerial fumigation in Colombia. Ever since the growth of the coca plant was outlawed by the

United Nations in 1961, states have been granted the power
not only to destroy coca when harvested illegally for drug
production, but also 'to kill it in the wild'. In her film *Falta
de Luz* (2020), Martin drew on archival footage to juxtapose
the history of the use of the herbicide glyphosate to target
marijuana crops in the mountainous national parks of Georgia
in the 1980s and that of the US-backed counter-narcotics
campaign to systematically eradicate the coca plant in the
forests of Putumayo in southern Colombia two decades later.
By interweaving temporalities and geographies, the artist merges
the memory of uncontaminated landscape with the legacy of
the chemical poisoning of land, water and bodies. Uncovering
the ecocidal violence of plant eradication in Colombia, the work
underlines the extent to which, in the artist's words, 'the war on
drugs is also a war on the natural world'.

The questionable neutrality of the scientific project of seed
archiving, the role of climate change in causing social and
political upheaval and the clash between the paradigms of
industrial agriculture and community permaculture were all at
issue in Palestinian artist Jumana Manna's film *Wild Relatives*
(2018). Her account began with the International Centre for
Agricultural Research in Dry Areas (ICARDA)'s 2015 decision
to request the return of the specimens it had deposited in the
Svalbard Global Seed Vault. This unprecedented move was
prompted by the war in Syria, which forced ICARDA to abandon
its own seed store in Aleppo and move its research across

80 Jumana Manna, *Wild Relatives*, 2018

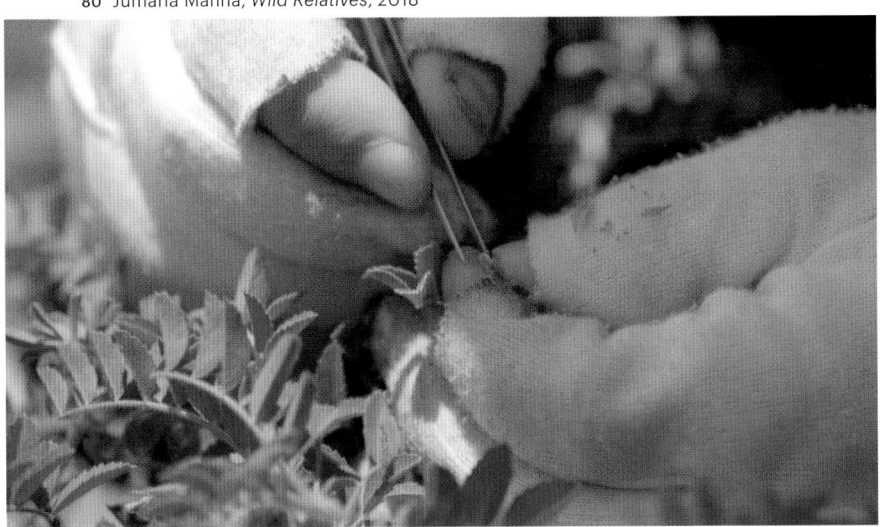

the border to Lebanon's Bekaa Valley. The film followed the seeds' journey from the Arctic doomsday vault to the displaced agronomical centre, where they were awakened and duplicated, and then their return to Svalbard for safe keeping. It drew attention to the global practice of seed archiving, which is only necessary due to the reduction in biodiversity caused by the switch to monocultural agriculture. The film also questioned the role of scientists in breeding thirsty crops that drained Syrian aquifers, making the country more vulnerable to severe droughts that fuelled the Arab Spring protests of 2011. As the permacultural methods of Lebanese farmers featured in the film demonstrate, it is the 'wild relatives' of industrially farmed crops, rather than their genetically modified cousins, that are best equipped to withstand the extreme conditions brought by climate change.

Artists in this chapter have revealed botany as distinctly embedded in the political projects of colonialism and decolonial struggles, as well as the tendency to elevate certain flower and tree species to a privileged place in the pantheon of national representation. Pharmaceutical companies' exploitation of plants as a genetic resource, the manipulation of seed varieties to suit the interests of monocultural agriculture and the criminalization of plant species as a health, security or economic threat in state-led ecocidal campaigns are shown as manifestations of the extractivist mindset. While climate change has heightened the political stakes around the ownership and control of plants, vegetal resistance is expressed through their capacity to overrun horticultural settings and make unexpected interspecies alliances.

Chapter 3
Self-Management of Plants

In 2008, a landmark decision in Swiss constitutional law affirmed the 'dignity of plants as living beings', establishing the principle that causing 'arbitrary harm to plants is morally impermissible'. However, by declining to protect plants from destruction for a 'rational reason', this partial expansion of planetary jurisprudence did not go so far as to question their instrumentalization. Equally, in seeking to apply the humanistic notion of individual dignity to beings of vegetal physiology, the decision squeezed plants into the narrowly anthropocentric categories of the Western legal tradition. By contrast, phytocentric approaches to vegetal wellbeing proceed from the understanding that plant life is 'complete exposure, in absolute continuity and total communion with the environment', which for theorist Emanuele Coccia in *The Life of Plants* represents 'the most intense, radical, and paradigmatic form of being in the world'. Furthermore, the emancipation of plants should not be seen merely as a matter of human benevolence, but as a condition that emerges through vegetal agency in shaping the environment. The refusal of weeds in particular to 'play by our rules', as Richard Mabey observed in *Weeds: The Story of Outlaw Plants*, 'makes them subversive and the very essence of wildness', traits that place them in the botanical vanguard of the planetary response to climate change.

    The self-management of post-industrial flora as a manifestation of resilience was at stake in Igor Eškinja's project *Do Plants Dream of the Future?* (2020), which took as its subject the vegetation that thrives in the post-socialist ruins of the Croatian port city of Rijeka. The capacity of weeds to prosper in proximity to humans, opportunistically populating new landscapes such as decaying factory buildings, roofs and other neglected urban infrastructures, was for the artist an indicator of their 'enormous

81

vitality and force, resourcefulness and energy in occupying and transforming space and life'. Eškinja uncovered the botanical and environmental history of the city, from the expulsion of nature with the beginning of industrial development and urbanization in the nineteenth century to the return of biodiversity to industrial sites abandoned since the 1990s, through the flourishing of self-seeding plants. Referring to the nineteenth-century vogue for wall coverings decorated with floral and exotic botanical motifs, the artist produced a series of wallpapers patterned with weed specimens now living in the industrial areas of the city. For cultural anthropologist Bettina Stoetzer, the 'ruderal worlds' that emerge spontaneously in inhospitable urban environments point to 'often unnoticed, cosmopolitan yet precarious ways of remaking the urban fabric'. By deliberating about a phytocentric future, Eškinja raised the question of whether ruderal plants, through their vigour, subversiveness and adaptability, might stand as signposts for the empowerment of cities in transition.

The plants that thrive in urban wastelands and abandoned development sites were also investigated by Danish artist Camilla Berner in her exhibition 'Still Alive' in Seoul in 2016, which asked how such sites are perceived by 'self-organising nature' itself. One photographic work in the show was prepared in Copenhagen and referenced the Korean flower arrangements

81 Igor Eškinja, *Untitled (Hartera)*, 2020

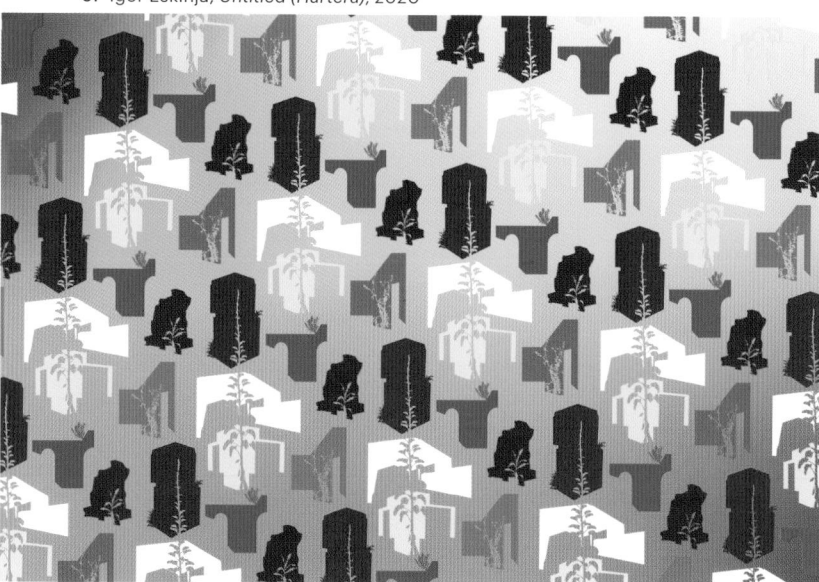

known as a *hwa-hwan*, traditionally made for celebrations such as weddings or birthdays, using roses, lilies or other colourful flowers. In the artist's version however, the assembly was meticulously put together with wildflowers, weeds and grasses collected from a post-industrial site intended for future gentrification. In Seoul, Berner researched the floral vegetation of similar locations, creating bouquets from these often overlooked, yet hardy and adaptable plants that also communicate the specific socio-economic circumstances of the site from which they originated. One such spot was the last remaining building site in the affluent commercial city district of Gangnam, which Samsung and Hyundai were competing to buy at the time, and therefore the artist could only reach the vegetation that was spreading under its fences. She placed each bouquet in a matching vase made by the Royal Copenhagen porcelain company, using the genre of still-life painting to interrogate the comparable position of wild plants in Danish and Korean culture. Appending a detailed list of species used in the composition of each *Plant Collection* challenged further their marginalized status in horticultural circles.

82

Reflecting on the extraordinary transformation of China's built environment in recent decades that have seen a ravaging spread of urbanization, Zheng Bo's intervention on the roof garden of the newly erected Sifang Art Museum in Nanjing entailed creating a refuge for weeds collected from the changing neighbourhood. By planting a *Weed Plot* (2016) for plants endangered by constantly advancing construction sites, the artist drew attention to the encroachment of ultra-modernity that disrupts people's connection with other species, pointing out that 'a hundred years ago you didn't need to go to a museum to reconnect with weeds'. The rapidity with which the conditions for vegetal life are being destroyed in the country's hi-tech urban sprawl is suggested by the fact that China currently pours more concrete in two years than the United States did over the whole twentieth century. The role of ruderal plants in the political imaginary is a recurrent concern in Bo's practice, on the one hand focusing on the issues of overlooked and marginalized, yet resilient and disobedient elements in the system, while on the other questioning inclusivity and eco-equality for all humans and non-humans.

Engaging with wild plants found within a twenty-minute walk of her studio in rural Goa, Indian artist Nandita Kumar anticipated a future in which forgotten plants could be reintegrated into the lives of local communities blighted by monocultures. Her interactive installation *The Unwanted Ecology* (2017) consisted of a glass jar containing dried samples of twenty plants denigrated as weeds, each of which was electronically

83

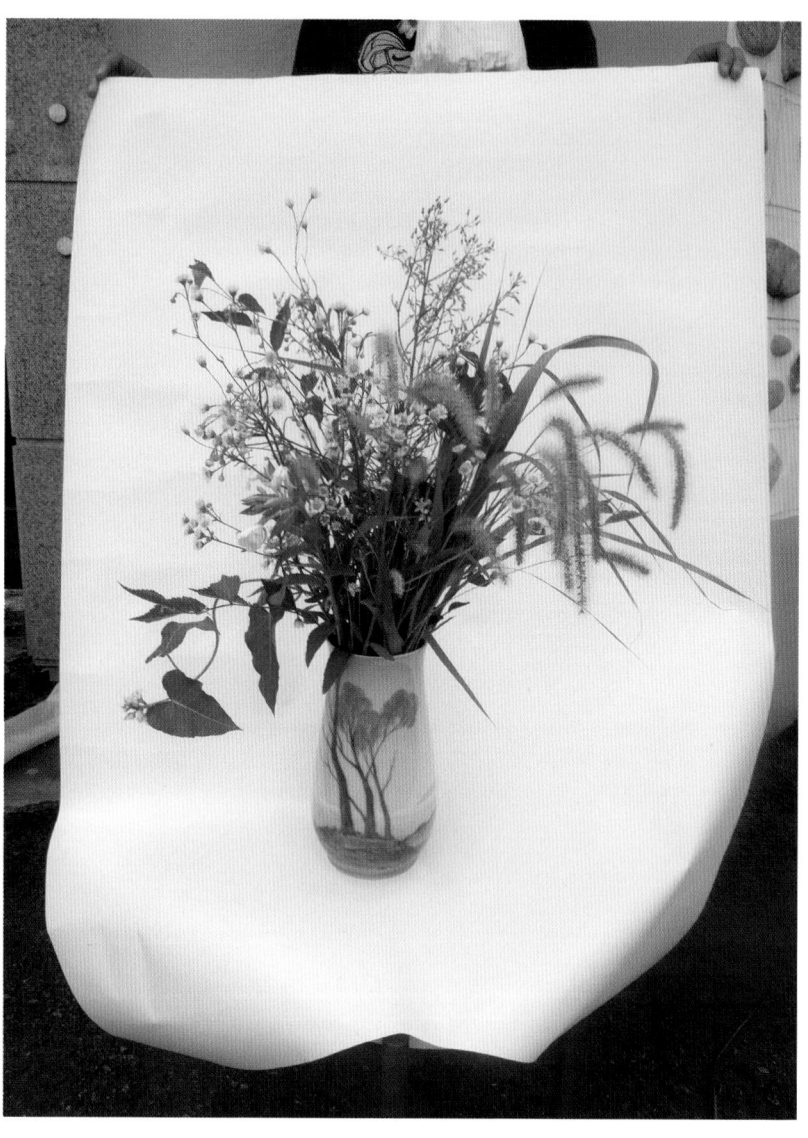

82 Camilla Berner, *Plant Collection no. 1030 Tongui-dong, Jongno-gu, Seoul 11.08.16*, 2016

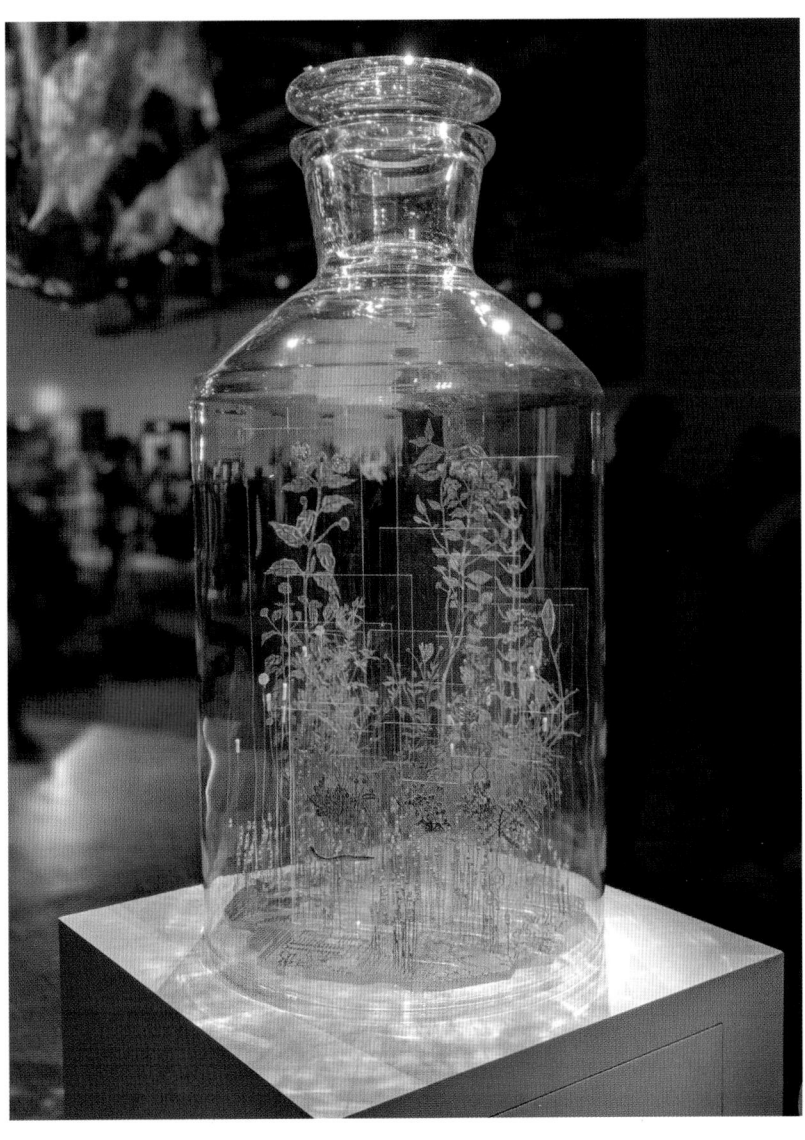

83　Nandita Kumar, *The Unwanted Ecology*, 2017

matched with a sound frequency. As visitors approached the jar, altering the atmospheric humidity, the sound levels emitted from this 'technologically reincarnated organism' also changed, re-enacting, in the artist's words, 'missed or invisible encounters between plants and people'. Alongside this sensorial attempt to rekindle appreciation for neglected plant species, the installation included a book with information about their nutritional and medicinal qualities, ethnobotanical knowledge that risks being lost as local healers disappear. Kumar also emphasized the resilience of these vegetal survivalists in the face of the high temperatures and drought conditions that are degrading the landscape as global warming intensifies.

The resilience of wild plants was also the subject of Annalee Davis's collaborative project *(Bush) Tea Plots* (2019–20). The work focused on the ecological damage caused by the monocultural farming of sugar on Barbados and wild plants' capacity to absorb toxins and restore harmony to an environment scarred by the physical and psychological legacies of slavery. Reflecting on the resurgence of wild botanicals she observed on walks through the abandoned sugarcane fields behind her studio, the artist used a glass planter to make visible the biological action of uncultivated vegetation in nourishing and restoring layers of soil made barren by monocultural production. Davis also referred in the work to the hidden history of bush tea practices, in which healers used West African medicinal knowledge to provide herbal cures and spiritual relief to their communities. These medicinal plants came mostly from the small plots given over to slaves to grow their own food, which became in the words of Jamaican writer Sylvia Wynter a 'source of cultural guerrilla resistance to the plantation system'. These wild herbs represent for the artist an 'apothecary of resistance' with the ability to counteract the devastating effects of the plantation system on the life of the island, while challenging at the same time reliance on imported pharmaceuticals during the post-plantation era.

Non-extractivist approaches to medicinal plants were at the core of Uriel Orlow's work *Learning from Artemisia* (2019–20), which took as its case in point the plant *Artemisia afra* that grows in various parts of Africa. Despite the fact that the herbal infusion of this indigenous plant is known to be effective in the treatment and prevention of malaria, it is not recommended as a medication by the World Health Organization, which tends to favour drugs produced by the pharmaceutical industry. The project was originally realized in the context of the Lubumbashi Biennale, where the artist worked with a women's cooperative of artemisia growers to plant a small garden, with a local painter to create an accompanying mural and with a band to perform

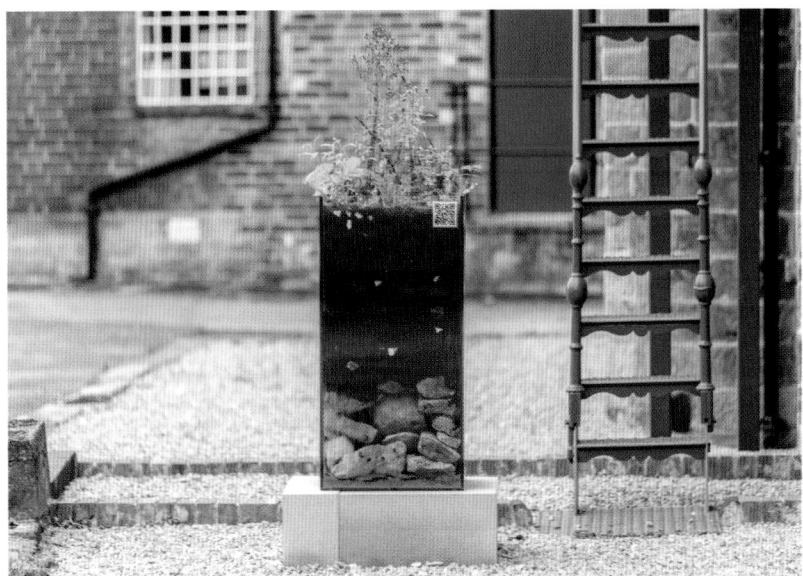

84 Annalee Davis, *(Bush) Tea Plot – A Decolonial Patch for Mill Workers*, 2020

a song about the beneficial qualities of the plant. In his research, Orlow juxtaposed anti-malarial drugs patented on the basis of pharmacological extraction of the component artemisin from the Chinese variety of the plant, to which the parasites that cause the illness are increasingly resistant, with the tea brewed from the whole plant in a sustainable and non-intrusive way. Against the background of colonial history and the post-colonial economy of the Democratic Republic of Congo, which has been coloured by various forms of extractivism, the artist proposed to learn from *Artemisia afra* about a non-exploitative relationship with the natural world and to reimagine modern medicine through forms of plant solidarity.

French artist Suzanne Husky drew on her background in landscape gardening to realize *Jardin à la française sauvage* (2013), a work that entailed reinventing the seventeenth-century French formal garden in the chateau park of Domaine de Chamarande as an experiment in botanical wilderness. The layout of her floral labyrinth referenced the history of French horticulture in the age of Louis XIV, when, as Chandra Mukerji asserted in *Territorial Ambitions and the Gardens of Versailles*, gardens were a microcosm designed to showcase the military and political power of the Sun King, and a 'model of material domination of nature' in which land was 'surveyed and measured and stamped as something under human control'. However, in

85

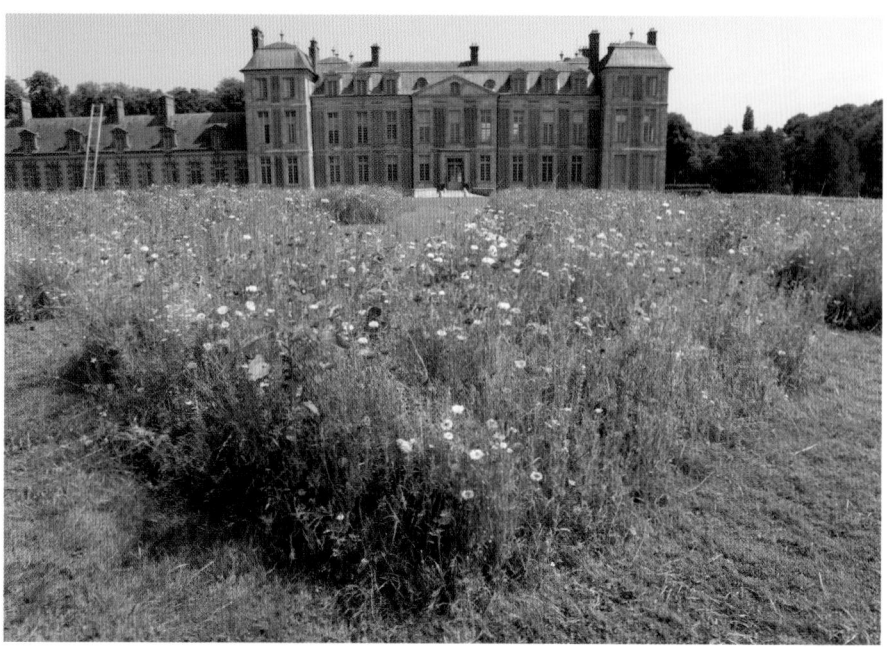

85 Suzanne Husky, *Jardin à la française sauvage*, 2013

Husky's ecocentric version, plants were chosen not for their self-aggrandizing effect, but based on the 'needs of the soil, the cycle of life and the relation of spaces with their environment', with the selection of wild grasses and perennial meadow flowers intended to provide a habitat and winter food resource for birds and insects. Challenging the political and aesthetic instrumentalization of vegetal life, the wildness of this French formal garden is also a premonition of a future in which only plants able to adapt to a changing climate will survive.

The wellbeing of plants in a world transformed by human interventions resides in their emancipation from being poisoned with chemicals, uprooted for urban development, meddled with genetically, or displaced from home soils and endangered by climate change. Rekindling appreciation for neglected vegetation that has found its ecological thriving spot in the wreckage of deindustrializing cities, artists in this chapter have confronted horticultural prejudices against uncultivated and self-managed plants. As global warming endangers the supply chains and social systems of the hi-tech world of carbon capitalism, the flourishing of ruderal vegetation in harsh, human-altered environments also carries a message about the potential for decentralized and non-coercive models of climate adaptation.

Chapter 4
Plants on the Move

The nationalist and anti-globalist agendas that prevail in populist political currents have been transposed onto botanical realms, in which plants with different geographic histories get labelled as non-native or invasive and subjected to public campaigns of eradication. The notion of native purity has, however, been corroded by climate disruption that is bringing in its wake the unstoppable resettlement of species across the planet, while the ecological crisis has sharpened the critique of the subdiscipline of biology that deals with invasive species, disputing the assumption that redistributed species pose a vital threat to native flora and fauna. In an article published in *Nature* in 2011, entitled 'Don't judge the species on their origins', a community of ecologists led by Mark A. Davis demanded the abandonment of the 'native-versus-alien species dichotomy', putting forward the corrective view that such external changes to local ecosystems actually tend to increase their biodiversity. Advocates of the 'new wild' accept that responsibility for deliberate or accidental assistance in the migration of species is a consequence of social, political and economic interference with the natural world. Intervening in the entangled domains of politics, science and ecology, artists have challenged the demonization of so-called invasives. They have uncovered complex histories of their planetary journeys and engendered collaborative scenarios in which the pioneering agency of non-native plants is released to restore and revivify devastated post-industrial environments.

In *Inheritors of the Earth*, ecologist Chris D. Thomas observed that the biotic exchanges set in motion by Columbus are effectively 'reuniting the biological world' to form a 'virtual continent' or 'new Pangaea', dissolving the distinction between native and non-native plants. The history of this process was

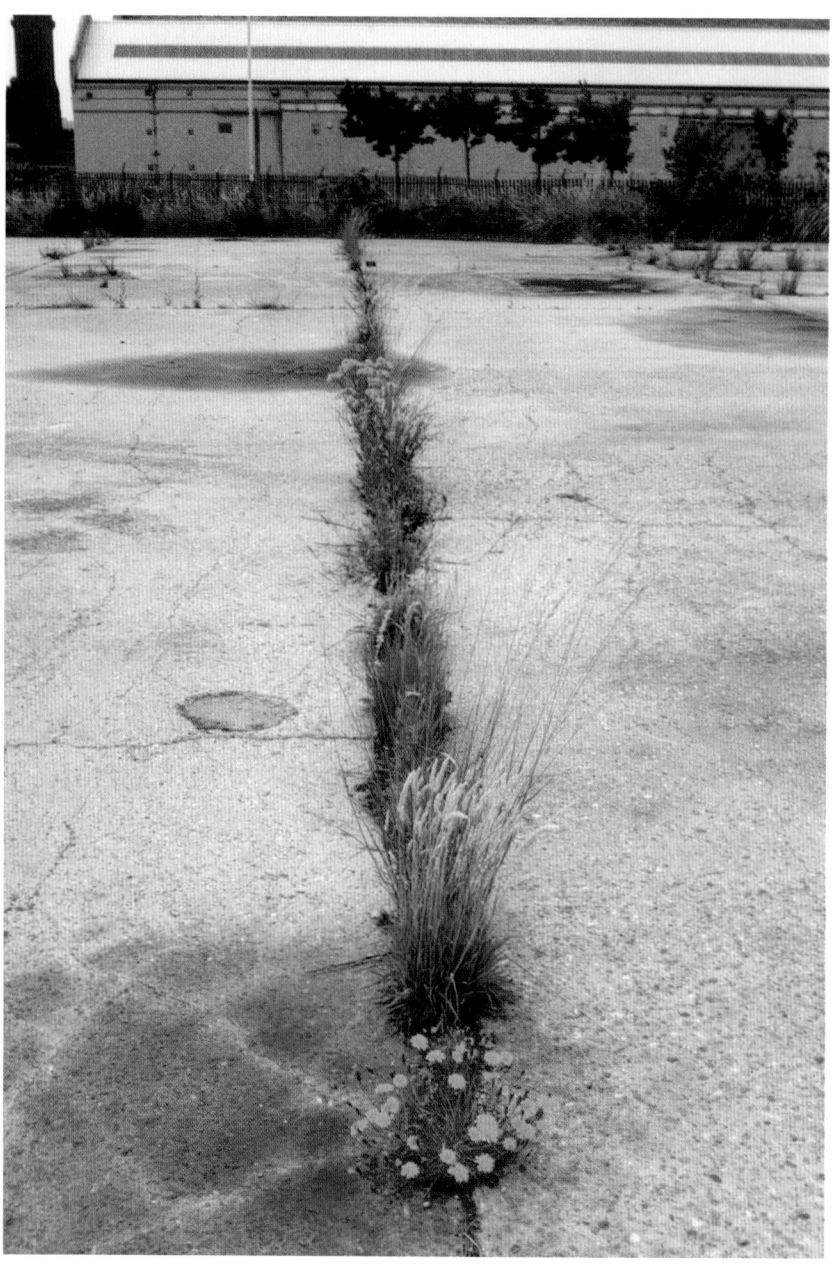

86 ABOVE Maria Thereza Alves, *Seeds of Change: Liverpool*, 2004
87 OPPOSITE Libby Harward, *Ngali ngariba*, 2019

investigated by Brazilian artist Maria Thereza Alves in her long-term project *Seeds of Change* (since 1999), which shed light on the transcontinental histories of 'ballast flora'. The artist examined the journeys of seeds hidden in the soil, sand and rocks loaded onto empty cargo ships and then unloaded on arrival in port, allowing the dormant seeds to germinate in new lands. This invisible movement of seeds was, as she discovered, closely linked to the triangular trade in enslaved Africans, since by the mid-eighteenth century slave traders found it more profitable to sail empty on the trip back from America to Europe, necessitating a full load of ballast to stop their ships capsizing. Alongside charts and archival documentation, Alves's installations have included non-native plants that sprout from seeds germinating in earth taken from local ballast sites in European port cities including Marseilles, Liverpool, Dunkirk and Bristol. Reflecting on the more-than-human temporalities of plants, which enable seeds to remain dormant for decades or even centuries before germinating, Alves raised the question of when exactly seeds become 'native' and how 'socio-political histories of place determine the framework for belonging'.

In her sound work *Ngali ngariba* (2018–19), which translates as 'we talk', Libby Harward set out to give voice to indigenous plants transported from colonial territories to European hothouses, by enabling them to pose the question 'Why am I here?' in their native languages. For example, the Australian black wattle tree asked visitors, 'Minyangu ngari gadji?' in

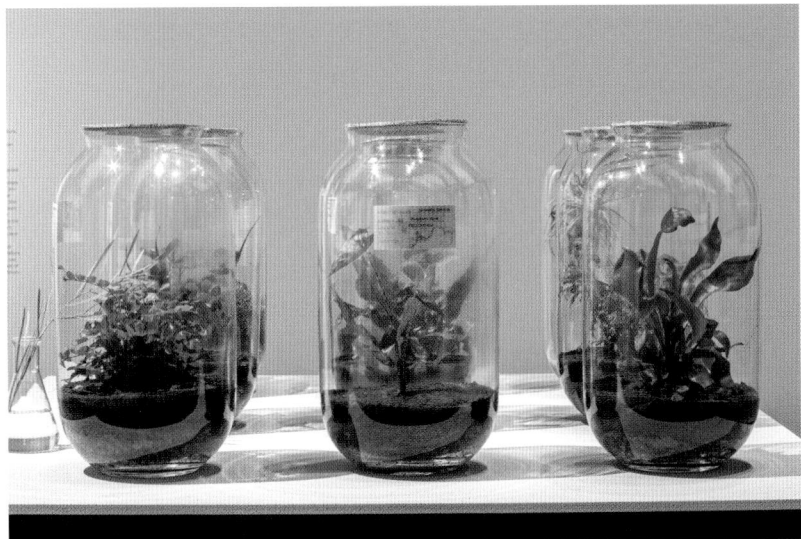

the language of the Ngugi people of the Quandamooka, from whom the artist is also descended. For her installation at the Gropius Bau Museum in Berlin in 2019, living specimens were sourced from the city's botanical gardens. The work belongs to the series *Already Occupied* (since 2017), which explores aboriginal sovereignty, contesting the founding deception of *terra nullius* that in 1770 enabled James Cook to claim Australia for the British Crown because it was empty and belonged to no one, despite the 80,000-year history of First Nations on the continent. Giving exotic plants the chance to contest their violent uprooting and relocation to serve the interlocked scientific and commercial interests of colonial powers, the work pointed to the more-than-human aspects of decolonization.

Societal attitudes towards plant species that have escaped the confines of garden environments to flourish in the wild were explored in Camilla Berner's project *The Exotic Becomes Ordinary and the Ordinary Exotic* (2019). The work was an indoor and outdoor installation for a museum in the Norwegian city of Stavanger. Outside, the artist displayed non-native plants sourced from a nearby building site that are today regarded in Norway as high-risk invasives, despite the fact that in many cases they were first introduced as exotic garden varieties. Referencing the nineteenth-century fashion for ornamental plants from distant lands, Berner grew them in a greenhouse modelled on the Wardian case, a colonial invention for the safe transport of plants on long sea voyages. Displayed nearby was a map of the world with information about the botanical origin of these feral plants. Inside the museum, Berner arranged a selection of today's exotic ornamental plants on pallets, bringing to mind their journey from intensive nurseries along global freight networks to supermarket shelves. As scientist Stefano Mancuso has noted in *The Incredible Journey of Plants*, it is above all the fact that 'the expansive thrust of life cannot be contained' that makes it impossible to keep plant species 'enclosed inside fenced-off areas, such as botanical gardens or nurseries'. In that sense, an additional question raised by the work was whether some of these newly imported non-native species might over time also make the transition from admired decorations in suburban gardens to the unruly category of dangerous invasives, while remaining biologically the same.

Taking the form of a performative reading session in two voices, Cooking Sections' work *The Next 'Invasive' is 'Native'* (2018) investigated the hysteria around the spread of Japanese knotweed in the United Kingdom. They juxtaposed alarmist media representations of the 'most invasive', 'killer', 'horror weed' with scrupulous analysis of the plant's complex natural

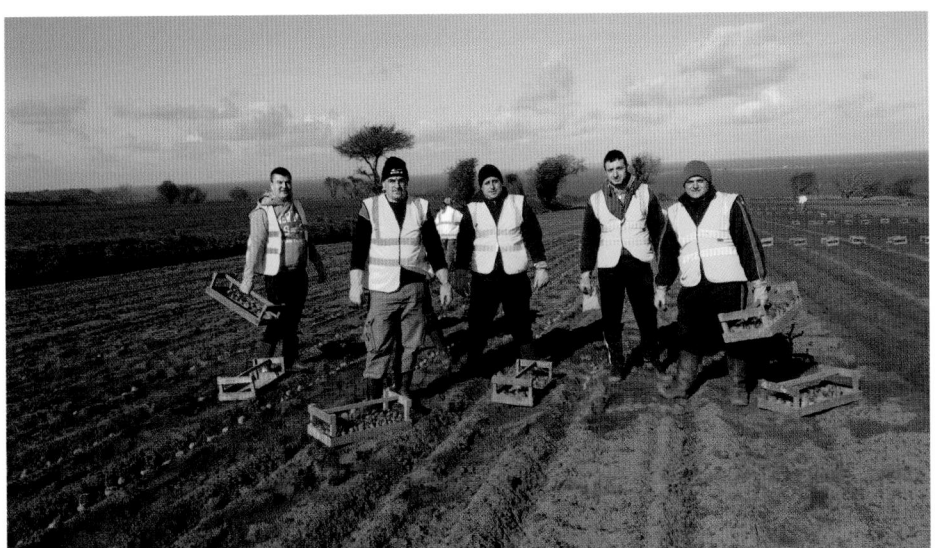

88 Alicja Rogalska, *Alien Species: Jersey Migrant Worker Archive*, 2017–18

and cultural history and its embeddedness in economic and urbanistic processes. As the lecture revealed, before Japanese knotweed began its imaginary assault on British suburbia, the plant that originally flourished on the nutrient-poor lava slopes of Japanese volcanos had been a favoured exotic addition to Victorian landscape gardens, having been introduced to the country via an unsolicited donation to the botanical collections of Kew in 1850. 'Empire redesigned the wild,' proclaimed one of the lines in the script, pointing to the artists' guiding interest in the interference of colonial legacies with the global distribution of species. The recent cultural, environmental and economic history of knotweed suggests the agency of the 'new wild' in reconfiguring landscapes degraded by colonialism and industrial development. Cooking Sections also speculated about the threshold necessary for an alien plant to become naturalized: 'Three years? Thirty years? 300 years? 3,000 years? 30,000 years?' Indicating the arbitrariness of such criteria for establishing a plant's 'degree of belonging', they determined that in the long run 'most native flora could actually be seen as "alien invaders"'.

London-based Polish artist Alicja Rogalska uncovered the contradictions in routinely applied distinctions between the notions of native and non-native, as attributed to both plants and people, in her *Alien Species: Jersey Migrant Worker Archive* (2017–18). The work's title referred to the Aliens Restriction

88

Act of 1920, which imposed strict conditions on all foreign nationals living in or visiting the island of Jersey in the English Channel, forcing them to carry 'alien cards' until the 1960s. It engaged specifically with the current wave of migrant labourers from Eastern Europe who pick Jersey's most important crop – the Royal Jersey potato, the only variety of this transatlantic newcomer to benefit from a European Union Protected Designation of Origin trademark. A complex interplay between the politics of civic and botanical classification was already indicated in an 1835 volume, *The New Botanist's Guide to the Localities of the Rarer Plants of Britain*, in which the author declared that 'species originally introduced by human agency' that presently 'exist in a wild state' now constitute 'a part of the British flora, with just as much claim as the descendants of Saxons or Normans have to be considered a part of the British nation'. First used as animal fodder, the potato was a notable vegetal protagonist in the contested histories of the 'Columbian exchange', the colonial exploitation and global transfer of people, animals and plants during the sixteenth and seventeenth centuries. The example of the Jersey Royal showed the newcomer species being fully adopted in the culture of its new territory, a gesture that has not been extended to the migrant workers who tend it.

The arbitrariness with which resettled species are adopted or rejected by populist political movements to serve their wider campaign of stoking fears about the contamination of national culture by foreign influences was elucidated in Kristóf Kelemen and Bence György Pálinkás's *Hungarian Acacia* (2017). The work took the form of a fictionalized documentary theatre piece telling the 'story of an alien species that became Hungary's most patriotic tree'. The black locust, or false acacia tree, arrived in Hungary 300 years ago from North America, first taking root in aristocratic gardens and spreading across the country to the extent that it is now widely considered to be the 'most Hungarian tree'. Notably, it was in the wake of the Second World War that the black locust began to proliferate, finding fruitful ground in ruined post-war landscapes, where it thrived as a spontaneous pioneering tree. When in 2014 the European Union discussed placing the tree on a blacklist for the 'prevention and management of the introduction and spread of invasive alien species', the Hungarian government reacted unexpectedly by leaping to the defence of the black locust. It pronounced the tree to be a Hungaricum, an official brand for entities of cultural, culinary or strategic significance to the Hungarian nation. Through choral chanting, educational slam poetry and multimedia projections, *Hungarian Acacia*

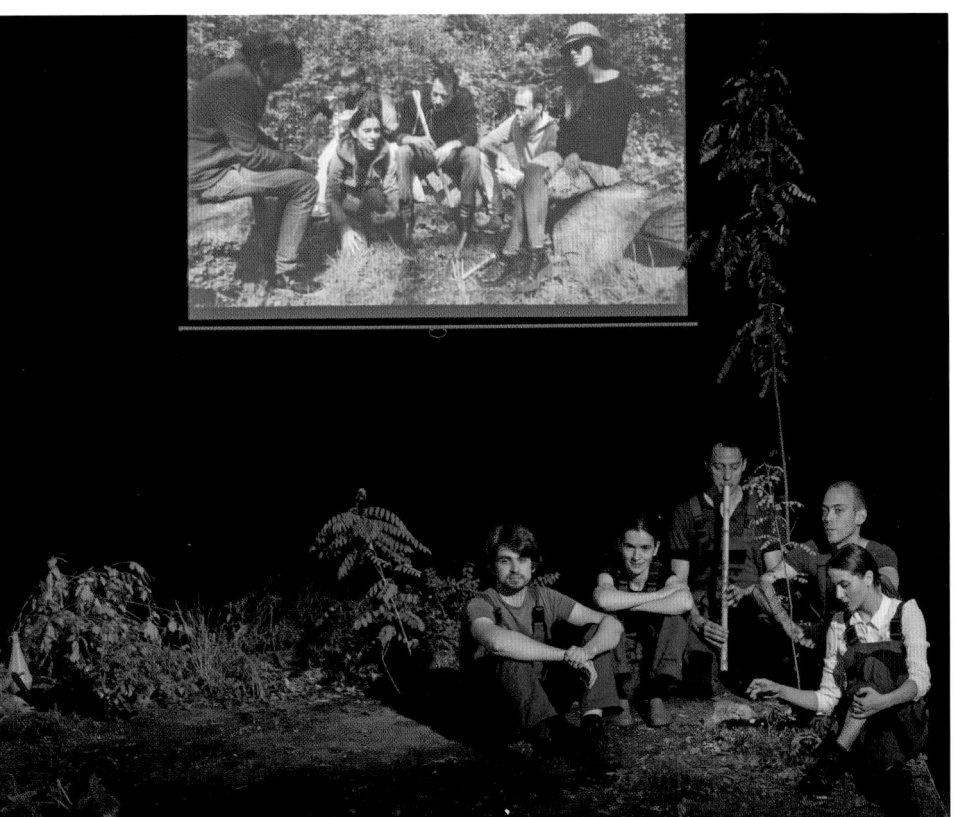

89 Kristóf Kelemen and Bence György Pálinkás, *Hungarian Acacia*, 2017

dramatized the entangled natural and human histories of the tree, concluding that if the black locust could become a Hungaricum, then 'anybody who can take root in Hungarian soil can be Hungarian'.

90   Hanna Rullmann and Faiza Ahmad Khan's film *Habitat 2190* (2019) interrogated the rationale behind building a nature reserve on the site of the former Jungle migrant camp in Calais. The camp functioned as a temporary refuge for more than 7,000 asylum seekers determined to cross the English Channel, before it was brutally cleared by French police in October 2016. The artists used interviews and archival documents to narrate how 20 centimetres of topsoil was stripped back to return the landscape to its condition seventy years before. Their work pointed to a convergence between the conservationist agenda of removing newcomer plants to restore the region's native flora and the political aim of erasing the migrant

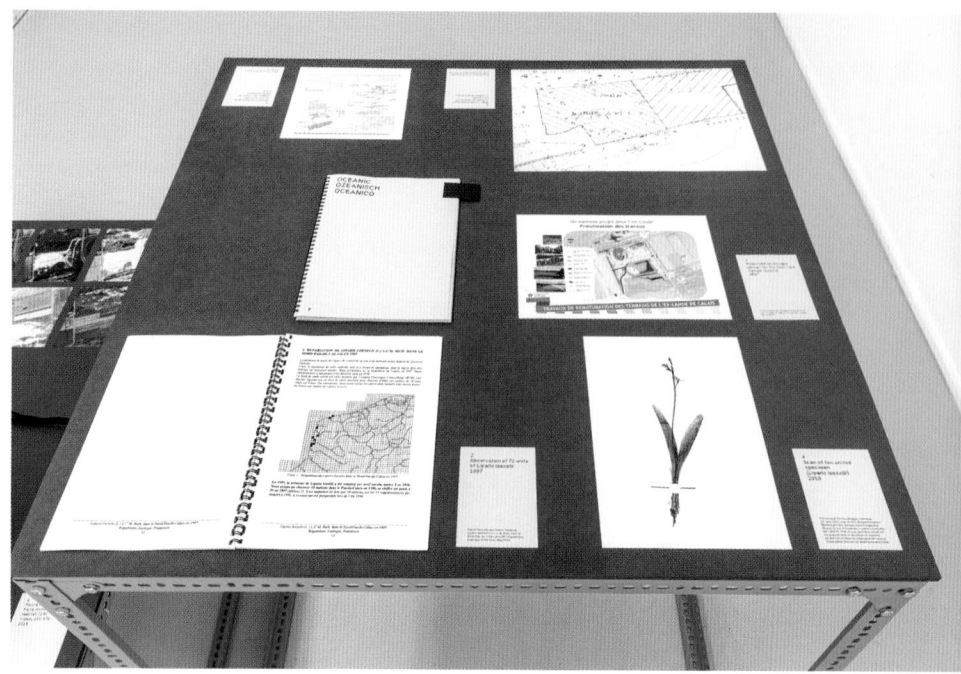

90 Hanna Rullmann and Faiza Ahmad Khan, *Habitat 2190*, 2019

presence. Indifference to human and botanical migrants can be detected in the words of a local conservationist, who states that 'after the refugees left, we found invasive species in some spots and wanted to prevent those plants from growing'. The construction of sandbanks and ditches, ostensibly to restore the topography of the landscape according to centuries-old maps, also coincided with the authorities' wish to erect anti-migrant barriers around the site. Revealing the plan to rewild this wasteland as a case of the 'weaponization of nature and conservation management' to enhance territorial security and camouflage border violence, the film pointed also to the futility of attempts to restrict the movement of people or plant species at a time of spiralling climate crisis.

Diana Lelonek's project *Seaberry Slagheap* (2018) proposed a strategy to reinvent the environment, economy and self-image of Konin in central Poland, an area scarred by the devastation of open-cast mining and afflicted by the social consequences of the rapid decline of industry during the post-communist period. Relying on the propensity of the resilient and high-yielding shrub to flourish on the bleak slagheaps, the artist designed a range of superfood products using the fruit of this non-native plant. Sea buckthorn, as it is also known, has migrated westwards from the harsh conditions of the Siberian steppes and, like many other pioneering plants, it is found on the European Union's list of alien and invasive species, because of the threat it apparently poses to the native vegetation of sand dunes. However, as Fred Pearce, author of *The New Wild*, has emphasized, the resilient and adaptive qualities of 'aliens' make them best suited to deal with 'the ecological mess humans leave behind', and they are nature's 'best chance of healing the damage done by chainsaws and ploughs, by pollution and climate change'. Pointing to the agency of pioneering plants in restoring biological processes, Lelonek advocated natural solutions to climate disaster, while by featuring the scenes of devastation on the labels of the produce, the artist also expressed awareness of the danger of art's complicity in covering up the ecological crimes of extractivism.

Encroaching planetary crisis has focused minds on the ecological benefits brought by new arrivals that reverse biodiversity loss and on the crucial work of so-called invasive species in restoring degraded landscapes. Artistic engagements with newcomer plants have considered the effects of the 'Columbian exchange' in unleashing the global intermixing of species, explored botanical perspectives on decolonization and pointed to the limits of horticultural control in the face of the dynamism and adaptability of plants. Other projects have unearthed the complex overlays of the histories of migrating plants and people, dissected the demonization of so-called invasive species and explored ways of collaborating with the plant pioneers of the new wild to model transformative ecological solutions. In the absence of concerted action to halt global warming, the planetary course is set to indiscriminately turn human and non-human Earth-dwellers into climate refugees, dissolving any residual distinction between natives and non-natives.

Chapter 5
Arboreal Worlds

One of the earliest campaigns in the history of modern environmentalism was motivated by care for trees and, significantly, was initiated by artists. In 1852 the painters of the Barbizon School, led by Théodore Rousseau, drew up a petition to Napoleon III of France to demand the Fontainebleau Forest be protected from the harvesting of wood for industrial purposes and disruption from an influx of Parisian day trippers. In response a decree was issued declaring that areas of the forest of special interest to artists should be 'left unmanaged', in other words, protected from exploitation. Since petrol-powered chainsaws replaced the felling axe, the disappearance of forest habitats has only accelerated, with biologist David George Haskell noting in his diary *The Forest Unseen* that 'logging kills many of the inhabitants of the woods, and their populations take decades, sometimes hundreds of years to recover'. The extractivist and instrumentalizing approach towards trees associated with industrial modernity stands in sharp contrast to traditional and indigenous attitudes towards forests. Indigenous ecologist Robin Wall Kimmerer notes that the 'ethic of reciprocity was cleared away along with the forests', calling in her book *Braiding Sweetgrass* for 'acts of restoration, not only for polluted waters and degraded lands, but also for our relationship to the world'. In the spirit of their nineteenth-century predecessors, contemporary artists have addressed the causes and effects of deforestation and the exposure of trees to worsening droughts and fires, drawn attention to their contested role in mitigating climate change and advocated for the revival of a culture of care and respect for interconnected arboreal worlds.

Anca Benera and Arnold Estefan's black-and-white film *No Shelter from the Storm* (2015) depicted two lonely figures traversing a mountainous terrain of scarred woodland while whistling the mournful melody of the popular American anti-war song 'Where Have All the Flowers Gone?'. The particular poignancy of the tune derived from the fact that the lyrics originated in a pre-war Ukrainian Cossack folksong and the footage was shot on the borderlands between Romania and Ukraine during a time of recent armed conflict on the territory of the post-Soviet country. Through the sound of distant chainsaws the work also directed attention to the current wave of extreme deforestation in these Carpathian woodlands, where allegedly a timber mafia funnels illegally cut trees from old wood forests into the supply chain of the world's biggest furniture company. In the film the poetic melody reverberating across ravaged hillsides crystallizes the sobering insight that, while in the past forests provided refuge in times of need, today they only stand as reminders, as the artists put it, of the 'human condition of our age'. Recalling ancient laws according to which the uprooting of trees was 'a declaration of total war without a chance for reconciliation', Michael Marder has emphasized the function of trees in providing shelter in times of need and pointed to the severity of uprooting communities who are 'prevented from seeking meaning and refuge (even) in the vegetal world'. The assault on forest, made possible by opportunistic alliances between extractive capitalist and oligarchic political interests, is transforming landscapes, ecosystems and communities, leaving no place to shelter from the planetary peril of climate change.

 The vulnerability of the Mata Atlântica, the green corridor that hugs Brazil's Atlantic coast, to deforestation and development was addressed in Rio-based Catalan artist Daniel Steegmann Mangrané's installation *Living Thoughts* (2019). The work consisted of dozens of hand-blown glass containers shaped like branches suspended in mid-air and dispersed in the exhibition space, with orchids, ferns, cactuses, mosses and bromeliads growing out of the transparent trunks. One of the most biodiverse environments on Earth and home to more than 8,000 endemic plant species, the forest has already been reduced to seven per cent of its original area through the spread of intensive agriculture and the growth of the megacities of São Paulo and Rio de Janeiro, while transferring the responsibility for care of indigenous lands to the Ministry of Agriculture has signalled the loosening of already meagre measures of environmental protection. Steegmann Mangrané brought into focus the resilience and adaptability of epiphytic plants, which derive nutrients and moisture from the atmosphere rather than the soil and are helped by fellow forest beings to find a niche among the branches. More vividly still, through the absence of the support trees on which epiphytes depend, he drew attention to the precariousness of dense forest ecosystems that are dematerializing before our eyes, leaving behind a fragmentary patchwork of isolated botanical specimens.

Amar Kanwar's *The Sovereign Forest* addressed conflicts between local communities, government and corporations over the control of agricultural lands, forests, rivers and mineral resources in the Indian state of Odisha, which have accelerated in the era of neo-liberal globalization. The centrepiece of the work is *The Scene of Crime* (2011), a forty-two-minute film composed of short sequences shot in territories acquired by the state government and mining corporations for industrial sites. In the artist's words, it offers 'an experience of landscape just prior to erasure', since 'every location, every blade of grass, every water source, every tree' is slated to disappear. An atmosphere of menace hangs over the slowly changing footage of depopulated rural landscapes, in which plant species, river sources and micro-geographies are named and recorded as evidence. Due to the fact that the region has the largest accessible reserves of bauxite in the world, international steel

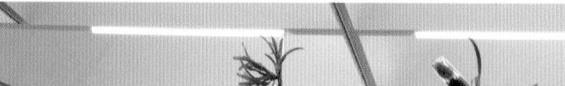

91 Daniel Steegmann Mangrané, *Living Thoughts*, 2019

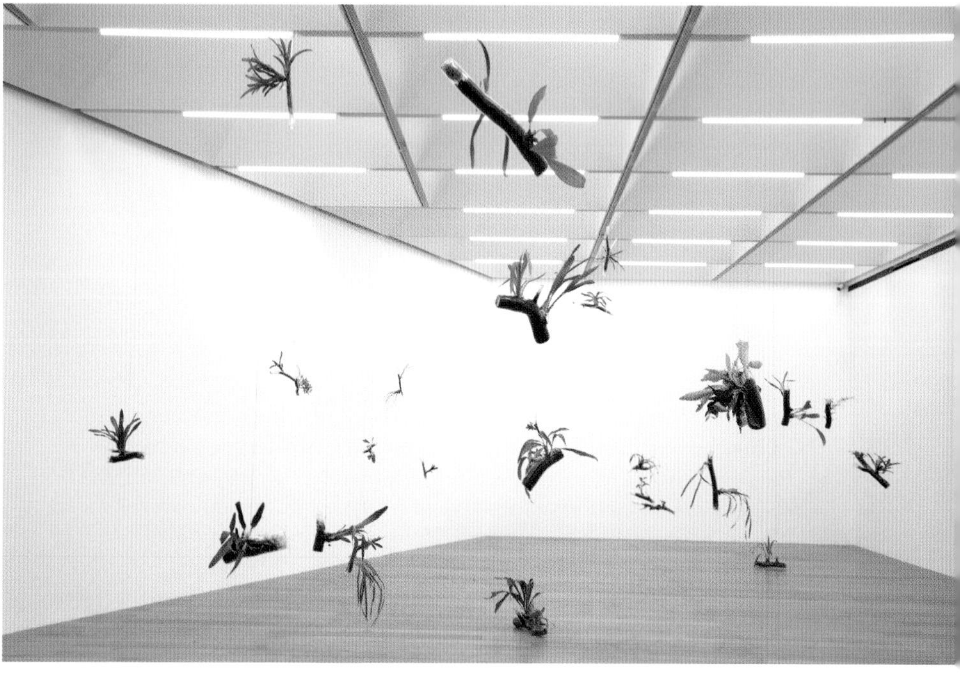

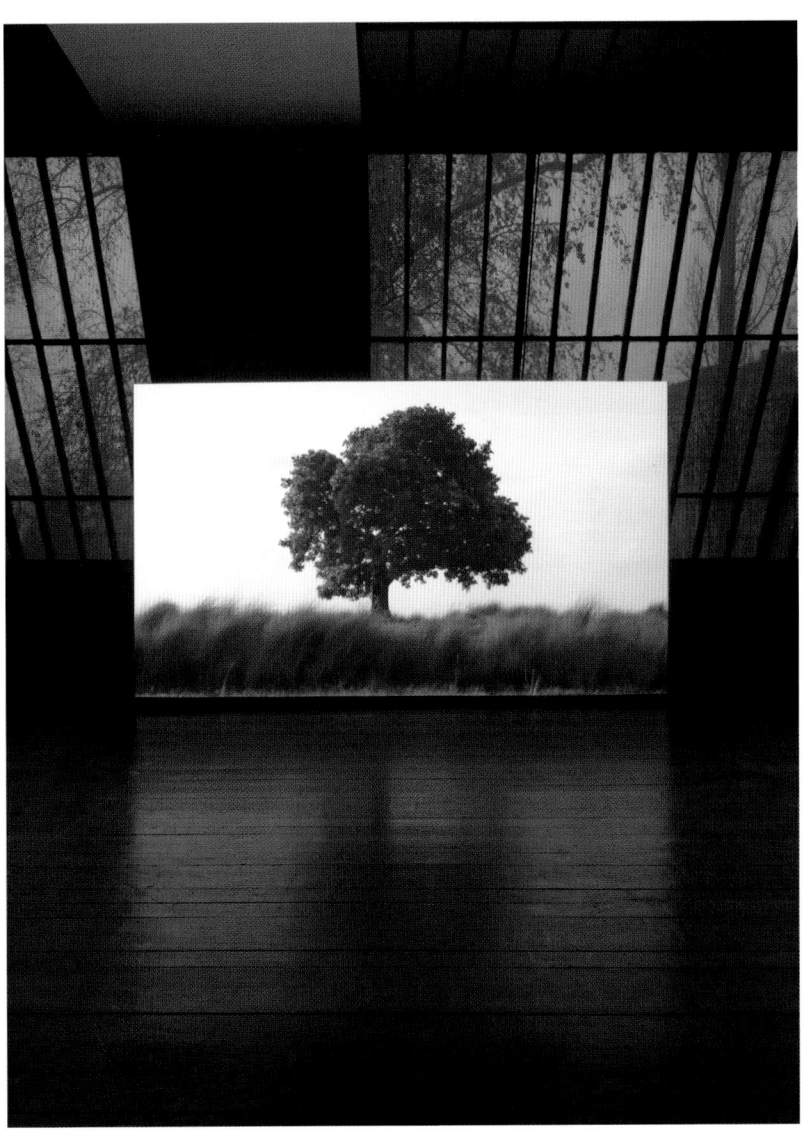

92 Amar Kanwar, *The Scene of Crime,* 2011

Arboreal Worlds

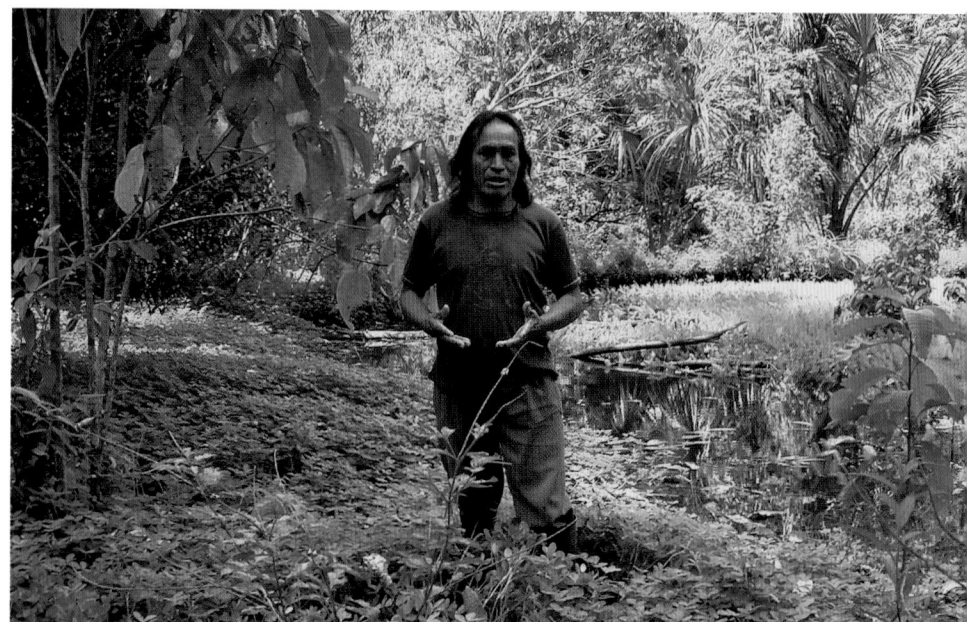

93 Ursula Biemann and Paulo Tavares, *Forest Law*, 2014

corporations have adopted a long-term strategy, factoring into their calculations the delays caused by community resistance and the time required to cultivate amenable politicians and corrupt local bureaucracies. The threat to the sovereignty of the forest can therefore be considered, as Kanwar revealed, a premeditated crime.

    A close reading of *The Natural Contract* by French philosopher Michel Serres, the declaration on the Rights of Nature in chapter seven of the Ecuadorian Constitution (2008) and the legal cases of forest rights brought by the indigenous people of the Ecuadorian Amazon are all intertwined in the installation *Forest Law* (2014) by Ursula Biemann and Paulo Tavares. Among the protagonists speaking to camera in the two-channel video work was the leader of the Sarayaku people, who gave an account of collective actions to protect the forest from the incursions of extractivist industry. These included establishing peace camps and using the recent expansion of planetary jurisprudence to encompass the rights of nature to challenge the activities of mining companies in international courts. Legal disputes over the burying of explosives in a part of the forest viewed by the authorities as 'empty', but which for the Sarayaku is a sacred zone reserved for the repopulation of

93

animal species, represent an irreconcilable clash between the capitalist mentality and indigenous understanding of the living forest. In the face of concerted attempts by corporate capital and state power to exploit the oil, mineral and timber wealth of the forest, the film drew attention to the struggles of the Sarayaku people in defending their ancestral territories and arboreal worlds.

The indifference of the constructors of modernist infrastructures to the living organisms and natural entities obstructing their path of economic growth and technological progress was at issue in Hungarian artist Kitti Gosztola's series of ink drawings *Right Tree Right Place* (2013–14).

94

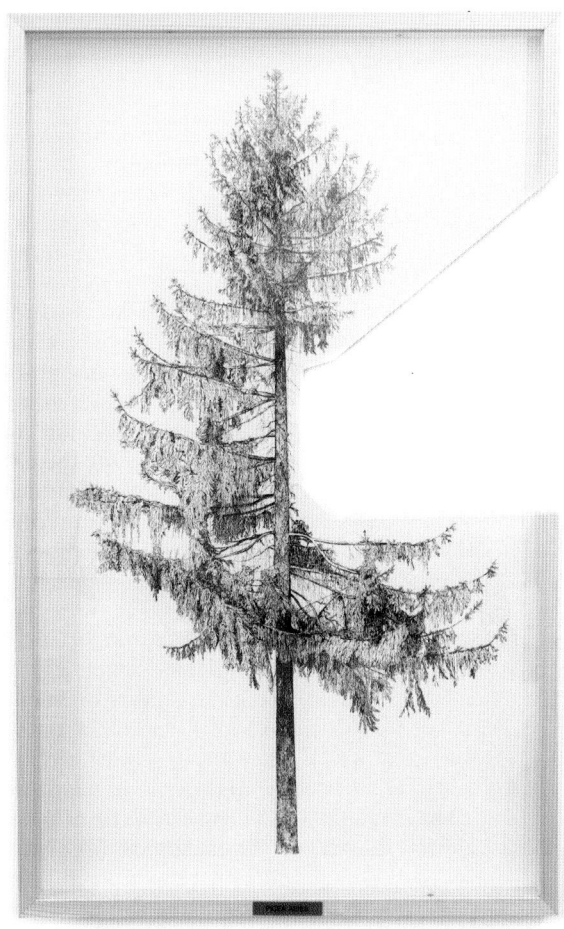

94 Kitti Gosztola,
Picea abies, 2013

The title of the work derived from a headline on the website of an energy company, posted in a section about what kind of trees should be planted underneath electricity cables. Showing what happens when trees find themselves in the 'wrong place', the artist depicted specimens that have had large parts of their canopy surgically removed because they block power lines, roads and other urban infrastructure. Gosztola's series of mutilated tree portraits are framed in a way to repeat the geometric shape of the brutal cut, using the same wood as the specific tree, with a small brass plaque indicating its Latin name. The irregular framing tangibly amplifies the sense of woundedness, with the artist cautioning that this is not merely 'an aesthetic issue', since the intervention almost always 'leads to the slow death of the tree'.

Taking as a case study the management of trees in New York City, Cooking Sections' performative lecture and exhibition project *Offsetted* (2019) questioned the logic of 'environmental gentrification' and the economic interests embedded in this 'urban forest'. Referring to the 2017 New York Street Tree Map, which counted 678,183 specimens growing in the city, the artists disclosed that the underlying reason for this cartographic undertaking was 'to provide tools for the developers'. Namely, by using a Tree Carbon Calculator, the authorities were able to estimate each tree's capacity for stormwater interception, air pollution removal and CO_2 reduction, and therefore put a price tag on them, so that developers or industrialists who are obliged to mitigate their environmental damage can pay to offset the harmful effect of their activities. In that way the trees have become 'objects of transaction', with an estimated value of $109,625,536.06, which means the city management could actually benefit from environmental destruction. By drawing attention to the transformation of trees into tradable assets while unsustainable economic practices continue uninterruptedly and the systematic causes of climate change are ignored, Cooking Sections raised the question of the de-financialization of the environment and the right of trees not to serve as carbon offsets.

Further complicating the picture of trees as oxygen producers and carbon sinks, Latvian artists Rasa Smite and Raitis Smits drew attention in *Atmospheric Forest* (2020) to the fact that trees breathe and therefore also emit carbon dioxide. Carbon is also released back into the atmosphere when trees die through drought, forest fires or accelerating biological processes, which underpins the journal *Nature*'s announcement on its cover in March 2020 that 'the ability of tropical forests to sequester CO_2 is in decline'. Smite and Smits's

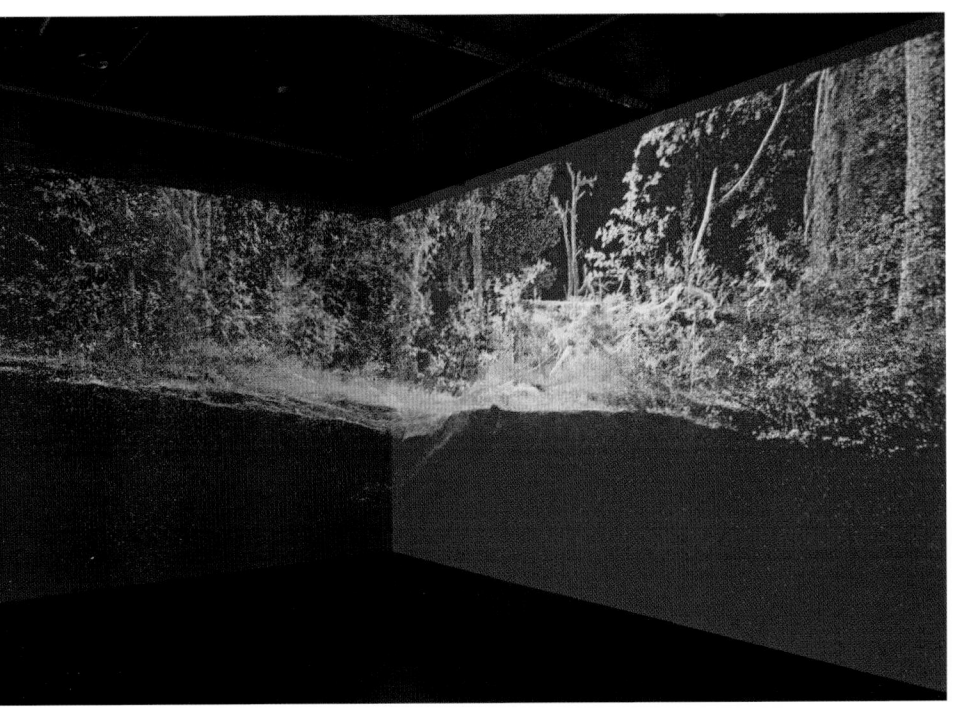

95 Rasa Smite and Raitis Smits, *Atmospheric Forest,* 2020

multimedia installation visualized and sonified findings about the relationship between forest and climate, based on the research they conducted in Pfynwald, an ancient Swiss Alpine forest, where they analysed the effects of drought on weather conditions in the valley. Evidence about the interaction between climatic conditions and pine-tree emissions suggested specifically that stressful situations, such as extended dry spells, influence the production of resin and trigger the release of volatile organic compounds that are responsible for the characteristic scent of the forest. By visualizing the data collected from observations of pine trees during one growing season, the artists revealed the connection between environmental factors and arboreal physiology, showing that with climate change the forests are likely to turn more fragrant in the future.

The challenges posed by climate chaos defy narrowly technocratic approaches that instrumentalize trees as climate sinks, requiring instead a change in societal attitude to arboreal beings that involves looking also to indigenous knowledge and practices of forest life. The forest drawings

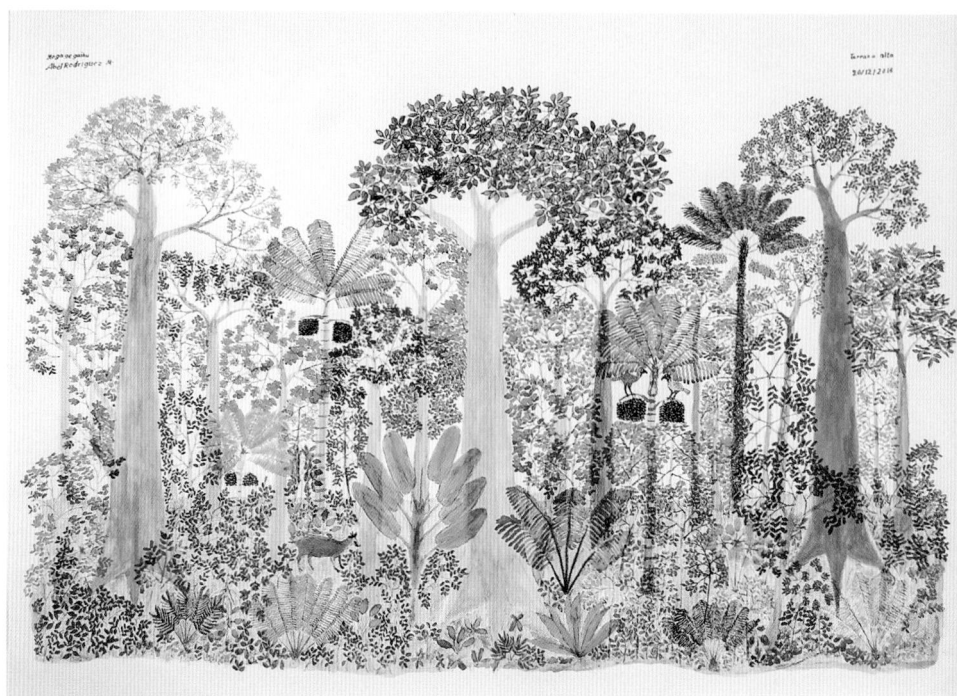

96　Abel Rodríguez, *Terraza Alta III*, 2018

of Mogaje Guihu, who westernized his name to Abel Rodríguez
after being forced by armed struggle to flee to Bogotá from
his ancestral lands in the Colombian Amazon, depict the
rainforest as a biodiverse and interconnected world thriving
with life. In contrast to the botanical illustrations made by
colonial explorers, whose scientific categorization paved the
way for economic exploitation, Guihu made his drawings from
memory. In works such as *Terraza Alta III* (2018), he represents
the forest from the inside, drawing on long years of learning its
ways and botanical knowledge acquired through oral tradition.
Dual annotations in both his native Muinane language and
Spanish record the sensuous complexity of the indigenous
relationship to forest plants, which fulfil a multiplicity of roles
by providing nourishment and materials for clothing and
homebuilding, as well as being used for healing and in spiritual
rituals. As anthropologist Eduardo Kohn put it in *How Forests
Think*, getting food in the forest 'involves people intimately
with one of the most complex ecosystems in the world – one
that is chock-full of an astounding array of different kinds
of interacting and mutually constituting beings'. By sharing

96

such forest knowledge with non-indigenous people, the artist confronted the extractivist attitudes to the natural world codified in scientific botany, while making visible the chains of mutual reliance on which planetary wellbeing depends.

It is becoming increasingly clear that the biogeochemical dynamism of forests unleashed by breaking the ecological contract has made them unpredictable participants in the drama of climate change. Ruthless deforestation, short-sighted profiteering and the financialization of the climate crisis have been addressed by the artists discussed in this chapter, who highlight the endangerment of our common terrestrial home. They also explore the tension between the environmental protection of trees through an expanded planetary jurisprudence and the opportunism of state and commercial actors. As the artists have shown, moving towards ecological transformation entails reawakening the sense of connection with urban trees and forest worlds and rekindling attentive and reciprocal relations to silvine beings.

Part IV
Animal Solidarities

97 Revital Cohen and Tuur Van
Balen, *Leopard, Impala*, 2016

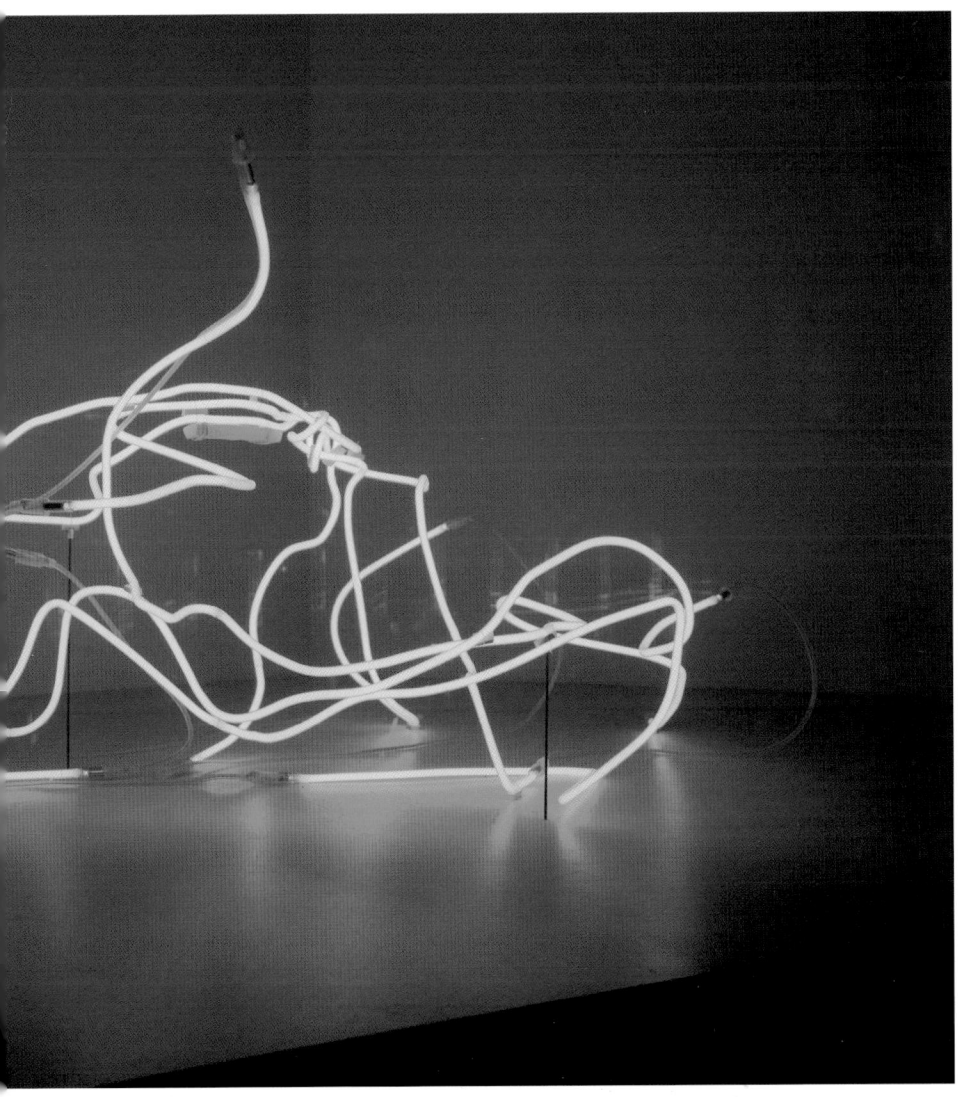

Chapter 1
Animals in the Museum

Natural history museums have from the outset seen their
mission as to promote scientific research and public knowledge
of the natural world, however the climate emergency, a
reckoning with the legacies of slavery and colonialism and
changing attitudes to non-human species are bringing a radical
reassessment of their role. In the mid-eighteenth century, when
London's Natural History Museum was established under the
mantle of the British Museum, 'nature and culture became
organised into distinct, independent realms', as museologist
Fiona Cameron has pointed out, noting also that many such
institutions have continued to 'support the notion of a
human-centred world, a separate "given" nature and
constructed culture'. Significantly, these two institutions,
established in the era of the British Empire, were founded on
the donated collection of books and artefacts, but also plants,
animals, shells and rocks, amassed by Irish physician and
colonialist Sir Hans Sloane from the profits of slavery. The
opening in 1793 of the Museum of Natural History in Paris
heralded the modern practice of stuffing animals for display or
taxidermy, a term derived from the Greek words for arrangement
and skin. More than a century later, the monumental dioramas
of taxidermized elephants, lions and gorillas in the Africa
Hall of the American Museum of Natural History in New
York reflected not just the benign aims of preservation and
education, but also, as Donna Haraway has detected, the
influence of eugenic theories of racial purity and the social and
gender hierarchies of 'white and male supremacist monopoly
capitalism'. For artists, natural history collections are urgent
sites for critical reconsideration and decolonial thinking in light
of their troubling pasts and the unfolding ecological crisis of
climate change and mass extinction.

97   In their work *Leopard, Impala* (2016), Revital Cohen and
Tuur Van Balen investigated the legacy of the Royal Museum
for Central Africa in Tervuren, Belgium, which was opened in
1898 as the Museum of Congo by King Leopold II, infamous
for his brutal and exploitative colonial rule. Describing the
exhibition in which tropical taxidermized animals were placed
'next to statues of naked African children', the artists claimed
that the display 'still shapes how many Belgians imagine both
Congo and the whole African continent'. Their intervention
into the collection entailed taking the preserved animals
to a local hospital and making an X-ray scan in order to
reveal the steel structure within them, exposing the artificial
construction of natural history as a site of cultural practice.
In particular, they drew attention to the taxidermist's
inventive handling of animal skins to create an imagined
hunting diorama of a leopard attacking an impala. Referring
to the lifelines in cave depictions of animals by prehistoric
hunters, they recreated the X-ray lines in neon tubes that
are coated in rare earth metals, as a further reference to the
extractivist operations of colonial histories. Investigating
the intersection of blackness and animality in her book *Afro-
Dog: Blackness and the Animal Question*, Bénédicte Boisseron
has postulated that they share the status of 'nonhuman
and nonwhite', asserting further that it is necessary 'to first
acknowledge and embrace the inextricable compoundedness
of race and animality in order to then defiantly inhabit or
transcend it'.

98   In one of the five vitrines of his installation *Measure and
Control* (2013), Paris-based artist Kader Attia assembled an
unsettling museum exhibit consisting of a taxidermized
cheetah standing on a plinth beside an African tribal mask and
a photograph of a middle-aged white man holding a cheetah
cub in his lap. The work set up a contrast between Western
practices of displaying the stuffed bodies of exoticized wild
animals as hunting trophies to demonstrate the mastery of
white civilization over colonized nature and African customs
of making animal masks that channel the spirit of their non-
human subjects without capturing or killing them. The framed
photograph, in which a white saviour caresses what we imagine
to be the cheetah's orphaned young, is suggestive of zoo
captivity as a further instrument in the shaping of colonialist
interactions with non-Western cultures and non-human
animals. The specimens and objects carefully juxtaposed in
the other four museum display cases, including monkeys, birds,
insects, ethnographic artefacts and a telescope, bring into
focus the role of natural history and ethnographic museums

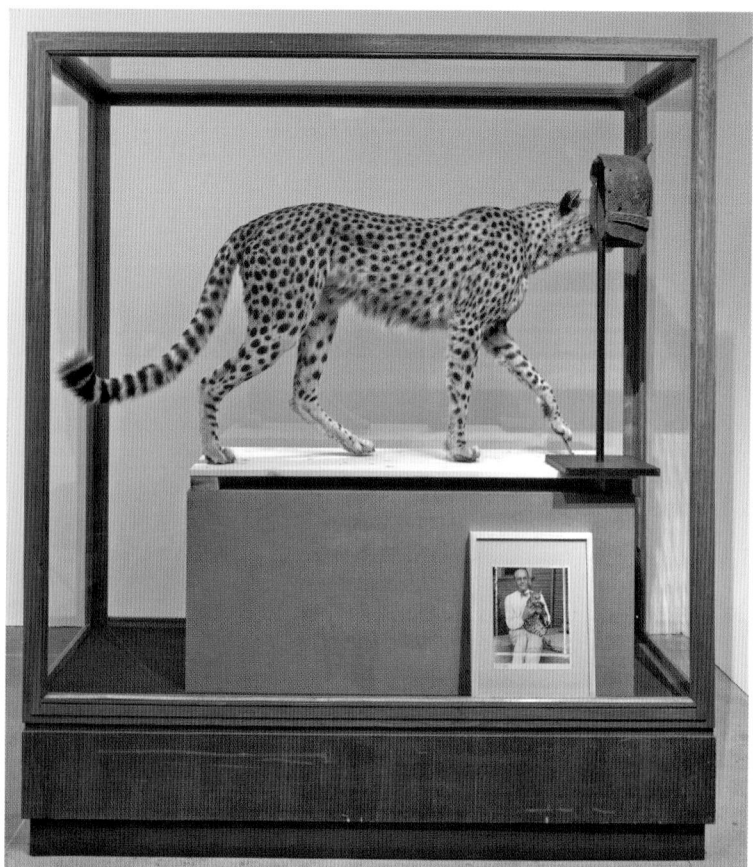

98 Kader Attia, *Measure and Control*, 2013

in articulating the monolithic logic of Western universalism and silencing the polyvalent knowledges of other terrestrials.

Petrit Halilaj's installation *Poisoned by men in need of some love* (2013) juxtaposed the tiers of political and natural histories of his native Kosovo narrated through the fate of the taxidermy collection in the capital Pristina's Natural History Museum. The collection of more than 1,800 specimens of local fauna, including owls, brown bears, otters, lynx and carp, was built up over two decades after the museum was founded in 1951, coinciding with the height of power of Yugoslavia's lifelong president Tito. Following the disintegration of Yugoslavia and the war in Kosovo in the 1990s, the collection was removed from the permanent display, making space for an apparently timelier ethnographic exhibition of folk traditions, while the

stuffed animals were walled up in hidden rooms. The fact that
the artist's own youthful life was also turned upside down by
the ethnic conflict at home and the experience of dislocation
as a refugee in Albania and Italy gave another layer of context
to the work. Having managed to secure access to the sealed-off
museum storage, Halilaj watched as the boxes of the taxidermy
collection were opened, secretly filming the poorly conserved
specimens to reveal mould growing on the animals' fur. Apart
from the films, the installation consisted of sculptures of
the found species that the artist remade using a mixture of
mud and animal excrement, symbolically communicating his
disagreement with the changing ideologies that have marked
the human and non-human worlds.

It was against the backdrop of another period of political
upheaval during the French Revolution that two elephants
named Hans and Parkie were captured and brought to the
Museum of Natural History in Paris. A couple of months later,
in May 1798, musicians performed a live concert for them in
the Jardin des plantes, to probe whether human music would
provoke a reaction in animals. In their film *Apotomē* (2013), the
Puerto Rico-based artist duo Jennifer Allora and Guillermo
Calzadilla revisited this singular episode from a period when
'the concepts of man, life and nature and the boundaries
between them' were reassessed in relation to 'war, captivity,
slavery, and other forms of social and political domination'.
Set in the subterranean storage of the Zooteque, where
thousands of taxidermized animals and the bones of the
two elephants are kept, the film follows vocalist Tim Storms,
known for having the world's deepest voice, as he sings
the music of the original concert to the elephant remains.
The insight of the Enlightenment musicians has been
confirmed by modern science, with Frans de Waal pointing
out in *Are We Smart Enough to Know how Smart Animals Are?*
that 'the elephant's Umwelt is largely acoustic and olfactory',
while their ability to hear 'far below human hearing range'
enables them to communicate across the longer distances
that infrasound travels. In *Apotomē*, the artists relied on the
singer's unique low vocal range, inaudible to humans but
sensed by elephants, as a nonrepresentational gesture
towards intra-species communication, while confronting
untenable assumptions about human superiority and
exceptionalism embedded in the praxis of institutions like
the Zooteque.

Observing that although the world is inhabited by numerous
species, history has always been written from the 'perspective
of a small minority, humans', writer Laura Gustafsson and

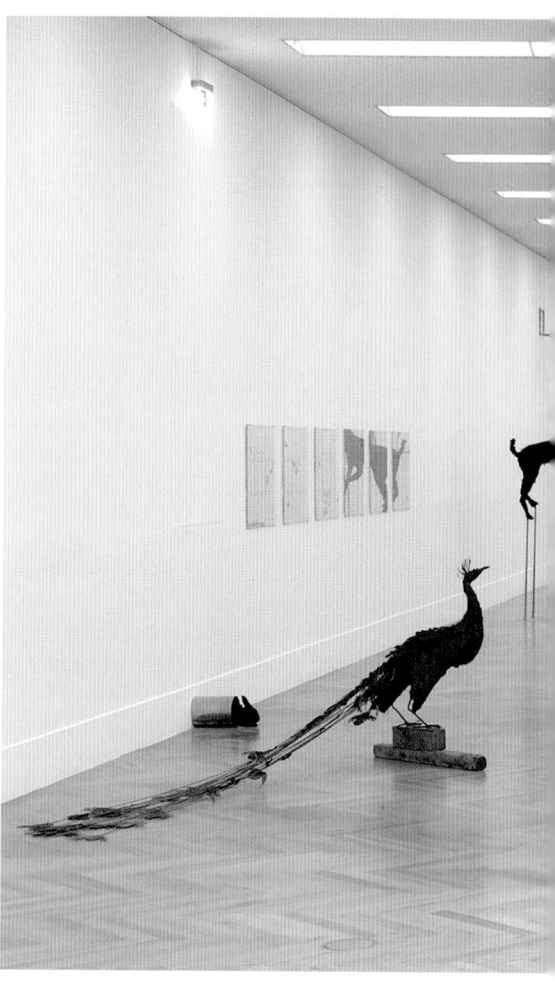

99 Petrit Halilaj, *Poisoned by men in need of some love*, 2013

artist Terike Haapoja collaborated to create the first museum for a 'non-human form of life'. The installation of *The Museum of the History of Cattle* (2013) divided this animal history into three periods: the semi-mythical era of the great Auroch, when the prehistorical ancestors of the cow roamed freely over Eurasian grasslands; the historical era of the Holocene during which 'human culture was revolutionised thanks to the bovine contribution in work'; and an ahistorical present of 'collective isolation' of cows in factory farms. The display also traced the parallels between the racist application of the Darwinian concept of natural selection to humans through eugenics and the development of selective breeding

100

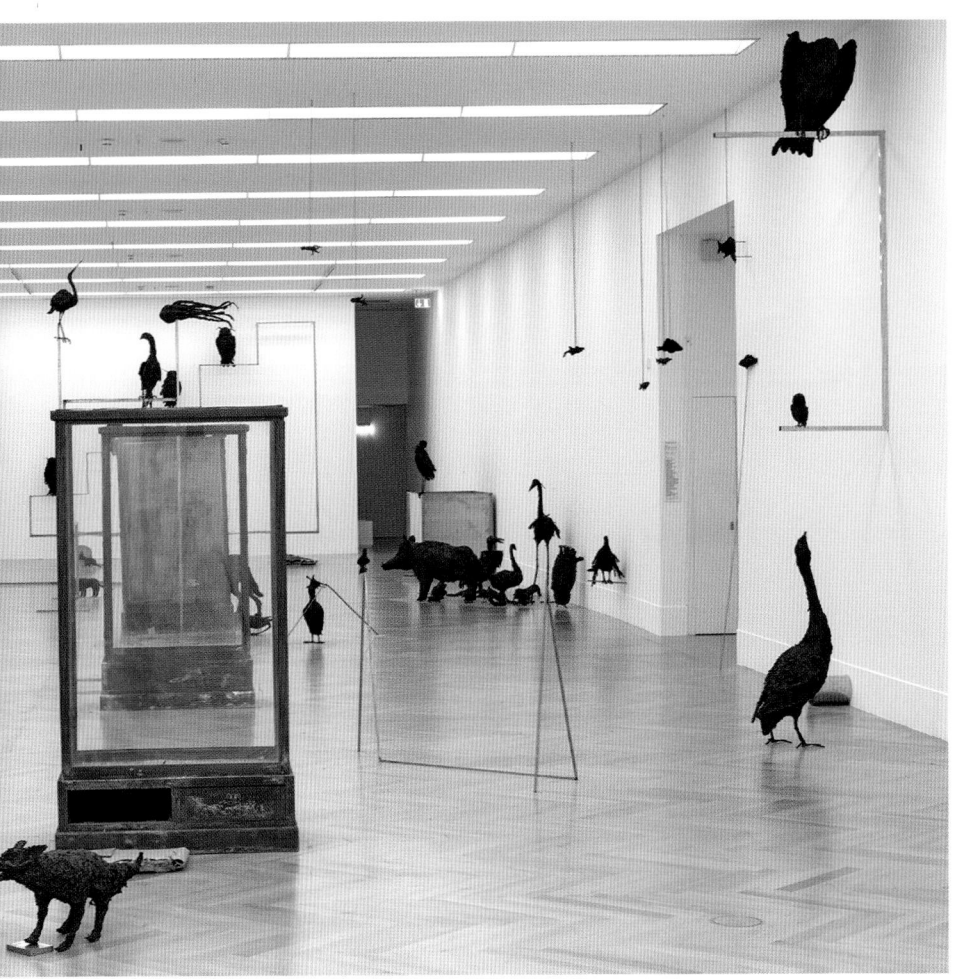

practices for cattle. Visitors could learn, for example, that while the eugenic 'breeding of humans' was outlawed after the Second World War, 'animals of other species' were excluded from the protection of the UN Declaration on Human Rights of 1948, with the consequence that their 'breeding, forced sterilisations, regulation of birth rates, and so forth are still allowed'. By articulating the history of cattle on their behalf, the museum reframed anthropocentric narratives and made visible the connections between the oppression of humans and the exploitation of other species.

London-based artist Sonia Levy's interest in 'new paradigms for multispecies living, environmental conservation and

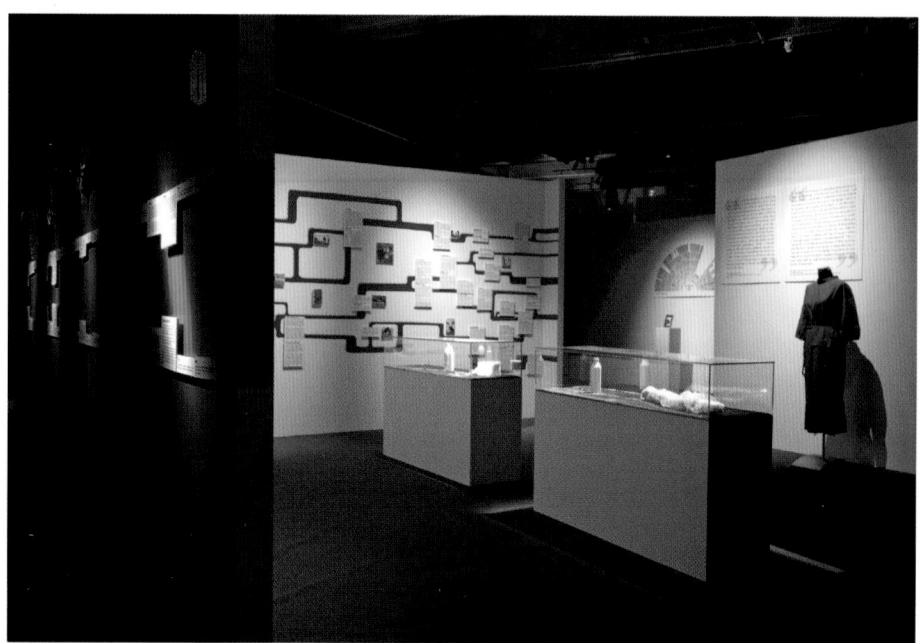

100 Gustafsson&Haapoja, *The Museum of the History of Cattle*, 2013

natural history that are emerging in the wake of the New
Climatic Regime', as theorist Bruno Latour has termed the
unfolding effects of the current ecological transformation,
101   was the motivation for her project *For the Love of Corals* (2018).
Conceived as a cinematic inquiry, the work followed for a
year a team of marine biologists breeding corals in captivity
at the Horniman Museum and Gardens in London. In special
tanks in the museum's basement, they have recreated the
optimal climatic conditions for corals, simulating those of
the Great Barrier Reef, including the effects of the lunar cycle.
Corals are marine invertebrates that live in close colonies
inseparable from their environment, while the reefs they build
for themselves and other species are bleached by warming
oceans as a devastating result of climate change. The marine
biologists' programme to grow corals in vitro is indicative
of the new roles opening up for natural history museums
in regeneration programmes and preserving species from
extinction. For the artist, the scientists in her film also form
a new multispecies assemblage with the corals, since through
the coral 'intensive care unit' they also 'become entangled
in sharing a space for living, working and world-making,
expanding the range of possible worlds in common'.

The founding of the travelling pop-up *Natural History Museum* in 2014 by the US artist collective Not An Alternative was an attempt to institute non-exploitative, anti-extractivist and decolonial practices of representing more-than-human species. Drawing on the confluence of contemporary scientific and indigenous approaches to ecological crisis, this mobile museum acts as a platform to realize exhibitions and public programmes that investigate the natural world from an activist and environmental justice perspective. While stationary museums have tried to hide their connections to extractivism and colonialism by cloaking themselves in the 'innocence of political neutrality', as founding member Steve Lyons put it in *Museum Activism*, this critical initiative makes visible their historical responsibility in collecting and displaying plundered objects. An exhibition realized in collaboration with the Lummi Nation in 2018 centred on a carved whale totem designed to raise awareness of the plight of the killer whale or orca, a species they revere as 'our people that live under the sea', but which is now endangered by the disappearance of the salmon on which it feeds and the toxic pollution of the ocean. By acknowledging the leadership of Native Nations in confronting climate emergency and revealing its systemic roots in the

102

101 Sonia Levy, *For the Love of Corals*, 2018

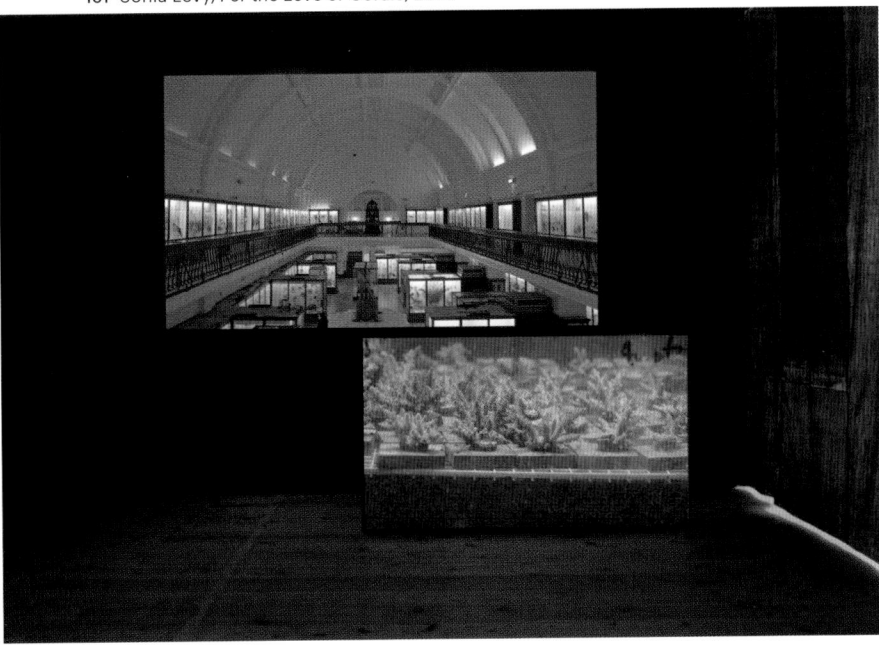

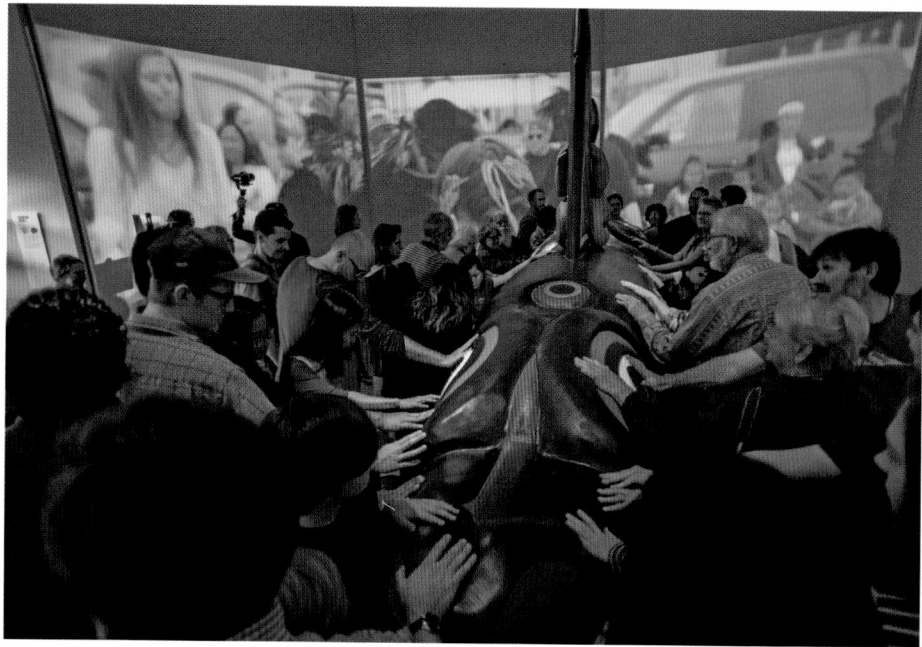

102 A totem pole blessing ceremony led by members of the Lummi Nation
at the opening of 'Whale People: Protectors of the Sea', 2018

extractivist economy, *The Natural History Museum* advocates
for a radical and transformative approach to museological
representation at a time of ecological crisis.

The accession of animal specimens into the collections of
national museums of natural history was from the outset bound
up with the violence of colonialism, as the art practices discussed
in this chapter reveal. Discriminatory attitudes towards the
non-human species objectified in exhibition dioramas went hand
in hand with the perpetuation of an ideology of racial supremacy
that sought to justify imperialist domination, while the decision
to display or hide from view collections of taxidermized animals
has also followed changing political winds. Dismantling the
edifice of the traditional natural history museum, artists have
explored the potential of non-anthropocentric natural histories
to reveal the dynamic and in recent times increasingly fraught
relationship between humans and animals. Updating these
institutions for a time of climate emergency, they have advocated
abandoning the pretence of scientific disinterestedness to
actively side with endangered species in their struggle against
anthropogenic extinction and decolonizing the museum in
the name of the excluded.

Chapter 2
Non-Human Persons

The antagonistic attitude towards non-humans in Western worldviews was contrasted by anthropologist Philippe Descola in *Beyond Nature and Culture* with the capaciousness of indigenous cosmologies that 'treat certain elements in the environment as persons endowed with cognitive, moral and social qualities analogous to those of humans'. Descola also referred to the Amazonian fieldwork of Eduardo Viveiros de Castro investigating the multi-perspectivism of the animist way of being in the world, which recognizes the similarity of all sentient beings, whether human or animal, in having a subjective sense of personhood, while acknowledging the multiplicity of different lifeforms. The seventeenth-century naturalists' tendency to relegate animals to an inferior category in the speciesist hierarchy, reserving for humans – and among them generally white European colonizers – the exceptional ability to express emotions, feel pain, make relationships and take decisions, prepared the ground for the intensive exploitation of non-humans in the modern capitalist era. In factory farms, as described in Alex Blanchette's book *Porkopolis*, animals have been subjected to a regime of total control designed to extract every last sliver of profit from industrialized animal bodies. The space for autonomous non-human life has shrunk further with the spread of surveillance technology, while accelerating environmental destruction and the destabilizing of Earth systems are dramatically affecting wild animals. Campaigns for the restoration of dignity to non-human persons have looked to the expansion of legal protections and animal rights, while also recognizing that to be effective these must be accompanied by wide-ranging measures such as the deindustrialization of agriculture and the restoration of habitats, along with the revival of human–animal relations based on compassion, kinship and care.

'The more species uploaded, the less species in the world' is how Dutch artist Melanie Bonajo summarized the momentous transformation of the 'physical animal kingdom into a virtual, imaginary, symbolic realm'. Her long-term research project into the online proliferation of images of animals investigated how the internet has altered the way animals are perceived, posing the question of what kind of analysis would emerge if uploaded images and videos of non-human animals were to be interpreted. Her publication *Non-Human Persons* (2015) catalogued these pictures first according to categories such as animals and air, animals and alcohol, and animals and stuffed animals, then ordered them in relation to books, cameras, cars, obesity, plastic bags, swimming pools and so on. At issue here was the trajectory of animals from non-sentient objects to hyper-subjective online entertainers, while Bonajo also drew attention to how the internet animal craze is contributing to the mistreatment of animals in the wild. The yellow background on which the images were arranged referenced the *National Geographic* magazine, standing for so-called objective scientific representation of the natural world, which in the artist's opinion meant that 'nature was captured without actually questioning the lens through which it is being observed, namely a western, heteronormative, capitalist, imperialist, white supremacist, patriarchal lens'. In the related video installation *Progress vs Sunsets: Reformulating the Nature Documentary* (2017), the main protagonists are children, who whimsically articulate the reconfigured relationship between human, technological and natural realms.

In reaction to the widespread 'reductionist interpretation of nonhuman beings, which legitimizes extensive human exploitation of and lack of consideration for them', British artist Fiona MacDonald started working collectively with human and non-human beings as Feral Practice to explore interspecies relationality and ethics. Their project *Foxing* (2017) dealt with the polarizing phenomenon of urban foxes, who as a result of the loss of their natural habitat have adapted to city life. It focused in particular on London, where they have resided since at least the 1930s. The exhibition display included a red fox pelt, installed in an outdoor cabinet alongside two scrolling signs emphasizing the divisive vocabulary attached to these animals by their human neighbours: majestic/marauding, sly/ thrilling, elegant/killer, beautiful/psycho. 'Fox News' was set up as a webpage collecting vulpine news items, such as speculation about the repeal of the ban on fox hunting with hounds. The gallery installation

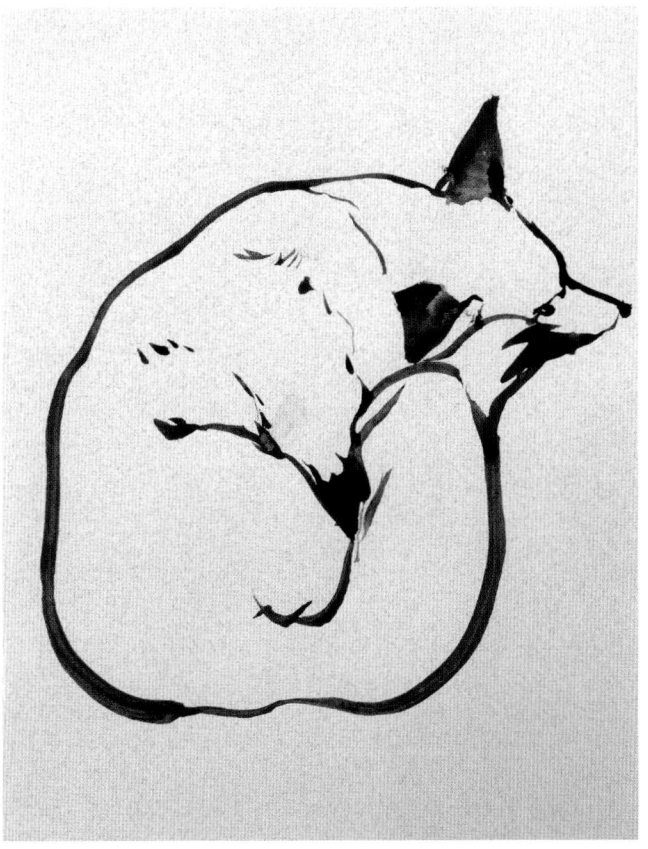

103 Fiona
MacDonald :
Feral Practice,
Diego, 2016

included drawings and video of foxes under the care of the
rescue charity 'The Fox Project', while a stained canvas on the
gallery floor displayed the painterly traces left by the foxes
visiting the artist's garden at night. Visitors were invited to
participate in an event at which they learned more about urban
foxes and practised how to 'walk like a fox, trot like a fox,
talk and eat like a fox', in order to imaginatively extend their
understanding of the complex existences of these non-human
city dwellers. Vulpine encounters in the more-than-human
contact zones of the urban environment could also be said
to point to the resilience and agency of the feral in the liminal
spaces of a hyper-controlled world.

Uncovering the entangled and enduring history of
human–animal collaboration in the city was at stake in
Vienna-based artist Anna Jermolaewa's installation *Hermitage
Cats* (2013). It consisted of forty photographs of feline employees

104

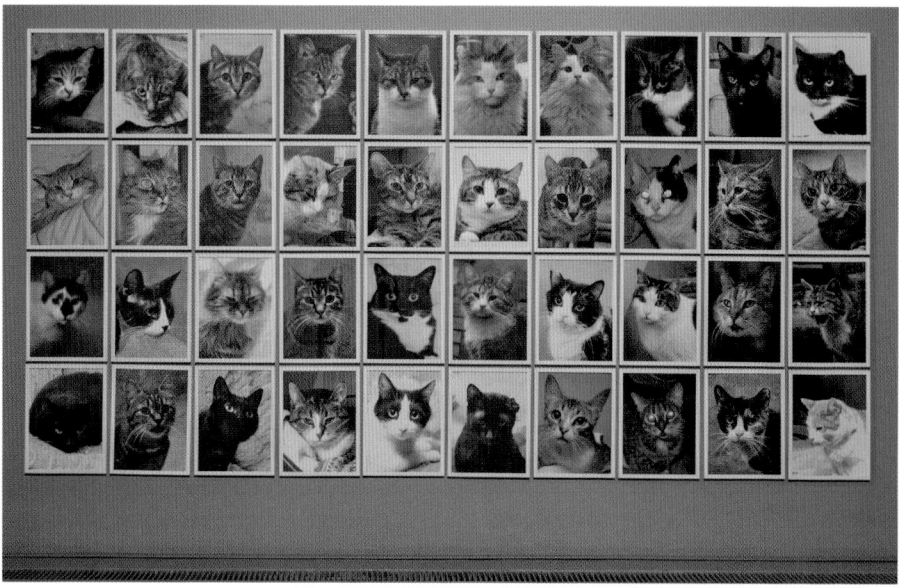

104 ABOVE Anna Jermolaewa, *Hermitage Cats*, 2013
105 OPPOSITE Lin May Saeed, *Pangolin*, 2020

of the Hermitage in St Petersburg, a video and a textual collage. Cats were first brought to the Winter Palace in 1745 from the city of Kazan on the orders of Empress Elizabeth, who 'had a great fear of mice and rats', and they have lived and worked on the premises to the present day. The orderly grid of cat portraits is reminiscent of a roll of honour, alluding to the grim period during the siege of Leningrad in the Second World War when the city's entire population of cats was consumed by the starving inhabitants. After the siege was lifted, the authorities reputedly sent thousands of cats by train from Siberia to the city, which had been overrun by rats. The format of the photographs also referenced the practice of celebrating 'heroes of labour' on factory billboards, implicitly raising the question of the attitude to animals under socialism. While socialist ideology was anthropocentric in its prioritization of the interests of the working class, to the extent that animals could be considered workers, the communist revolution could potentially be extended to them. Writing about 'Communism with a Nonhuman Face', theorist Oxana Timofeeva drew on Soviet utopian poetry to argue that revolution 'goes beyond the human and human rights, towards animality', noting also that as long as 'inequality remains untouched at the interspecies level, equality of people, too, can never be realized'.

The Liberation of Animals from their Cages is a sculptural series by German–Iraqi artist Lin May Saeed through which she problematizes the questions of animal rights, animal liberation and speciesism, citing suffragette and anti-vivisection activist Lizzy Lind af Hageby as her heroine. In this long-term project, a variety of animals – from elephants in chains to chickens in poultry farms and seals in zoos – are the subjects of works realized as large-scale paper cut outs, steel reliefs or life-size animal sculptures. In the sixteenth work in the series, *Moschophoros (gate)* (2015), which referenced in its title the ancient Greek statue of the calf-bearer, Saeed cut out silhouettes of factory-farmed cattle bursting free from their chains with the help of masked human allies equipped with wire cutters. In the artist's words, 'there is no justification for keeping animals in prison, not for animal experimentation, not for food, in either intensive or so-called species-appropriate farming – only freedom can be species appropriate'. The artist has also sculpted animals in styrofoam – a fragile non-biodegradable material made of petroleum, symbolic of the consumerist throwaway culture responsible for the current ecological crisis and extinctions – and placed them on wooden structures resembling cages or shipping crates. Among the most recent works in the series is *Pangolin* (2020), depicting the Asian and African mammal distinctive for its body covered in hard protective scales made of keratin. Pangolin meat is

105

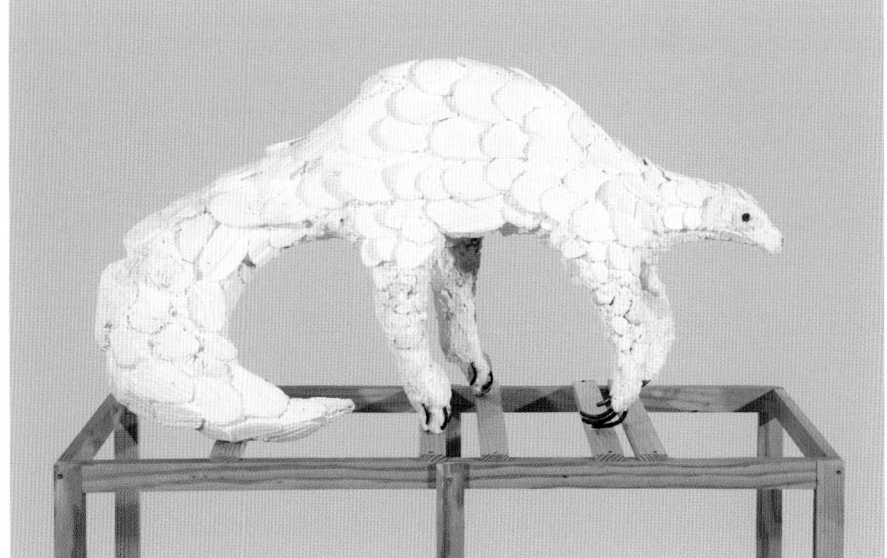

considered a delicacy in some Southeast Asian countries, while its scales are used in traditional Chinese medicine. Since they are one of the most heavily trafficked animals, pangolins are today an endangered species, however their status might change as a paradoxical result of alleged links to the spread of coronavirus halting the illegal consumption and trade.

The legal rights of non-humans were the subject of the courtroom performance *The Trial* (2014) devised by Laura Gustafsson and Terike Haapoja, based on the 2013 Perho wolf-poaching case that saw twelve Finnish hunters convicted of illegally hunting wolves. In their participatory re-enactment, actors playing the men were put on public trial and sentenced to imprisonment for eight years, with the judges also asked to consider whether compensation should be paid to the Perho wolf pack. While in medieval Europe live animals were taken to court for their criminal activities, more recent legislation is centred on the Animal Welfare Act, which although safeguarding their wellbeing, still categorizes them as legal property with little concern for the independent interests of animals. This artistic project interrogated the extent to which the existing anthropocentric law shapes our relationship to non-humans and how new ways of thinking about nature jurisprudence that are emerging from the convergence of indigenous customs and environmental crisis might transform the status of animals into legal persons. Reflecting on the typical attribution of rights to 'all persons' in national constitutions, the authors of *Zoopolis: A Political Theory of Animal Rights*, Sue Donaldson and Will Kymlicka, have commented that 'to achieve justice for animals, we need to move them from the property box to the personhood box'. Unabated public interest in this issue is evident from the fact that in 2020 Finland was taken to the European Court of Justice for continuing the cull of wolves despite their protected status. Meanwhile, in the Punjab, India, the high court has recognized the legal personhood of all animals, including avian and aquatic species.

106 Brazilian artist Jonathas de Andrade's film *O Peixe (The Fish)* (2016) is made up of repetitive sequences in which Amazonian fishermen go through the process of catching a fish, which they then gently caress and hold firmly to their bare chest until it dies. Although shot in the style of an ethnographic documentary about Amazonian tribes, the tender-cruel ritual performed on the asphyxiating fish was invented by the artist. Exposing the voyeurism of Western anthropologists' fascination with indigenous practices of ritual slaughter, the film suggested a correlation between the ethnographer's power

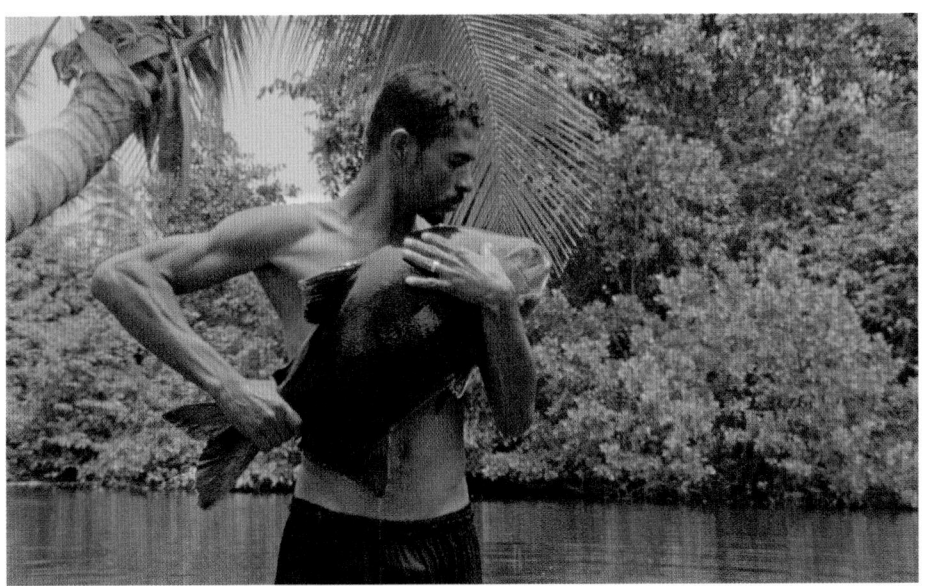

106 Jonathas de Andrade, *O Peixe (The Fish)*, 2016

over the observed and that exercised by the fisherman over his catch. The fictional ritual in *The Fish*, nevertheless resulting in the death of its non-human participants, mimics animist practices recorded by anthropologists in which indigenous hunters soothe or cajole their prey to reconcile it to the loss of life. This brings to the surface the tension between defenders of animal rights and advocates for indigenous customs, since while both groups reject myths about the inferiority and non-sentience of animals, they disagree on the rightness of killing them. As Claire Jean Kim has pointed out in *Dangerous Crossings: Race, Species, and Nature in a Multicultural Age*, the urgency of resolving such differences comes from the fact that 'meantime, the forces of neoliberal capitalism face few obstacles as they transform racialized others, nonhuman animals, and the earth into "resources" in the game of perpetual capital accumulation'.

The impact of climate change on all terrestrials has cast debates over the treatment of non-humans in a world transformed by colonialism and capitalism in a new light. Moved by the story of a group of macaque monkeys who in 1972 were resettled from the cold yet changing climate of the mountains in the vicinity of Kyoto to a reserve in Texas, Japanese artist Shimabuku decided to pay them a visit in their new setting in the southern United States. After spending

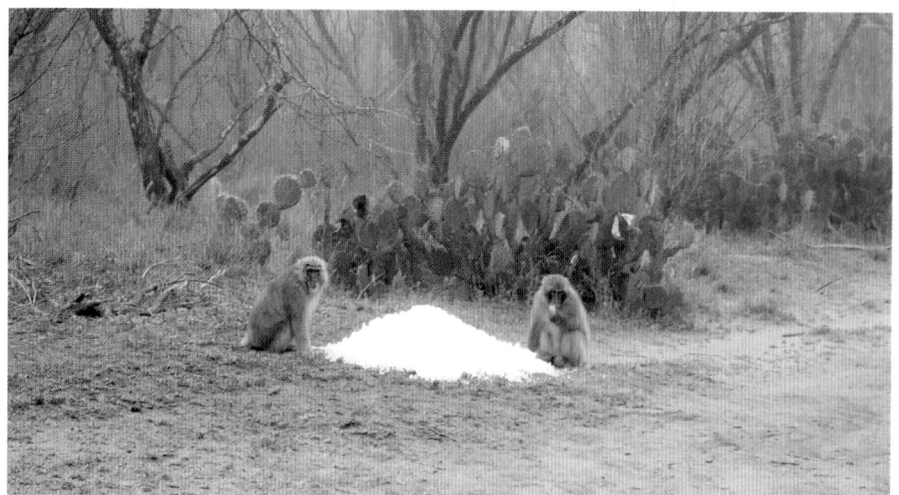

107 Shimabuku, *The Snow Monkeys of Texas: Do snow monkeys remember snow mountains?*, 2016

several days with them in their adopted environment populated by cactuses and cougars, the artist wondered whether they still remembered their old habitat. His video *The Snow Monkeys of Texas: Do snow monkeys remember snow mountains?* (2016) recorded the reaction of the monkeys to a heap of snow and ice brought to them under the Texan sun. It shows the American-born primates cautiously approach, touch and taste a substance that they have never experienced before, but which used to define their ancestral home. While the monkeys were saved from the deteriorating environment in Japan, this ephemeral encounter is a reminder that, as for the human animals with whom they share the gift of sentience, there is no escape from the planetary crisis of climate change, while the memory of thick winter snow fades for our species too.

The artistic practices discussed here have proposed a critical rethinking of relations with other-than-human species. The intensification of the exploitation and mistreatment of animals that is manifest in farming practices, habitat loss, illegal hunting and the trade in wild animals is accompanied by the spread of uncaring and exploitative attitudes, reflected in animal memes that negate the dignity of non-humans by denying them the privacy of their species-specific existence. At the same time, heightened awareness of climate change is instigating a reorientation visible in movements for non-human rights and personhood and calls for the critical embrace of untamed, wild and feral forms of interspecies coexistence.

Chapter 3
Countering Extinction

The rate at which species go extinct can be seen as a barometer of the health and stability of Earth systems. While during stable periods the level of background extinctions is slow and negligible, in the history of the planet there have been five previous mass extinction events when, as environmental writer Elizabeth Kolbert put it in *The Sixth Extinction*, 'there's a crash and disappearance rates spike', eliminating a significant proportion of existing biota. With mammals, birds, fish, amphibians and insects now dying out at up to a thousand times the background rate, resulting in the loss of two thirds of wildlife since the 1970s, the world is witnessing in real time a catastrophic sixth mass extinction, this time as a consequence of the toxic impact of humans on the liveability of the Earth. The destruction of planetary biodiversity should not be taken as a 'general human capacity' but rather, as Ashley Dawson, author of *Extinction: A Radical History*, has commented, as a 'product of the global attack on the commons, a capitalist frenzy on the planet that tilts towards increasingly intense environmental catastrophe'. Counter-extinction endeavours have either followed the eco-modernist path of combining genetic material from preserved specimens with that of their living relatives to reverse species loss or have centred on the rewilding of diminished habitats by reintroducing missing species and restarting natural processes. Artists have engaged with extinction as a planetary phenomenon that threatens to turn the blue planet into a lifeless Martian red and also as a downward spiral experienced by individuals and communities in specific geolocations, while also exploring potential recovery scenarios.

A Labrador duck, Pyrenean ibex, Tasmanian tiger, Irish elk, aurochs, Steller's sea cow, pied raven, Japanese Honshu

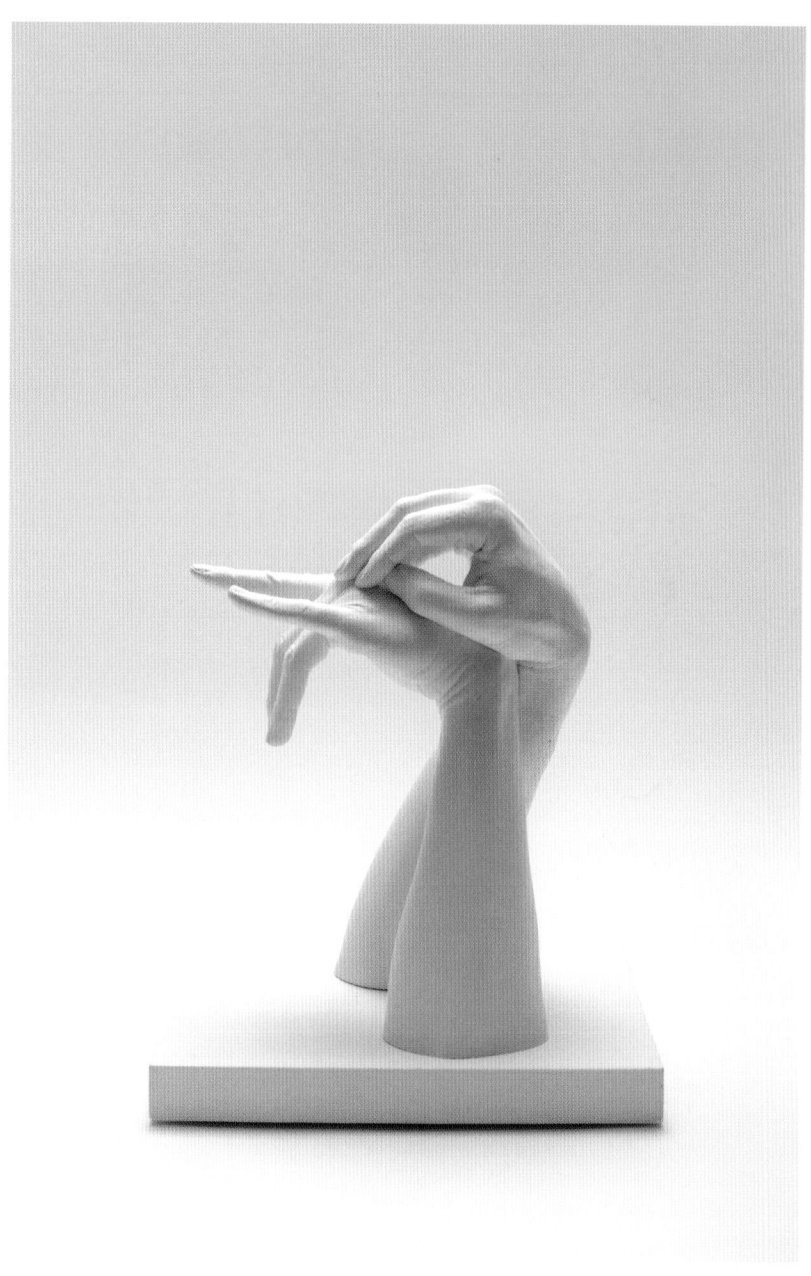

108 Marcus Coates, *Syrian Elephant*, 2018

wolf, Pinta Island tortoise, Atlas bear, golden toad, Javan tiger, Yangtze River dolphin, Syrian elephant, Lake Pedder earthworm and passenger pigeon all feature in *Extinct Animals* (2018) by British artist Marcus Coates. The work consists of a collection of sixteen sculptures of hands clasped together in poses that, when illuminated, cast a shadow revealing the animal in question. Although far from exhaustive, this list is illustrative of the fact that species are disappearing in diverse geographies all over the planet and across animal kingdoms, from birds to marine life, from large mammals to amphibians. Remaking the shapes of animal species with human hands points undoubtably to the main culprits in this sixth wave of mass extinction. The fact that the artist used his own hands as a model indicates the understanding that, however different in scale, everyone partaking in the globalized consumerist way of life is playing a part in the depletion of the natural world. As an evocation of their ethereal spirits, the work is a tribute to the extinct species, whose shadowy projections are a ghostly reminder of a collective loss.

Uzbek filmmaker and artist Saodat Ismailova's film *The Haunted* (2017) opens with a statement about the extinction of the Turan tiger, whose demise, we discover, started with the Russian Tsarist colonization of the Central Asian territories of Turkestan in the nineteenth century and continued during Soviet times, with the last sightings of the subspecies occurring in the 1960s in the region of Karakalpakstan. Conceived as a cinematic encounter with the mythical tiger whose imaginary presence pervades the grand landscapes along the Amu Darya River, the film takes the form of a soliloquy in which a female voice is heard whispering to the feline spirit: 'My descendants will know you, I will not need to tell them about you, they will inherit my memory, that is engraved deep into my skin.' Although it is no longer roaming the vast expanses of the region, according to the artist, the tiger still inhabits the collective memory and dreams of local people, as when you speak to them about the Turan tiger, 'it is unclear when the reality finishes and a tale begins'. Narratives of extinction are often accompanied by reflection on the 'turning points in cultural histories', and as such stories unfold, as Ursula K. Heise has noted in *Imagining Extinction*, 'part of national identity and culture itself seems to be lost along with the disappearance of nonhuman species'.

Struck by the news that the skeleton of the last Javan rhinoceros on mainland Asia had been found in Đồng Nai Province in 2010 with its horn chopped off, Ho Chi Minh City-based artist Tuan Andrew Nguyen started to research the

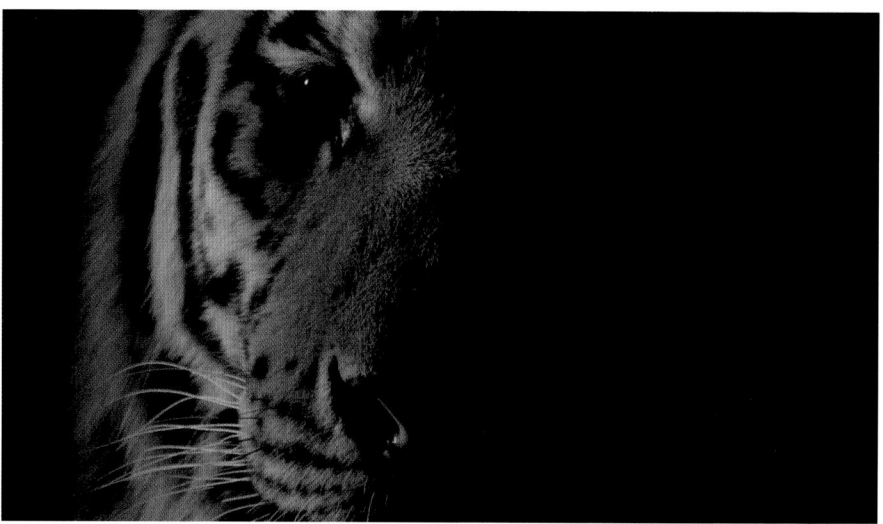

109 Saodat Ismailova, *The Haunted*, 2017

socio-political context of Vietnam, 'one of few places on the planet with such high levels of biodiversity and yet with one of the highest rates of animal extinction among all the nations of the world'. The resulting body of work, *Empty Forest* (2017), comprised of sculpture, installations and the two-channel video *My Ailing Beliefs Can Cure Your Wretched Desires*, dealt with the environmental impact of traditional medicinal practices based on beliefs in the mythical healing powers of rhino horns, deer antlers, pangolin scales and turtle shells. Although there is no scientific evidence for their curative properties, poachers have continued their illegal hunting and trade in these endangered animals. In Nguyen's supernatural compositions, combining real and mythological creatures, the extinct animals roam the empty forest. The spirit of the hornless rhino tells the last softshell turtle that he had hoped his 'murder would start a revolution, but it didn't', so his only redemption is to 'be a revolutionary' against the 'oppressive human species' and to 'keep other animals from suffering the same fate'.

   The manifold transformations of a territory once marked by now extinct predators are addressed in *Reserve* (2020), a film by Barcelona-born artist Gerard Ortín Castellví, delivered as a mosaic of interlinked episodes. Descriptions of wolf pits or traps, which can still be found in the north of the Iberian Peninsula and might be hundreds of years old, are juxtaposed in the film with images of modern-day leisure archers practising the ancient hunting technique with a bow and arrow and using animal models as targets. The audio includes a recorded phone conversation about inquiries into buying 'humanely sourced' wolf urine from the United States, which is used as a predator substitute to prevent animals from, for instance, crossing the road and causing traffic accidents. This is played against images of animal carcases delivered to reserves as food for vultures and other scavengers, who in the absence of big predators are left without a reliable food source. Hinting at the interchanging role of humans as exterminators, manipulators and rescuers, *Reserve* sketches a picture of the profoundly changed ecosystem left behind after the extinction of keystone species. As George Monbiot pointed out in *Feral: Rewilding the Land, Sea and Human Life*, 'top predators and keystone species unwittingly reengineer the environment', but when animals such as wolves disappear, 'this self-reinforcing process goes into reverse'.

The audio-visual work *The Unseeables (a tale of extinction in three birds)* (2020) by Feral Practice used narration and filmed performance, alongside footage of taxidermized museum exhibits, to put forward three case studies of UK birds that have gone extinct, and the attempts to bring them back to life using strategies of genetic de-extinction, reintroduction and conservation education. The first episode dealt with the great auk, the once plentiful 'penguin of the north' that used to nest in the northern islands of the Atlantic. In the 1840s the

110 Tuan Andrew Nguyen, *My Ailing Beliefs Can Cure Your Wretched Desires*, 2017

There is a certain kind of violence
in the way they look at things...

flightless bird was hunted down for its soft feathers, eventually disappearing due to volcanic eruptions and the desire of museums to extend their natural history collections. The species is today on the list of potential candidates for genetic de-extinction, to be achieved by combining scraps of its DNA with the genome of razorbills. The main character of the second story is the great bustard, famed for its extravagant male mating dance, which went extinct in Britain in the 1800s because it was 'delicious'. Since 2004 there have been attempts at rewilding this species in military training grounds in Wiltshire, first with Transvolgan bustards, then more successfully with Spanish bustards. The reintroduction also entails the assisted nesting and breeding of chicks indoors for greater survivability rates. Finally, the ground-nesting corncrake met its threat in the 1950s in the form of the industrial mower, which its chicks could not compete against for speed. Since the 1990s farmers in England have received financial support if they agree to mow their meadows from the centre out, allowing time for the birds to escape. Interrogated in this work is the question of whether, in the artist's words, recent ecological ideas such as rewilding could help to 'understand landscapes as self-creating masterpieces of which humans can never be masters'.

The last Kaua'i ʻōʻō bird died in 1987, however, since its lonely mating call recorded in the 1970s was uploaded onto a social

111 Gerard Ortín Castellví, *Reserve*, 2020

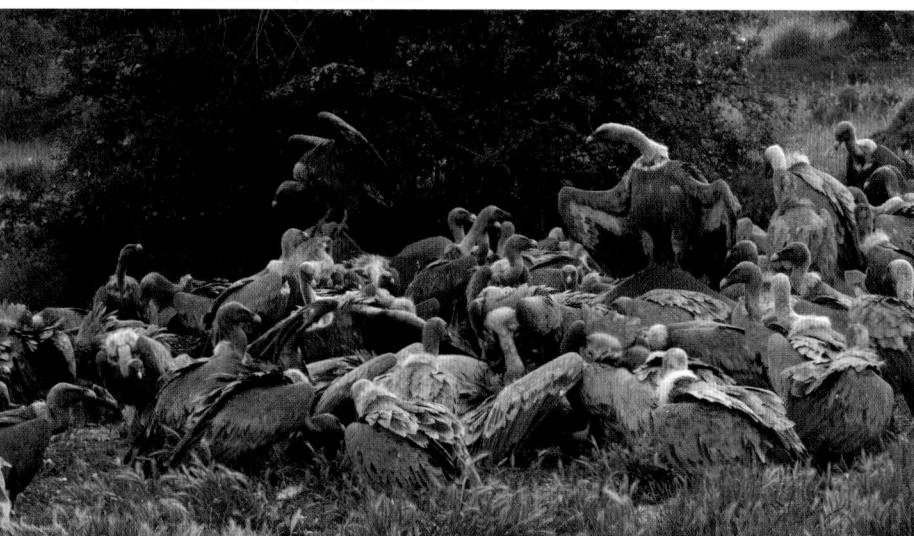

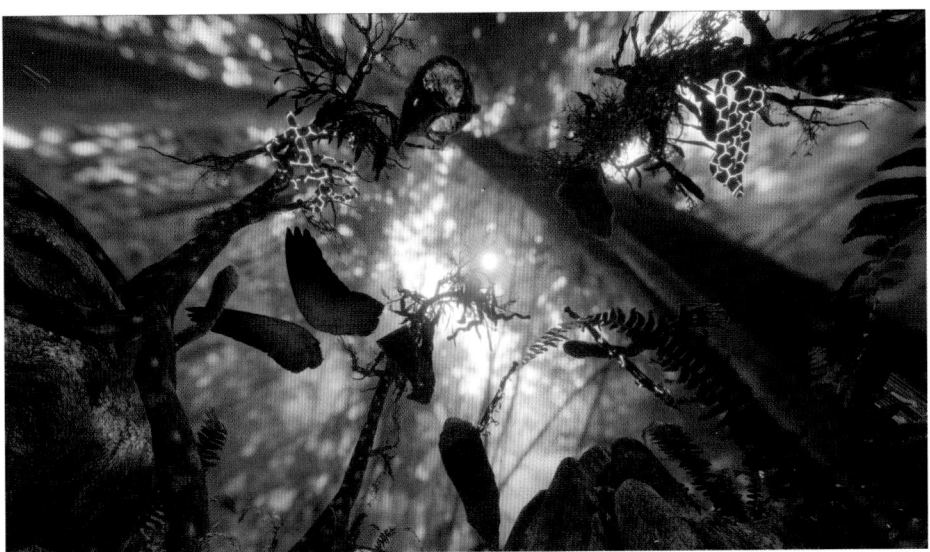

112 Jakob Kudsk Steensen, *Re-animated*, 2018–19

media site in 2009 and went viral, it has become one of the
most emblematic examples of extinct species. 'Responding to
its call' is how Danish artist Jakob Kudsk Steensen described
112   his motivation for *Re-animated* (2018–19), which used VR
technology to create a digital reconstruction of the species
and its habitat on the Hawaiian island of Kaua'i. Along with
interactive audio and environmental effects, the viewer's own
breath and voice impact the virtual atmosphere, turning this
scenario into an individualized experience. The artist drew on
archival research in the holdings of the American Museum
of Natural History, interviews with scientists and 3D scans of
flora and fauna to develop this hyperreal imaginary ecosystem,
using his skills as a 'digital gardener' and algorithms to
restore extinct species to the island. In its approach, the
work references computer simulation models used by climate
scientists to envisage future scenarios for life on Earth,
which, according to the artist, one day 'may become unbound
by the physical conditions governing our present reality'.
        The world devoid of human presence surveyed in US artist
113   Matthew C. Wilson's sci-fi documentary *Geological Evidences*
(2017) appears at first sight to have been struck by a cataclysmic
disaster exceeding even the worst-case global warming scenario
of 4°C modelled by the International Panel on Climate Change.
The work is filmed in futuristic infrared, the spectrum of the
electromagnetic radiation absorbed and emitted back towards

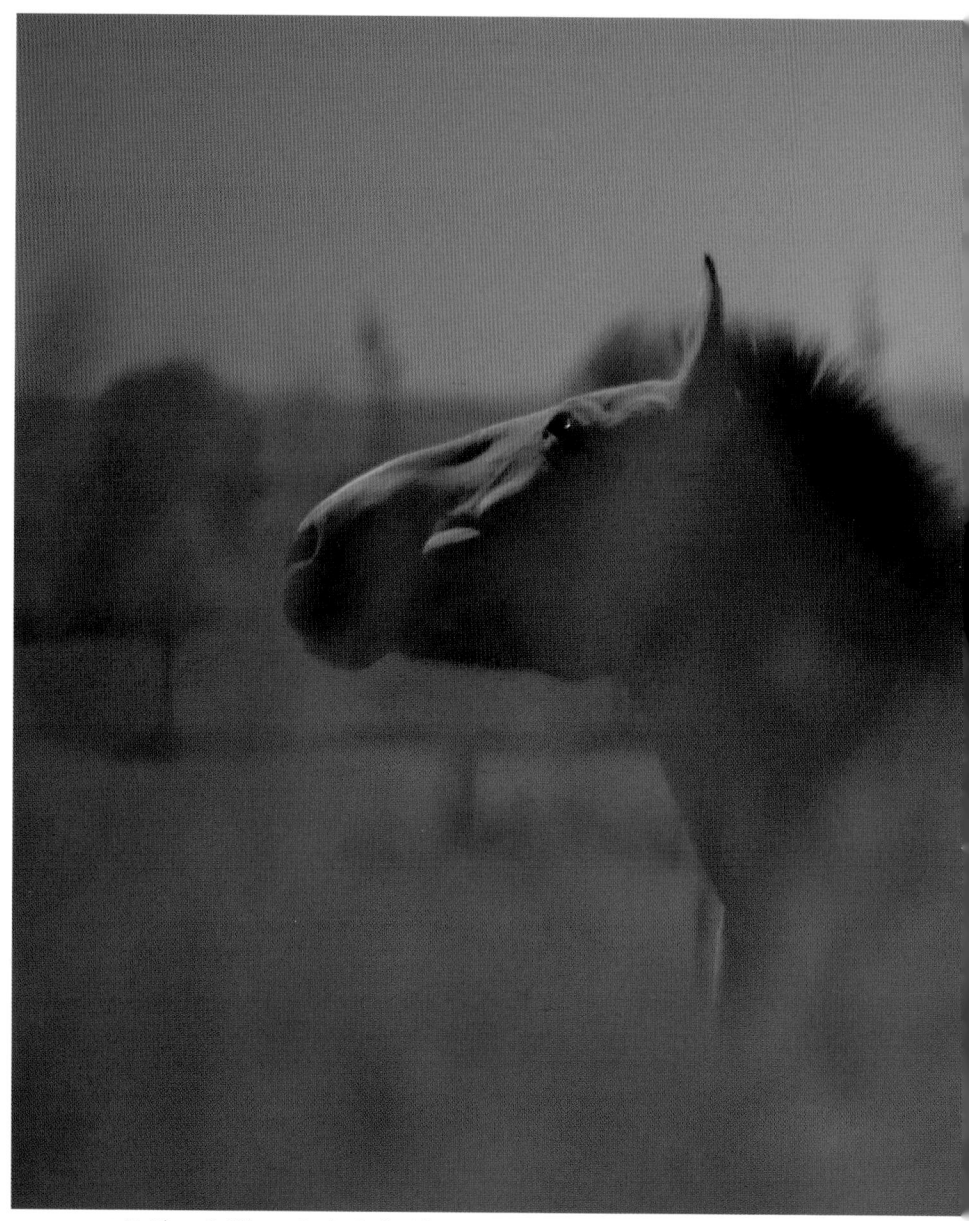

113 Matthew C. Wilson, *Geological Evidences*, 2017

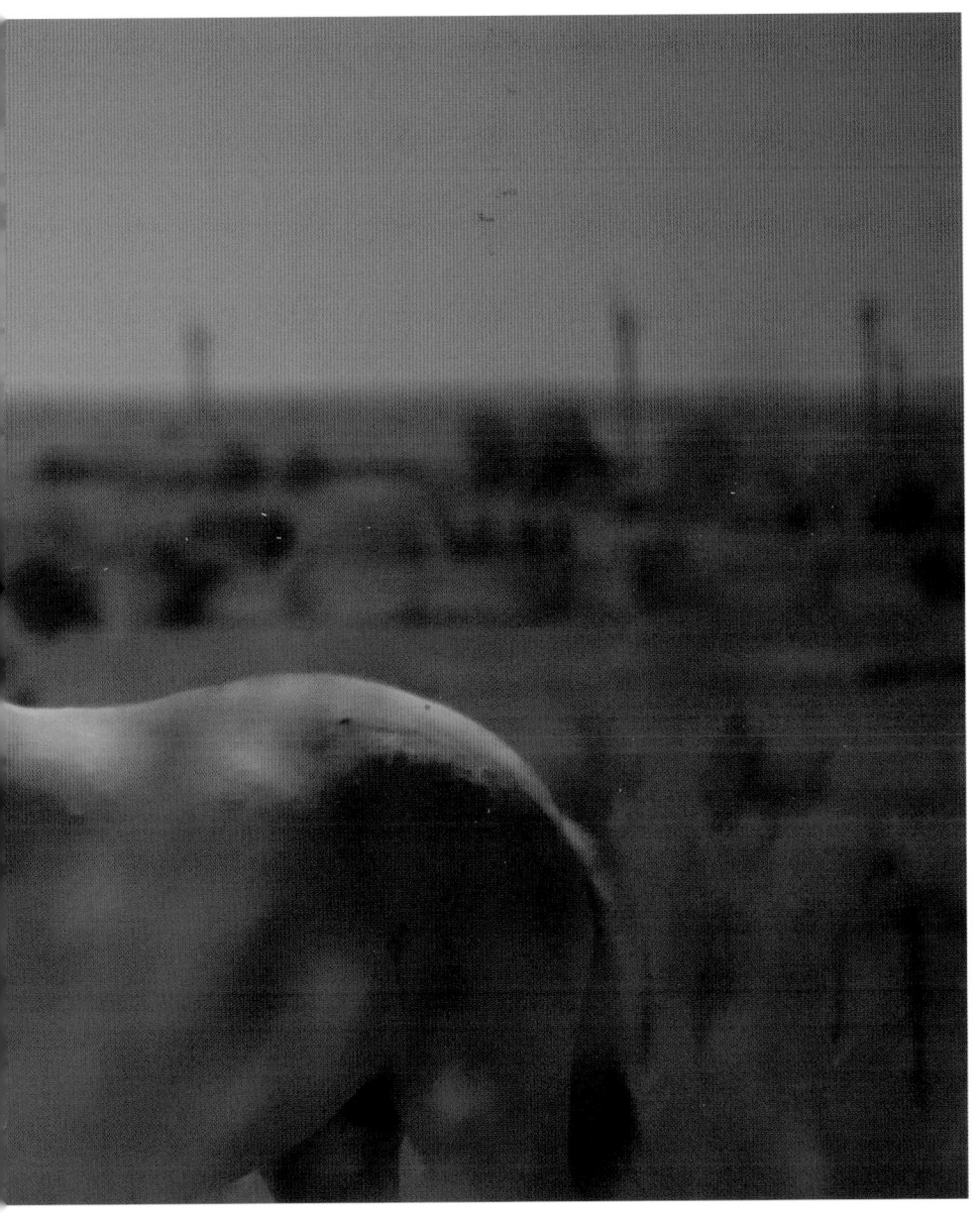

Earth's surface through the greenhouse effect. The camera hovers over scenes of rusting mining machinery and defunct satellite dishes that for the Western culture of the neo-liberal Anthropocene symbolized mastery of nature and technological progress. However, it is not the pathos of industrial ruins that catches the eye of the unseen observer, but rather the signs of biogeochemical processes continuing and restarting. There are shots of tadpoles swimming in a runoff pool, ants traversing clods of soil, wild plants propagating in an abandoned polytunnel and Palaeolithic wild horses grazing beneath stilled wind turbines. As this film suggests, the hopes for ecological resurgence in the wake of climate breakdown lie not with technological wizardry, but in the endurance and agency of terrestrials who have learned to survive and flourish beyond the capitalist logic of extraction and exploitation.

In view of the fact that 'humans, other animals, and a diversity of other species are woven together in coforming multispecies communities', extinction should, according to theorist Thom van Dooren, be seen as a more-than-human biocultural loss, since the breakdown of traditional 'ways of life' also extends to other species. Today the mass extinction of species no longer stands as a separate or competing issue on the agenda of the world's most pressing environmental concerns, but as inextricably connected to climate change. The revival of endangered species through restarting natural processes in diminished environments appears both as an ecocentric alternative to technocratic attempts to reverse species extinction through genetic engineering and as the future prospect of spontaneous rewilding in a truly post-human world.

Chapter 4
Political Ornithology

At the centre of the dystopian fable with which Rachel Carson began her 1962 exposé of the effects of chemical pollution on the land was the dreadful prospect of a *Silent Spring*: 'On the mornings that had once throbbed with the dawn chorus of robins, catbirds, doves, jays, wrens and scores of other bird voices, there was now no sound; only silence lay over the fields and woods and marsh.' Nearly six decades later, at the height of the coronavirus lockdown of spring 2020, the sudden audibility of morning birdsong as noise levels and air pollution were drastically reduced was a harbinger of the potential for nature to rebound when humans step back. Calls and songs carry information about a singer's species, 'geographic origin, group membership, even its individual identity', noted Jennifer Ackerman in *The Bird Way*. They enable birds to use 'sound in ingenious ways to share information, negotiate boundaries, and influence one another's behaviour'. The enigma of bird cognition and their ability to learn have been investigated against the backdrop of the threat posed to avian cultures by climate change and habitat loss, with the adoption of a critical stance towards the historical tendency to perceive birds as metaphors for human visions of the other world, the soul, freedom and peace, and as national symbols. Accepting birds as fellow members of the multispecies community of planet Earth has implications that point beyond protection and conservation to the emergence of a more-than-human cosmopolitics that takes their many voices into account.

Something Happened on the Way to Heaven (2019–20) was the body of work produced by Angolan artist Kiluanji Kia Henda during his art residency on the Italian island of Sardinia, reflecting on the overlays of the island's natural environment and its position in the Mediterranean at the crossroads of

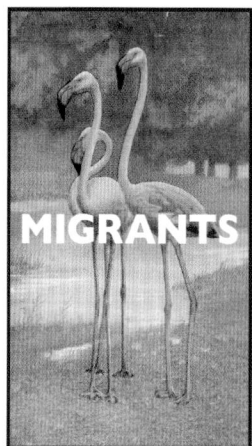
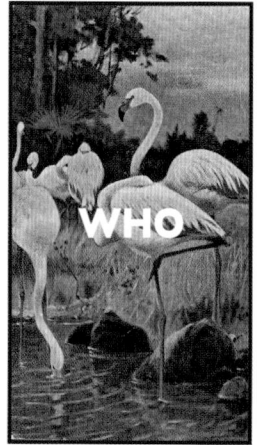
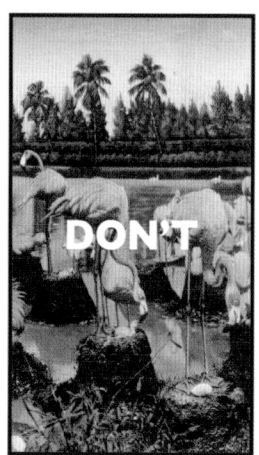
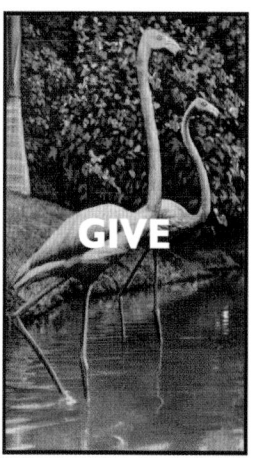
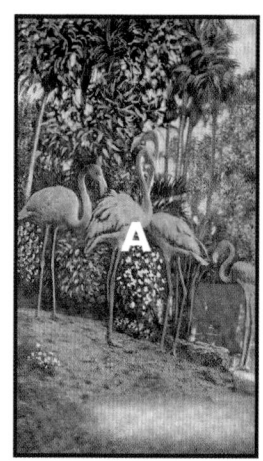
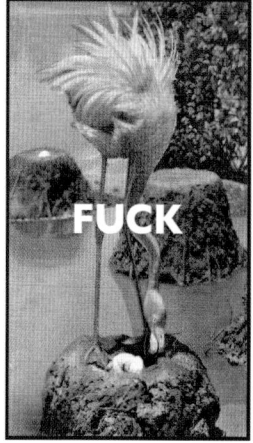

migratory routes. Belonging to the series were six photographs of enlarged vintage postcards depicting flamingo birds feeding, resting, bathing and tending to chicks, each inscribed with one word that when read together gave the work its title: *Migrants Who Don't Give a Fuck*. Breeding on Sardinia and wintering in Angola, these migratory birds have an enviable freedom of movement that is not equally enjoyed by all members of the human species. Describing his experience of the Mediterranean island as 'a heavenly landscape', the artist pointed out that 'there is no concept of paradise without there also being a hell'. He referred to the remains of twentieth-century military infrastructure on the island, as well as the ongoing crisis of migrant crossings of what in Latin was known as *mare nostrum*, or our sea. The symbolism of pink flamingos, which since their reincarnation as plastic garden ornaments in the 1950s have stood as capitalist icons for the consumerist dream of optimism and escape to exotic tourist destinations, is contextualized in this work in relation to the social injustice experienced by climate refugees and others for whom borderless mobility is illusory.

Drawing attention to the unsuspected diversity and abundance of avian imagery that can be found embossed in metallic gold on national travel documents was the focus of *Amateur Bird Watching at Passport Control* (2016–19) by New York-based Belarusian artist Alina Bliumis. She identified forty-three states whose passports feature living or extinct, realistic or anthropomorphic feathered creatures on their covers, including the flamingo for the Bahamas, a vulture for Mali, a dodo for Mauritius, doves for Cyprus and sisserou parrots for Dominica. For her graphic series, the artist extricated the species from the state insignia and drew them anew to highlight how the natural world is enmeshed in national representations. Birds are commonly used as potent state symbols by projecting avian characteristics onto national identities. For instance, Australia has the emu, as 'it is thought never to take a step backwards', while the eagle's 'reputation for strength and ferocity' has been counted on by nations including Germany, Mexico, Zimbabwe, Albania and the USA, according to author Jeremy Mynott. In *Birdscapes: Birds in Our Imagination and Experience*, he put this prevalence down to the fact that 'birds are above all creatures of the air, the realm between that of gods and humans in which they move with such ease', noting that it is 'the power of flight, surely, that we most envy and admire, in our conscious lives as in our dreams'. In that sense, Bliumis's work pointed to the

114 OPPOSITE Kiluanji Kia Henda, *Migrants Who Don't Give a Fuck*, 2019

irony that those travelling with passports do not have the avian privilege of flying without consideration of national borders, despite the auspicious emblems on their documents.

The tension between living species and their symbolic role in the creation of nationalist imagery was examined by Hungarian artist Szabolcs KissPál in his work *Greater Hungaries* (2013), which entailed outlining the astoundingly long flight paths of saker falcons on maps of the European continent. These cartographic inscriptions were based on data collected from electronic tags placed on individuals of this endangered species, which is assumed to be the closest extant relative to the mythical Turul bird of Hungarian national mythology. While in the original myth, the Turul led the Magyar tribes from Central Asia into the Carpathian basin during the tenth century to show them the land of their future country, a thousand years later, thanks to a European ecological programme, it is now possible to trace the flying habits of their real counterparts and map out with irony 'the possible territory of Greater Hungary'. In the related film *The Rise of the Fallen Feather* (2016), the artist referenced the recent revival of Turul symbolism in patriotic

116

115 BELOW Alina Bliumis, *Amateur Bird Watching at Passport Control*, 2019
116 OPPOSITE Szabolcs KissPál, *From Fake Mountains to Faith (Hungarian Trilogy), Chapter 2, The Rise of the Fallen Feather*, 2016

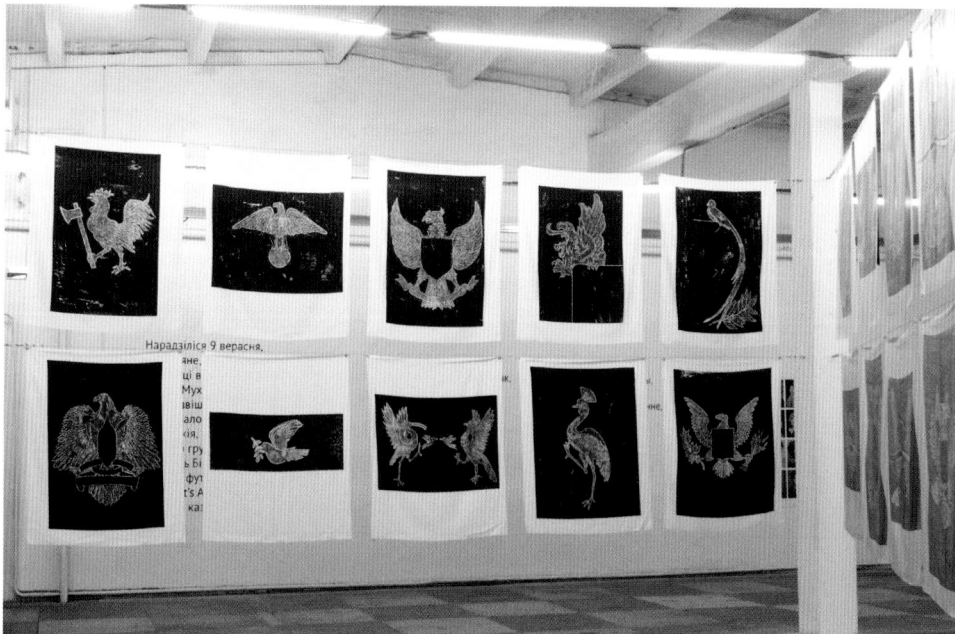

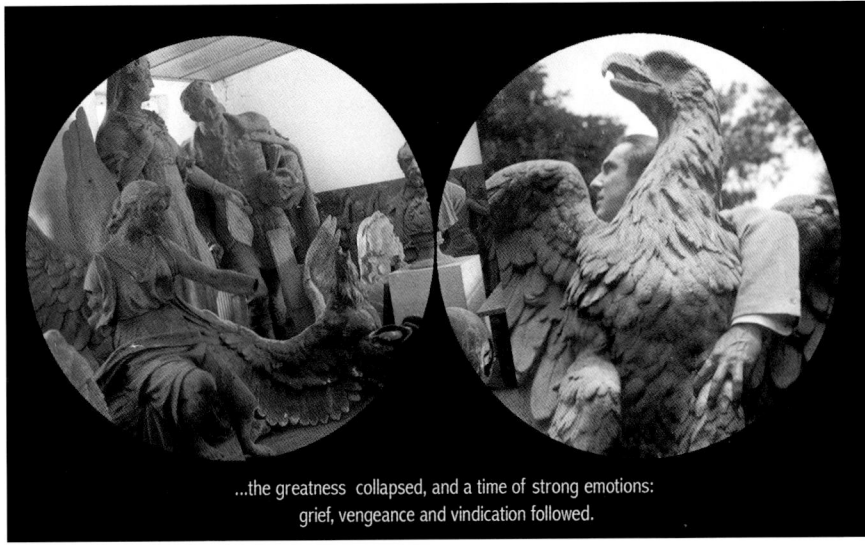

...the greatness collapsed, and a time of strong emotions:
grief, vengeance and vindication followed.

paraphernalia and new public monuments that have sought
to rehabilitate Hungary's revanchist interwar leader Admiral
Horthy. The commentary that runs through the work examined
the discrepancy between the biological and the symbolic,
uncovering the ideological distortions at play in the nationalist
attribution of metaphorical functions to birds.

Another tagged Hungarian bird almost caused a diplomatic
scandal when in 2013 it made international headlines that read:
'Stork suspected of being a spy detained by police in Egypt'.
A native of Hungary, the stork set off on its migratory route
via Israel to the shores of Lake Victoria in East Africa, where it
overwinters. However, it was captured in southern Egypt when
the electronic device detected on its back was mistaken for
espionage equipment. This was the starting point of Berlin-
based Egyptian artist Heba Y. Amin's performative lecture
and ongoing artistic project *The General's Stork* (since 2016),
which investigated how the contemporary military–industrial
complex is driven by aerial surveillance, while showing that
the bird's eye view of the landscape was also integral to the
colonial project. It also revisited the case of Lord Allenby, the
British High Commissioner in Cairo and a general who led
the Egyptian Expeditionary Force in 1917 to capture Jerusalem
from the Ottomans, a victory achieved with the help of leaflets
dropped from airplanes calling for surrender. Connecting the
non-belligerent takeover to biblical prophecy, the artist pointed
to archival footage showing the general off duty with his pet

117

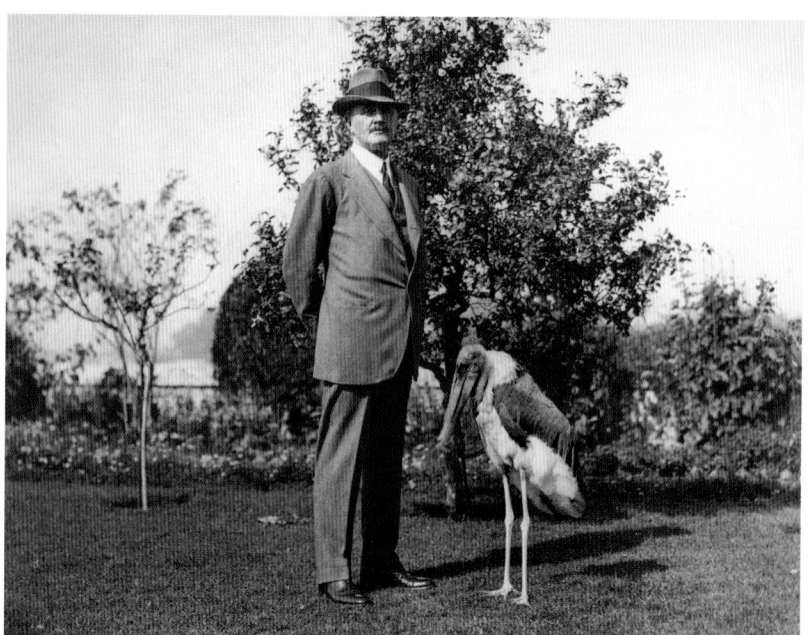

117 Heba Y. Amin, *The General's Stork I*, 2020

marabou stork, which he pats on the head. By bringing together these disparate episodes, which saw two storks incidentally caught up in militaristic operations, the artist hinted at the ultimate desire to appropriate the natural abilities of birds for drone warfare that seeks conquest from the sky.

Directing our attention even further towards cosmic realms is the video work *The Great Silence* (2014) by Allora & Calzadilla. The duo collaborated with science fiction writer Ted Chiang to narrate a heartrending story about the human obsession with establishing connections with life in the universe, while failing to communicate with other terrestrials on Earth. Written from the perspective of parrots, it is set in Río Abajo forest in Esperanza, Puerto Rico, where the last wild population of critically endangered *Amazona vittata* parrots live in the vicinity of the Arecibo Observatory, the world's largest single-aperture radio telescope, which transmits and receives radio waves to and from outer space. The birds explain that the 'great silence' refers to the paradox that although the universe is so vast that intelligent life 'must surely have arisen many times', there is no sign of life elsewhere. They speculate that 'intelligent species actively try to conceal their presence' to avoid hostile invaders, a strategy that the parrots support, since humans have driven them to the verge of extinction and therefore 'soon the

118

rainforest may be as silent as the rest of the universe'. By seeing the world from the parrots' point of view, the work drew attention to the discrepancy between humans' aspirations for advancement through cutting-edge technologies and the incredible ignorance they display towards other intelligent life on Earth.

Addressing the arbitrariness of the treatment of non-human species, Swiss artist Robin Meier's work *Collective Feeding* (2019) dealt with the fate of a small population of house crows, *Corvus splendens*, who settled near the Port of Rotterdam around 1994, when a pair of them most likely arrived from their 'native' Indian subcontinent as stowaways on a commercial container ship. In 2014, two decades after their 'unassisted arrival' and peaceful coexistence, when their number had grown to about forty, the Dutch authorities gave orders for the crows to be eradicated on the grounds that it was necessary to prevent possible future damage to crops and wildlife. *Collective Feeding* was realized during an art festival in Sri Lanka, in the vicinity of Colombo Port City, possibly the spot from which the crows took off on their transoceanic journey to Hoek van Holland. Conceived as a performance that consisted of 'two wind instruments, two megaphones, wild crows, rice and eggs', it was carried out during consecutive evenings on a roof terrace, where the house crows were treated to food and music. In his book *The Wake of Crows*, Thom van Dooren devoted a

119

118 Allora & Calzadilla, *The Great Silence*, 2014

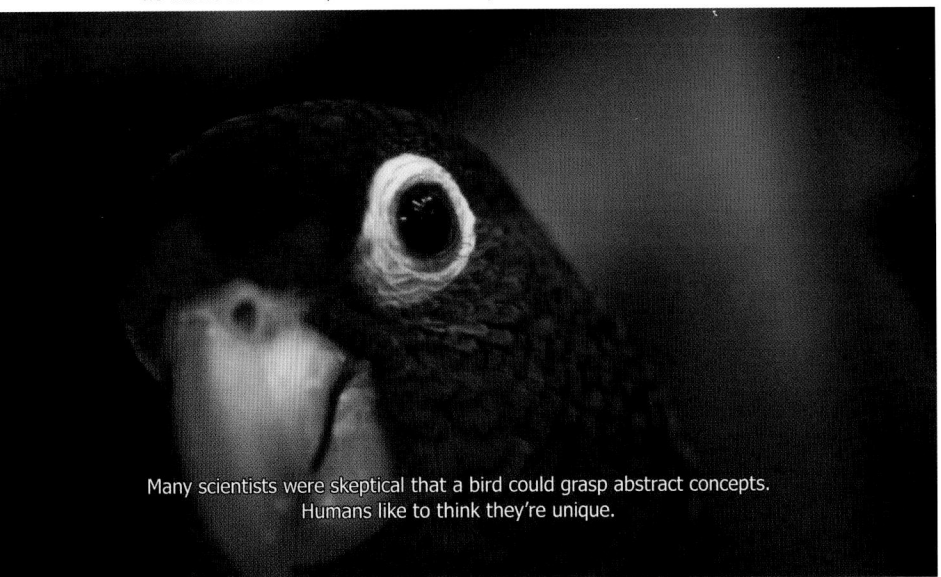

Many scientists were skeptical that a bird could grasp abstract concepts. Humans like to think they're unique.

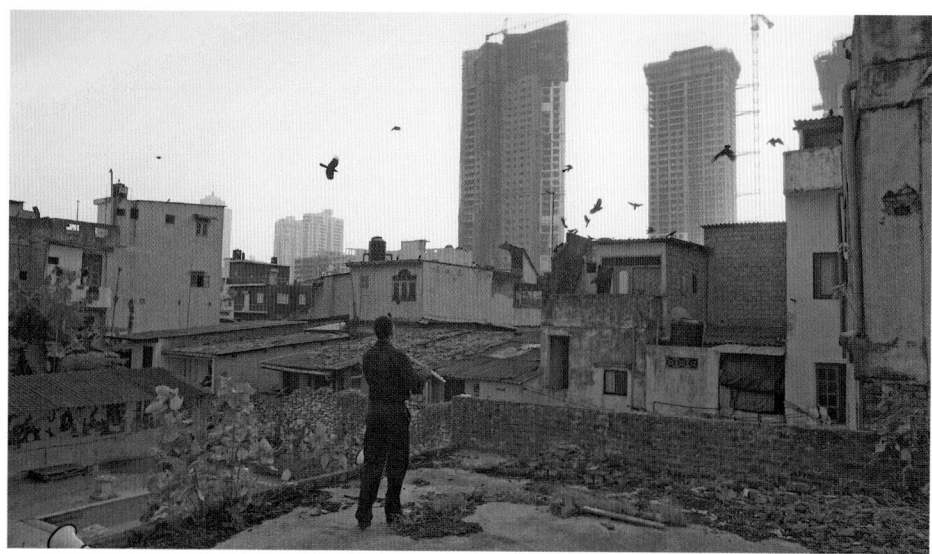

119 Robin Meier, *Collective Feeding*, 2019

chapter entitled 'Unwelcome Crows' to the Dutch episode,
revealing the acts of hospitality towards the birds as a form
of appropriation and identifying the Port of Rotterdam as the
'engine of the Anthropocene'. Van Dooren called for a new
framework for thinking about ecological futures, which should
be 'constructed by fragile collectives that cannot claim absolute
knowledge, power, or authority' and therefore hold open 'the
question [of] who acts and to whose benefit'.

   A conversation between seven birds – a heron, tree sparrow,
roseate tern, great black-backed gull, cuckoo, dotterel
and blackbird – was set in motion by Marcus Coates in
Conference for the Birds (2019). Played by wildlife experts and
ornithologists, their exchanges touched on avian topics such
as migration, breeding, chicks and predation, as well as the
effects of climate change on the natural environment. A roseate
tern, a representative of a small breeding colony on Coquet
Island in Northumberland that is on the brink of extinction,
expressed his concern that the fish he feeds on are retreating
further north due to rising sea temperatures. Other birds
agreed, commenting that 'there is a natural order to things,
but mankind is creating an unnatural disorder'. Some were
quick to point to the 'proliferation of cats in gardens' and
the dangers they pose to their offspring. The enlarged bird
heads in the installation were made after the engravings of
Thomas Bewick, author of the 1797 book *A History of British*

Birds, while reanimating them was for the artist an exercise in understanding that when speaking from the perspective of another animal, we 'rely on subjective experience' to communicate across species boundaries. The possibility of meaningful exchange between species on matters of shared concern is also the precondition for the emergence of a planetary cosmopolitics that, in the words of Bruno Latour, would take account of the 'complexities of the pluriverse' by embracing 'literally, everything – including all the vast numbers of nonhuman entities'.

Anca Benera and Arnold Estefan's series of drawings *Urban Wildlife* (2012–14) depicted scenes of birds nesting on elements of urban infrastructures, abandoned vehicles or street furniture, each accompanied by a news clipping that hinted at the consequences such practices might have on human citizens. For example, on one sheet a BBC headline that read 'Cash machine stolen. No suspect identified' was juxtaposed with an image of collard doves nesting on security cameras. Another paired a news item from the *Telegraph* about the suspension of a postman with an image of a great tit nesting in a post box. It is through the wit and humour of the found images and matching press cuttings that the artists drew attention to birds' adaptability to new circumstances, or the phenomenon of the 'synanthropization' of wild populations to human-created conditions. With its serendipitous avian interruptions to the usually seamless operations of the globalized world, on the one hand this work demonstrated the resilience of species to changing habitats and their opportunistic spirits, while on the other it could be seen as a call to take into account the interests and needs of non-human city dwellers.

The tendency within certain human cultures to see birds as symbolic of notions such as national belonging or the yearning for freedom reflects the qualities of actual avians, who soar above borders and give careful consideration to where they build their nests. Birds take on the additional burden of representing the collective trauma of climate change, measured also in the vertiginous drop in bird numbers, including of species previously regarded as common. Artists have uncovered the ways in which birds have been called upon to represent contrasting political projects, exert influence on the unfolding of historical events, are caught up in processes of urbanization and globalization and, when given a voice, speak uncomfortable truths to humanity about ecological responsibility.

Chapter 5
Magnified Natures

The discipline of biology changed substantially during the twentieth century thanks to the new technology of the transmission electron microscope, which had powers of magnification 5,000 times those of light microscopes, while the genomics revolution based on DNA sequencing has since provided new ways of inspecting complex microbial worlds. As a result, as the authors of *The Hidden Half of Nature* have pointed out, scientists are now 'seeing that complex microbial communities drive many things we depend upon, from soil fertility to a healthy immune system', with microbes consisting of ancient archaea, bacteria, fungi, protists and viruses making up 'half the weight of the life on earth'. This magnified nature brings a new understanding of how integral microbes are in the web of life, forcing us to rethink the imagined autonomy of individuals. In her study *Symbiotic Planet*, evolutionary theorist Lynn Margulis defined symbiosis as a 'system in which members of different species live in physical contact', forming holobionts as assemblages of a host and other organisms, in light of which she concluded that 'we need to be freed from our species-specific arrogance'. Drawing on this work in developing her theory of the Chthulucene, Donna Haraway proposed that the epochal geological turn be considered as 'intense commitment and collaborative work and play with other terrans', suggesting with the name chthulu 'diverse earth-wide tentacular powers'. Accordingly, as she further asserted in *Staying with the Trouble*, all critters of the Terra are 'compostists' engaged in the 'mixing and turning of [the] terran compost pile', while making kin in the Chthulucene is a form of multispecies coexistence.

Claire Pentecost's ongoing series of drawings *Old Friends and Unloved Others* (since 2013) is focused on creatures in biological and cultural ecosystems that are often unappreciated, despised and feared, depicting in detail magnified spiders, slugs, bugs, mosquitos, microbes, bacteria, viruses or worms. The 'old friends' in the title refers to the hypothesis of scientist Graham Rook who, positing that the human body is made up of a shared ecosystem with microbial partners, 'which are involved in the development and function of essentially every organ, including the brain', drew attention to the fact that symbiotic relationships are also vital in the immediate environment, as they help regulate the immune system. However, changes in human surroundings that have seen natural elements such as wood and clay being replaced by increasingly synthetic household objects, anti-bacterial cleaners and pesticides are having an unprecedented impact on the 'old friends' and therefore on the health of humans, other species and the planet. The second part of the title cites the environmental humanities study of the 'death of the disregarded', understood as extinctions of the creatures that are less visible, less beautiful and therefore described as 'unloved others' which do not capture our imagination as much as whales or panda bears, although our daily lives depend on them. Pentecost's interest in microbial life was sparked by her investigation of soil, where she 'encountered the prodigious world of microbes, specifically bacteria and fungi' whose activities are 'crucial to all other life forms' and the cycles of death and new life. Through her unsettling drawings, the artist compels the viewer to confront both fears and ignorance and to embrace composting and co-dependence with other critters.

Finnish artist Alma Heikkilä's large-scale paintings deal with microscopic organisms and natural processes that evade human perception, yet through their tireless activity constantly transform the world. For the artist this offers a corrective view of the Anthropocene, since 'humans play such a minor part in the biosphere', while 'the basis of life is constantly created and remade by microbes'. Among the canvases that constituted her site-specific exhibition at the Museum of Contemporary Art Kiasma in Helsinki in 2019 was *in the air – into the lungs*, which was stretched across a long window and depicted dark microbial life forms against the natural light. Another work, *warm and moist | decaying wood*, was painted in colours that resemble human flesh, pointing to the decaying wood as a fruitful biotope for insects and fungi. If approached as a form of institutional critique from a microbiological symbiotic point of view, Heikkilä's work could be viewed as shattering the myth of artistic individuality, bearing in mind that we are profound holobionts. Through their wooden frames and

120

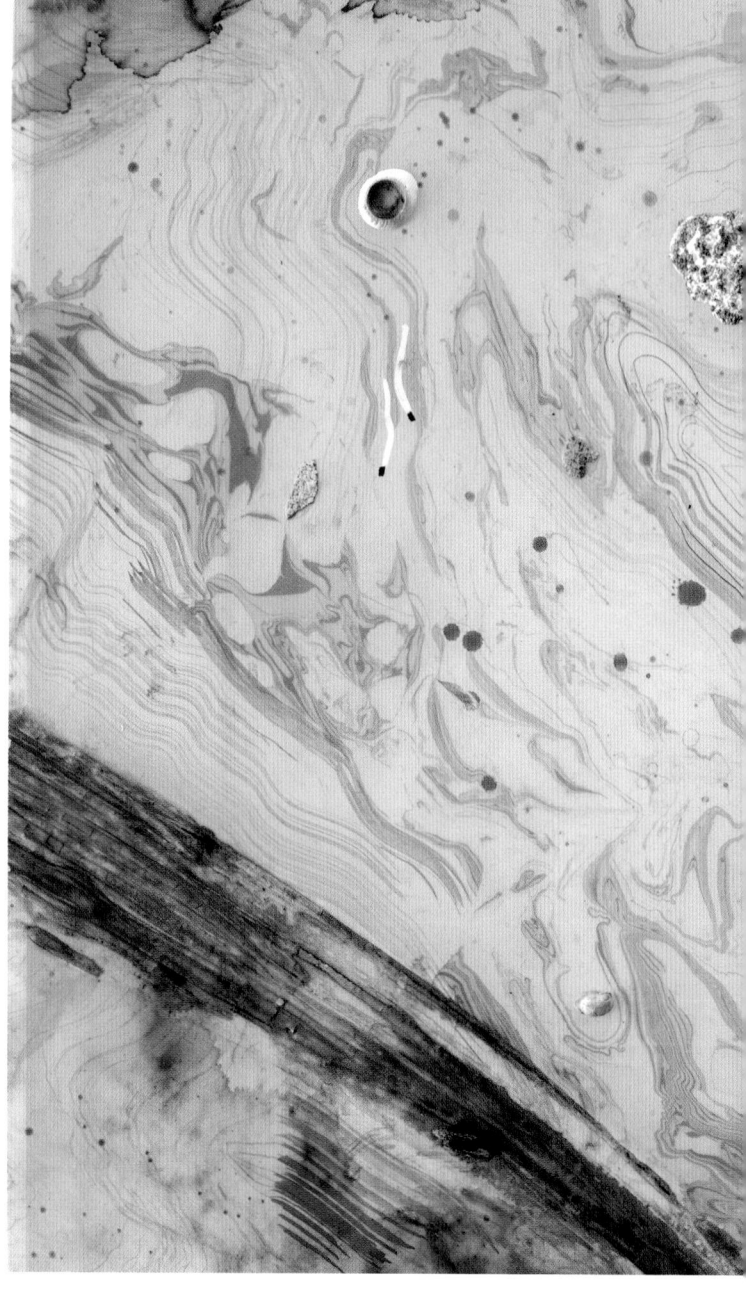

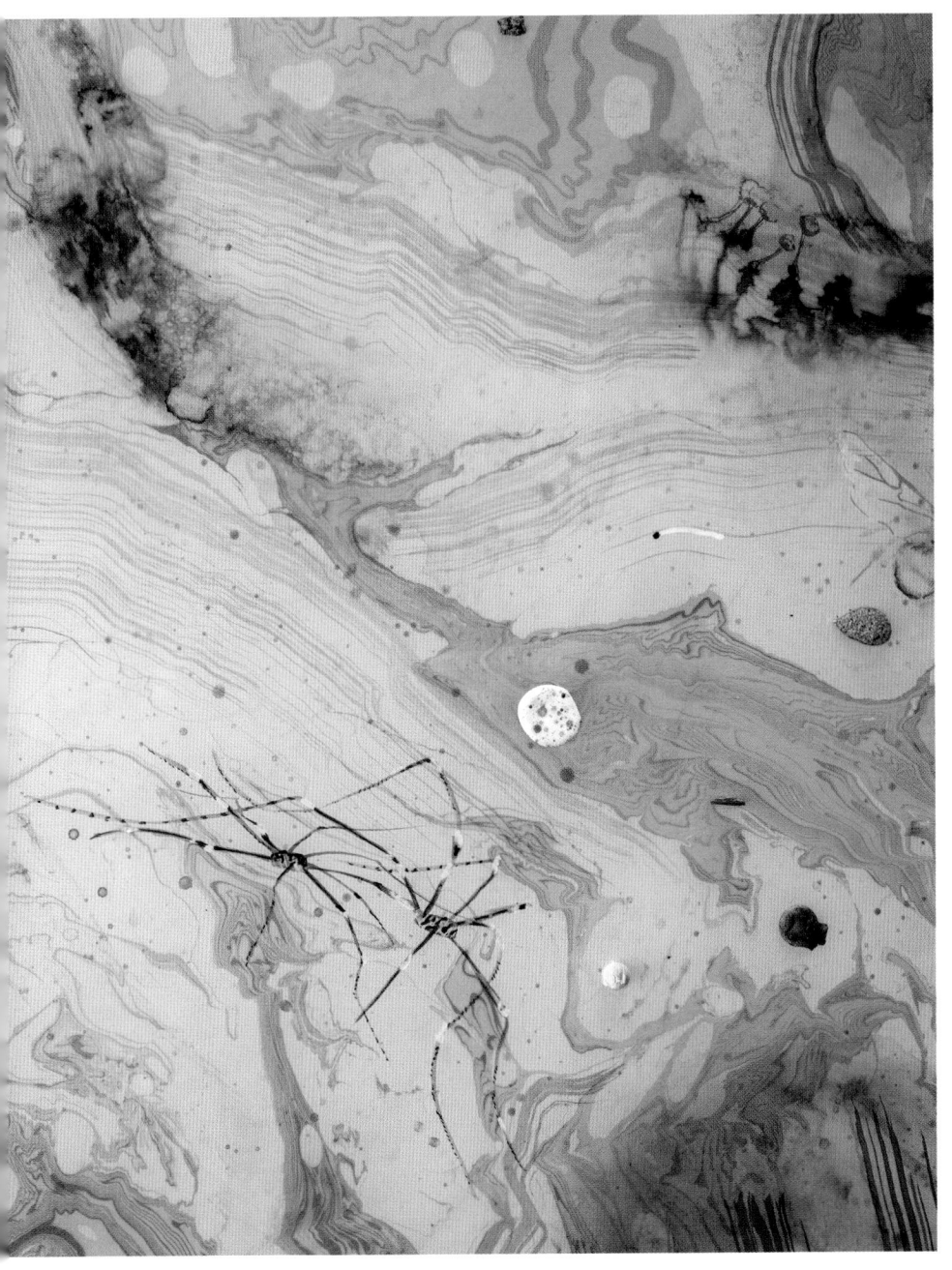

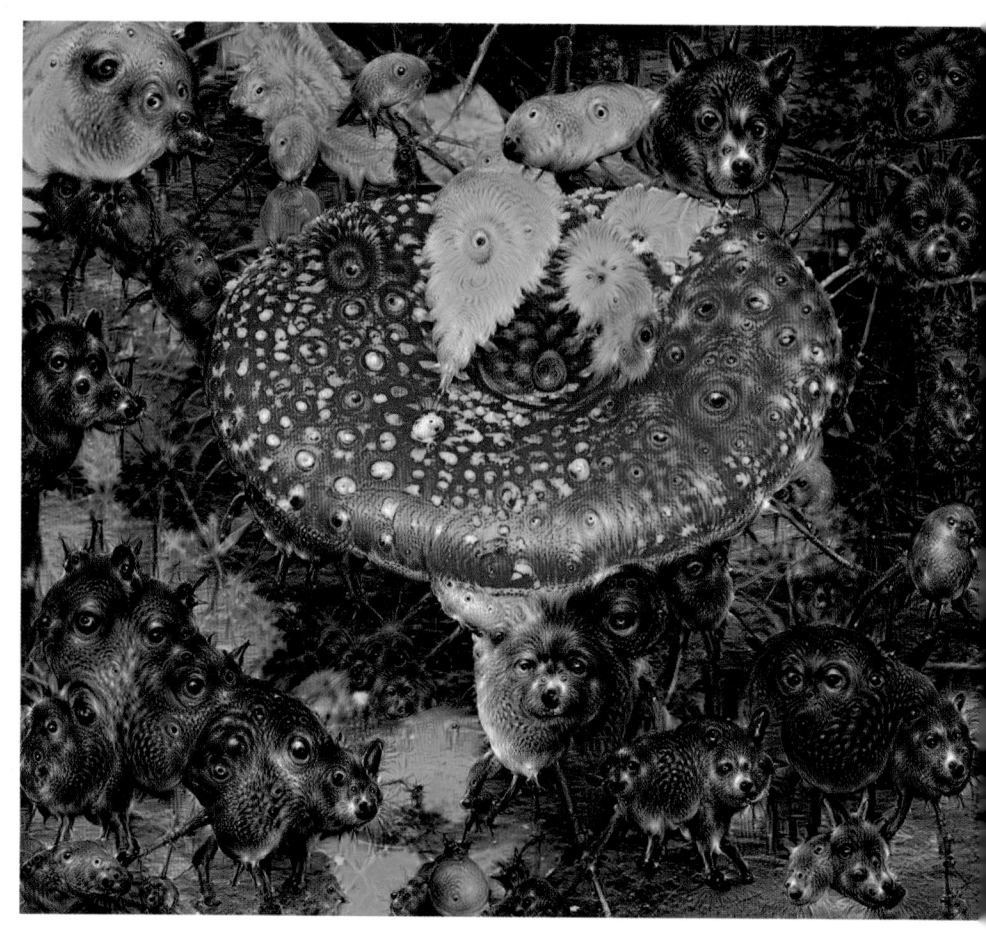

121 Eloïse Bonneviot and Anne de Boer, *The Mycological Twist,
Five Amazing Tricks to Get Rid of Perception*, 2016

pigments, the paintings partake in past and present microbial processes, since the pristine museum environment is also a place where bacteria, fungi and viruses are at work, while the exhibition production contributed to CO_2 emissions. According to the artist, understanding the invisible world of microbes is a precondition for dealing with climate change, requiring us to stop thinking about humans as separate individuals and instead recognize our dependence on life-supporting microorganisms. Writing in the catalogue to the exhibition, scientist Scott F. Gilbert underlined that each of us is 'not only an organism, we are also a biome, a collection of ecosystems', a bodily consortium of species whose 'partnerships are necessary for survival'.

At a moment when 'the world's climate is going haywire and industrial progress has proved much more deadly to life on earth than was imagined a century ago', the ability of wild mushrooms to thrive in human-disturbed landscapes has, as anthropologist Anna Tsing noted in *The Mushroom at the End of the World*, much to teach us about 'collaborative survival in precarious times'. The potential of 'mushrooms to save the world' was the starting point of Berlin-based artists Eloïse Bonneviot and Anne de Boer's project *The Mycological Twist*, an artistic investigation of fungal cycles of deterioration and regeneration happening in subterranean zones. In *Five Amazing Tricks to Get Rid of Perception* (2016), they looked at how mushrooms could be used to eliminate pests, regulate health and decompose waste, as well as to 'enhance our vision and experience of hyper-connected bodies'. In that sense, Merlin Sheldrake has noted in his book *Entangled Life* that because they are 'eating rock, making soil, digesting pollutants, nourishing and killing plants, surviving in space, inducing visions, producing food, making medicines, manipulating animal behaviour and influencing the composition of Earth's atmosphere', fungi are 'changing the way that life happens'.

The formative role of microorganisms in Earth systems is also addressed in the work of German artist Susanne M. Winterling, whose research is focused on marine bioluminescence. This natural phenomenon of light emissions is caused by dinoflagellates, single-cell aquatic organisms that are considered algae, although they have characteristics of both plants and animals and constitute a large proportion of planktonic biomass. The alien qualities of such lifeforms have also been noted by anthropologist Stefan Helmreich, who, in *Alien Ocean: Anthropological Voyages in Microbial Seas*, attributed their otherness to the fact that marine microorganisms 'inhabit contexts, scales, worlds and microcosms inaccessible to prosthetic-free human experience'. To display her findings in gallery settings, Winterling has built up immersive installations consisting of several works, such as: *Planetary opera in three acts, divided by the currents* (2018), comprised of an audio piece of natural and synthetic sounds including hydrophone recordings of algae; *Planetary loop of gravitation* (2018), a video projection using 4K technology depicting enormous floating particles; and the textile installation *Flags of the miracular (welcome to the algae empire)* (2018). According to the artist, these microorganisms are indicators of *aqua viva*, the living water referred to by Caribbean fishermen, as their exposure to pollution and climate change makes them a litmus test for the health of the oceans.

122

    The destabilizing effects of anthropogenic climate change on the dynamic balance of natural systems were addressed by German artist Antje Majewski in her large-scale painting *Passagen* (2019), which replicated the winding passageways painstakingly carved into trees by bark beetles. The artistic qualities of these insects' tree-carving skills are also reflected in their names, with *Ips typographus* deriving from the Greek for book printer and *Pityogenes chalcographus* meaning copperplate engraver. In undisturbed ecosystems, bark beetles mostly live in dying hosts and contribute to the decomposition of organic matter. However, they have also been beneficiaries of more frequent and extended periods of drought in recent years, when monoculturally grown spruce trees become weak and therefore offer them optimal breeding grounds. For the authors of *Feral Atlas: The More-Than-Human Anthropocene*, 'climate seems a clear culprit' in the proliferation of bark beetles, with warming winter temperatures allowing them to expand northwards in North American forests at a rate of 40 kilometres per year, while by killing off trees the insects are making woodland even more 'susceptible to high-intensity fires'. Apart from documenting the path of destruction carved by the bark beetle in the forests of the German region of Tharandt, Majewski has also devised practical strategies for the rewilding of affected areas by planting wild fruit trees to restart the symbiotic processes of multispecies communities.

123

    In the essay 'Microscopic Colonialism', part of his larger body of research into the relationship between infectious diseases and modernism, *Terra Infecta*, architect Andrea Bagnato analysed viral diseases including Ebola, malaria and HIV. He related their spread to the colonial transformation of landscapes and capitalist networks of production, as a consequence of which 'viruses and bacteria began to circulate as well'. Tehran-born artist Natascha Sadr Haghighian's installation *passing one loop into another* (2017) juxtaposed

124

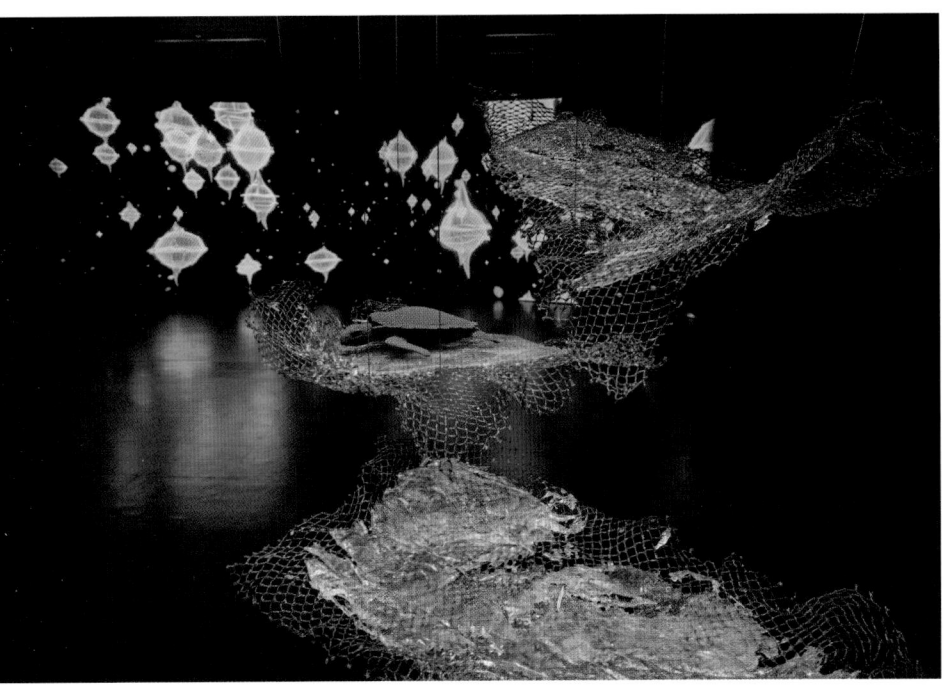

122 Susanne M. Winterling, *Meditation on Terraforming (a tribute to Marie Tharp)*, 2018, *Shield Warrior For Biodiversity*, 2018, and *Planetary loop of gravitation*, 2018

the first sighting of the Asian tiger mosquito in Italy with the signing of the General Agreement of Tariffs and Trade (GATT) in the early 1990s, which was also the moment when global institutions woke up to the threat of climate change. Discovering the Southeast Asian mosquito to be a carrier of pathogens and diseases such as the Zika virus, the Italians attempted to combat its spread by relying on the local *Pipistrellus* microbat that feeds on insects. Haghighian's work consisted of a larger-than-life model of the tiger mosquito landing on a tablet connected to three other screens, all resting on a tower of textile reels with yarn from Prato, the Italian centre of the global textile trade, in a space that resonated with the hunting calls of the nocturnal microbat. Referencing in its title the widespread technique for making string figures, the work demonstrated the interwoven aspects of economy, politics, ecology and microbial transits along global trade routes.

The focal point of Pedro Neves Marques's digital animation *Aedes aegypti* (2017) was a mosquito that carries Zika and dengue viruses. In the video it appears surrounded by a toxic

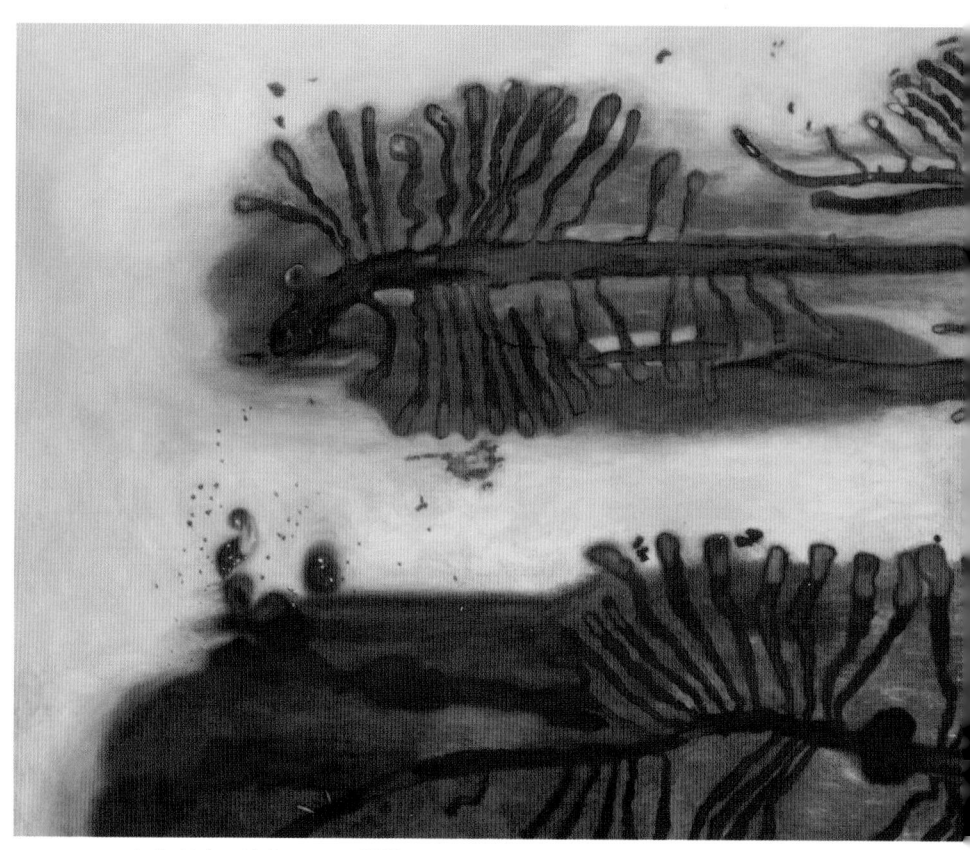

123 Antje Majewski, *Passagen*, 2019

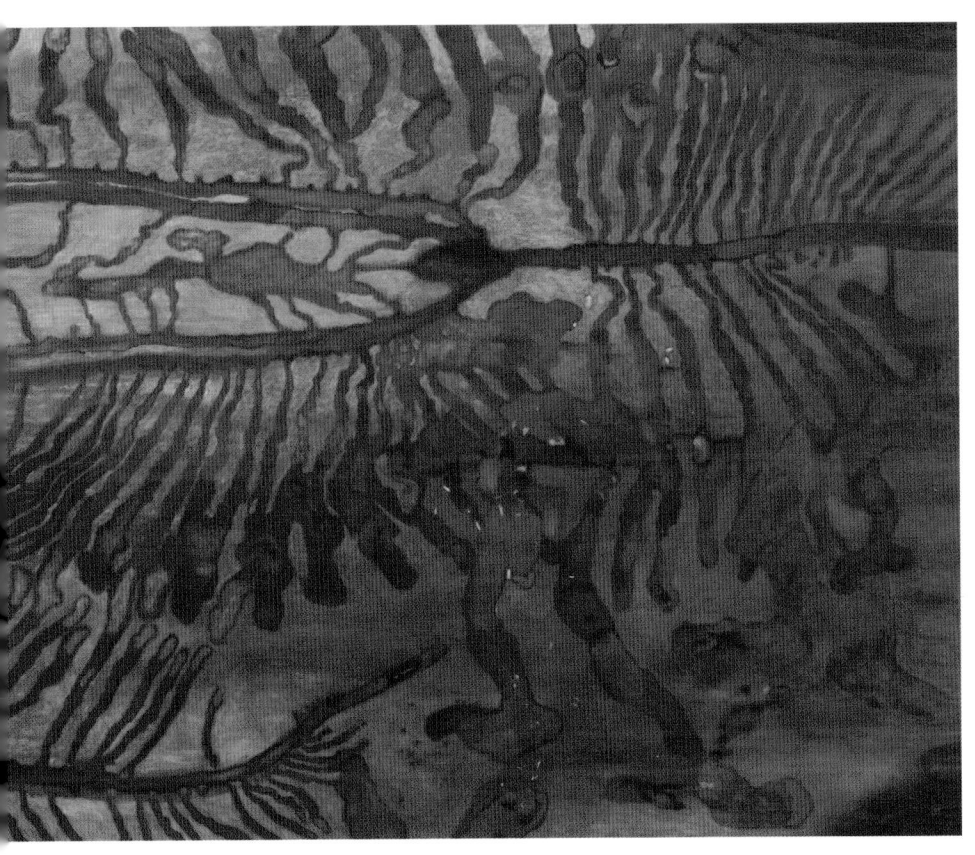

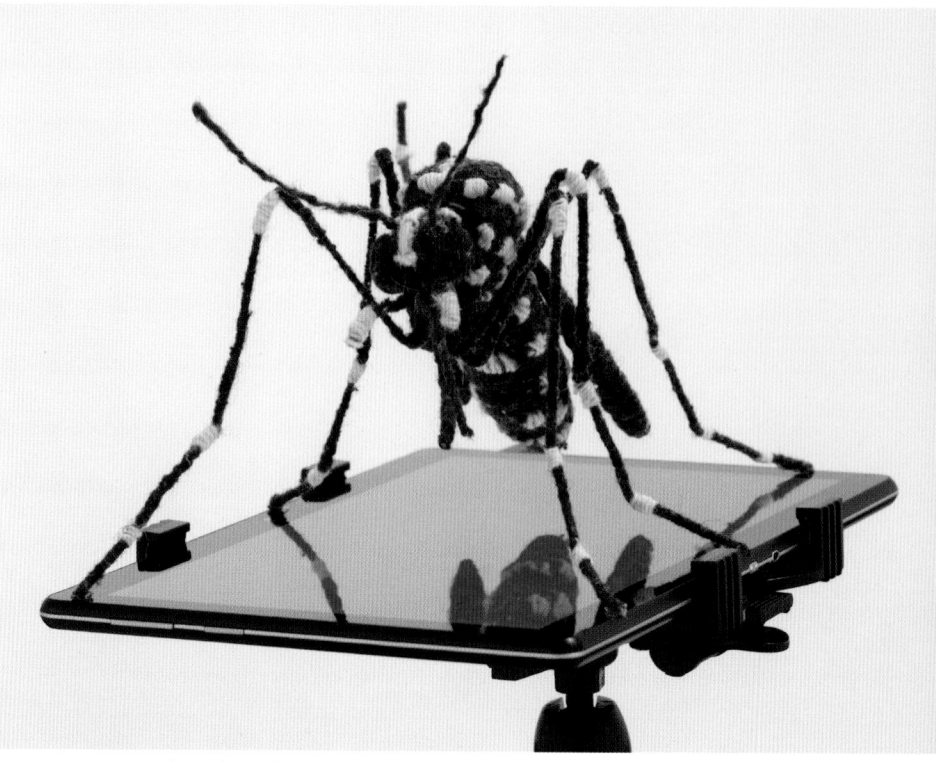

124 Natascha Sadr Haghighian, *passing one loop into another*, 2017

cloud of dispersed chemicals, in interchanging scenes of
sucking blood on human skin and engaging in a dance of
copulation. The artificial atmosphere of this hyperreal work
emphasized the fact that the mosquito itself is a 'post-natural
insect', since the main protagonist is a genetically modified
variety. The artist referred to biotechnological procedures that
entail inserting a particular gene into male mosquitos. After
being released into the wild, they mate with females and pass
on the lethal gene, which ensures that the female and the
offspring die and therefore obstruct the virus's transmission.
The field trials have been carried out in countries such as
the Cayman Islands, Malaysia and Brazil, where Western
biotech companies have set up their laboratories, repeating
the colonial matrix. The related audio-video installation
The Bite (2018) situated the epidemics of Zika virus within
the populist politics of Brazil, inserting President Bolsonaro
into the 3D visualization of the virus. Incorporated in the
film is footage of genetic manipulations in a laboratory,

along with video portraying a triangular relationship between cis and transgender people. Issues of intimacy, love and care in times of epidemics are combined in this work with environmental, biotechnological and political crises, even before the coronavirus outbreak brought greater attention to their interconnection.

Artists discussed in this chapter have pointed to the vital contribution of microbes to processes of decomposing and decay in providing the soil for new beginnings, while disclosing human bodies as holobionts and sites of symbiotic co-dependencies. Investigations of the subterranean world of fungi, the marine realms of aquatic microbes and the pathways of forest insects have revealed the unsuspected density of such micro-ecosystems and the mutual exposure of their inhabitants to the planetary dislocations of climate change. The opportunism of viruses in trafficking between animal hosts has become enmeshed in biotechnological strategies for the containment and control of accelerating global outbreaks. Pointing to the structural similarity between the coronavirus and climate crises in his book *Corona, Climate, Chronic Emergency*, Andreas Malm has noted that 'left untreated, both afflictions become self-amplifying – the more people infected, the more will be infected; the hotter the planet, the more feedback mechanisms heat it up further – and once underway, the sole way to terminate such spiralling burns is to cut the fuse'.

Part V
Pluriversal Ecologies

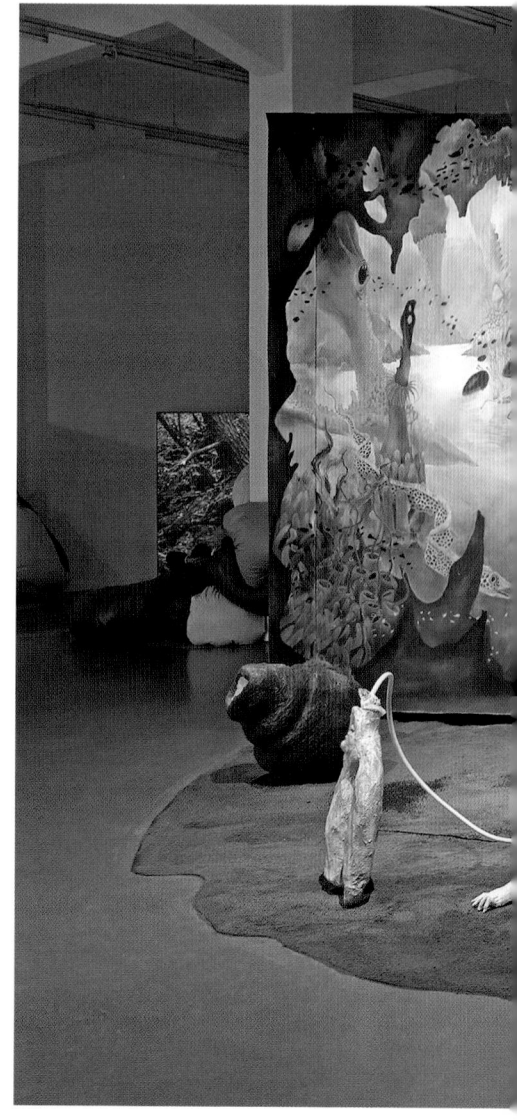

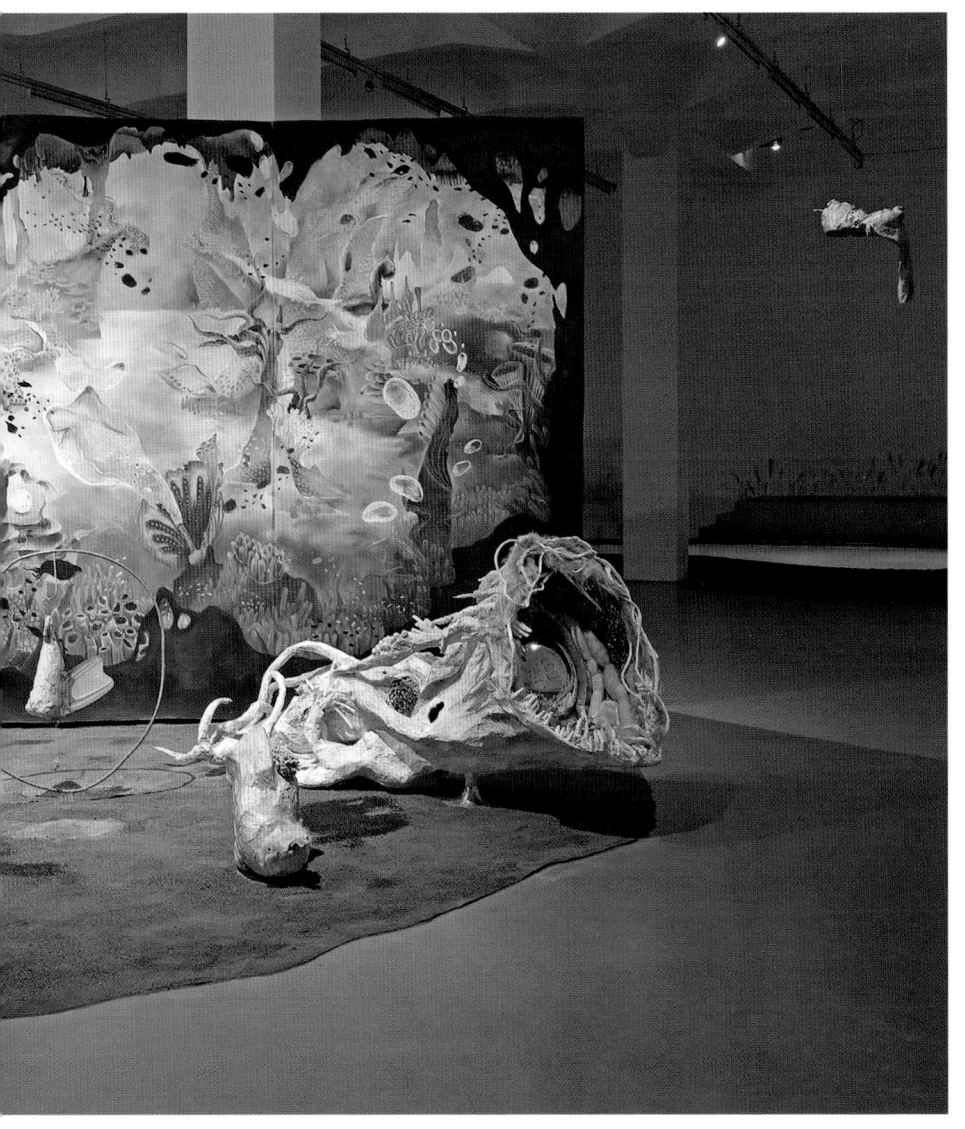

Chapter 1
Entangled Terrestrials

The global pandemic of 2020 has put the question of human exceptionalism squarely back into focus, with the virus exposing the collective – yet socially unequal – vulnerability of human bodies, as well as the surprising susceptibility of all-powerful capitalist technologies and infrastructures to disruption by non-human agents. In other words, the presumption that human life can be categorically distinguished from the wider world breaks down in light of the understanding of human bodies as sites of multispecies kinship relations and therefore already entangled in more-than-human communities. As theorist Achille Mbembe has pointed out, 'to return to the body is also to come back to earth', understood 'not as land but as event', belonging to all its inhabitants, 'without distinction of race, origin, ethnicity or even species'. Correspondingly Bruno Latour has proposed 'the Terrestrial with a capital T' to denote a reshaping of planetary politics that is able to 'accommodate the multiplicity of beings belonging to the terrestrial world'. At the same time, such entanglements are also imbricated with the technosphere, which since colonization, modernization and globalization has, according to theorist Yuk Hui, determined the 'relation between human and non-human beings, human and cosmos, nature and culture'. Calling for the dismantling of the idea of a 'mono-technological culture', he has proposed the notion of 'cosmotechnics', understood as the 'unification between the cosmic order and the moral order through technical activities', pointing to the existence and history of a plurality of technological cultures. At issue here are propositions and gestures for changing attitudes and actions towards other terrestrials, as well as opening up new pathways to connect with the world by exploring other-than-human perspectives.

The unfamiliar worlds brought into being by Australian artist Madison Bycroft in their double installation *There There, There Now / Field* (2020) are in active revolt against the rule of Western modernity, calling into question the historical dualisms that have divided human subjects with identities and cultures from the non-humans they subjugate with their gaze. *Field* depicted an underwater scene with sculptures of hybrid aquatic organisms with crab claws and human features against a coral reef background swirling with amorphous ocean creatures, a watery cosmos brought to life by a soundscape of music, poems and acoustic samplings. On the reverse side of the circular installation the backdrop of *There There, There Now* was a futuristic scene of volcanic rocks and abstract sculpted forms bathed in the purple-pink light of a low full moon, in front of which sat a sloth with a drum and a farting baboon with his rear turned towards the viewer. What is destabilized here are the boundaries between human and animal, culture and nature, living and inanimate, but also the whole apparatus of establishing boundaries, categories and hierarchies that since the colonial era has sought to impose the narrow outlook of scientific rationalism onto boundless indigenous cosmologies. These scenographic constellations demand to be viewed not as outlandish but with curiosity and in acceptance of the more-than-human territories that lie beyond the reach of Western ontology.

In an age of ecological crisis, the impossibility of compartmentalizing life and maintaining the boundaries between the atomized individual idealized by modern Western culture and more-than-human flows, lifeforms and intelligences was addressed in Laure Prouvost's *Deep See Blue Surrounding You* (2019). Realized for the Venice Biennial, this immersive installation saw visitors enter the French pavilion through an underground storeroom and don theatrical masks before treading their way through an otherworldly terrain scattered with unlikely objects, from eggshells and seaweed to discarded mobile phones, all props from the mesmerizing film at its centre. Entitled *They Parlaient Idéale* (2019), the video was conceived as a 'road trip to the subconscious' undertaken by a group of people of different ages and ethnicities on a feverish journey from the downtrodden suburbs of Paris to the canals of Venice via a mysterious underworld. They relate their experiences in a fluid mixture of French, English, Dutch and Arabic, as well as through dance and rap. It is not just the boundaries of social, racial and generational difference that are liquified in the film, but also the divide between human and non-human, through the figure of the octopus as a leitmotif

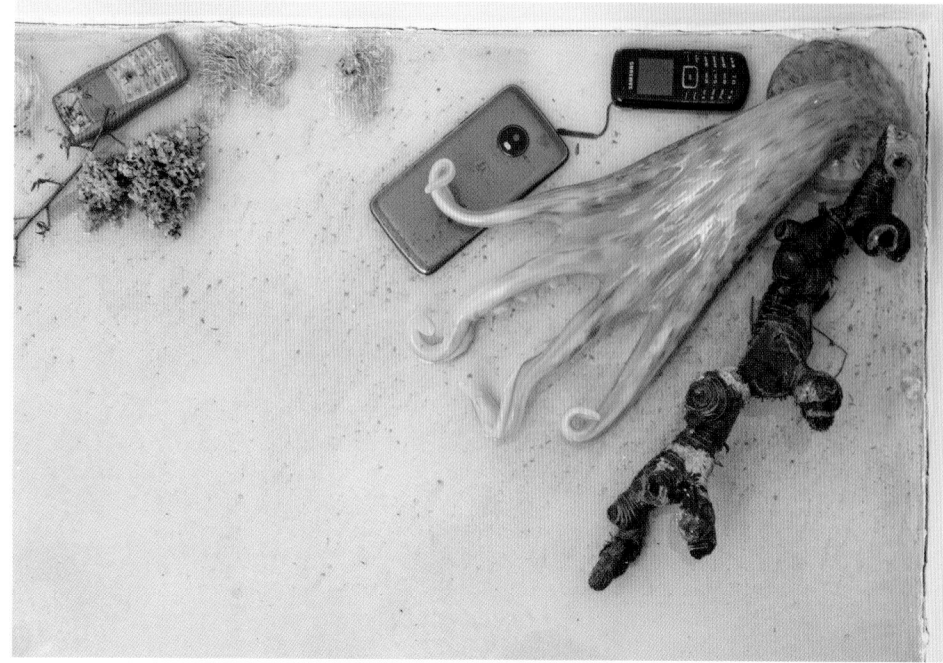

126 Laure Prouvost, *Deep See Relique n°10*, 2019 (detail)

and living presence in the work. Visitors found their way through the exhibition space by following the tentacles to the octopus's head, while in the film the cast of adventurers move forward like the octopus, 'touching the world, feeling while thinking'. The myth of human exceptionalism lies discredited and discarded in this visionary ode to tentacular intelligence and more-than-human sensibility.

With its purposely enigmatic title, London-based artist 127 Heather Phillipson's hallucinatory film *put the goat in the goat boat* (2014) brought into focus the gap between references to nature in everyday language and the biophysical realities of the natural world. Concepts and figures of speech, such as 'finding your better nature' or 'going back to nature' are singled out in headings that appear over images of living organisms whose controlled existence in artificial environments, such as botanical gardens or zoological enclosures, contradicts the cultural longings for an untouched, wild and separate realm of the natural. Surprised to find herself naked in front of a field of staring cows, the narrator asks them, 'What do you think?', and against closeups of a human body reassures herself that 'excess hair is acceptable' and 'there is no nudity in nature'. The cows respond not with metaphysics, but with the more mundane comment that 'you and your kind are trying to eat us all up'. To be human at a time when it is no longer tenable to maintain the illusion of separation from the natural world entails taking an active stance towards the exploitation of fellow terrestrials. As the artist has insisted, 'before being humans, or ideas, or genders, we are, primarily, animals', while the treatment of non-human animals constitutes 'one of the greatest unacknowledged atrocities – tragedies – of our time'.

Korean-born Anne Duk Hee Jordan is a Berlin-based artist whose practice arises from her interests in nature, science, philosophy and technology, as well as her professional experiences of fishing, rescue diving and being a chef. This is manifest in her work, which ranges from edible landscapes to robotic sculpture and video installations, exploring the manifold forms of coexistences, multispecies entanglements and instances of climate adaptation that encompass plants, animals, humans, microorganisms and machines. In her evolving series *Artificial Stupidity* (since 2016), as a cynical comment on artificial intelligence, the artist transforms organic and non-organic material into animated machines, creating space for 'non-intelligent' technologies. A case in point is *Water Crab* (2017–ongoing), which was conceived as a dysfunctional cleaning robot, alluding to the vain efforts to solve environmental problems, especially in relation to

128

127 Heather Phillipson, *put the goat in the goat boat*, 2014

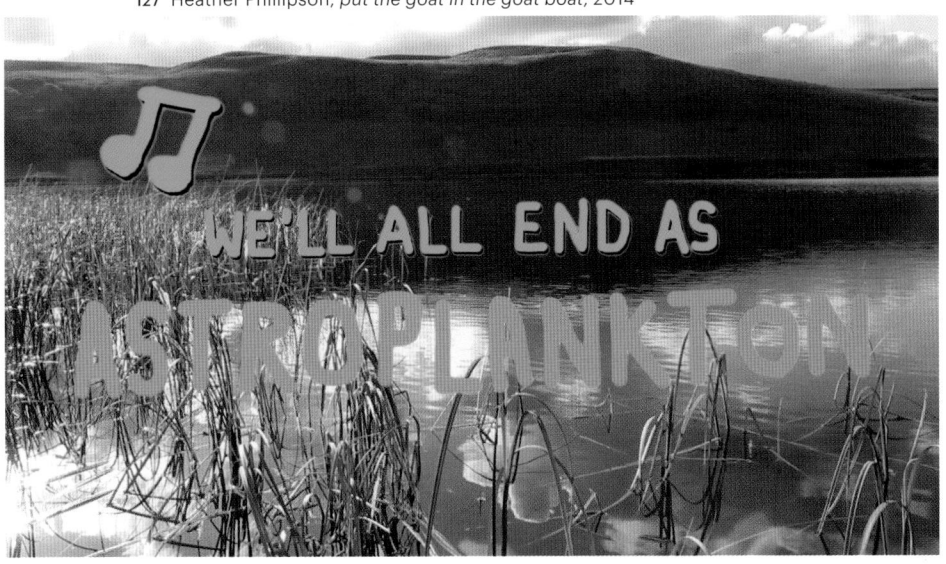

pollution of the oceans and the effect climate change has on marine life. Also part of the series is *Critters* (2018), a family of robotic creatures reminiscent of enlarged oceanic organisms, which are there to 'remind us of what we do not know about the marine world'. The moving aluminium *Teapot* (2019) is a sonic sculpture whose sound recreates wind, which starts with a breeze but can turn into a huge storm and therefore symbolizes climate change. Referencing Donna Haraway's *Staying with the Trouble* and the appeal of making kin as 'perhaps the hardest and most urgent' task for the Chthulucene, Jordan demonstrates in her practice the interdependent processes of giving and taking in Earth's ecosystems and the need to 'cope with the strangers'.

New York-based Thai artist Korakrit Arunanondchai questions in his work the effects of the Anthropocene on human subjectivity, problematizing the complex overlays of globalized cultures and the contentious interplay of Eastern philosophy, ecological realms and technological developments. His performative and multimedia practice encompasses the

128 Anne Duk Hee Jordan, *Water Crab*, 2017–ongoing

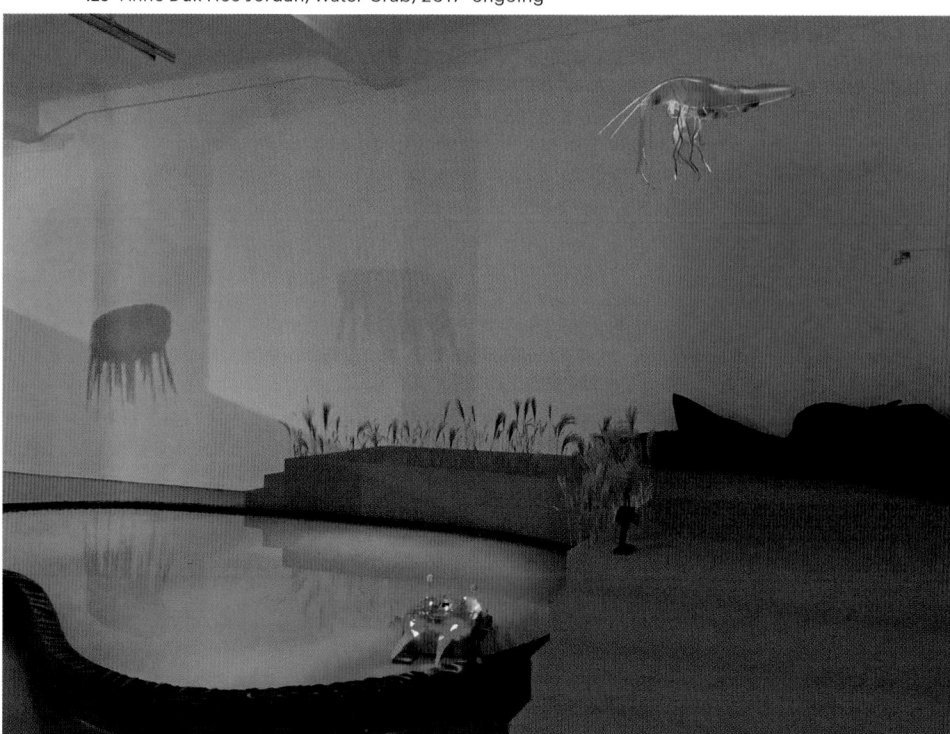

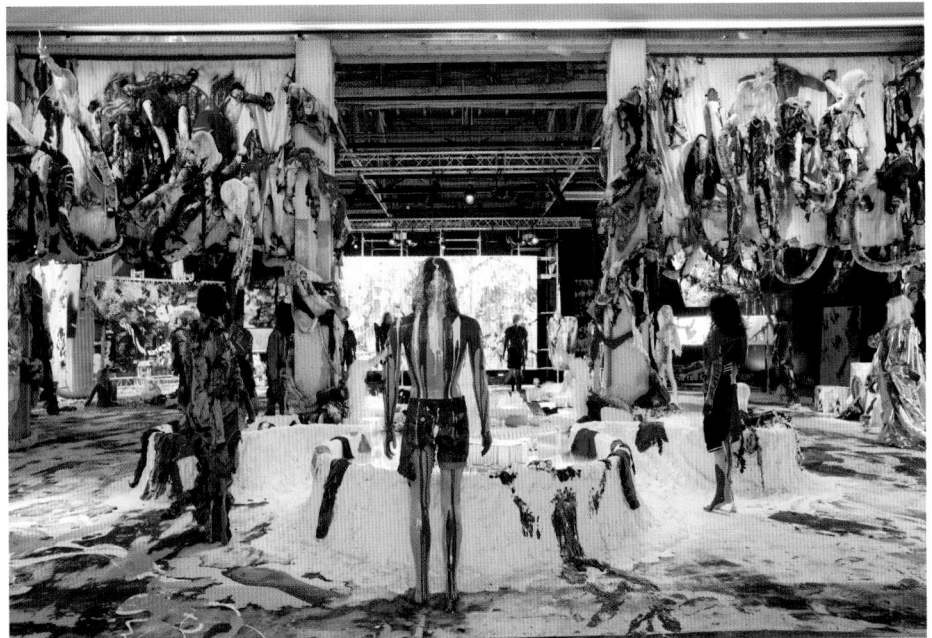

129 Korakrit Arunanondchai, *Painting with history in a room filled with people with funny names 3*, 2015

domains of the private and the social, the autobiographical and the political, while keeping reality and fiction inseparable. This is exemplified in *Painting with history in a room filled with people with funny names 3* (2015), a bold and unsettling exhibition environment which consisted of paint-splashed mannequin sculptures, expressive canvases mounted on scaffolding as TV studio sets and a film projection, epitomizing the informational overload and saturation of contemporary culture. Equally dense is the film part of the work, in which the artist is personified as a Thai painter wearing torn denim, as a symbol of youth and music subculture. He engages in a conversation with a drone named Chantri, a figure inspired by the Hindu and Buddhist mythological bird Garuda, which has recorded views of Thailand's scenic islands and riversides, cityscapes and crocodiles in the zoo. The work probed the discrepancies between Eastern and Western worldviews, such as around the convergence of spirituality and machines, pointing to the fact that although everyone is interconnected in the digital sphere, there are many faces of technology and, depending on which culture one approaches it from, everyone else appears to have funny names.

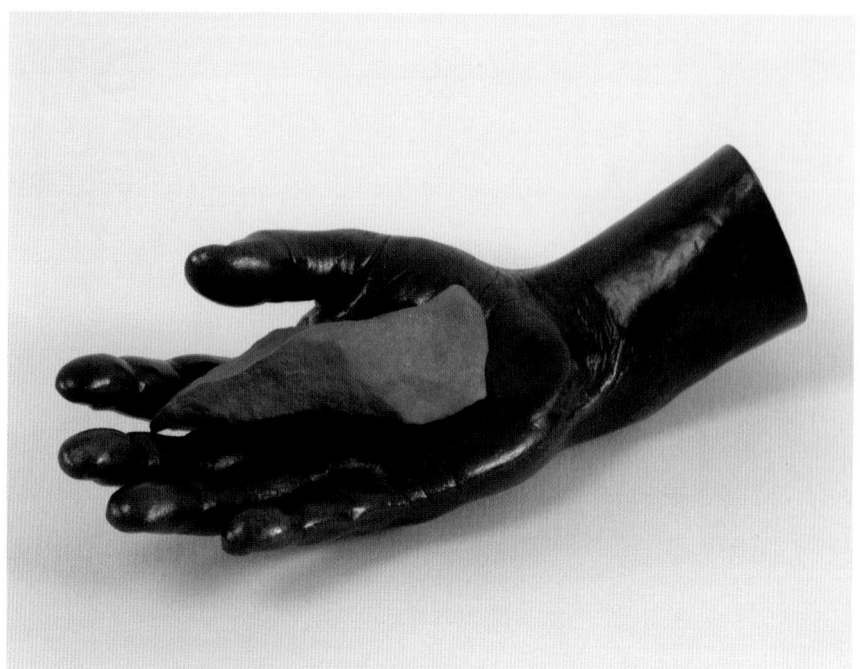

130 Marjolijn Dijkman, *That What Makes Us Human*, 2016

Noting that for the first time in human history 'we have the capacity to destroy conditions for survival' and making reference to the mass extinction event 65 million years ago when an asteroid wiped the dinosaurs from the face of the planet, theorist Noam Chomsky famously observed that 'today we are the asteroid'. Dutch artist Marjolijn Dijkman's animation *Prospect of Interception* (2016) speculated about the impact an asteroid colliding with the Earth might have on future life. Comprised of a two-hour textual narration subtitled in various world languages beneath an image of the floating cosmic body, the film incorporated conflicting quotations from over a hundred historic and living authors from the disciplines of astronomy, cosmology and spirituality. The related sculpture *That What Makes Us Human* (2016) consists of a bronze cast of a human right hand holding a life-size titanium copy of one of the Canyon Diablo meteorites that landed on Earth about 50,000 years ago, fitting into the hand as if it were a flint tool used by Palaeolithic humans at the time of the impact. For the artist this represented a conjuncture with the evolutionary path from early humans to modern times, with the progressive development of consciousness, technologies and ambition

130

now expanding to aspirations to conquer, colonize and extract even the cosmos. Another analogy was also at play here, arising from the fact that the strength of the asteroid of which this meteorite is a fragment was similar to the energy released by the first hydrogen bomb, bringing to the fore the question of technologies of war and humanity's potential for destruction reaching into outer space. The artist left open the question of whether the use of tools and the ability to reason are what distinguishes humans from other species, or whether it is rather their uniquely destructive force.

The Terrestrial breaks down the boundaries between the familiar dualisms and categorical hierarchies of Western modernity, shattering the myth of the atomized individual and dissolving social, racial, generational and species-bound differences. Artists discussed in this chapter have highlighted the destabilization of the notion of nature in popular culture, probed the linguistic transformations heralded by interspecies communication and acknowledged troubled coexistences. Questioning the potency of the technosphere and showing its limits, they have pointed to the inevitability of hybridity in Anthropocene conditions, in light also of the recognition that technology has many faces and disconcerting histories.

Chapter 2
Reparative Histories

The Anthropocene thesis has brought to the fore the call to overcome the long separation of human and natural histories in Western modernity predicated on the dominance of reductive and instrumentalizing attitudes towards nature. At the same time, anthropologist Marisol de la Cadena has proposed the notion of the 'anthropo-not-seen' to describe both the devastation of indigenous worlds that do not 'ontologically separate humans (or culture) from nonhumans (or nature)' and the resistance to today's unparalleled levels of destruction. While there are more than 370 million indigenous people on the planet, the institutions of colonial modernity have, as curator Katya García-Antón has pointed out, expertly insisted on the 'localness of indigenous experience, in order to fragment, isolate and render invisible these intellectual processes from the world's stage'. The unevenness with which the effects of climate disaster are distributed demonstrates the extent to which racism and imperialism have structured what theorist Françoise Vergès has called the 'racial Capitaloscene'. Another divergent history is signalled by the term socialist Anthropocene, reflecting the fact that for much of the twentieth century there were competing versions of industrial modernity, while the rapid restoration of capitalism to post-communist countries overshadowed socialist prospects. As explored here, the dismantling of West-centric accounts of global expansion, scientific progress and economic development has created space for the emergence of new narratives that are decolonial, anti-racist and ecological.

Broaching the vastness of geological timescales and the materiality of terrestrial forces, Vancouver-based academic and artist Denise Ferreira da Silva and Berlin-based artist Arjuna Neuman's film *4 Waters: Deep Implicancy* (2019) traced

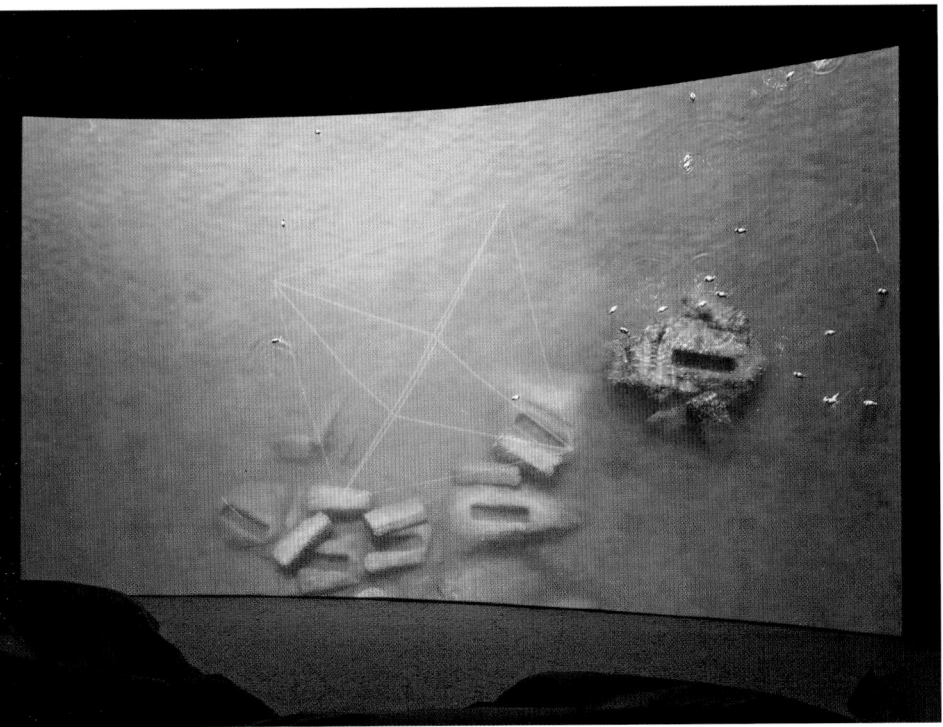

131 Denise Ferreira da Silva and Arjuna Neuman, *4 Waters: Deep Implicancy*, 2019

the movement of people, species and matter across oceans and over millennia. Video footage and oral accounts of the perilous ordeal of Syrian refugees journeying in overcrowded boats across the Mediterranean to escape chemical warfare opened up a discussion of the epistemological roots of the callous indifference to their suffering in fortress Europe. Observing that 'this very same crossing gave birth to the Western mind', the artists pointed to the tendency since Plato to 'contain air, water, earth and fire within abstract forms' as a source of the 'total violence' of the modern world. Across the Atlantic, the earthquake that struck Haiti in 1784 was explored as a seismic prefiguration of the Haitian Revolution, and as such doubly invisible to a Western teleology that has long ignored the uprising of self-liberated slaves against French colonial rule and the historical agency of natural forces. Images of vibrant microscopic life and a fisherman's tale of a thousand years of attentive human–sea relations in the Indian Ocean disclosed a state of primordial entanglement before the world was divided up by colonial modernity.

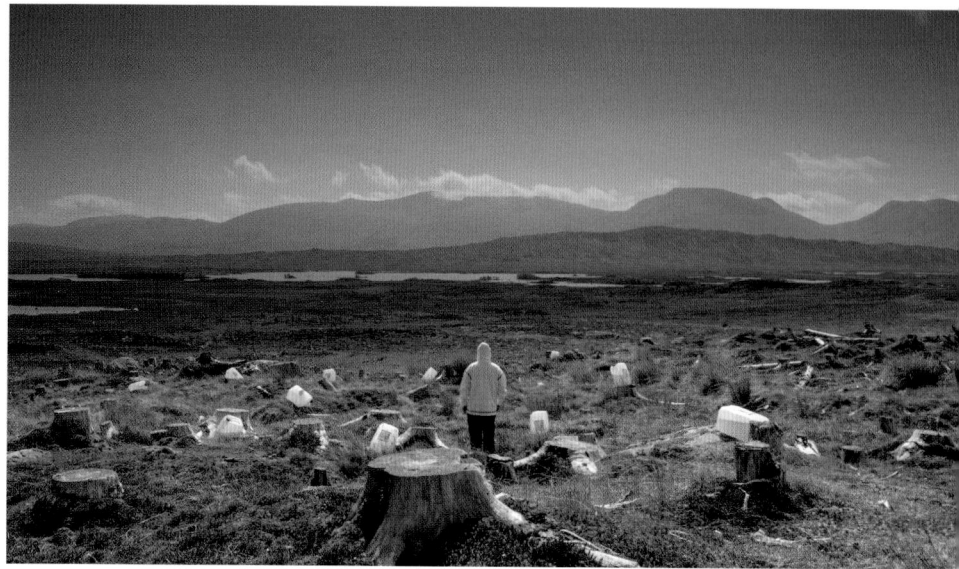

132 John Akomfrah, *Purple*, 2017

The planetary drama of climate change is projected across six screens in the panoramic installation *Purple* (2017) by British artist of Ghanaian descent John Akomfrah. Newly shot footage of scenes of environmental disaster, from the melting of the ice sheet in Greenland to the engulfing of the Marquesas Islands by rising ocean levels, is combined with archival footage of mid-twentieth-century television documentaries that appear today as an unintentional record of the ecological blindness of industrial modernity. A recurrent motif interspersed in this filmic tapestry of wilderness loss and societal dislocation are shots of solitary figures set before grandiose landscapes that have been endangered by human intervention. There is a visual reference here to the landscape paintings of Romanticism, but while the heroic explorers and poetic hikers of the nineteenth century gazed down upon the sublime bounty of untouched nature, Akomfrah's latter-day wanderers appear listless and uncertain faced with the environmental wreckage left by an economic system based on expansion and extraction. The camera lingers on the powerlines and fossil fuel furnaces that are a visual link to the artist's childhood lived in the shadow of London's Battersea Power Station during the 1960s, at a time when few made the connection between the industrial majesty of the iconic landmark and the 'daily dose of carbon monoxide poisoning' inflicted on the local residents.

The phrase 'I can't breathe' is invoked in The Otolith Group's film *INFINITY minus Infinity* (2019) as a direct reference to the last words of Eric Garner, an unarmed black man choked to death by New York police in 2014, but also to allude to the toxic effects of air pollution, which due to environmental racism disproportionately impact black communities. Incorporating dance, performance, music, poetry recitals and digital animation, this audio-visual assemblage by the London-based artist duo of Anjalika Sagar and Kodwo Eshun explored the transhistorical connections between 'the unpayable debts of racial capitalism' and the 'ongoing crimes of climate catastrophe'. The film established a historical timeline that reveals the UK government's strategy of creating a 'hostile environment' for migrants as one of many racist crimes enacted by British imperial capitalism in the aftermath of the abolition of slavery in 1833. Colonialism is exposed as the ultimate cause of climate change, but also, through its erasure and devaluing of indigenous and black lives, as a political obstacle to building global solidarities in mitigating the effects of rising temperatures on vulnerable communities.

Consisting of over twenty members, the Karrabing Film Collective is a grassroots indigenous media group founded in 2013 and based largely in the Belyuen community in Australia's Northern Territory. Their name references 'low tide' in the Emmiyengal language, a moment when, according to Elizabeth A. Povinelli, anthropologist and long-term collaborator of the group, 'all kinds of potentialities spring forward'. Their approach to filmmaking is described in her *Geontologies* as a means to analyse contemporary settler colonialism by 'continually probing its forms and forces', while seeking a way to maintain and enhance the Karrabing's 'manner and mode of existing'.

The film *The Mermaids, or Aiden in Wonderland* (2018) follows a speculative scenario in which only Aboriginals can survive long periods outdoors, while the white race has no immunity to the toxic contamination and capitalist degradation it has produced, taking the form of an epidemic of toxic mud. A young indigenous boy, Aiden, who was taken away as a baby to be a part of a medical eugenics experiment, is returning to his family and on the way encounters entangled futures and pasts. The fragmentary episodes of this dangerous journey lead through Aboriginal lands scarred by the brutal actions of multinational chemical companies and extractive industries and the charred remains of forests devastated by the wildfires of climate breakdown. An elder whom the boy meets on the way tells him that 'before white people came, the world was alright, the mermaids would come out in the moonlight', pointing to the recuperative power of storytelling.

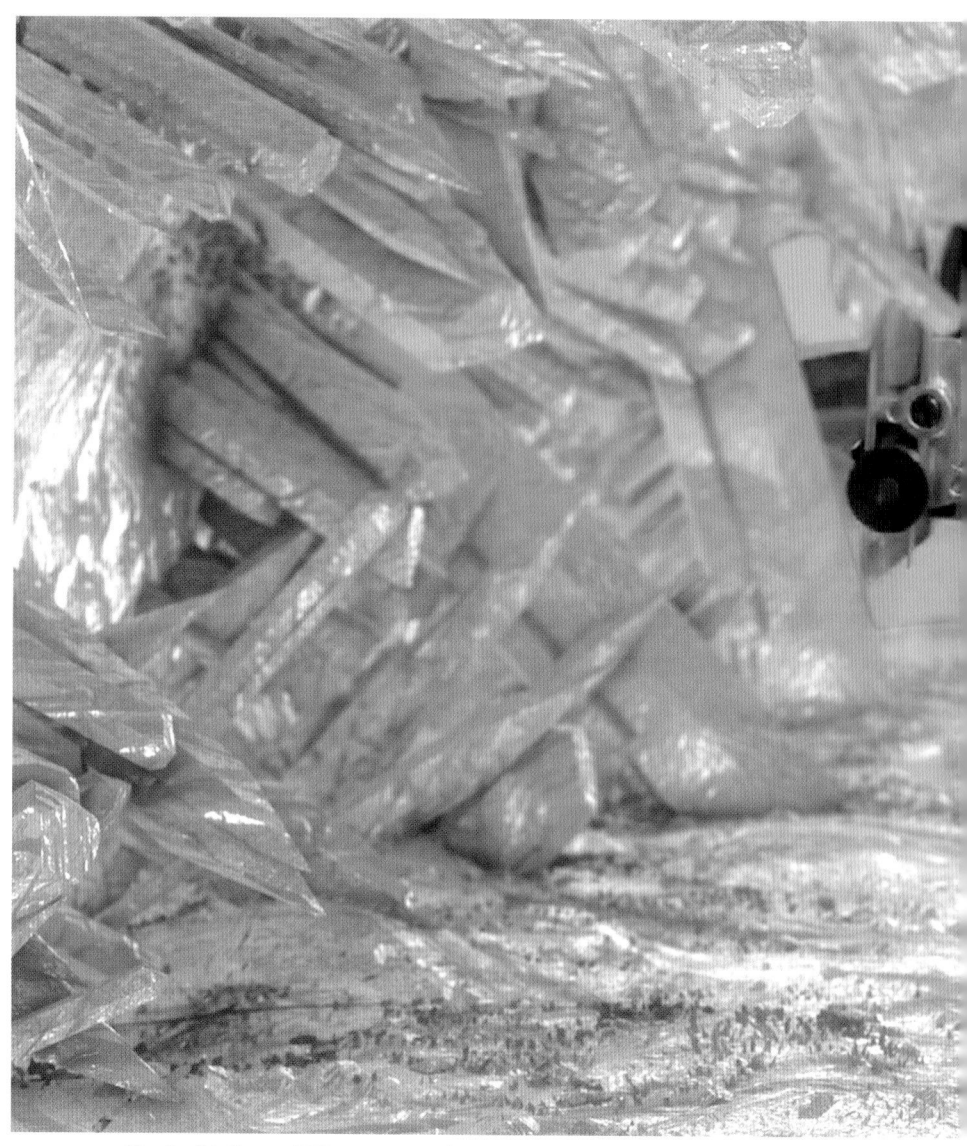

133 The Otolith Group, *INFINITY minus Infinity*, 2019

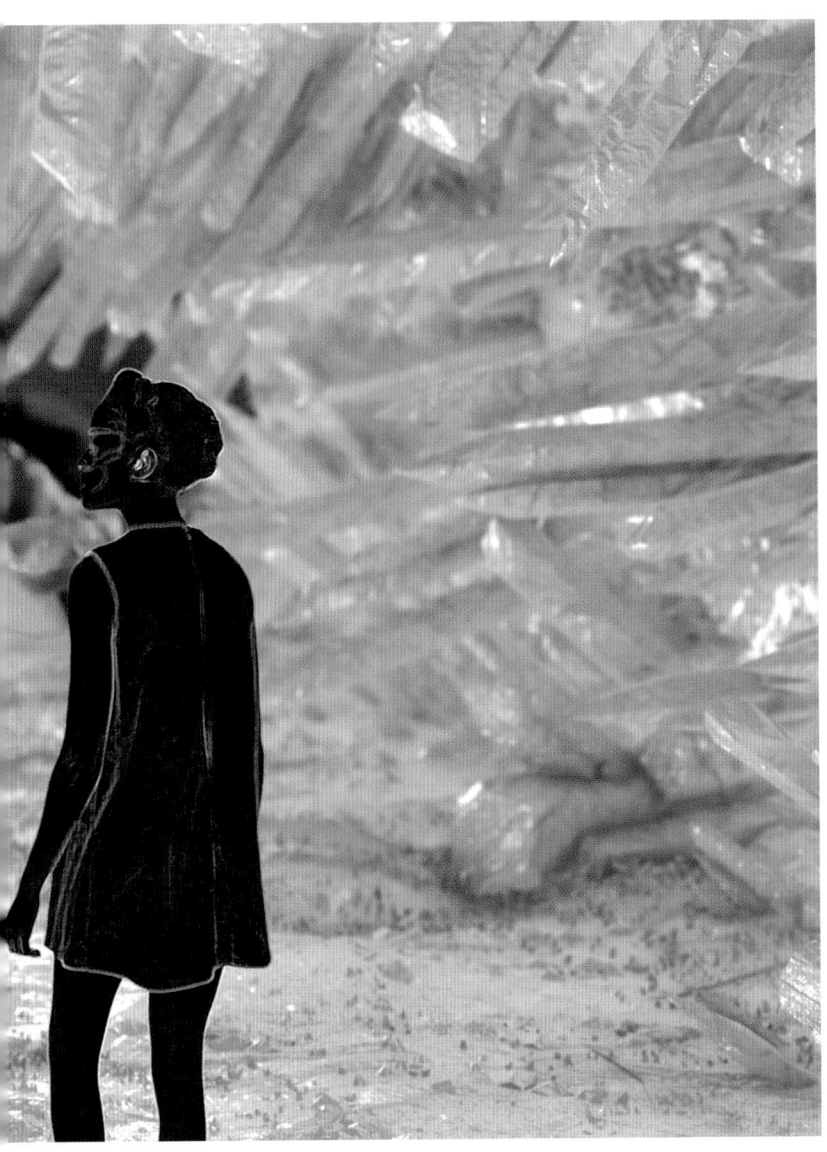

'My work is like singing a Sámi yoik: there's no beginning and no end. It's like a circle,' observed Britta Marakatt-Labba, a visual artist born in 1951 as one of nine children in a reindeer-herding family on the Swedish side of Sápmi, where she is still based. The cyclical mode of her practice is visible in the exhibition 'History in Stitches' in Lunds konsthall in 2018. It gathered her embroidery works spanning several decades, which depict intertwined scenes of landscapes, everyday life or mythological events to illuminate the long-suppressed heritage, culture and worldviews of her community. Her 24-metre tapestry *History* (2003–7), permanently installed in Tromsø University, narrates the history and cosmology of the Sámi people, starting with the forest and the animals that live in it, then relating how it was populated by indigenous hunters and herders, before the history of domination, unrest and militarization unfolded. Indicatively, many of Marakatt-Labba's textile works also address political and environmental struggles. *The Crows* (1983) dealt with the protest movement against the damming of the Áltá River in Finnmark in the early 1980s, while *Movement* (2016) engaged with the mining industry's extractivist conquest of the region and its effects on the city of Kiruna, the centre of which is currently being relocated to avoid sinking into the cracks caused by the iron ore mines that are still being exploited. Marakatt-Labba's practice reveals indigenous people's struggles against the suppression of their cosmologies, histories and traditional knowledges within nation states,

135

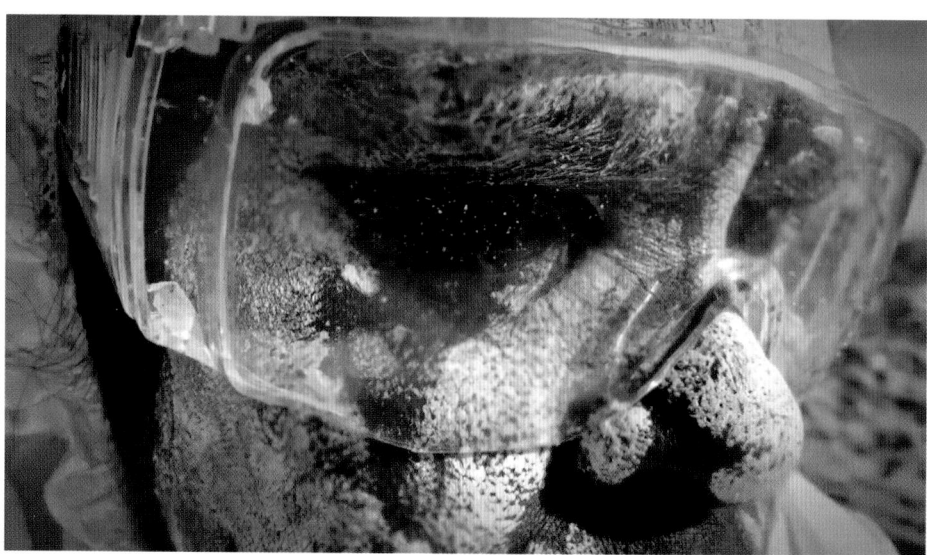

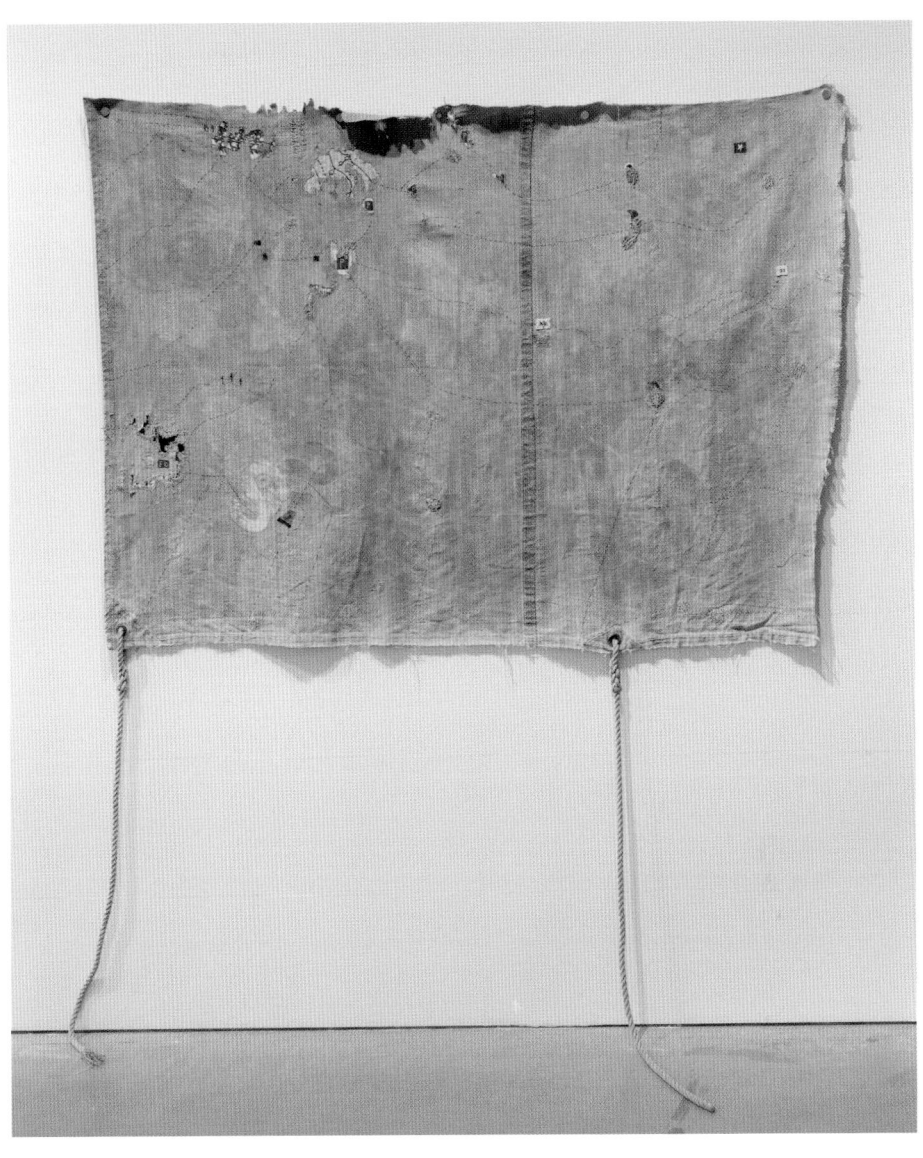

134 OPPOSITE Karrabing Film Collective, *The Mermaids, or Aiden in Wonderland*, 2018
135 ABOVE Britta Marakatt-Labba, *Movement*, 2016

Reparative Histories

as well as demonstrating how unfolding climate change is endangering their survival.

The discordant processes of rapid modernization in China and the effects that intertwined political, technological and economic forces exert on social and natural landscapes unfold as the grand narrative in Liu Chuang's three-channel video installation *Bitcoin Mining and Field Recordings of Ethnic Minorities* (2018). The energy-intensive cryptocurrency mining that takes up to seventy percent of the world's computing power is largely distributed across southwestern China, a mountainous area that is rich in hydropower and also inhabited by a number of ethnic minorities. Aerial footage of the river valleys and dam infrastructures was combined with images of Bitcoins, abstractions of technological transmissions and field recordings of indigenous people, while the references also included archival footage, science fiction cinema and anthropological research. Highlighting the tension between tradition and high technology, as well as the discrepancy between the illusion of immateriality of virtual realms and the reckless harvesting of electricity for digital transactions, the work also left open the possibility of alliances between the autonomous strivings of minorities and the online currency that operates outside centralized financial systems. In a moment when all three screens stall on the image of a spider painstakingly weaving his web, it becomes clear that the geoengineering drama is also being played out at the expense of Earth's systems and non-human species.

The starting point for Czech artist Zbyněk Baladrán's investigation of the alternate modernity of the socialist Anthropocene was the alteration and subsequent erasure of a socialist-era peace slogan on a viaduct in Prague. In the early 1990s the Cold War anti-militarist sign 'For Europe without Wars' was modified by crossing out two Czech letters to transform the message into 'For Crude Oil without War' in order to draw attention to the link between dependence on fossil fuels and the Gulf War. Noting that the graffitied version had recently been painted over in grey, the artist identified the hue of the oil-based grey paint as corresponding to the colour RAL 7035 and traced the history of this colour coding to its origins in imperial Germany. The fact that it had replaced the colour mixing systems developed under socialism was indicative for Baladrán of the 'reliance of local industry on the German economy'. At the same time, the minimalist grey rectangle that overwrote both Cold War fears of nuclear war and later public awareness of the threat posed by conflicts over natural resources now stood as a pervading 'expression of powerlessness'. Found photographs of socialist coal-mining

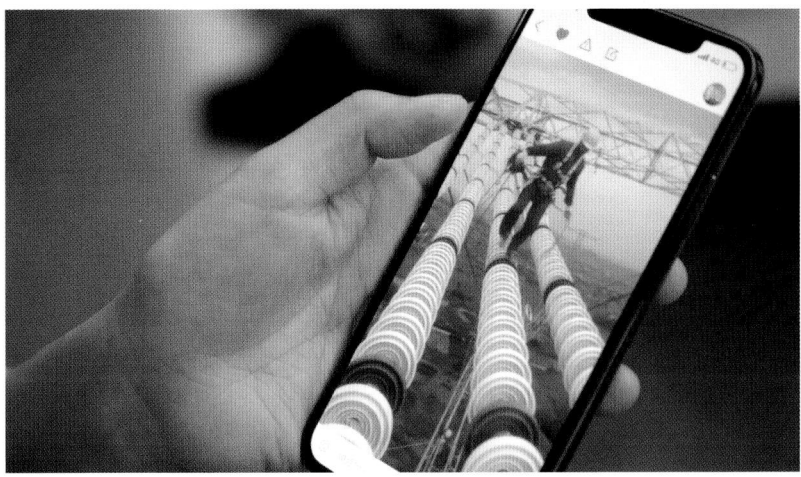

136 Liu Chuang, *Bitcoin Mining and Field Recordings of Ethnic Minorities*, 2018

infrastructures taken in the 1970s, at a time when Central European colour samplers were in use, were the basis for the artist's related series of diagrams entitled *Jevons Paradox* (2020), which revealed a 'coded history of the industrial age – and its alternatives too'. Referring to the paradox by which the efficiencies brought by technological advances always lead to increased consumption of natural resources, the artist disclosed the ideology of historical and technological progress shared by both Cold War industrial systems and the hi-tech green capitalism of today.

The historical roots of the capitalist mechanism for managing catastrophic risk were unearthed in Dutch artist Femke Herregraven's *Corrupted Air* (2018). One of the two lightboxes at the centre of her installation showed data from the book *Natural and Political Observations Made Upon the Bills of Mortality*, published in 1662 by John Graunt, a pioneering epidemiologist who used London's mortuary statistics to estimate the rise and spread of the plague and other illnesses. The other lightbox displayed a list of all the catastrophe bonds issued since 1996 on the global re-insurance market, a financial instrument invented to protect insurance companies from massive pay-outs after natural disasters such as extreme weather events. Through this juxtaposition, the artist exposed the roots of the complex predictive modelling of cat bonds, which speculate on the material and human costs of future cataclysms. An accompanying spatial composition consisting of abandoned furniture covered with plastic sheets was a reference to a billionaire's bunker, described by the artist as 'a hiding

137

138

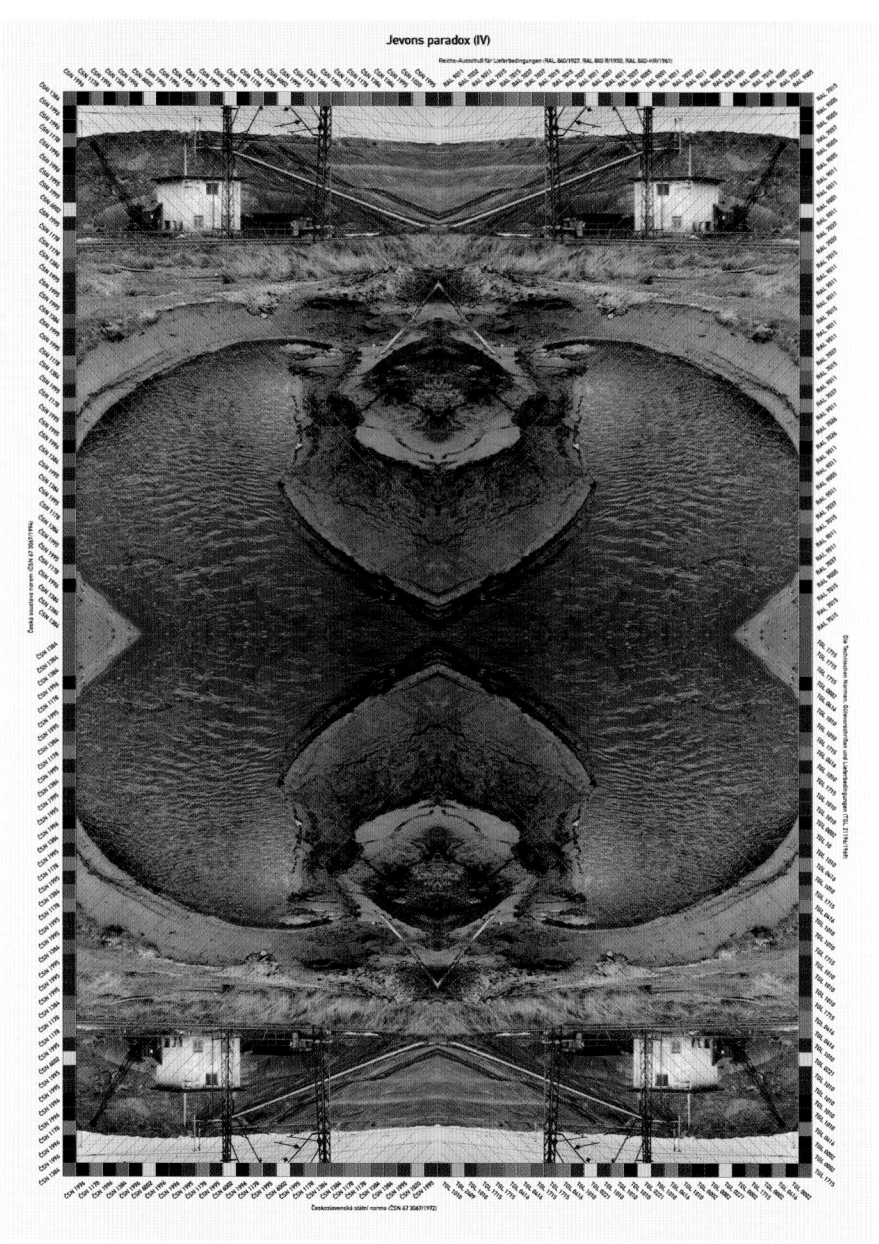

137 ABOVE Zbyněk Baladrán, *Jevons Paradox IV*, 2020
138 OPPOSITE Femke Herregraven, *Corrupted Air*, 2018

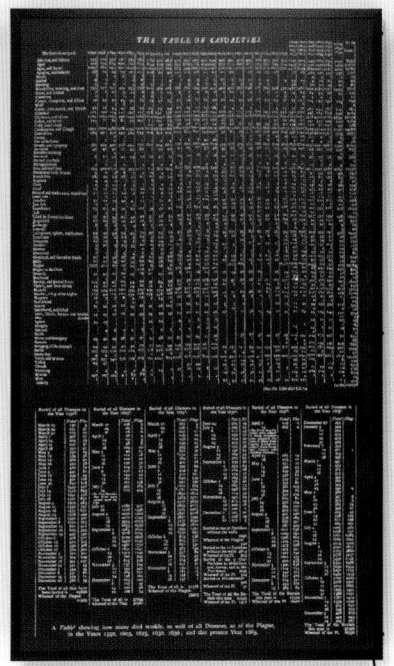
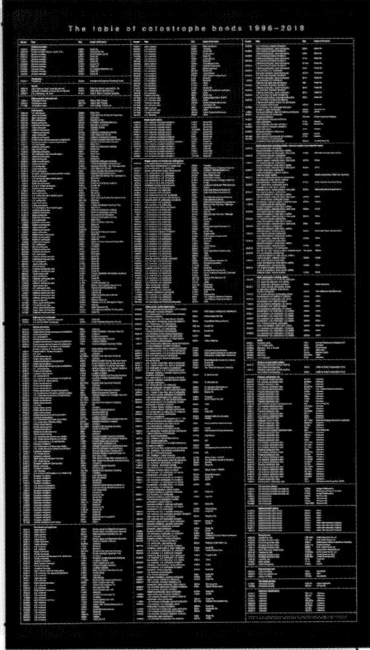

place for the ultra-wealthy in the event of large-scale social
unrest or sudden ecological collapse'. Through this constellation
Herregraven drew attention to the opportunism of financial
capitalists who seek short-term profit from the suffering of
others while insulating themselves against risk, as well as to the
longer-term unviability of insurance policies for meteorological
aberrations made ever more frequent by climate change.

Driving attempts to remake planetary history is the
realization that the damage done to shared worlds by racial
exploitation and extractivism can only be remedied by
what theorist Ariella Aïsha Azoulay has called 'unlearning
imperialism'. Dismantling the narratives of colonial modernity,
artists have revealed personal embeddedness in the unfolding
of environmental histories, the dynamic between racial
capitalism and climate change and the short-sightedness
of climate disaster profiteering. Against the background
of environmental destruction and financial speculation,
the works discussed here provide the building blocks for
a reparative history of pluriversal worlds with the potential
for a social and ecological transformation of terrestrial life.

Chapter 3
Green Protocols

Ecological responsibility is for the artists and collectives
discussed in this chapter a matter of imagining alternatives,
providing instructions for their realization and actually putting
them into practice. Reclaiming communal space as a form of
resistance to consumerism and expansion, they devise strategies
to restore food sovereignty, construct self-built homes and craft
herbal remedies, coming together in intentional communities
to counteract social anomie and disconnection from nature.
By reactivating the relation between place, community and
ecosystem in both urban and rural contexts, these artistic
methodologies create non-hierarchical social models and
equitable circuits of exchange, reviving and adapting traditional
nature-centric skills and livelihoods for new circumstances.
Such situated, self-organized and collaborative practices could
be seen as instances of 'world making', which, as anthropologist
Arturo Escobar has asserted, contribute to 'radical societal
transformation' according to the principles of 'degrowth,
commoning and the *Buen Vivir*', meaning both good life and
collective wellbeing. Relinquishing the modern Western
compulsion to control and dominate the natural world and
breaking the hold of the competitive mindset open a pathway to
planetary reconnection, which, as soil steward Leah Penniman
has suggested in *Farming While Black*, is about coming to the
land with 'humility and gratitude in your hearts' to establish
a caring, reverent and reciprocal relation to the Earth.

₁₃₉ The experimental documentary *Nocturnal Gardening* (2016)
is the last part of *Night Soil Trilogy*, a series of immersive film
installations by Melanie Bonajo that addressed 'the huge
disconnection most Western people feel to nature'. It told the
story of four women as agents of change, each of whom has
developed pioneering practices to reassemble communities,

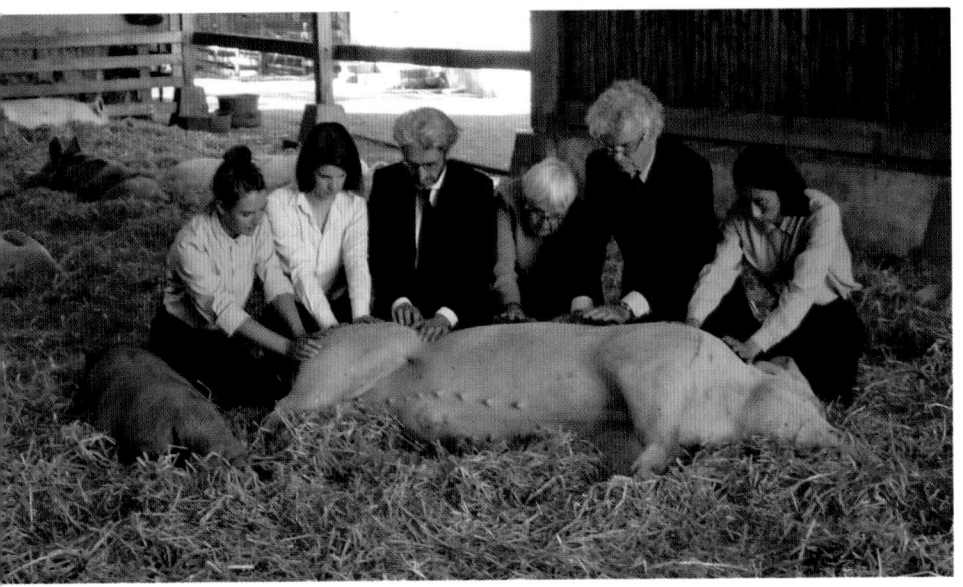

139 Melanie Bonajo, *Night Soil – Nocturnal Gardening*, 2016

reconnect with nature and restore non-capitalist ways of being in the world. The first is bringing up her family in union with plant spirits, foraging and harvesting fruits of the forest and applying its healing powers. The second woman left her city career to rediscover her family's farming roots, establishing a farm where pigs are stroked and cuddled and appreciated to counteract the monstrosities of the meat industry. Another started a black community organic gardening project to oppose 'food apartheid' in the United States, cultivating resistance to racism, capitalism and other kinds of oppression through spiritual activism and reconnection to the land. Finally, we hear from a Navajo woman whose call is to 'uplift all indigenous people' and reunite them with the Earth and with their relatives the plants, horses, clouds and trees, declaring that whoever thinks 'life is sacred' can partake in this 'indigenous renaissance'. Bonajo's work laid out alternative ways of living in tune with plants and animals, explored new forms of togetherness and advocated for new social movements based on 'commitment, compassion and patience'.

Tamás Kaszás's practice revolves around artistic propositions that destabilize the boundaries between wild and domesticated, traditional and modern, technological and crafted in order to re-enlighten the lost utopian core of the anarcho-socialist project of an egalitarian society built on communal principles. His ongoing series of graphic sheets, which are intended as 'visual aids' to empower 'historical consciousness', draw on the aesthetic and political outlook of left-wing groups of the 1920s, as well as the thousand-year history of peasant protests and the material relics of 'actually existing socialism'. For instance, *Famine Orchards* (2013) depicted a person planting a fruit tree in the grounds of a socialist housing estate, while in *Farming on the Golf Course* (2014) vegetables were grown on manicured lawns, with a handcart used not for putters and wedges, but instead for carrying a hoe, pick, rake and scythe. Another issue in the foreground of Kaszás's interests is that of habitation, as expressed in *Home Made Home Manifesto* (2011), which critiqued the dominance of specialized architecture, pointing to the long history of self-made homes. His agitational poster *Contemplatio × Never Work* (2007) was an invitation to redirect fixations away from the swiftly moving trends of contemporary living and to slow down, in order to pay attention to one's immediate community, natural surroundings and fellow species.

Artistic engagements with the rural have addressed the impact of extractivism, the exploitation of labour, the problems of industrial agriculture and the effect of economic migration on farming communities. *Sowing Somankidi Coura: A Generative Archive* (2015–20) is the long-term collaborative project between Paris-born artist Raphaël Grisey and photographer Bouba Touré, who lives between Paris and Mali. It deals with the exemplary model of the Malian self-organized farming collective Somankidi Coura, which the artists document through texts, photographs and recordings and promote through exhibitions and publications. The cooperative was founded in 1977 by a transnational group of fourteen former African migrant workers and activists, who first met in Paris at the Cultural Association of African Workers in France and shared concerns about the effects of recurring droughts in the Sahel region in Africa. They studied alternative economic and farming practices and, after undertaking agricultural training in the French countryside, agreed with the Malian local authorities to take on 60 hectares of land along the Senegal River near the village of Somankidi. They turned the farm into sections with polyculture gardens, pastures and arable areas, while their activities also entailed cofounding the Rural Radio of Kayes and running educational programmes for the local population. In the artists' view this is a 'story of the creation and creolisation of farming technologies and practices' to enable the region to 'sustain its ecosystems and provide people with food sovereignty and to integrate the migration economy into the making of new futures'.

140

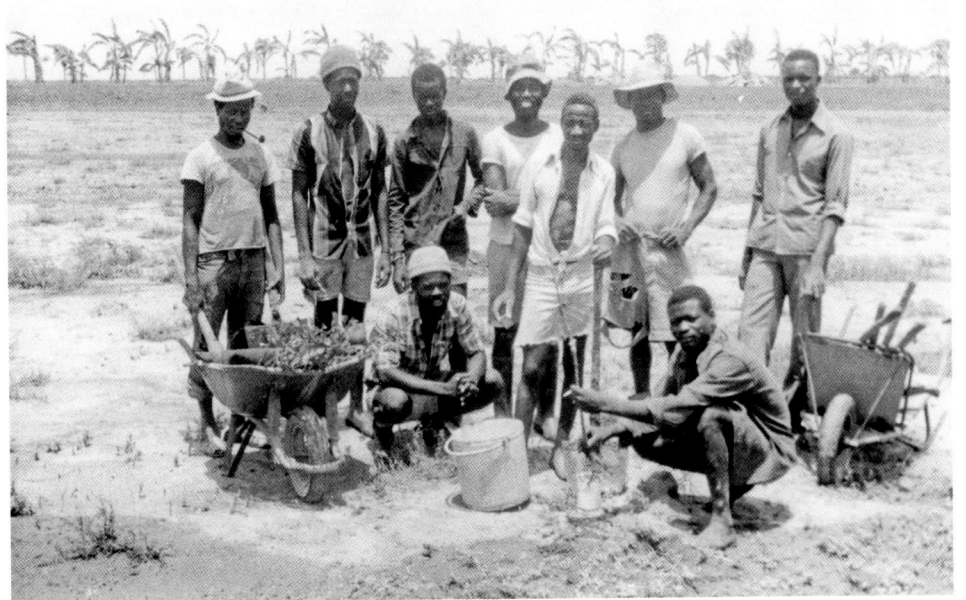

140 Bouba Touré, *Planting trees in (the cooperative of) Somankidi Coura*, 1977

Founded in 1995 by artist Amy Franceschini, Futurefarmers is a San Francisco-based collective of diverse practitioners, from artists and anthropologists to architects and farmers, who are committed to 'hands-on exploration of how people and things, neighbours and grains effect each other'. Their project *Seed Journey* (2016–17) entailed a sea voyage from Oslo to Istanbul onboard a nineteenth-century wooden sailing boat containing a precious cargo of ancient grains, from seeds saved from the Vavilov Institute Seed Bank during the Siege of Leningrad to archaeological finds of Finnish rye from the roof beams of a Norwegian sauna. Using grains as a compass to determine the stages of the journey, the rotating crew dropped anchor along the way at various host institutions, where meetings were organized with seed savers, palaeobotanists, activists and progressive farmers. One such *Seed Ceremony* was held in Belgium around a 500-year-old grain discovered in a church in Pajottenland, named Bruegel grain after the painter who depicted the pastoral life of the region. Stored in an hourglass, the sample of grain was taken on board to partake in the onward travel and contribute to rethinking questions around agriculture, autonomous farming and alternative networks of producers and consumers, as well as larger issues around

141

the stewardship of the land, air and water. Anthropologist Michael Taussig, who was also on board, described the aim of the low-tech, sustainable journey as 'not to oppose technology and science but to shift control and oversight of the means of production from the few to the many'.

Aspiring to 'create a countryside and art system I would like to live in', artist and agroecologist Fernando García Dory initiated the *Inland* project in 2009 as a rural arts organization and vehicle for the investigation of interconnected questions of territories, geopolitics and culture. The collective is active in three different locations: an abandoned village in the northern mountains of Spain, the Centre for the Approach of the Rural in Madrid and a medieval abbey on Mallorca. The group publishes books, produces shows and makes cheese, operating as 'an open space for land-based collaborations, economies and communities-of-practice as a substrate for post-Contemporary Art cultural forms'. Education also constitutes an important aspect of their activity, with a curriculum including a

141 Futurefarmers, *Seed Ceremony: Bruegel Awakens, Belgium,* 2017

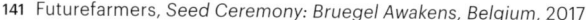

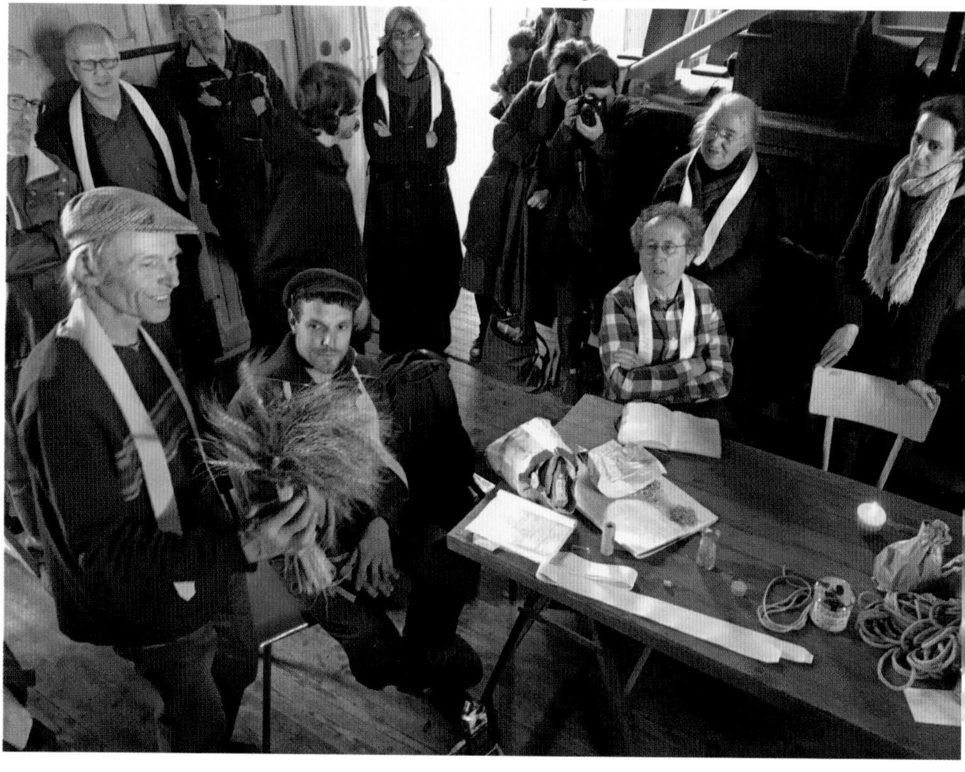

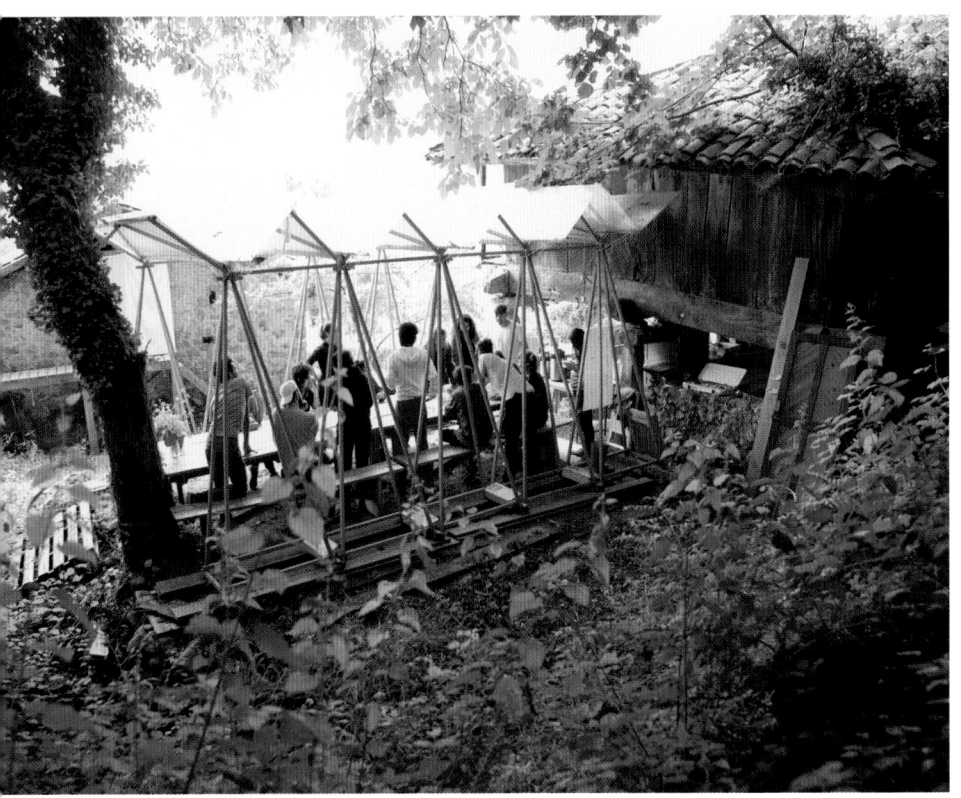

142 Fernando García Dory, *Inland*, 2009–ongoing

Shepherd's School, a School for Peasant Leaders and Rural
Self-Reliance Basic Courses, all of which are centred on the
reinvention of the rural as a capacious alternative to precarious
urban living. This has particular relevance for Spain, where
depopulation and land desertion as a result of rural exodus to
industrial cities have been especially notable. *Inland* took this
as an opportunity to envision a model of development that is
more sustainable in a social, environmental and cultural sense.

   In the era of climate disorder, as writer Ashley Dawson has
put it in *Extreme Cities*, a just transition from the inhospitable
metropolises of the Anthropocene to 'ecocities' depends on
'the most basic questions of survival: who has the right to
breathe clean air, to grow up in an environment free from
toxic pollutants, to have access to healthy food'. Taking the
form of a floating edible landscape on a barge moored in New
York City, Mary Mattingly's *Swale* (since 2016) raised pertinent
questions about social and economic inequalities in relation

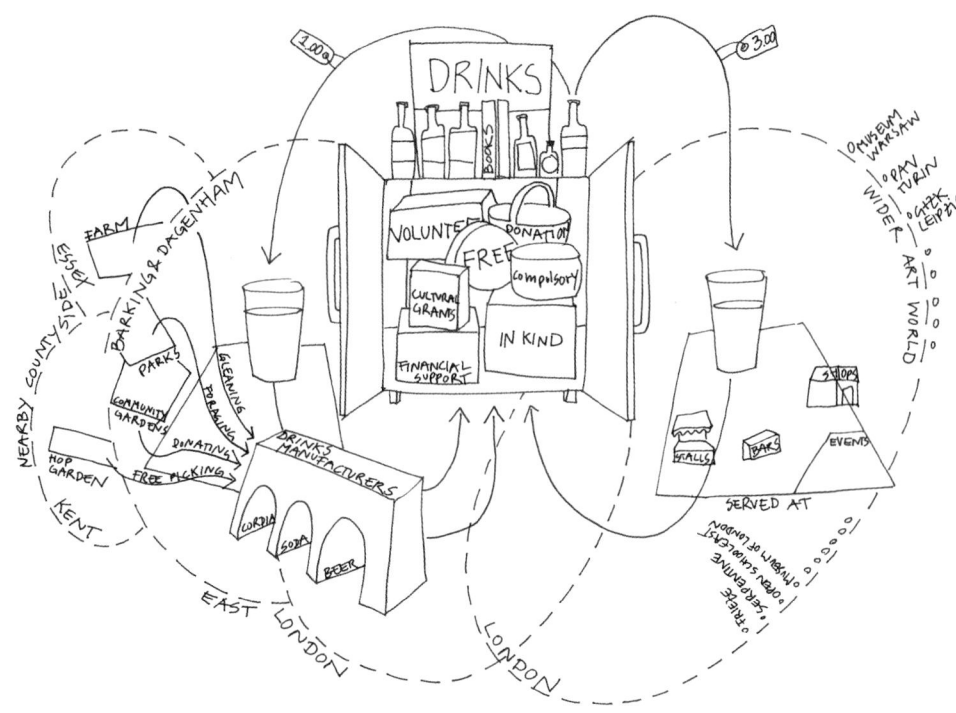

143 Kathrin Böhm, *Economy as a Drinks Cabinet or Explaining Company Drinks'
Diverse Economies,* 2018

to nutrition and access to fresh fruit and vegetables in an
urban setting. Circumventing local land laws that forbid
the growing or picking of food on New York's public land by
cultivating her garden on a waterborne vessel, the artist invited
local communities to reconnect with the experience of freely
foraging for edible and medicinal plants, from strawberries and
blackberries to kale, lettuce and chamomile. This floating plot,
which uses solar power and recycles its own water, is an artistic
prototype with the potential to be scaled up and adapted to
different environments. At the same time, it's a social model for
cultivating more attentive relations to the natural world, since,
in the artist's words, 'care about soil, care about plants and care
about water all come together when we pick food ourselves'.

Kathrin Böhm is a London-based member of MyVillages,
which she co-founded in 2003 with Wapke Feenstra and Antje
Schiffers to advocate for a new understanding of the rural as
a site of polyvocal knowledge production. The art collective
also investigates the potential of commoning as the 'most

reasonable economic and cultural option for survival'. Their principles of 'new ruralism', which functions in dynamic interrelation with the urban, can be detected in the project *Company Drinks*, which was initiated by Böhm in 2014. Conceived as a form of artistic intervention into everyday economic circuits, it drew on the history of East Londoners who, until the mechanization of harvesting in the 1950s, travelled in their thousands to Kent in late summer to work as hop pickers, with mostly women and children exchanging city life for a few weeks in the countryside. Based in Barking Park, this community enterprise is engaged in a full production cycle of growing, foraging, processing, branding and trading drinks made from elderflowers, cherry blossoms or knotweed, all growing in London. Theorist and contributor to the project Katherine Gibson has called for the development of 'a different vocabulary and language of economy' that can register the variety of ways in which goods are 'produced, transacted, distributed, financed and owned' outside of the 'capitalocentric frame'. Operating according to such alternative economic principles, *Company Drinks* could be seen as a testing ground for achieving more ecological livelihoods.

Derived from the French acronym for Zone to Defend, ZAD is the name of a community that for more than a decade has occupied 4,000 acres of countryside near the city of Nantes in order to prevent a biodiverse wetland from being destroyed by the building of a new airport, which through increased aviation emissions would have been a significant contributor to global warming. What also had to be defended, against repeated attempts by the police to violently evict the activists and farmers of the ZAD, was 'Europe's largest laboratory of commoning', a collective experiment in anti-capitalist and ecological self-organization that, in the words of Naomi Klein, 'models a different way to live together and with the land'. This fusion of direct action to confront the machinery of fossil fuel capitalism with the building of shared ecological worlds is described by artist and ZAD resident Jay Jordan, cofounder with Isabelle Frémeaux of the Laboratory of Insurrectionary Imagination, as combining 'the yes and the no, creation and resistance'. Watching over the land is a 20-metre lighthouse constructed as an affront to the authorities on the site of the planned control tower and as a defensive structure to slow down would-be evictors, but also more symbolically as a beacon of resistance, 'its beam welcoming people to safe haven and showing the dangers of the storms of the Capitalocene'.

Rethinking existential wellbeing based on post-extractive and post-growth principles of collectivity and solidarity has

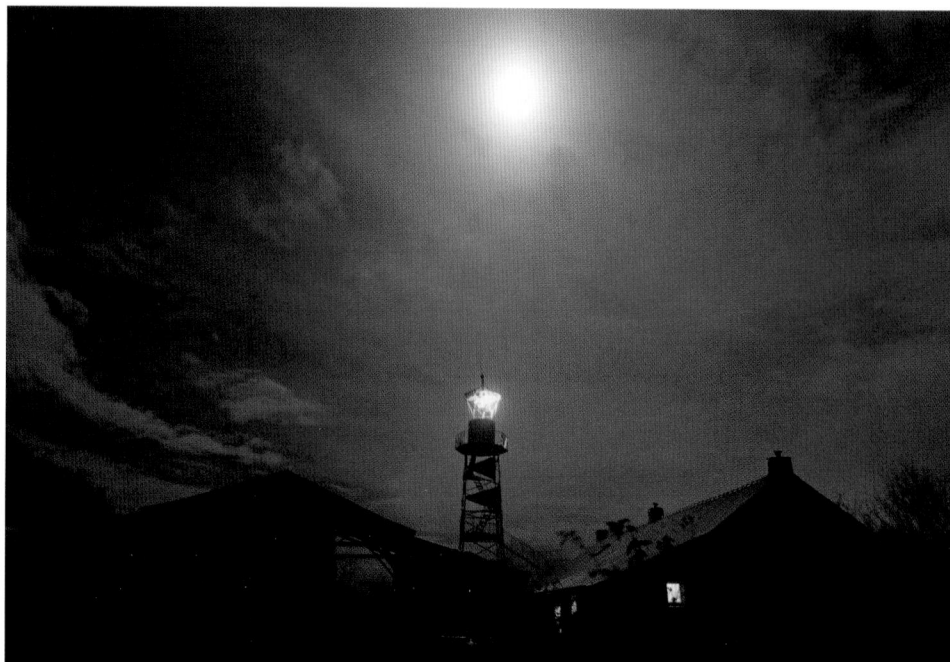

144 The Lighthouse at the ZAD, built where they wanted to put the control tower, 2018. Photo Jay Jordan, 2021

entailed establishing alternative social and economic models, from habitation to sustenance. Artist practices discussed here have displayed inventiveness in overcoming bureaucratic and systemic barriers in order to reclaim space and agency in rural and urban settings. Procedures for putting ecologically sound and socially just ways of living and working into practice have also followed the path of reconnection to nature by restoring ways of being in the world in relation to plants, animals, land and spirits.

Chapter 4
Climates of Transformation

Despite climate change being a global phenomenon that
threatens biological life across the planet, the impacts of
rising temperatures and sea levels are felt unequally. Islanders
in the global South and communities living in hot dry zones
experience climate change not as a future danger, but as an
existential reality that limits and determines life choices
in the present. Climate disorder is converging with and
exacerbating social and economic injustices that originate in
centuries of exploitation and discrimination, dating to the era
of colonialist conquest and the long-burning aftermaths of
European domination. As a result, as indigenous theorist Kyle
Powys Whyte has observed, climate risks are often perceived
by indigenous peoples 'through their experiences of already
being deeply harmed by the economic, industrial, and military
drivers behind anthropogenic climate change'. For frontline
communities, there can be no solution to global warming
without social and environmental justice for those who did
the least to cause it and are most exposed to its immediate
effects. Achieving climate justice is also closely bound up
with addressing other forms of inequality, with eco-feminists
identifying and challenging the patriarchal logic of domination
that underpins both gender discrimination and ecological
destruction, while contesting the heteronormative order is also
opening up an array of queer ecological possibilities. Rejecting
top-down, technocratic strategies of climate mitigation that
shore up existing social, political and economic structures,
climate justice activists are working with communities to build
transversal alliances and cross-sectional solidarities to bring
about a just ecological transformation.

Working with the coastal community on her native island
of Bantayan in the Philippines, Martha Atienza, an artist of

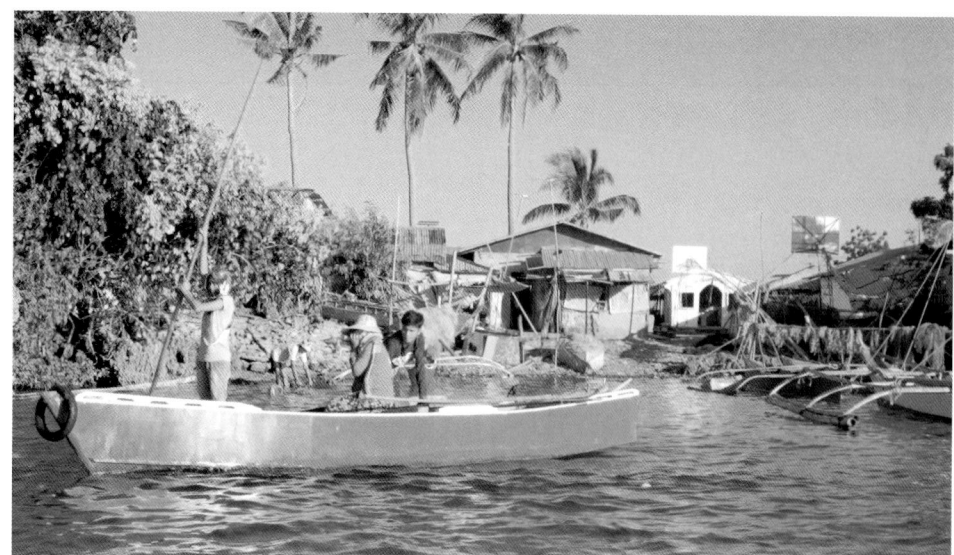

145 Martha Atienza, *Panangatan 11°09'53.3"N 123°42'40.5"E 2019-10-24 Thu 6:42 AM PST 1.29 meters High Tide, 2019-10-12 Sat 10:26 AM PST 1.40 meters High Tide,* 2019

Filipino and Dutch origins, drew on collective insights and shared creativity to tackle the pressures of environmental crisis engulfing the islands. Since the deadly Typhoon Yolanda devasted the islands in 2013, causing population dislocations and economic hardship, more super storms have continued to descend on the country. The revoking of the islands' protected Wilderness Area status on the pretext of rebuilding the affected regions was met locally with suspicion, provoking fears of further capitalist exploitation. Atienza's panoramic video *Panangatan 11°09'53.3"N 123°42'40.5"E 2019-10-24 Thu 6:42 AM PST 1.29 meters High Tide, 2019-10-12 Sat 10:26 AM PST 1.40 meters High Tide* (2019) is a cinematic record of the devastation and decay caused by rising sea levels. The information in the title of this five-hour film, shot while circling the island's coastline, serves as a form of archiving and a reference to the local population's seafaring way of life. The collectively realized *Equation of State* (2019) was a kinetic installation with mangrove shrubs, which used appropriated karaoke machines to lift the plants in and out of the water to the rhythm of the tide, an ad hoc solution that the artist refers to as 'island technology'. The work questioned the reintroduction of mangroves as a natural means to absorb greenhouse gases and protect against floods, suggesting that the input and participation of the local community are crucial in dealing with climate change, rather than relying solely on solutions imposed from above.

145

Two giant sea turtles suspended in space were a means for Oto Hudec to start a conversation about migration in his landlocked homeland of Slovakia. Named *Tartaruga I* and *Tartaruga II* (2017) after the Portuguese word for turtle, each of the clay sculptures carried on its back a collection of model houses. The first set was based on homes in a village on the Cape Verde islands and perched on a blue shell, while the second replicated buildings in the crowded neighbourhood of Cova da Moura in Lisbon and stood on an earthy brown one. The hanging sculptures refer to the oceanic migrations undertaken by the world's oldest reptiles and recall the non-Western and indigenous mytheme of the World Turtle that supports the living world. The turtle is also the symbol of the Cape Verde archipelago and a representation of the life of its migrants who travel great distances from their islands of origin. The clay houses were made during ceramic workshops that the artist put on for young people from Cape Verde who now live in the suburbs of Lisbon, as a way of exploring the connections between these two geographically remote but culturally connected sites. Hanging in a Central European gallery and building also on the artist's work with Roma communities, the turtles were designed to provoke feelings of empathy for migrants of different ethnicity and an understanding of how the challenges of droughts and failed harvests intersect with the economic and environmental legacies of racism and colonial exploitation.

Since 2009 Maria Theresa Alves has worked with the Museo Comunitario del Valle de Xico (Community Museum of Xico Valley), a hub of indigenous cultural resistance to unrelenting processes of colonial erasure, to collectively unearth the complex geo-colonial histories of the lacustrine region of Chalco near Mexico City. Inaugurated at Documenta (13) in 2012, the multifaceted project *The Return of a Lake* focused on the reappearance of Chalco's lake a century after it was drained by a Spanish immigrant. Iñigo Noriega Laso amassed a fortune from his environmental and social crimes, which led to the displacement and dispossession of the twenty-eight indigenous communities that lived around the lake. In what could be perceived as an act of nature's ecological revenge, the return of what is now known as Lake Tláhuac-Xico, as a result of land subsidence and underground water exploitation, has brought a further raft of environmental problems, from flooding to a lack of drinking water and the cracking and cratering of the ground. Alves has worked with the Xico community to bring about the rehabilitation of the lake through environmental and cultural remediations that challenge the geoengineering plans of the state authorities, such as by remaking the indigenously engineered

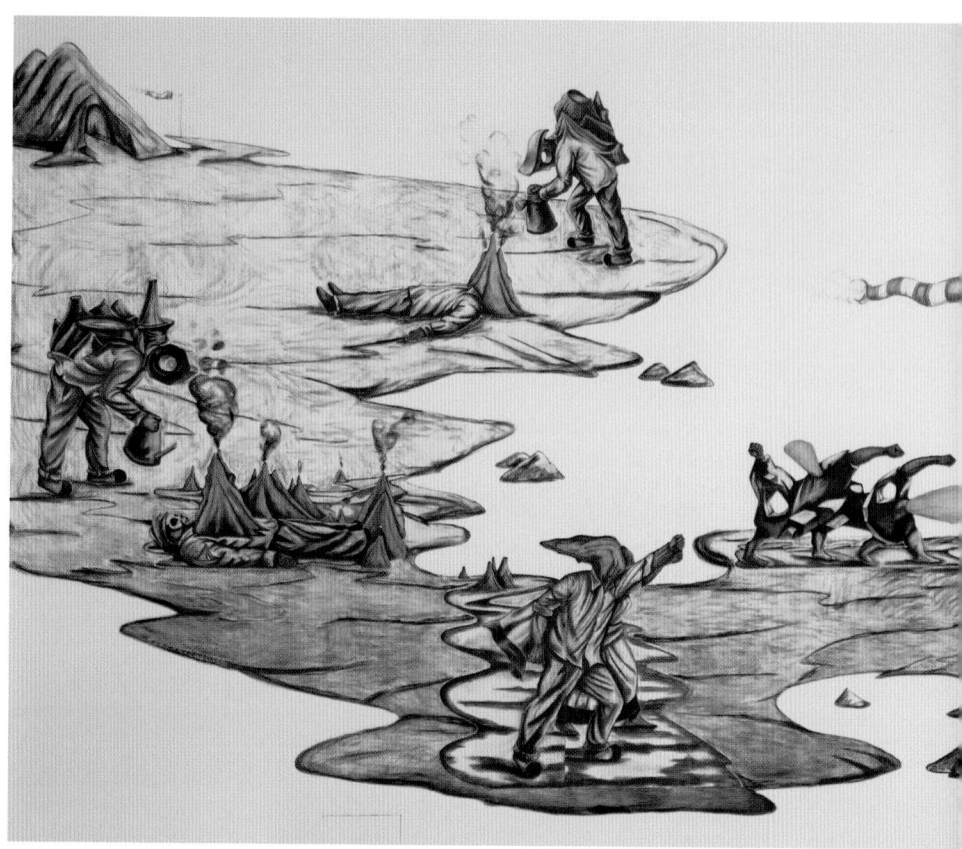

hydro-agricultural islands, or *chinampas*, that covered the lake in the pre-Hispanic era. Such indigenous technologies belong to the corpus of traditional ecological knowledge, which, as Julia Watson has described in *Lo-TEK Design by Radical Indigenism*, are engineered to 'sustain rather than exploit resources, fostering symbiosis between species by making biodiversity the building block used to construct green technologies'. Alves has made use of publishing, exhibition making and the critical space of the artistic sphere to support the Xico in their struggle against colonial and neo-colonial operations that continue to be a pervasive reality for the indigenous community.

Considering drawing to be a 'quick medium' and art practice itself as a form of 'political gesture', Prabhakar Pachpute often uses charcoal for his large-scale murals executed directly on gallery walls. His works are concerned with agrarian crisis, troubling labour issues and the ecological devastation currently

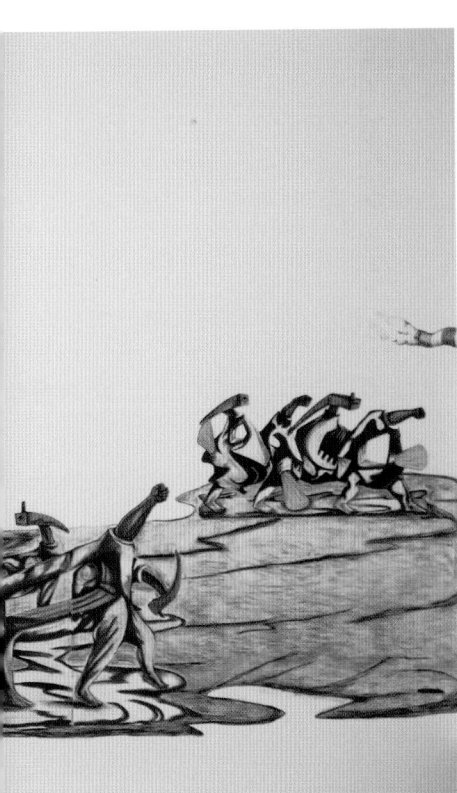

146

taking place in India. Born into a family of miners in Chandrapur district in Maharashtra, known as the country's coal belt, Pachpute's personal quest to find answers to the economic and environmental challenges faced by farmers and miners in his hometown is the motivation behind his work. Enlarged, disproportional and unsettling figures that are part-machine, part-animal and part-human populate desolate, barren and exhausted post-industrial landscapes to deliver a dystopian vision of the abuse of power and its destructive force. In his ongoing and evolving series *Sea of Fists* (since 2018) he has focused on protest campaigns for land rights and social justice, such as the 180-kilometre peaceful march of more than 40,000 farmers from Nashik to Mumbai in 2019, or actions in which farmers buried themselves in pits to protest against forced land acquisitions in Rajasthan in 2020. The figures depicted in these works march forward unstoppably with their fists raised.

This corresponds to Pachpute's conviction that by relying on their own bodies and coming together to demonstrate, they turn their revolt and resistance into an indication of hope that will necessitate change.

Women's voices take centre stage in Marwa Arsanios's film series *Who is Afraid of Ideology?* (2017–19), which explores the ecological dimension of the military and social struggles of the Kurdish Women's Liberation Movement. The first film, shot against a bleak winterly landscape in Iraqi Kurdistan, dealt with the experience of guerrilla warfare. In it, women fighters described the skills needed to survive in the mountain wilderness and how each member of the movement developed environmental consciousness in practising self-defence, 'which is very organic and normal and comes from nature'. A sequence that describes the properties of the plants in a medicinal herbarium forms the introduction to the second film, which is set in Jinwar, a women-only commune in northern Syria. This utopian eco-feminist village surviving precariously in the midst of a war-torn country is the setting for an experiment in putting ecological principles into practice in a non-patriarchal, egalitarian society. We learn that there is justice now 'because these lands belong to the people', while according to Kurdish beliefs, 'ants, birds, snakes, humans and foxes have the right to live on this soil'. The connection made in the film between the regime's imposition of a system of monocultural farming of cotton or grain and a culture of political passivity – with the

147 Marwa Arsanios, *Who is Afraid of Ideology? Part II*, 2019

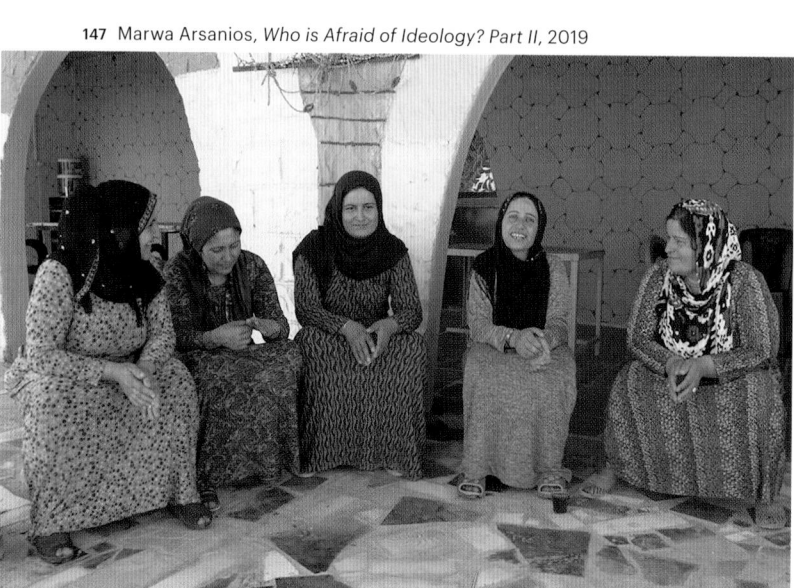

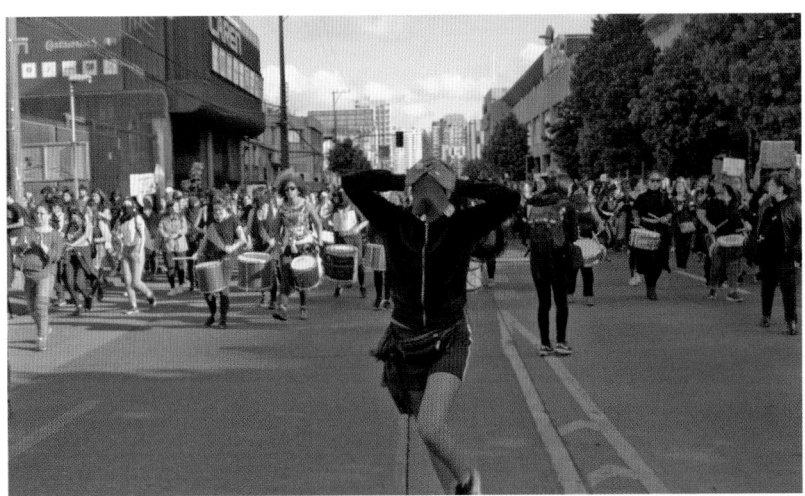

148 Barbara Marcel, *Humo sobre los humedales* (Smoke over the wetlands), 2019–20

planting of diverse crops associated by contrast with the ability to
stand up for rights against the state – is an insight that holds true
for environmental justice movements across the world.

148   The footage of the film *Humo sobre los humedales* (Smoke over
the wetlands) (2019–20) was recorded by Barbara Marcel during
her art residency in Chile in autumn 2019, at a time when the
country had to cancel the UN Climate Conference COP25 amidst
widespread social unrest sparked by a rise in metro fares in the
capital Santiago. The protests laid bare the tension between the
city's claim to the greenest public transport network in Latin
America and stark levels of social inequality in one of the countries
most exposed to the effects of climate change. Utilizing the form of
the essay film as a tool to instigate 'decolonial ecological thinking',
Marcel interwove documentation of feminist street protests,
individual reflections on the uprising and footage of the activist
work of Radio Humedales, an eco-feminist community radio
station in the city of Concepción that mobilizes women in defence
of the local wetlands, or *humedales*, of the Bío Bío region. The
film celebrates the revolutionary energy of the women marchers,
whose dances and songs reverberate with the 'scream of a silent
voice' and the 'strength of a mountain range', in a rallying call
against the oppression of indigenous people and 'stolen natures'.
Through their support of 'a non-capitalist use of land', as feminist
theorist Silvia Federici observed, 'women are today the main social
force standing in the way of a complete commercialization of
nature'. Underlined in the film is the fact that the climate crisis

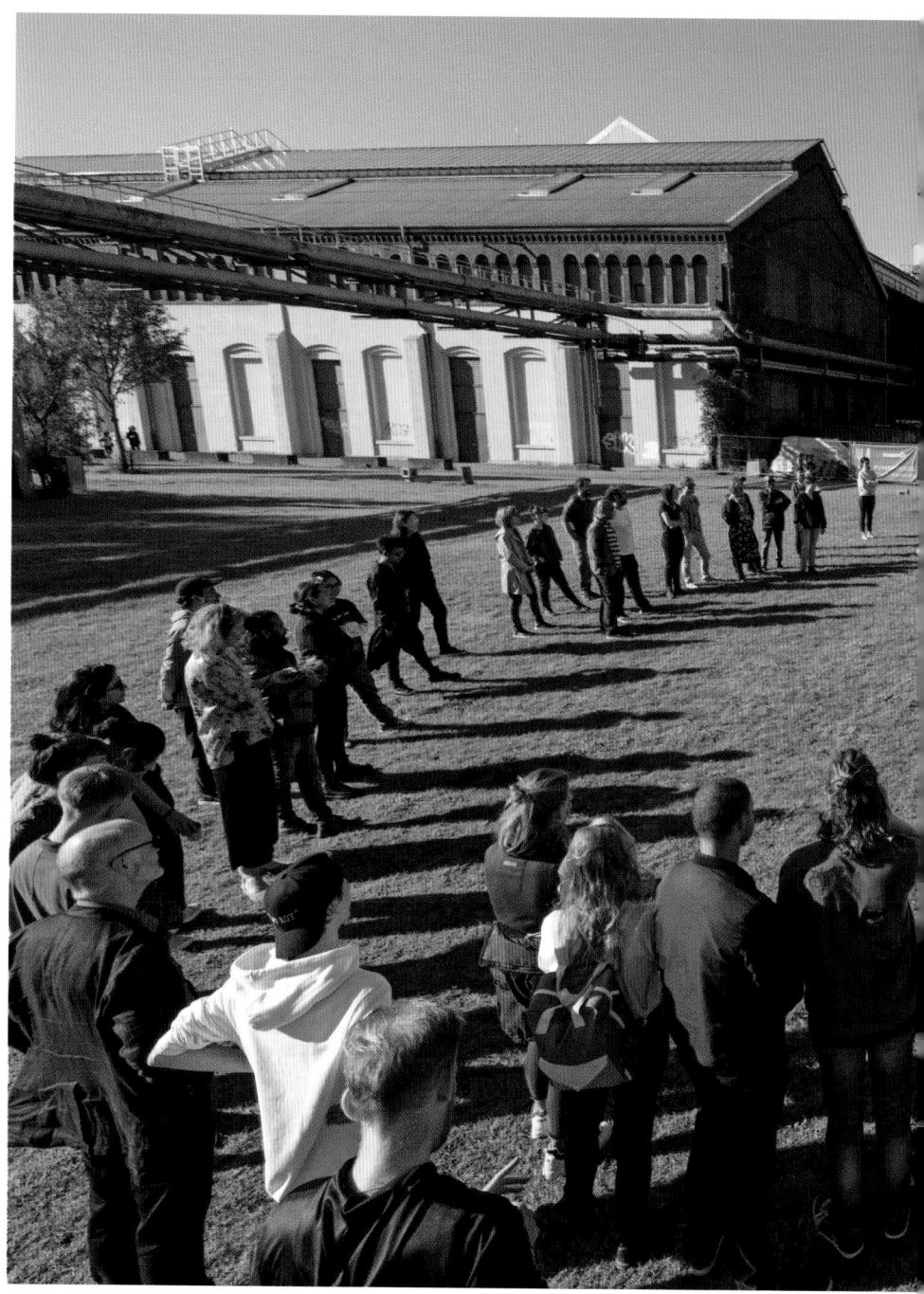

149 Jonas Staal in collaboration with Florian Malzacher, *Training for the Future*, 2019

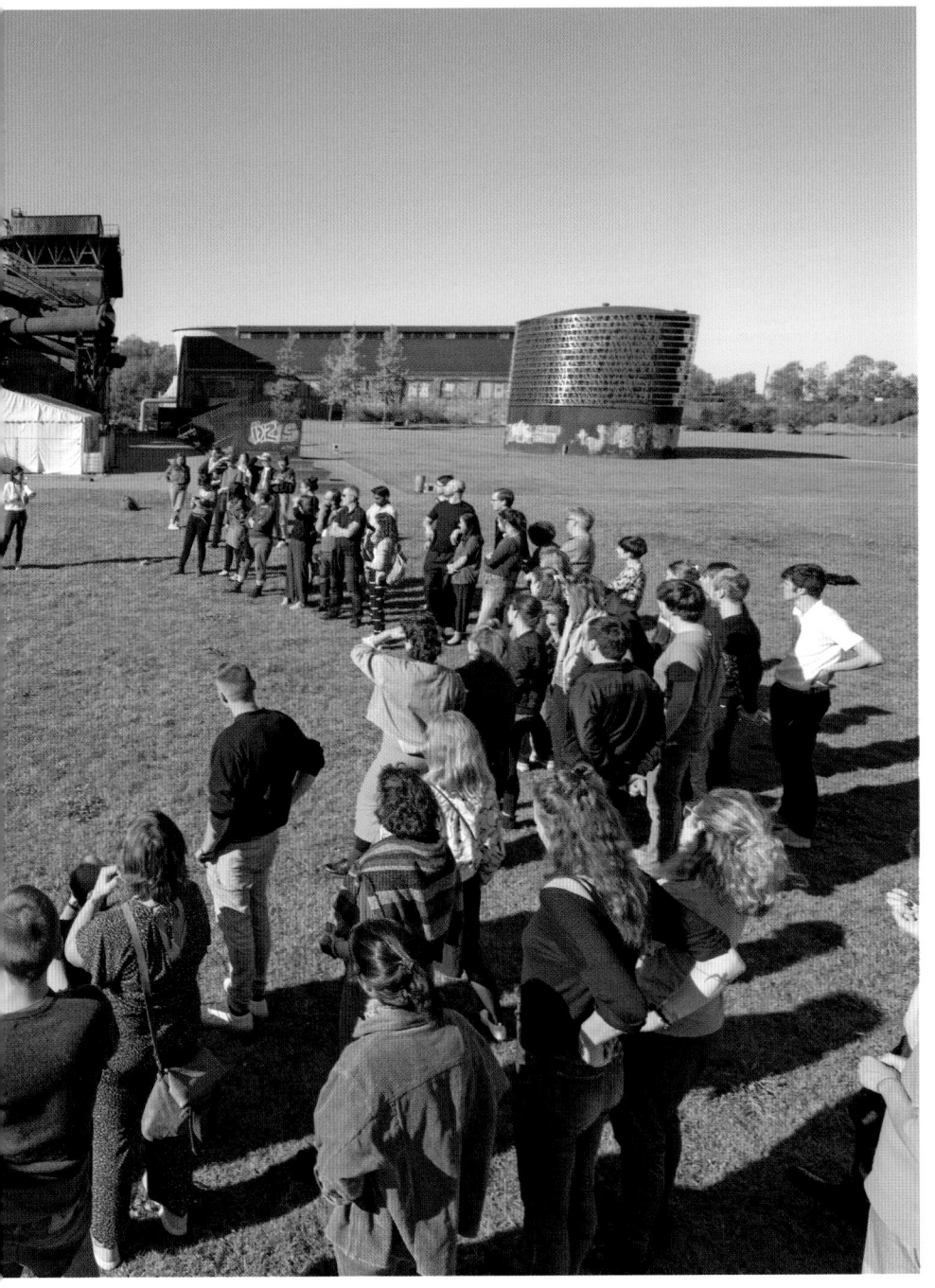

Climates of Transformation

cannot be treated separately from deeply entwined issues of gender inequality and social injustice.

Dutch artist Jonas Staal uses his theoretical and practical work to develop templates for rethinking and reactivating relations between art, propaganda and democracy in light of the interconnected crises of politics, economy and ecology enveloping the planet today. In his participatory projects, which revolve around summits, assemblies, unions and academies, Staal has probed the emancipatory potential of artistic and political organizing to strengthen alliances and cross-sectional solidarities. His project *Training for the Future*, which took place in autumn 2019 within the framework of Ruhrtriennale in the German town of Bochum, was envisaged as a utopian training camp in which participants were turned into trainees, acquiring skills for acting out alternative scenarios in order to 'reclaim the means of production of the future'. Through select coaching by invited instructors, among them artists, activists and theatre makers, the participants were acquainted with concrete exercises to tackle present-day troubles. These included practising 'choreographies of togetherness', learning how to use voice to express collective demands, reclaiming love from capitalist commodification, understanding the extent of surveillance and the exploitative agenda of data mining on the internet, as well as undertaking steps towards decolonizing society and imagining more sustainable terrestrial futures. For Staal, the unfolding climate catastrophe should be recognized as 'a deep and real transformative force that opens pathways towards comradely coexistence and sympoietic collaboration between the various agents – human, nonhuman and other-than-human' to constitute a new cosmopolitical ecosystem.

The struggle to achieve climate justice, as the authors of *Climate Futures* have put it, entails 'fighting at the front lines, promoting intersectionality, developing coalitions and infusing systemic analysis of the roots of the crisis'. Artists discussed here have worked from within marginalized communities, empowering local strategies for climate adaptation, rather than relying on ill-fitting technocratic solutions imposed from above and elsewhere. The urgency of the climate emergency has seen art practised as a political gesture and the institutional system of the art world repurposed to give sustenance and support to embattled communities. The climate of transformation is revealed as a struggle of bodies as well as ideas, as a campaign that calls on the insights and practices of eco-feminisms, queer ecologies and movements for land and indigenous rights, and as a transversal mobilization of communities and allies for the planetwide social and environmental justice on which the future of all terrestrials depends.

149

Chapter 5
Eco-Futurisms

Situating their ecological parable *The Collapse of Western Civilization* in the distant future, historians of science Naomi Oreskes and Erik M. Conway coined the phrase 'penumbral age' to describe the 'shadow of anti-intellectualism that fell over the once-enlightened techno-scientific nations of the Western World during the second half of the twentieth century, preventing them from acting on the scientific knowledge available at the time and condemning their successors to the inundation and desertification of the late twenty-first and twenty-second century'. That scientists are resorting to science fiction to warn of the danger of climate-denying populists and disaster profiteers obstructing the global response to climate change is a measure of the gravity of the ecological crisis. Indeed, the future of the planet is becoming increasingly unreliable and practically 'unimaginable outside the framework of science fiction', as T. J. Demos has asserted in *Beyond the World's End*, since we are 'in the midst of a world-historical, cosmological event, an event that is quickly making the world we once knew historical'. Addressed in this chapter are climate uncertainties that threaten to make the biosphere unliveable, critical exposures of technocratic futurological speculations and terraforming projects, as well as contestations of post-human biotechnological dystopias. The ending of the universalizing world of white dominance, glimpses into post-petroleum temporalities and defiant scenarios of indigenous survivance constitute the panopticon of possible futurity.

In 2017 US artist Daniel Keller and filmmaker Jacob Hurwitz-Goodman followed a group of 'techno-futurists, libertarians, environmentalists, anarcho-capitalists and Burners' who call themselves 'Seasteaders' to a resort in Tahiti to document their conference. The resulting film *Seasteaders* (2018) recorded the panellists promoting their vision of exiting the existing society and building an artificial floating city, while trying to convince the Polynesian nation to support their project, because it's 'a magical place that would fulfil all our requirements'. The Seasteading Institute was founded in 2008 by Patri Friedman with financial support from billionaire investor Peter Thiel, co-founder of PayPal, with the idea to establish a fluid world run by ultra-libertarian microgovernments, taking advantage of the fact that although land is already controlled by various states the oceans are still free to be colonized. For Keller, this was 'essentially a fantasy escape plan for a permanent minority to circumvent a representative democracy, which is inherently unsympathetic to their devotion to tax evasion and secession'. In his study of futurity, art theorist Sven Lütticken described these kinds of escapist manifestations as 'speculo-accelerationist neo-futurisms' in which 'the global über-class is to abandon any notion of society or solidarity on a dying planet'.

Set in Brazil, a world stage where social inequalities, political usurpation and biotechnological prospecting converge, Pedro
Neves Marques's film *Semente Exterminadora* (Exterminator Seed) (2017) presented the futuristic frontier of extraction and exploitation. It tells the story of the relationship between Capivara, an oil rig worker evacuated back to land after a disastrous oil spill, and a female android called Twy, who

150 Daniel Keller and Jacob Hurwitz-Goodman, *Seasteaders*, 2018

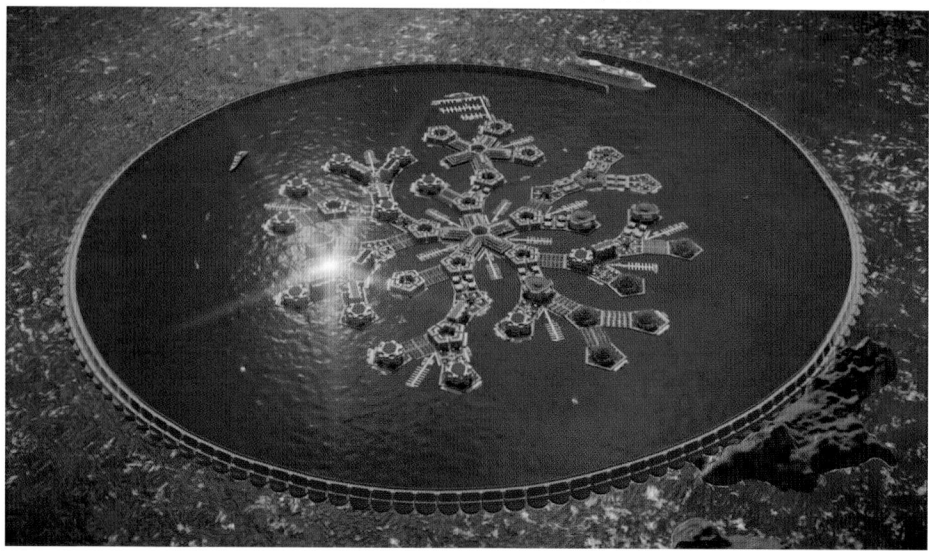

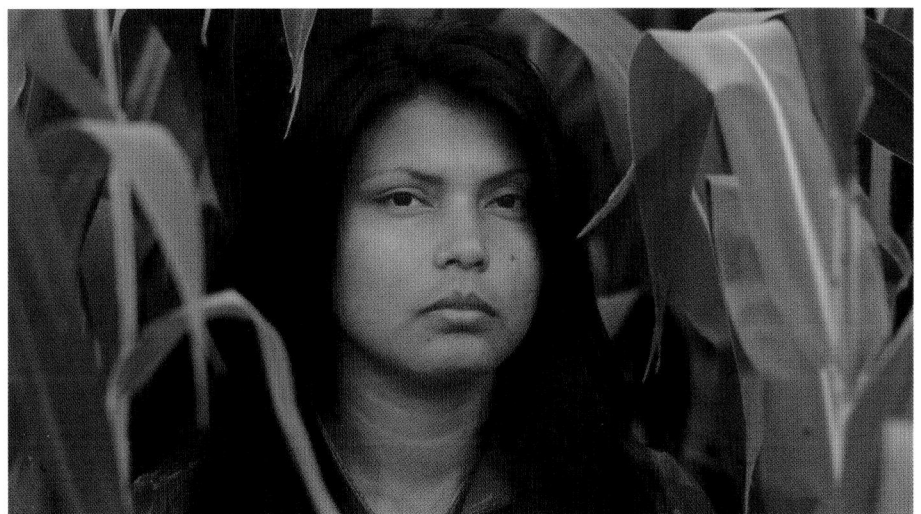

151 Pedro Neves Marques, *Semente Exterminadora* (Exterminator Seed), 2017

convinces him to travel back with her to the region of Mato Grosso in search of work in the soya and corn plantations. Sheltering in a rundown shack next to the vast and impersonal cornfields, the android, who is played by a member of the indigenous Guajajara nation, explains to the uncomprehending human worker about the infertility of transgenic plants and the financial calculus behind the replacement of traditional farmers by post-human robots. Although the scenario belongs to science fiction, the footage of the vast machine of industrial farming in the largest soya-producing state in Brazil, where agricultural expansion is inseparable from deforestation in the Amazon biome, is suggestive of the degree to which biological and cultural realms are already automated and under biotechnological control. Rather than replicating the mentality of the colonial matrix of power, the artist has called for a science fiction that is 'rooted in the present, anthropologically aware, and open to the multiplicity of non-Western futures'.

Growing up between the United States and Qatar and experiencing first-hand the direction in which petro-capitalist cultures were heading, Sophia Al-Maria added the term 'Gulf Futurism' to the circulation of analogous notions, as it became apparent to her that some Western imaginaries of the future already exist in the hyper-modern cityscapes and ultra-consumerist lifestyles of the Gulf States. Al-Maria's two-part video work *The Future Was Desert* (2016) emerged from her interest in deep time, the distant future and eco-science

152

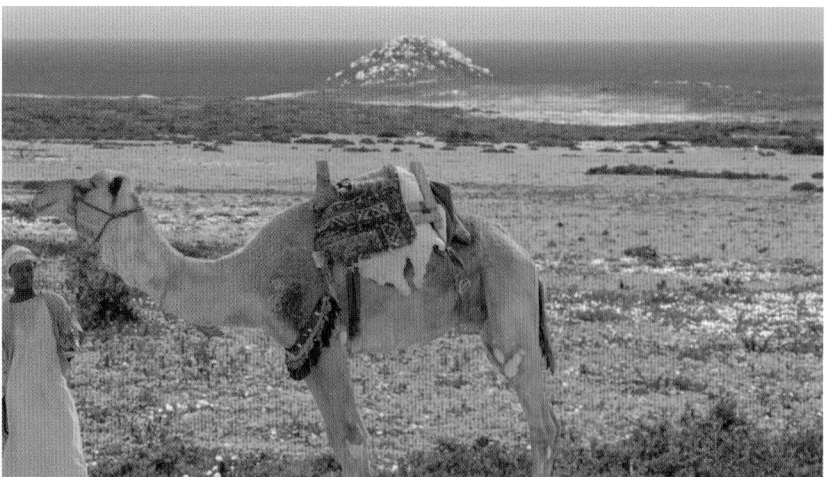

152 Sophia Al-Maria, *The Future Was Desert Part 2,* 2016

fiction literature, including the work of Ursula K. Le Guin and Octavia E. Butler. Contending that the keys to the future are to be found in the past, the figures of the archaeologist and astronaut are put into correlational reciprocity, with one digging into ancient silt, while the other leaves prints in the new dust of another planet. A robotic voiceover reveals that 'we have committed planetary suicide' against a flickering stream of images of futuristic supercars superimposed onto sand dunes. In the second part, the narrator discloses that 'to enter the desert is to exit time', indicating what the future will look like, however, we are also reminded that 'before memory' the Sahara was a savanna and the Gulf a garden. Just as other planets are perceived as uninhabitable and desolate deserts, the desertification processes happening here as a result of anthropogenic global warming and aided by droughts, deforestation and aggressive agriculture are on course to turn the Earth into a barren sphere. As this work suggests, the contest between the biogeochemical processes set in motion by a transforming climate and the geoengineering efforts to control and dominate them are most starkly displayed in the Gulf States.

The social and political implications of moving away from a petrocapitalist economy built on exploiting the solar energy trapped over millennia in fossil fuels was addressed in Tamás Kaszás's *Sci Fi Agit Prop* (2010–12) series, which warned of the economic, technological and ecological collapse towards which the world is hurtling. Presenting contrasting scenarios for a post-petroleum social order, one of the pair of graphic prints *After Oil* predicted a *New Slavery*, a labour-intensive dystopia in which people are forced to take the place of fossil fuel-dependent technologies, by literally carrying on their backs the relics of carbon civilization. An alternative future is depicted under the heading *Folk Science*, in which people adapt by using hand-crafted tools designed on the principles of traditional knowledge, easing the burden of transportation through cooperation and social equality. Which path society heads down, as theorist Timothy Mitchell observed in *Carbon Democracy*, depends on 'the political tools with which we address the passing of the era of fossil fuel'. The bifurcated futurity of Kaszás's 'pseudo-communist' agitprop illustrates the high-stakes struggle over the social and political trajectories of climate emergency. Drawing on pre-modern folk epistemology and reclaiming the experience of an economy of scarcity under state socialism, as well as thriving on the serendipitous misconceptions that arise from cultural collisions, the artist opened up vistas and provided the tools for eco-futurist imagining.

Relegating the notion of linear time to the project of Western colonial modernity, Philadelphia-based collective Black Quantum Futurism, led by Camae Ayewa and Rasheedah Phillips, set out to envision ways of living and experiencing reality through the 'manipulation of space-time in order

153 Tamás Kaszás, *Sci Fi Agit Prop*, 2010–12

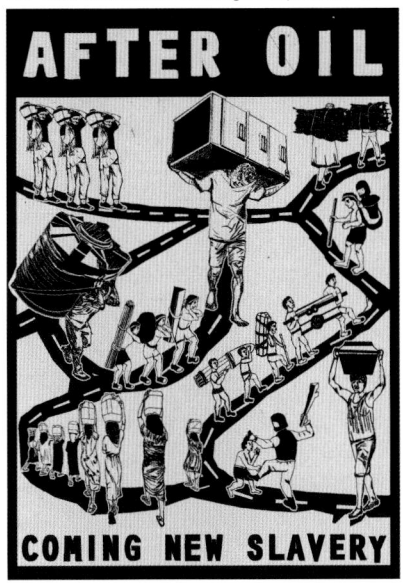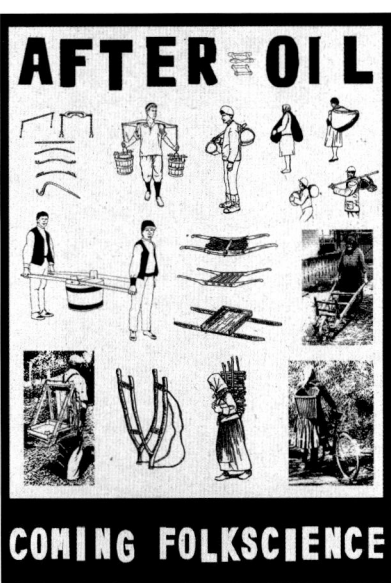

to see into possible futures'. In their practice, African and Afrodiasporan temporalities are coupled with the principles of quantum physics to reveal the intermingling of pasts, presents and futures, establishing 'a creative plane that allows for the ability of African-descended people to actually see "into," create, or choose the impending future'. Their exhibition 'All Time is Local' in 2019 featured projects that combine experimental soundscapes, sculptural installations, performative lectures and community-based events. Among these was *Black Space Agency* (2018), which was conceived to recover and activate memories of the autonomous black spaces and temporalities of North Philadelphia, uncovering the hidden histories of local scientists and businesspeople against the backdrop of the space race of the 1960s. By collapsing temporalities, it also disclosed the challenges posed to community spaces by the recent wave of gentrification, while opening up a liberatory exploration of Afro-futuristic possibility. An installation of antique clocks and watches incorporated press clippings about black women activists and healers from different eras, juxtaposed with wall inscriptions carrying chrono-political messages such as the empowering invocation 'a clock ticking, a storm brewing, forcing change'.

Finding a silver lining in privileged white fantasies of escaping climate disaster, exemplified by schemes to terraform Mars by detonating nuclear bombs to melt its icecaps and create a breathable atmosphere for zealous colonizers, Thirza Cuthand's film *Reclamation* (2018) envisioned an alternative scenario in which queer indigenous people are the main protagonists in the ecological reworlding of a ruined planet. In the video, the artist – who is of Plains Cree, Scottish and Irish descent – depicts the moment after the mass exodus of white settlers to Mars, in which the original inhabitants of North America are left behind to cope with the aftermath of the colonial-extractivist project and set about trying to rehabilitate the land and restore communities. One of the participants in the fictive documentary explains that the settlers suddenly gave up and left, adding that since they are 'colonizers, I feel more for the planet Mars than for them'. Wearing gas masks to protect against toxic residues, a queer indigenous couple are shown clearing up the 'garbage left by white people', caring for abandoned farm animals and finding ways to feed themselves locally through foraging and gardening. With the colonizer gone, the work of 'decolonizing the community' goes much more quickly, resulting also in the disappearance of the white settler prejudice towards the non-binary identities of 'two-spirit people'. The recovery of the Earth through natural

154

155

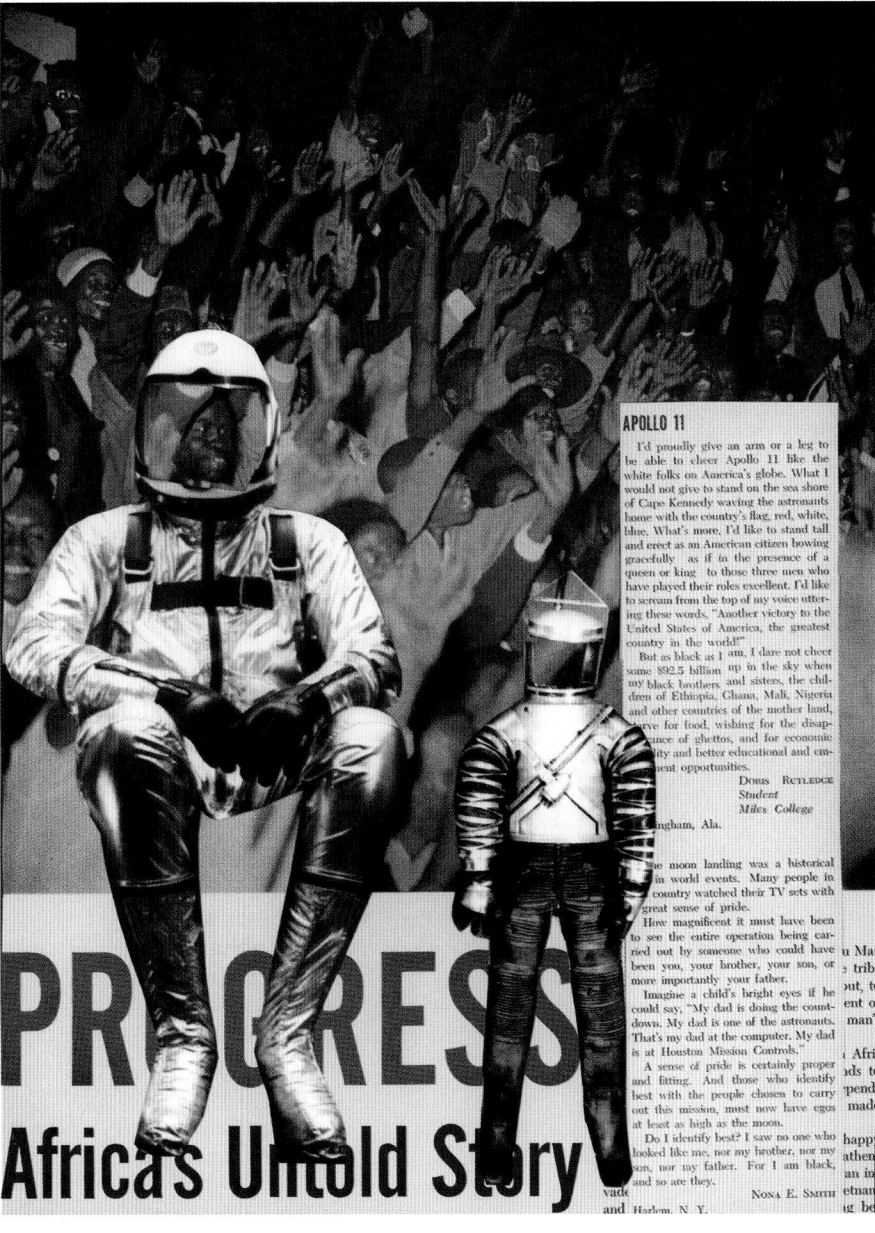

APOLLO 11

I'd proudly give an arm or a leg to be able to cheer Apollo 11 like the white folks on America's globe. What I would not give to stand on the sea shore of Cape Kennedy waving the astronauts home with the country's flag, red, white, blue. What's more, I'd like to stand tall and erect as an American citizen bowing gracefully as if in the presence of a queen or king to those three men who have played their roles excellent. I'd like to scream from the top of my voice uttering these words, "Another victory to the United States of America, the greatest country in the world!"

But as black as I am, I dare not cheer some $92.5 billion up in the sky when my black brothers and sisters, the children of Ethiopia, Ghana, Mali, Nigeria and other countries of the mother land, serve for food, wishing for the disappearance of ghettos, and for economic quality and better educational and employment opportunities.

                   Doris Rutledge
                   Student
                   Miles College
ingham, Ala.

The moon landing was a historical in world events. Many people in country watched their TV sets with great sense of pride.

How magnificent it must have been to see the entire operation being carried out by someone who could have been you, your brother, your son, or more importantly your father.

Imagine a child's bright eyes if he could say, "My dad is doing the countdown. My dad is one of the astronauts. That's my dad at the computer. My dad is at Houston Mission Controls."

A sense of pride is certainly proper and fitting. And those who identify best with the people chosen to carry out this mission, must now have egos at least as high as the moon.

Do I identify best? I saw no one who looked like me, nor my brother, nor my son, nor my father. For I am black, and so are they.

                   Nona E. Smith

and Harlem, N. Y.

PROGRESS

Africa's Untold Story

154 Black Quantum Futurism, *Black Space Agency*, 2018

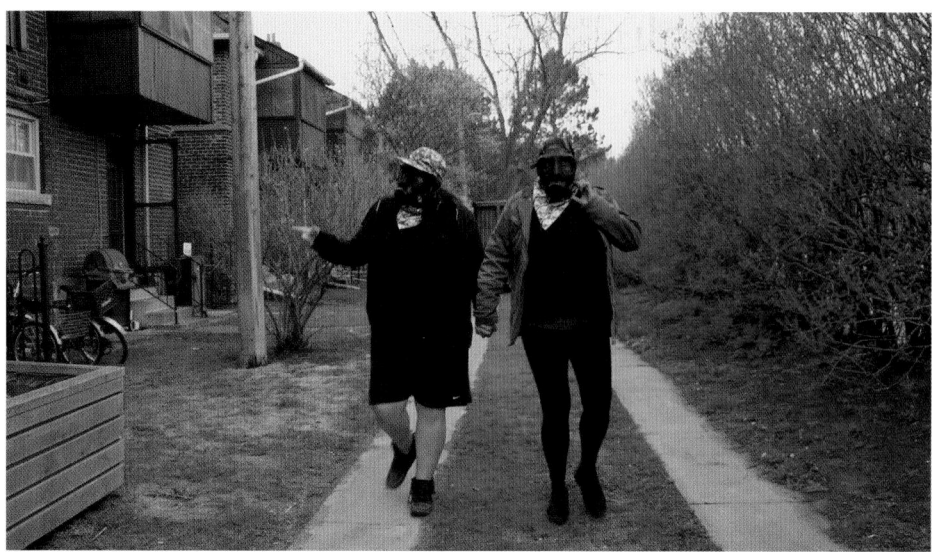

155 Thirza Cuthand, *Reclamation*, 2018

healing processes is so intense that its restorative energy
reverberates in the protagonists, whose only fear is that 'one
day the colonizers might return'. Through warmth, humour
and inclusivity, the film radiates the message that if structures
and habits of domination were abruptly relinquished, the world
could recover its cosmic balance.

The drama of biogeochemical processes set in motion
by anthropogenic changes to the planet's climate is played
out against post-human technoscientific efforts to control
and dominate these usurpations, while in its shadow other
scenarios coexist and are being enacted. The artistic practices
discussed here, cognisant of the fact that science fiction is
rooted in current concerns, have looked to the past for pointers,
anticipating emancipatory futures built on historical struggles
and the situated experiences of the oppressed. Liberating the
futuristic imaginary from the linearity of progressive time, artists
have challenged Western modernist utopias that perpetuate
present and past exclusions and hierarchies, making possible
through a subversive cosmotechnics the collision of the pre-
modern past with post-petrol futures. A multitude of Afro-,
indigenous and eco-futurisms envision the tentative prospect
of a pluriversal futurity, while the reclamation of the ruined
planet is revealed as a chronopolitical question that depends
on overcoming inertia and procrastination in the face of
climate change.

Conclusion

What the art practices discussed in this book have revealed is the deep-seated understanding that climate change is inseparable from the multiple ecological, social and economic crises of an interconnected world that is spiralling out of control. The source of these troubles cannot be reduced to a single cause, even one so all-encompassing as human usurpation of natural processes, since the Anthropocene itself cannot be understood apart from the economic order of capitalist extractivism driven by petroculture, the pernicious influence of the military–industrial complex and the crimes and long-lasting consequences of slavery and colonialism in unleashing modern forms of exploitation and cultivating the disconnect from nature. Overturning this divisive logic of rationalist modernity, artists have uncovered a multitude of ways in which humans are interconnected with the natural order, from exploring what is shared with animals and plants to shattering the myth of individuality through understanding organisms as sites of microbial kinship and cooperation. This has been taken even further to detail how the building blocks of human bodies are made up of the same chemical elements as mountains and oceans. Correspondingly, the response to the planetary dimensions of climate change requires not a one-sided or solely technocratic approach, but a systemic change in orientation and attitudes to the natural world by transforming behaviours and political priorities to achieve climate justice for all terrestrials.

This understanding of a pervasive interconnectedness has been brought about by emergent epistemologies that also stand in a critical relation to Western standpoints, reflecting the convergence of contemporary science and historically side-lined indigenous and traditional knowledges and wisdoms. This is reflected in the structure of the book, which devotes sections to the re-epistemologizing of knowledge about natural entities, plants and animals, which artists have approached with a variety of techniques. Such perspectives are enriched by opening up to the insights of non-Western science, as well as the work of scientists in the fields of Earth sciences, plant neurobiology or ecocentric cybernetics, whose research was disregarded or redirected by the pull of dominant economic and political interests. Art practices have brought to the fore the multiplicity of non-human agency, exploring the ways in which rivers, mountains, glaciers and other natural entities recognized by indigenous cosmology as Earth beings have the power to shape realities, histories and environments. Also going against reified Western beliefs about human exceptionalism, they have brought to light the extent to which plant and animal sentience and intelligence can eclipse that of humans.

Extending the concerns of environmentalism beyond conservation, artists have formulated a different set of questions about non-human rights, planetary jurisprudence and cosmopolitical justice deriving from an expanded understanding of agency, intelligence and personhood. It is also apparent that expanding legal rights to animals, flowers, the sky or glaciers is only meaningful if the conditions for their existence and flourishing are ensured, above all by slowing down climate change, reversing habitat loss, reducing the dispersal of toxic waste and emissions and halting the disfiguring of the natural landscape by extractive industries. An array of artistic considerations have been directed towards liberating and rescuing natural entities and species from the confines of ideological exploitation, and from their instrumentalization for political purposes and the nationalist project, as well as unmasking their appropriation within the oppressive edifices of Cold War and colonial histories. Artists have also exposed the mechanisms of electronic colonialism and digital speciesism, showing how hypersubjectified animal memes are linked to the mistreatment of animals in the wild and how intrusive surveillance technologies are for the natural world. The concealed contribution of virtual worlds to climate change has been revealed by artists in terms of the mining and exhaustion of rare Earth minerals and the invisible, energy-intensive and emissions-escalating footprint.

The climate crisis arose from centuries of a cultivated indifference towards the effects of human actions on the environment, accompanied by the branding of ecology as soft politics. While earlier environmental campaigns emphasized the need to take into account what legacy will be left for future generations, the speed with which the environmental crisis, global warming, biodiversity loss and extinctions are unfolding has brought forward the discussion, firmly locating it in the present. Artistic projects have drawn attention to the manifold consequences of the destruction of biodiversity, showing extinction not just as a biological loss, but also as impoverishing the culture of human communities in which species played an enormous and often unacknowledged part and as diminishing the variety of non-human cultural practices. Many artistic approaches have been guided by principles of care and tending, enacting gestures and procedures for attending to the wellbeing of animals, plants, rivers and oceans, as well as marginalized and oppressed communities across the globe. Anthropological studies in beyond-human indigenous cosmologies have been drawn upon by artists to reveal the complexity of ecosystems in which physiological and spiritual dimensions coexist, heightening empathy and solidarity necessary for rebuilding and rekindling caring and reciprocal relations to many worlds. As itself a form of radical care, eco-activism is revealed in this book as a multitude of positions and practices, from engaged drawing and filming to community trainings and public protests, all of which contribute to bringing about systemic change.

The growth-oriented extractivist system, which was hardwired into colonialist expansion, flowed through both capitalist and socialist modernities, and gained new momentum in the era of economic globalization, is now headed into outer space. Resorting to science fiction, artists have laid bare the way such terraforming utopias perpetuate earthbound structures of white privilege and social injustice, while generating a multitude of inclusive and liberatory scenarios for an alternative futurity. Partial and segmented proposals for technocratic climate adaptation thrive on neutralizing voices and movements for radical ecological transition, turning off microphones to criticism and imposing trade-offs between democracy and survivance. However, the recognition that there can be no 'ecology in one country', since the effects of climate change are planetary, has only spurred efforts to stop environmental devastation one place and one struggle at a time, with situated artistic practices providing the connecting thread between them. Against the backdrop of the velocities of extractivism and its competitive ethos, the artists have indicated the potential for different attitudes and protocols based on collaboration, solidarities and collective efforts to turn climate disaster into an opportunity to bring about the conditions for a terrestrial pluriverse to emerge.

Further Reading

Isabelle Stengers, *Another Science is Possible: A Manifesto for Slow Science* (Cambridge: Polity, 2017)

Part I: Chapter 2

Ignacio Acosta, ed., *Ignacio Acosta: Copper Geographies* (Barcelona: Editorial RM, 2019)

T. J. Demos, *Decolonising Nature: Contemporary Art and the Politics of Ecology* (Berlin: Sternberg Press, 2016)

Macarena Gómez-Barris, *The Extractive Zone: Social Ecologies and Decolonial Perspectives* (Durham, NC: Duke University Press, 2017)

Naomi Klein, *This Changes Everything: Capitalism vs. the Climate* (New York, NY: Simon & Schuster, 2014)

Andreas Malm, *Fossil Capital: The Rise of Steam Power and the Roots of Global Warming* (London: Verso, 2016)

J. R. McNeill, ed., *Environmental Histories of the Cold War* (Cambridge: Cambridge University Press, 2010)

Clare Molloy, Philippe Pirotte and Fabian Schöneich, eds, *Otobong Nkanga: Luster and Lucre* (Berlin: Sternberg Press, 2017)

Jason W. Moore, *Capitalism in the Web of Life: Ecology and the Accumulation of Capital* (London: Verso, 2015)

Nadim Samman and Boris Ondreička, eds, *Rare Earth* (Vienna: Thyssen-Bornemisza Art Contemporary, 2015)

Part I: Chapter 1

Anca Benera and Arnold Estefan, eds, *Debrisphere* (Bucharest: Punch, 2018)

Andrew Berardini, ed., *Emilija Škarnulytė: Sirenomelia* (Berlin: Sternberg Press, 2021)

T. J. Demos, *Against the Anthropocene* (Berlin: Sternberg Press, 2017)

Maja and Reuben Fowkes, 'Cracks in the Planet: Geo-ecological Matter in Eastern European Art', in Urška Jurman and Christiane Erharter, eds, *Extending the Dialogue*, (Berlin: Archive Books, 2016)

Katerina Gregos, ed., *Maarten Vanden Eynde: Digging up the Future* (New Haven, CT: Yale University Press, 2020)

Simon L. Lewis and Mark A. Maslin, *The Human Planet: How We Created the Anthropocene* (London: Pelican Books, 2018)

Armin Linke et al., eds, *Blind Sensorium. Il paradosso dell'Antropocene* (Matera: Fondazione Matera-Basilicata, 2020)

Nicholas Mangan, *Limits to Growth* (Melbourne: Monash University Museum of Art, 2016)

John McNeill and Peter Engelke, *The Great Acceleration: An Environmental History of the Anthropocene* (Cambridge, MA: Harvard University Press, 2016)

Jussi Parikka, *A Geology of Media* (Minneapolis, MN: University of Minnesota Press, 2015)

Nicholas Mirzoeff, *How to See the World* (London: Pelican Books, 2015)

Pope Francis, *Laudato Si: On Care for Our Common Home* (Vatican: Our Sunday Visitor, 2015)

Elizabeth A. Povinelli, *Geontologies: A Requiem to Late Liberalism* (Durham, NC: Duke University Press, 2016)

Part I: Chapter 3

Inke Arns, ed., *World of Matter* (Berlin: Sternberg Press, 2015)

Adam Carlson, Imre Szeman and Sheena Wilson, eds, *Petrocultures: Oil, Politics, Culture* (Montreal: McGill-Queen's University Press, 2017)

Clive Hamilton, *Earthmasters: The Dawn of Climate Engineering* (New Haven, CT: Yale University Press, 2013)

Sandro Mezzadra and Brett Neilson, *The Politics of Operations: Excavating Contemporary Capitalism* (Durham, NC: Duke University Press, 2019)

Timothy Mitchell, *Carbon Democracy: Political Power in the Age of Oil* (London and New York, NY: Verso, 2011)

Oliver Ressler, ed., *Barricading the Ice Sheets. Artists and Climate Action in the Age of Irreversible Decision* (Vienna: Camera Austria, 2020)

David Wallace-Wells, *The Uninhabitable Earth: A Story of the Future* (London: Penguin, 2019)

Part I: Chapter 4

Amanda Boetzkes, *Plastic Capitalism: Contemporary Art and the Drive to Waste* (Cambridge, MA: MIT Press, 2019)

Christophe Bonneuil and Jean-Baptiste Fressoz, *The Shock of the Anthropocene: The Earth, History and Us*, translated by David Fernbach (London: Verso, 2016)

Heather Davis and Etienne Turpin, *Art in the Anthropocene: Encounters Among Aesthetics, Politics, Environments and Epistemologies* (London: Open Humanities Press, 2015)

Jennifer Gabrys, *Digital Rubbish: A Natural History of Electronics* (Ann Arbor, MI: University of Michigan Press, 2011)

Jennifer Gabrys, Gay Hawkins and Mike Michael, eds, *Accumulation: The Material Politics of Plastic* (New York, NY and London: Routledge, 2013)

Katarina Gregos, ed., *Maarten Vanden Eynde: Digging up the Future* (New Haven, CT: Yale University Press, 2020)

Diana Lelonek, *A New Archeology of Liban and Plaszow* (Warsaw: Foundation for Visual Arts, 2019)

Vance Packard, *The Waste Makers* (New York, NY: IG Publishing, 1960)

Joanna Warsza, ed., *Janek Simon: Synthetic Folklore* (Berlin: Sternberg Press, 2020)

Jan Zalasiewicz, *The Earth After Us: What Legacy will Humans Leave in the Rocks?* (Oxford: Oxford University Press, 2008)

Part I: Chapter 5

Cooking Sections, *The Empire Remains Shop* (New York, NY: Columbia University, 2018)

Maja and Reuben Fowkes, eds, *Ilona Németh: Eastern Sugar* (Berlin: Sternberg Press, 2021)

Paul Josephson et al., *An Environmental History of Russia* (Cambridge: Cambridge University Press, 2013)

Matteo Lucchetti, *Marzia Migliora: The Spectre of Malthus* (Gallarate: MA*GA Art Museum, 2020)

Sidney W. Mintz, *Sweetness and Power: The Place of Sugar in Modern History* (London: Penguin, 1985)

Jason W. Moore and Raj Patel, *A History of the World in Seven Cheap Things: A Guide to Capitalism, Nature, and the Future of the Planet* (Berkeley, CA: University of California Press, 2017)

Vandana Shiva, *The Violence of the Green Revolution: Third World Agriculture, Ecology and Politics* (Chicago, IL: University of Chicago Press, 1991)

Part II: Chapter 1

Elena Agudio, Marleen Boschen and Lorenzo Sandoval, eds, *Agropoetics Reader* (Berlin: The Institute for Endotic Research Press, 2020)

Sebastian Cichocki and Jagna Lewandowska, eds, *The Penumbral Age: Art in the Time of Climate Change*, exhibition guide (Warsaw: Museum of Modern Art in Warsaw, 2020)

Ros Gray and Shela Sheikh, eds, 'The Wretched Earth: Botanical Conflicts and Artistic Interventions', special issue of *Third Text*, nos 151–52 (March–May 2018)

Kristina M. Lyons, *Vital Decomposition: Soil Practitioners and Life Politics* (Durham, NC: Duke University Press, 2020)

John McNeill, *Something New Under the Sun: An Environmental History of the Twentieth Century* (London: Penguin, 2000)

Maria Puig de la Bellacasa, *Matters of Care: Speculative Ethics in More Than Human Worlds* (Minneapolis, MN: University of Minnesota Press, 2017)

Emily Eliza Scott and Kirsten Swenson, eds, *Critical Landscapes: Art, Space, Politics* (Berkeley, CA: University of California Press, 2015)

Alexandra Toland, Jay Stratton Noller and Gerd Wessolek, eds, *Field to Palette: Dialogues on Soil and Art in the Anthropocene* (Cleveland, OH: CRC Press, 2018)

Kathryn Yusoff, *A Billion Black Anthropocenes or None* (Minneapolis, MN: University of Minnesota Press, 2018)

Part II: Chapter 2

Carla Acevedo-Yates, *Carolina Caycedo* (New York, NY: DAP, 2021)

Peter Coates, *A Story of Six Rivers: History, Culture and Ecology* (London: Reaktion Books, 2013)

Marco Daniel et al., *Thao Nguyên Phan: Monsoon Melody* (Milan: Mousse Publishing, 2019)

Maja and Reuben Fowkes, *River Ecologies: Environmental Arts and Humanities on the Danube* (Budapest: Translocal Institute, 2015)

Gunvor Guttorm and Harald Gaski, eds, *Let the River Flow: An Indigenous Uprising and its Legacy in Art, Ecology and Politics* (Oslo: Office for Contemporary Art, 2020)

Laurence C. Smith, *Rivers of Power: How a Natural Force Raised Kingdoms, Destroyed Civilisations, and Shapes our World* (London: Penguin, 2020)

Richard White, *The Organic Machine* (New York, NY: Hill and Wang, 1995)

Part II: Chapter 3

Rachel Carson, *The Sea Around Us* (Oxford: Oxford University Press, 1951)

Elizabeth M. DeLoughrey, *Allegories of the Anthropocene* (Durham, NC: Duke University Press, 2019)

Jennifer Gabrys, *Program Earth: Environmental Sensing Technology and the Making of a Computational Planet* (Minneapolis, MN: University of Minnesota Press, 2016)

Stefan Helmreich, *Alien Ocean: Anthropological Voyages in Microbial Seas* (Berkeley, CA: University of California Press, 2008)

Stefanie Hessler, *Tidalectics: Imagining an Oceanic Worldview through Art and Science* (Cambridge MA: MIT Press, 2018)

Stefanie Hessler, ed., *Prospecting Ocean* (Cambridge, MA: MIT Press, 2019)

Astrida Neimanis, *Bodies of Water: Posthuman Feminist Phenomenology* (London: Bloomsbury, 2017)

Enrique Ramírez, *Océan 33°02'47"S / 51°04'00"N* (Paris: Editions Pylone, 2013)

Nadim Samman, ed., *Julian Charrière: Second Suns* (Berlin: Hatje Cantz Verlag, 2018)

Part II: Chapter 4

Barnaby Drabble, ed., *Along Ecological Lines: Contemporary Art and Climate Crisis* (Manchester: Gaia Project Press, 2019)

Dahr Jamail, *The End of Ice: Bearing Witness and Finding Meaning in the Path of Climate Disruption* (New York, NY: The New Press, 2019)

Martin J. S. Rudwick, *Earth's Deep History: How It Was Discovered and Why It Matters* (Chicago, IL: University of Chicago Press, 2016)

Peter Wadhams, *Farewell to Ice: A Report from the Arctic* (London: Allen Lane, 2016)

David Wallace-Wells, *The Uninhabitable Earth: A Story of the Future* (London: Allen Lane, 2019)

Part II: Chapter 5

Christian Alonso, ed., *Mutating Ecologies in Contemporary Art* (Barcelona: University of Barcelona, 2019)

Monika Bakke, ed., *The Life of Air: Dwelling, Communicating, Manipulating* (London: Open Humanities Press, 2011)

Steven Connor, *The Matter of Air: Science and Art of the Ethereal* (London: Reaktion Books, 2010)

Sasha Engelmann, *Sensing Art in the Atmosphere: Elemental Lures and Aerosolar Practices* (Abingdon: Routledge, 2020)

Jennifer Gabrys, *Program Earth: Environmental Sensing Technology and the Making of a Computational Planet* (Minneapolis, MN: University of Minnesota Press, 2016)

Mark Lynas, *The God Species: How Humans Really Can Save the Planet* (London: HarperCollins, 2011)

Tomás Saraceno: The Aerocene Project (Milan: Skira, 2018)

John E. Thornes, 'Cultural climatology and the representation of sky, atmosphere, weather and climate in selected artworks of Constable, Monet and Eliasson', *Geoforum* 39, no. 2 (March 2008)

Part III: Chapter 1

Teresa Castro, 'The Mediation of Plants', *E-Flux Journal*, no. 102 (September 2019)

Patricia Domínguez, *Gaia Guardians* (London: Thyssen-Bornemisza Art Contemporary, 2020)

Silvia Federici, *Beyond the Periphery of the Skin: Rethinking, Remaking and Reclaiming the Body in Contemporary Capitalism* (Oakland, CA: PM Press, 2020)

Stefano Mancuso and Alessandra Viola, *Brilliant Green: The Surprising History and Science of Plant Intelligence* (Washington, DC: Island Press, 2015)

Michael Marder, *Plant-thinking: A Philosophy of Vegetal Life* (New York, NY: Columbia University Press, 2013)

Boaventura de Sousa Santos, *Epistemologies of the South: Justice Against Epistemicide* (London: Routledge, 2014)

Line Marie Thorson, ed., *Moving Plants* (Rønnebæksholm, Næstved: Narayana Press, 2017)

Part III: Chapter 2

Ana Maria Bresciani, ed., *Jumana Manna: Small Big Thing* (Berlin: Sternberg Press, 2018)

Uriel Orlow and Shela Sheikh, eds, *Uriel Orlow: Theatrum Botanicum* (Berlin: Sternberg Press, 2018)

Londa Schiebinger, *Plants and Empire: Colonial Bioprospecting in the Atlantic World* (Cambridge, MA: Harvard University Press, 2004)

Judith Shapiro, *Mao's War Against Nature: Politics and the Environment in Revolutionary China* (Cambridge: Cambridge University Press, 2001)

Eyal Weizman, Anselm Franke and Forensic Architecture, eds, *Forensis: The Architecture of Public Truth* (Berlin: Sternberg Press, 2014)

Part III: Chapter 3

Emanuele Coccia, *The Life of Plants: A Metaphysics of Mixture* (Cambridge: Polity Press, 2018)

Bonnie Fortune, *An Edge / Effect: Art and Ecology in the Nordic Landscape* (Copenhagen: Half Letter Press, 2014)

Richard Mabey, *Weeds: The Story of Outlaw Plants* (London: Profile Books, 2012)

Katherine McKittrick, ed., *Sylvia Wynter: On Being Human as Praxis* (Durham, NC: Duke University Press, 2014)

Chandra Mukerji, *Territorial Ambitions and the Gardens of Versailles* (Cambridge: Cambridge Cultural Social Studies, 1997)

Bettina Stoetzer, 'Ruderal Ecologies: Rethinking Nature, Migration, and the Urban Landscape in Berlin', *Cultural Anthropology* 33, no. 2 (2018)

Part III: Chapter 4

Mark Davis et al., 'Don't judge species on their origins', *Nature* (June 2011)

T. J. Demos, Emily Eliza Scott and Subhankar Banerjee, eds, *The Routledge Companion to Contemporary Art, Visual Culture, and Climate Change* (Abingdon: Routledge, 2021)

Pedro de Llano, ed., *The Long Road to Xico: Maria Thereza Alves, 1991–2015* (Berlin: Sternberg Press, 2015)

Stefano Mancuso, *The Incredible Journey of Plants* (New York, NY: Other Press, 2020)

Fred Pearce, *The New Wild: Why Invasive Species will be Nature's Salvation* (London: Icon Books, 2016)

Chris D. Thomas, *Inheritors of the Earth: How Nature is Thriving in an Age of Extinction* (London: Penguin, 2018)

Part III: Chapter 5

Ursula Biemann and Paulo Tavares, eds, *Forest Law / Selva Juridica* (Ann Arbor, MI: University of Michigan Press, 2014)

David George Haskell, *The Forest Unseen: A Year's Watch in Nature* (London: Penguin, 2013)

Luce Irigaray and Michael Marder, *Through Vegetal Being* (New York, NY: Columbia University Press, 2016)

Robin Wall Kimmerer, *Braiding Sweetgrass: Indigenous Wisdom, Scientific Knowledge and the Teachings of Plants* (London: Penguin, 2020)

Eduardo Kohn, *How Forests Think: Toward an Anthropology Beyond the Human* (Berkeley, CA: University of California Press, 2013)

'Saturation Point: The ability of tropical plants to sequester CO_2 is in decline', cover of *Nature* (5 March 2020)

Michel Serres, *The Natural Contract* (Ann Arbor, MI: University of Michigan Press, 1990)

Rasa Smite and Raitis Smits, eds, *Virtualities and Realities: New Experiences, Art and Ecologies in Immersive Environments* (Riga: RIXC, 2019)

Petra Stegmann, ed., *Through a Forest Wilderness* (Postdam: Down with Art!, 2018)

Part IV: Chapter 1

Giovanni Aloi, *Speculative Taxidermy: Natural History, Animal Surfaces, and Art in the Anthropocene* (New York, NY: Columbia University Press, 2018)

Bénédicte Boisseron, *Afro-Dog: Blackness and the Animal Question* (New York, NY: Columbia University Press, 2018)

Fiona Cameron and Brett Neilson, eds, *Climate Change and Museum Futures* (London: Routledge, 2015)

Frans de Waal, *Are We Smart Enough to Know how Smart Animals Are?* (London: Granta, 2016)

Terike Haapoja and Laura Gustafsson, eds, *History According to Cattle* (Goleta, CA: punctum books, 2015)

Petrit Halilaj, *Poisoned by men in need of some love* (Brussels: WIELS Contemporary Art Centre, 2013)

Donna Haraway, 'Teddy Bear Patriarchy: Taxidermy in the Garden of Eden, New York City, 1908–1936', *Social Text*, no. 11 (1984–85)

Robert R. Janes and Richard Sandell, eds, *Museum Activism* (London: Routledge, 2019)

Bruno Latour and Peter Weibel, eds, *Critical Zones: The Science and Politics of Landing on Earth* (Karlsruhe: ZKM, 2020)

Part IV: Chapter 2

Alex Blanchette, *Porkopolis: American Animality, Standardized Life and the Factory Farm* (Durham, NC: Duke University Press, 2020)

Déborah Danowski and Eduardo Viveiros de Castro, *The Ends of the World* (Cambridge: Polity, 2019)

Philippe Descola, *Beyond Nature and Culture* (Chicago, IL: University of Chicago Press, 2013)

Sue Donaldson and Will Kymlicka, *Zoopolis: A Political Theory of Animal Rights* (Oxford: Oxford University Press, 2013)

Lori Gruen, *Critical Terms for Animal Studies* (Chicago, IL: University of Chicago Press, 2018)

Donna J. Haraway, *Staying with Trouble: Making Kin in the Chthulucene* (Durham, NC: Duke University Press, 2016)
Claire Jean Kim, *Dangerous Crossings: Race, Species, and Nature in a Multicultural Age* (Cambridge: Cambridge University Press: 2015)
Filipa Ramos, ed., *Animals* (London: Whitechapel Gallery, 2016)
Oxana Timofeeva, 'Communism with a Nonhuman Face', *E-Flux Journal*, no. 48 (October 2013)
Eduardo Viveiros de Castro, *The Relative Native: Essays on Indigenous Conceptual Worlds* (London: HAU, 2016)
Robert Wiesenberger, ed., *Lin May Saeed: Arrival of the Animals* (Williamstown, MA: Clark Art Institute, 2020)

Part IV: Chapter 3
Zoe Butt, ed., *Tuấn Andrew Nguyễn: The Empty Forest* (Ho Chi Minh City: The Factory Contemporary Arts Centre, 2017)
Ashley Dawson, *Extinction: A Radical History* (New York, NY: OR Books, 2016)
Richard Grusin, ed., *After Extinction* (Minneapolis, MN: University of Minnesota Press, 2018)
Ursula K. Heise, *Imagining Extinction: The Cultural Meanings of Endangered Species* (Chicago, IL: University of Chicago Press, 2016)
Elizabeth Kolbert, *The Sixth Extinction: An Unnatural History* (London: Bloomsbury, 2014)
George Monbiot, *Feral: Rewilding the Land, Sea and Human Life* (London: Penguin, 2013)
Isabella Tree, *Wilding: The Return of Nature to a British Farm* (London: Picador, 2019)
Thom van Dooren, *Flight Ways: Life and Loss at the Edge of Extinction* (New York, NY: Columbia University Press, 2014)

Part IV: Chapter 4
Jennifer Ackerman, *The Bird Way: A New Look at How Birds Talk, Work, Play, Parent and Think* (London: Penguin, 2020)
Julieta Aranda, Anton Vidokle and Brian Kuan Wood, eds, *Supercommunity: Diabolical Togetherness Beyond Contemporary Art* (London: Verso, 2017)
Rosi Braidotti and Maria Hlavajova, eds, *Posthuman Glossary* (London: Bloomsbury Academic, 2018)
Rachel Carson, *Silent Spring* (London: Penguin, 2000)

Bruno Latour, 'Whose Cosmos, which cosmopolitics?', *Common Knowledge* 10, no. 3 (2014)
Edit Molnár and Zoltán Kékesi, *From Fake Mountains to Faith (Hungarian Trilogy)* (Oldenburg: Edith-Russ-Haus for Media Art, 2018)
Jeremy Mynott, *Birdscapes: Birds in Our Imagination and Experience* (Princeton, NJ: Princeton University Press, 2009)
Thom van Dooren, *The Wake of Crows: Living and Dying in Shared Worlds* (New York, NY: Columbia University Press, 2019)

Part IV: Chapter 5
Donna Haraway, *Staying with the Trouble: Making Kin in the Chthulucene* (Durham, NC: Duke University Press, 2016)
Alma Heikkilä and Satu Oksanen, eds, *Alma Heikkilä: A Museum of Contemporary Art Publication* (Helsinki: Kiasma, 2019)
Lynn Margulis, *Symbiotic Planet: A New Look at Evolution* (New York, NY: Basic Books, 1998)
David R. Montgomery and Anne Biklé, *The Hidden Half of Nature: The Microbial Roots of Life and Health* (New York, NY: W. W. Norton & Company, 2016)
Deborah Bird Rose and Thom van Dooren, eds, 'Unloved Others: Death of the Disregarded in the Time of Extinctions', special issue of *Australian Humanities Review*, no. 50 (2011)
Merlin Sheldrake, *Entangled Life: How Fungi Make Our Worlds, Change Our Minds, and Shape Our Futures* (London: The Bodley Head, 2020)
Anna Tsing, *The Mushroom at the End of the World: On the Possibility of Life in Capitalist Ruins* (Princeton, NJ: Princeton University Press, 2015)
Anna Tsing et al., *Arts of Living on a Damaged Planet* (Minneapolis, MN: University of Minnesota Press, 2017)
Anna Tsing et al., *Feral Atlas: The More-Than-Human Anthropocene* (Redwood City, CA: Stanford University Press, 2021)

Part V: Chapter 1
Yuk Hui, *Art and Cosmotechnics* (New York, NY: e-flux, 2020)
Martha Kirszenbaum, ed., *Laure Prouvost: Deep See Blue Surrounding You* (Paris: Flammarion, 2019)
Bruno Latour, *Down to Earth: Politics in the New Climatic Regime* (Cambridge: Polity, 2018)

Achille Mbembe, *Critique of Black Reason* (Durham, NC: Duke University Press, 2017)
Heather Phillipson, *Whip-hot & Grippy* (Hexham: Bloodaxe Books, 2019)

Jonas Staal, *Propaganda Art in the 21st Century* (Cambridge, MA: MIT Press, 2019)
Julie Watson, *Lo-TEK Design by Radical Indigenism* (Cologne: Taschen, 2019)

Part V: Chapter 2

Ariella Aïsha Azoulay, *Potential History: Unlearning Imperialism* (London: Verso, 2019)
Mario Blaser and Marisol de la Cadena, eds, *A World of Many Worlds* (Durham, NC: Duke University Press, 2018)
Gary Carrion-Murayari and Massimiliano Gioni, eds, *John Akomfrah: Signs of Empire* (New York, NY: New Museum, 2018)
Katya García-Antón, *Sovereign Words: Indigenous Art, Curation and Criticism* (Oslo: Office for Contemporary Art, 2019)
Jan-Erik Lundström, ed., *Britta Marakatt-Labba: Embroidered Stories*, Kiruna: Koncentrat (2010)

Part V: Chapter 3

Ashley Dawson, *Extreme Cities: The Peril and Promise of Urban Life in the Age of Climate Change* (London: Verso, 2019)
Arturo Escobar, *Designs for the Pluriverse: Radical Interdependence, Autonomy, and the Making of Worlds* (Durham, NC: Duke University Press, 2018)
Katherine Gibson, Deborah Bird and Ruther Fincher, eds, *Manifesto for Living in the Anthropocene* (Goleta, CA: punctum books, 2015)
Raphaël Grisey with Bouba Touré, eds, *Sowing Somankidi Coura: A Generative Archive* (Berlin: Archive Books, 2020)
Myvillages, *The Rural* (London: Whitechapel Gallery, 2019)
Leah Penniman, *Farming While Black: Soul Fire Farm's Practical Guide to Liberation on the Land* (London: Chelsea Green Publishing, 2018)
Joanna Sokołowska, ed., *Exercises in Autonomy: Tamás Kaszás featuring Anikó Loránt (ex-artists' collective)* (Łódź: Museum Sztuki in Łódź, 2016)

Part V: Chapter 4

Maria Thereza Alves, *The Return of a Lake* (Cologne: Walther König Verlag, 2013)
Kum-Kum Bhavnani et al., eds, *Climate Futures: Reimagining Global Climate Justice* (London: Zed Books, 2019)
Silvia Federici, *Caliban and the Witch: Women, the Body and Primitive Accumulation* (New York, NY: Autonomedia, 2014)

Part V: Chapter 5

Eric C. H. de Bruyn and Sven Lütticken, *Futurity Report* (Berlin: Sternberg Press, 2020)
T. J. Demos, *Beyond the World's End: Arts of Living at the Crossroads* (Durham, NC: Duke University Press, 2020)
Kodwo Eshun, 'Further Considerations on Afrofuturism', *The New Centennial Review* 3, no. 2 (2003)
Suad Garayeva-Maleki and Heike Munder, eds, *Potential Worlds: Planetary Memories & Eco-Fictions* (Zurich: Migros Museum, 2020)
Naomi Oreskes and Erik M. Conway, *The Collapse of Western Civilization: A View from the Future* (New York, NY: Columbia University Press, 2014)
Rasheedah Phillips, *Black Quantum Futurism: Theory & Practice: Volume 1* (Philadelphia, PA: AfroFuturist Affair, 2015)

List of Illustrations

Dimensions are in centimetres, followed by inches, height before width before depth

1 Anne Duk Hee Jordan, *Water Crab*, 2017–ongoing (detail). Material: motors, mechanics, waste. Technical engineer: Andreas Marckscheffel. Photo Anne Duk Hee Jordan. Courtesy of the artist
2 Amie Siegel, *Quarry*, 2015. HD video, colour/sound (video still) © Amie Siegel. Image courtesy the artist and Thomas Dane Gallery
3 Nicholas Mangan, *A World Undone*, 2012. HD video, silent, 12:00 mins duration, continuous loop. Video still. Image courtesy the artist and Sutton Gallery, Melbourne
4 Anca Benera and Arnold Estefan, *Debrisphere: Landscape as an Extension of the Military Imagination*, 2017. Exhibition view mumok. Photo Klaus Pichler
5 Sasha Litvintseva and Daniel Mann, *Salarium*, 2017. Video still. Courtesy of the artists
6 Emilija Škarnulytė, *T1/2*, 2019. Video still. Courtesy of the artist
7 Armin Linke, *Blind Sensorium: Il Paradosso dell' Antropocene*, 2019. Fireman in the peatland, Kota Dumai (Sumatra), Indonesia, 2016. © Armin Linke. Courtesy of the artist
8 Tabita Rezaire, *Deep Down Tidal*, 2017. Video still. Courtesy of the artist
9 Lise Autogena and Joshua Portway, *Kuannersuit; Kvanefjeld*, 2016. Video installation. Courtesy of the artists
10 Otobong Nkanga, *The Weight of Scars*, 2015. 'Bruises and Lustre', MuHKA, 2015. Photo Christine Clinckx – MuHKA. Courtesy of the artist
11 Sammy Baloji, *Petits Chanteurs à la Croix de Cuivre*, 2020. Black & white print on paper, 110 × 165 (43⁵⁄₁₆ × 65). *Untitled*, 2018. Installation with 39 copper shell casings and exotic plants, various sizes. Installation view. Photo Daniel Zachrisson. Courtesy of the artist and Lunds Konsthall
12 Ignacio Acosta, *Copper Geographies*, 2012–16. Satellite view of Chuquicamata corporate mining town, Atacama Desert, Chile, c. 2011. Courtesy of the artist
13 APART Collective, *The Most Beautiful Catastrophe*, 2018. Courtesy of the artists and Prague City Gallery
14 Angela Melitopoulos and Angela Anderson, *Unearthing Disaster II*, 2015. Single-channel 4K video, 26 mins. Courtesy of the artists
15 Territorial Agency, *Museum of Oil*, 2016. Installation view ZKM | Center for Art and Media, Karlsruhe. Photo Harald Völkl / © ZKM | Karlsruhe
16 Zina Saro-Wiwa, *Karikpo Pipeline*, 2015. Video still depicting masquerade dancers on top of an abandoned flow station in Ogoniland. Courtesy of the artist
17 Kinotron Group, *Data Is the New Gas*, 2019. HD video. Courtesy of Oleksiy Radynski
18 Rachel O'Reilly, *Infractions*, 2019. HD video, split screen with text, Dolby 5.1, 1:03:00. Video still. Courtesy of the artist
19 Oliver Ressler, *Carbon and Captivity*, 2020. 4K video, 33 mins. Courtesy the artist, àngels Barcelona, The Gallery Apart, Rome
20 Monira Al Qadiri, *Deep Float*, 2017. Epoxy, acrylic, steel, 150 × 75 × 87 (59 × 29½ × 34¼). Image courtesy of the artist
21 Mary Mattingly, *Life of Objects*, 2013. Archival pigment print, 30 × 30 (11⅞ × 11⅞). Courtesy of the artist
22 Joana Hadjithomas and Khalil Joreige, *A State*, 2019. Part of the project *Unconformities* by Joana Hadjithomas and Khalil Joreige. 3 drilling cores, 45 metres and 25 years of waste and techno-fossils, shot at a rubbish dump in Tripoli, Lebanon. Digital photography 130 × 220 (51¹⁄₁₆ × 86⁵⁄₁₆). Courtesy The Third Line (Dubai) and In Situ fabienne leclerc (Paris)
23 Janek Simon, *Huaqiangbei Commercial Street: A Selection of Objects from Shenzhen*, 2019. Installation view. Courtesy of Ujazdowski Castle Centre for Contemporary Art and the artist
24 Maarten Vanden Eynde, *Plastic Reef*, 2008–13. Art Space Pythagorion, Samos, Greece, 2019. Photo Panos Kokkinias. Courtesy of the artist
25 Alberto Baraya, *Another Amapola, NY*, 2018. From the series *Herbarium of Artificial Plants*, 2001–ongoing. Courtesy of the artist
26 Diana Lelonek, *PET-environment*, 2017. Found object from the collection *Centre for Living Things*, 2017. Courtesy of the artist and lokal_30 gallery

56 Joan Jonas, *Reanimation*, 2012. Performance at Hangar Bicocca, Milan, Italy, 'Light Time Tales', 2014. Photo Moira Ricci. © ARS, NY and DACS, London 2022
57 Ieva Epnere, *Four Edges of Pyramiden*, 2015. HD video, 20 mins, colour, sound. Video still. © Ieva Epnere
58 Himali Singh Soin, *we are opposite like that*, 2019. Video still. Courtesy of the artist
59 Isuma collective, *Qapirangajuq: Inuit Knowledge and Climate Change*, 2010. Courtesy of Kingulliit Productions
60 Oto Hudec, *Concert for Adishi Glacier*, 2018. Still from HD video (8:50 mins). Archive of the artist
61 Dora Budor, *Origin II (Burning of the Houses)*, 2019, and *Origin III (Snow Storm)*, 2019. Installation view, 'I am Gong', Kunsthalle Basel, 2019. Photo Philipp Hänger. Courtesy of the artist and Kunsthalle Basel
62 Emily Parsons-Lord, *Different Kinds of Air, a Plant's Diary*, 2014. Performance documentation. Photo Peter Cheng. Courtesy of the artist and Proximity Festival
63 Hanna Husberg, *Often People Ask How Birds Are Affected by the Air*, 2017. Black Sesame Space (Institute for Provocation), Beijing, November 2017. Photo Sun Shi. Courtesy of the artist
64 Rohini Devasher, *Shadow Walkers*, 2010. Audio vignette, duration 15 mins. At the Spencer Museum of Art, 2016. Image credit: Ryan Waggoner. Courtesy of the Spencer Museum of Art
65 Amy Balkin, *PUBLIC SMOG IS NO SUBSTITUTE FOR DIRECT ACTION*, 2009. Billboard, Bonamoussadi, Douala, Cameroon. Part of Amy Balkin's *Public Smog* (2004–ongoing). Credits: Amy Balkin, with photography by Guillaume Astaix. Image: Benoît Mangin. Courtesy of the artist
66 Joana Moll, *CO2GLE*, 2014. Courtesy of the artist
67 *Flight with Aerocene Pacha*: Tomás Saraceno for Aerocene 21–28 January 2020, Salinas Grandes, Jujuy, Argentina Human Solar Free Flight as part of Connect, BTS, curated by DaeHyung Lee. Courtesy the artist and Aerocene Foundation. Photography by Studio Tomás Saraceno, 2020. Licensed under CC BY-SA 4.0 by Aerocene Foundation
68 Alexandra Pirici, *Describing in movement/ Observing through embodiment*, 2020. Research project. Video still of exercise *Crown shyness – branches of different trees avoid touching or covering each-other, growing together around each-other, negotiating space and access to light*. Performed by Maria Mora, Farid Fairuz, Alexandra Pirici. Courtesy of the artist

69 Christine Ödlund, *Stress Call of the Stinging Nettle*, 2010. Watercolour and pencil on paper, 85 × 197 (33⁷⁄₁₆ × 77⅛). Photographer Jean-Baptiste Béranger. Collection Michael Storåkers. © DACS 2022
70 Patricia Domínguez, *Eyes of Plants*, 2019. Video still. Commissioned by Gasworks, London. Courtesy of the artist. © ARS, NY and DACS, London 2022
71 Åsa Sonjasdotter, *The Order of Potatoes*, 2010. Photo Åsa Sonjasdotter. Courtesy of the artist
72 Woad and Japanese indigo, indigo-bearing plants best suited to a European climate, grown by Sigrid Holmwood, 2020
73 Zheng Bo in collaboration with plants, *Socialism Good*, 2016. Installation at CASS Sculpture Foundation. Image courtesy the artist and Edouard Malingue Gallery
74 Reena Kallat, *Siamese Trees*, 2018–19. Installation view Migros Museum of Contemporary Art, Zurich. Photo Stefan Altenburger. Courtesy Chemould Prescott Road and Reena Kallat Studio
75 Kapwani Kiwanga, *Flowers for Africa: Cameroon*, 2020. Protocol of assembly and display including archival iconography to guide the reconstruction of a floral arrangement consisting of cut flowers. © ADAGP, Paris and DACS, London 2022. Variable dimensions. View of the exhibition 'Prix Marcel Duchamp 2020', Centre Pompidou, Paris, 2020–21. Photo Aurélien Mole. Collection Galerie Poggi, Paris. Courtesy of the artist and Galerie Poggi, Paris
76 Uriel Orlow, *The Squirrel's Revenge*, 2015–16 (detail). Photograph, seed, loupe, concrete plinth. © Uriel Orlow. All Rights Reserved, DACS 2022
77 Joscelyn Gardner, *Mimosa pudica (Yabba)*, 2009. Hand-coloured stone lithograph on frosted mylar, 91.4 × 60.9 (36 × 24). Photo John Tamblyn. Courtesy the artist
78 Beatriz Santiago Muñoz, *Farmacopea*, 2013, 16mm, colour, silent. Duration: 5:38 mins. Courtesy of the artist
79 Hannah Meszaros Martin, *Falta de Luz*, 2020. Single-channel video projection, 23 mins. Direction, concept and production: Hannah Meszaros Martin. Editing: Manuel Correa and Hannah Meszaros Martin. Sound design: Emil Olsen. Music: Mhamad Safa. Interview 'Taita' conducted in collaboration with Andrés Monzón-Aguirre. Archival consultant: Emily Coxe
80 Jumana Manna, *Wild Relatives*, 2018. HD video 64 mins. Film still. Photo Marte Vold. Courtesy of the artist. © DACS 2022
81 Igor Eškinja, *Untitled (Hartera)*, 2020. Digital print on paper, variable dimensions. Part of the project *Do Plants Dream of the Future?* produced by

Drugo more within European Capital of Culture, Rijeka 2020. Courtesy of the artist and Drugo more

82 Camilla Berner, *Plant Collection no. 1030 Tongui-dong, Jongno-gu, Seoul 11.08.16*, 2016. Photography: Platine Fibre Rag 310g – Satin, 90 × 120 (35⁷⁄₁₆ × 47¼). Text: canson champagne 100 g, 17 × 36 (6¹¹⁄₁₆ × 14⅛)

83 Nandita Kumar, *The Unwanted Ecology*, 2017. Installation view, Centre Pompidou, Paris. Courtesy of the artist

84 Annalee Davis, *(Bush) Tea Plot – A Decolonial Patch for Mill Workers*, 2020. Haarlem Artspace Gallery, Wirksworth, UK. Materials: Glass vitrine, limestone blocks, limestone, soil, 18th- and 19th-century clay, and porcelain sherds, bobbin. Wild botanicals: Coltsfoot, Red clover, Horsetail, Yarrow, Meadowsweet, Lemon Balm, Mint Elderberries, Lady's Mantle, Self-Heal & Vervain. 101.6 × 71.1 × 71.1 (40 × 28 × 28). Photo Will Slater

85 Suzanne Husky, *Jardin à la française sauvage*, 2013. Sculpture park, Chamarande, France. 2,508 m² (3,000 square yards). Photo Suzanne Husky

86 Maria Thereza Alves, *Seeds of Change*, 1999–ongoing. *Seeds of Change: Liverpool*, 2004. Photo Maria Thereza Alves

87 Libby Harward, *Ngali ngariba*, 2019. Installation view, Gropius Bau. Photo Mathias Voelzke. Courtesy of the artist

88 Alicja Rogalska, *Alien Species: Jersey Migrant Worker Archive*, 2017–18. Photo Sabina Sudol

89 Kristóf Kelemen and Bence György Pálinkás, *Hungarian Acacia*, 2017. Photo Krisztina Csányi. Courtesy of the artists

90 Hanna Rullmann and Faiza Ahmad Khan, *Habitat 2190*, 2019. Accompanying research in the exhibition 'Hostile Environment(s): Atlas of Critical Habitats', ar/ge kunst, Bolzano, Italy. Photo Tiberio Sorvillo. Commissioned by Middlesbrough Institute of Modern Art. Courtesy of ar/ge kunst and the artists

91 Daniel Steegmann Mangrané, *Living Thoughts*, 2019. Glass branches, epiphytic plants (orchids, bromeliads, ferns, lichens and cactuses). Variable dimensions. Installation view at Nottingham Contemporary. Photo Stuart Whipps. Courtesy Mendes Wood DM and Esther Schipper, Berlin

92 Amar Kanwar, *The Scene of Crime*, 2011. HD video installation, colour, sound, 42 mins. Installation view: 'Amar Kanwar. The Sovereign Forest' at Thyssen-Bornemisza Art Contemporary (TBA21 – Augarten), Vienna, 2013–14. Courtesy of the artist and Marian Goodman Gallery. Photo Jens Ziehe / TBA21. Copyright: Amar Kanwar

93 Ursula Biemann and Paulo Tavares, *Forest Law*, 2014. Courtesy of the artists

94 Kitti Gosztola, *Picea abies*, 2013. Ink on paper, common spruce wood, plexiglass 62 × 99 (24⁷⁄₁₆ × 40). Courtesy of the artist

95 Rasa Smite and Raitis Smits, *Atmospheric Forest*, 2020. 'Critical Zones: Observatories for Earthly Politics.' © ZKM | Center for Art and Media Karlsruhe. Photo Tobias Wootton

96 Abel Rodríguez, *Terraza Alta III*, 2018. Ink on paper, 70 × 100 (27½ × 39⅜). Photo Sandra Vargas. Courtesy of the artist and Instituto de Visión

97 Revital Cohen and Tuur Van Balen, *Leopard, Impala*, 2016. Courtesy of the artists

98 Kader Attia, *Measure and Control*, 2013. Series of 5 vitrines. Vintage vitrine, stuffed animals, African masks, vintage photographs in frame, steel, wood. Exhibition view 'Reparatur. 5 Acts', KW Institute for Contemporary Art, Berlin, 2013. Courtesy of the artist, Galleria Continua and Galerie Nagel Draxler. Photo Simon Vogel. © ADAGP, Paris and DACS, London 2022

99 Petrit Halilaj, *Poisoned by men in need of some love*, 2013. Installation view at Bundeskunsthalle Bonn. PH: Simon Vogel / Cologne. Courtesy the artists and ChertLüdde, Berlin

100 Gustafsson&Haapoja, *The Museum of the History of Cattle*, 2013. Installation view, The Hall of Historical Time. Photo Terike Haapoja. Courtesy of the artists

101 Sonia Levy, *For the Love of Corals*, 2018. Obsidian Coast. Installation view. Courtesy of the artist

102 A totem pole blessing ceremony led by members of the Lummi Nation at the opening of 'Whale People, Protectors of the Sea', an exhibition by The House of Tears Carvers of the Lummi Nation and The Natural History Museum at the Florida Museum of Natural History, Gainesville, Florida, 2018. Photo Kristen B. Grace

103 Fiona MacDonald : Feral Practice, *Diego*, 2016. Walnut ink on paper, 33 × 25 (13 × 9⅞). Courtesy of the artist

104 Anna Jermolaewa, *Hermitage Cats*, 2015. Installation consists of 40 photographs, drawings, video. Installation view from 'Anna Jermolaewa: Good Times, Bad Times' at Zachęta National Gallery of Art, Warsaw, Poland. Photo: Bartosz Górka. Courtesy of the artist

105 Lin May Saeed, *Pangolin*, 2020. Styrofoam, steel, plaster, acrylic paint, wood. Overall: 137 × 108 × 36 (53¹⁵⁄₁₆ × 42½ × 14⅛); pangolin: 52 × 104 × 29 (20½ × 41 × 11⁷⁄₁₆). Courtesy of the artist and Jacky Strenz, Frankfurt. Image courtesy of the Clark Art Institute. Photo Thomas Clark

106 Jonathas de Andrade, *O Peixe (The Fish)*, 2016. 23 mins, 16mm transferred to 2K, video, sound, 5.1, 16:9 (1.77). Film still. Courtesy of the artist, Alexander and Bonin, Vermelho and Galleria Continua

107 Shimabuku, *The Snow Monkeys of Texas: Do snow monkeys remember snow mountains?*, 2016. Video installation: HD video (20 mins, colour, sound, 16:9), vinyl wall text and cactus pots. Courtesy the artist, Air de Paris, Romainville and Amanda Wilkinson, London

108 Marcus Coates, *Syrian Elephant*, 2018. Plaster, 34 × 25 × 28 (13⅜ × 9⅞ × 11). Courtesy of the artist and Kate MacGarry London

109 *The Haunted*, a film by Saodat Ismailova, 2017, 23 mins. Full HD. Countries of production: Uzbekistan, Norway

110 Tuan Andrew Nguyen, *My Ailing Beliefs Can Cure Your Wretched Desire*s, 2017. Two-channel video installation, 1080p each channel, colour, 5.1 surround sound, 18:51 mins. © Tuan Andrew Nguyen 2021. Image courtesy the artist and James Cohan, New York

111 Gerard Ortín Castellví, *Reserve*, 2020. Duration: 27 mins. Format: DCP. Still of vultures at a feeding station in Valderejo Natural Park (Araba, Basque Country). Courtesy of the artist

112 Jakob Kudsk Steensen, *Re-Animated*, 2018–19. VR still image. Courtesy of the artist

113 Matthew C. Wilson, *Geological Evidences*, 2017. UHD 4K near-infrared and colour video with sound, 10 mins. Commissioned by NEARCH with support from the European Commission. Courtesy of the artist

114 Kiluanji Kia Henda, *Migrants Who Don´t Give a Fuck*, 2019. Mixed media, inkjet print and silkscreen, 100 × 63 (39⅜ × 24³⁄₁₆) each. Courtesy of the artist and Galleria Fonti, Naples

115 Alina Bliumis, *Amateur Bird Watching at Passport Control*, 2019. Installation view: 'Alina Bliumis, Classification Patterns: Christian, Muhammad, Lee', 'ÿ' Gallery of Contemporary Art, Minsk, Belarus; curator Irena Popiashvili, 2019. Courtesy of the artist

116 Szabolcs KissPál, *From Fake Mountains to Faith (Hungarian Trilogy), Chapter 2, The Rise of the Fallen Feather*, 2016. Video still. Courtesy of the artist

117 Heba Y. Amin, *The General's Stork I*, 2020. Archival colour print, 100 × 80.9 (39⅜ × 31¹³⁄₁₆). Courtesy of the artist

118 Allora & Calzadilla, *The Great Silence*, 2014. Three-channel HD video installation. Dimensions variable, 16 mins 22 secs. © Allora & Calzadilla; Courtesy Lisson Gallery

119 Robin Meier, *Collective Feeding*, 2019. Colomboscope, Sri Lanka. © ADAGP, Paris and DACS, London 2022

120 Alma Heikkilä, *warm and moist | decaying wood*, 2019. Polyester, aluminium, hardwood, acrylic polymer emulsion, cotton, sand-based pigment from Hyrynsalmi, ink from black alder fruit, industrial pigments and inks, plaster, 308 × 240 (121¼ × 94½). Photo Finnish National Gallery/Petri Virtanen. Courtesy of the artist

121 Eloïse Bonneviot and Anne de Boer, *The Mycological Twist, Five Amazing Tricks to Get Rid of Perception*, 2016. Digital print on mesh. Courtesy of the artists

122 Susanne M. Winterling, *Meditation on Terraforming (a tribute to Marie Tharp)*, 2018. Suspended fishnets, resin. *Shield Warrior For Biodiversity*, 2018. 3D sand-printed green turtle statue. *Planetary loop of gravitation*, 2018. Computer generated imagery mapped projection for curved screen 4K, 9 mins. Installation view from 'Gravitational Currents & the Life Magic', Empty Gallery, Hong Kong. Image courtesy of the artist and Empty Gallery. Photo Michael Yu. © DACS 2022

123 Antje Majewski, *Passagen*, 2019. Oil on canvas, 197 × 510 (77½ × 200¾). Photo Jens Ziehe. Courtesy the artist and neugerriemschneider, Berlin. © DACS 2022

124 Natascha Sadr Haghighian, *passing one loop into another*, 2017. EUR-pallet, spools of thread, fleece, tablets with mounts, insect model, animation loops. Exhibition view Neuer Berliner Kunstverein (n.b.k.), 2020. Photo Jens Ziehe. Courtesy of the artist and Neuer Berliner Kunstverein

125 Madison Bycroft, *Field*, 2020. Installation, Kunsthaus Hamburg. Courtesy of the artist

126 Laure Prouvost, *Deep See Relique n°10*, 2019. Resin, Murano glass objects and found objects. Installation view: *Deep See Blue Surrounding You*, 58th International Art Biennial, Venice, May–November 2019. Photography by Cristiano Corte. © Laure Prouvost. All rights reserved, DACS 2022

127 Heather Phillipson, *put the goat in the goat boat*, 2014. Still from video. Courtesy of the artist

128 Anne Duk Hee Jordan, *Water Crab*, 2017–ongoing. Material: motors, mechanics, waste. Technical engineer: Andreas Marckscheffel. Photo Anne Duk Hee Jordan. Courtesy of the artist

129 Korakrit Arunanondchai, *Painting with history in a room filled with people with funny names 3*, 2015. Installation view, Palais de Tokyo, Paris. Photo Aurélien Mole. © Korakrit Arunanondchai 2021, courtesy the artist, Carlos/

Acknowledgments

The first words of this book were set down when the world came to a standstill in the spring of 2020. Making a virtue of necessity, field trips were exchanged for video calls to connect with practitioners in faraway places, while imaginary journeys to countless sites of struggle and resilience across the planet offered an antidote to the narrowing horizons of UK lockdowns. Along with an intensive period of research into the most recent art practices tackling the accelerating crises of climate breakdown, in writing this book we also drew on our long-standing curatorial and academic engagement with issues of sustainability, ecology and the Anthropocene. We're incredibly grateful therefore to have had the opportunity to learn from so many artists, scientists and environmentalists through the Environmental Arts and Humanities Initiative at Central European University, the programmes of the Danube River School and the Anthropocene Reading Room at the Translocal Institute for Contemporary Art and interdisciplinary exchanges at the Institute of Advanced Studies at University College London. Collaborative editorial and writing projects, encounters with research-based art practices in exhibition contexts and the international circuits of art conferences were also formative in developing our approach to art and climate change in continuous conversation with fellow curators, critics and theorists, to whom we are greatly indebted. At Thames & Hudson we would like to warmly thank Roger Thorp for his guidance and support, as well as Mohara Gill, Bethany Wright, Ilona de Nemethy Sanigar and the whole editorial team for the care they have taken in bringing this publication to timely fruition. Above all, it has been a joy and a privilege over the course of this research to get to know so many amazing artists from across the globe and have the chance to immerse ourselves in their extraordinary work.

Index

"This kind of book at this kind of price
is what art publishing should be about"
—*New York Times Book Review*

"An extraordinarily rich and varied series"
—Linda Nochlin

The World of Art series is a comprehensive,
accessible, indispensable companion to the history
of art and its latest developments, covering themes,
artists and movements that span centuries and
the gamut of visual culture around the globe.

You may also like:

Art in California
Jenni Sorkin

**The Art of Contemporary
China**
Jiang Jiehong

Black Art
Richard J. Powell

Caribbean Art
Veerle Poupeye

**Central and Eastern
European Art Since 1950**
Maja and Reuben Fowkes

Contemporary African Art
Sidney Littlefield Kasfir

Movements in Art Since 1945
Edward Lucie-Smith

**The Photograph as
Contemporary Art**
Charlotte Cotton

World of Art

For more information about
Thames & Hudson, and the World of Art
series, visit **thamesandhudsonusa.com**